D1802822

WITHDRAWN
HARVARD LIBRARY
WITHDRAWN

VARIATION IN MODERN STANDARD ARABIC IN RADIO NEWS BROADCASTS

A SYNCHRONIC DESCRIPTIVE INVESTIGATION INTO THE USE OF COMPLEMENTARY PARTICLES

ORIENTALIA LOVANIENSIA
ANALECTA
——— 117 ———

VARIATION IN MODERN STANDARD ARABIC IN RADIO NEWS BROADCASTS

A SYNCHRONIC DESCRIPTIVE INVESTIGATION INTO THE USE OF COMPLEMENTARY PARTICLES

BY

MARK VAN MOL

UITGEVERIJ PEETERS and DEPARTEMENT OOSTERSE STUDIES
LEUVEN — PARIS — DUDLEY, MA
2003

Library of Congress Cataloging-in-Publication Data

Mol. Mark van.
Variation in modern standard Arabic in radio news broadcasts: a synchronic descriptive investigation into the use of complementary particles / Mark Van Mol.
p. cm. -- (Orientalia Lovaniensia analecta; 117)
Includes bibliographical references.
ISBN 9042911581
1. Arabic language--Standardization. 2. Arabic language--Variation. 3. Arabic language--Particles. 4. Arabic language--Dialects. 5. Mass media and language--Arab countries. I. Title. II. Series.

PJ6074.5 .M65 .2002
492.7-dc21

2002066200

PJ
6074.5
.M65
2003

© 2003, Peeters Publishers & Department of Oriental Studies
Bondgenotenlaan 153, B-3000 Leuven/Louvain (Belgium)
All rights reserved, including the rights to translate or to
reproduce this book or parts thereof in any form.

D. 2002/0602/79
ISBN 90-429-1158-1 (Peeters, Leuven)

To my wife Mireille
and our beloved children
Charlotte
Christof
Elisabeth
Johannes
Annelies
Matthias
Michaël

FOREWORD

This study by Prof. Dr. Mark Van Mol is a significant contribution to our knowledge of the nature of Spoken Modern Standard Arabic and a model for language research, in particular for corpus linguistics. After surveys of traditional Arab and contemporary western grammatical traditions and of diglossia in Arabic, a detailed analysis of a limited number of syntactic structures representing current usage in the contemporary Arab World is presented, based on a corpus of well over 300,000 words of text from radio broadcoasts in Algeria, Egypt and Saudi Arabia. The research reveals insight into the nature of Modern Standard Arabic, namely, that, as shown by this study, regional changes on MSA are uniform and parallel, albeit there are regional differences in style.

An equally important contribution is the corpus linguistic methodology described here in great detail: an accounting of the steps involved in gathering and analyzing an extensive oral corpus. This involves tagging and inputting the data in a database in such a way as to retrieve the relevant data for the analysis. This is one of the great strengths of the conclusions: they are based on live data rather than received tradition or personal impressions.

Professor Van Mol has also used corpus linguistics in publishing a dictionary of MSA and Dutch using a corpus of over three million words of post-1980's prose, and is currently working on ARALL, Advanced Receptive Arabic Language Learning, a project to develop software to accelerate the acquisition of vocabulary.

Ernest McCarus
University of Michigan

February 2003

ACKNOWLEDGEMENTS

I owe many people thanks for their practical help or valuable comments. It is impossible for me to remember all those who were of help in one way or another. Without forgetting others I want to mention some people who were of great help. First of all I want to thank four Arabists who were so patient in recording cassettes of newscasts in different Arab countries over a long period of time. In Saudi Arabia recordings were made by Mark Mouton, in Egypt by Jos Smets and Professor Emilio Platti and in Algeria by the late Father Karel Deckers. Without their recordings this study could not have been conducted.

I also want to thank Miss Mieke Claus for bibliographical references. Mr. Hans Paulussen spent many hours discussing and developing the software for this investigation. He also was a very critical reader of the manuscript and gave many valuable comments. I also want to thank Professors Urbain Vermeulen, Emilio Platti, Manfred Woidich and Julia Ashtiyani for their pertinent comments. Professor Woidich also gave interesting bibliographical references. I also want to thank Professor Billiet for his advice on statistics and Professor Lamiroy for advice on linguistics. I am also grateful to Jan Cumps who reviewed the whole manuscript for the English. I want to thank deeply Professor Ernest McCarus. Not only did he review the English language of the manuscript but he also gave a tremendous amount of critical remarks concerning the content of the manuscript.

Last but not least I thank many people for their moral support. In the first place, my wife Mireille, but also Wilfried and Patrick.

Deo Gratias – الحمد لله.

TABLE OF CONTENTS

FOREWORD VII

ACKNOWLEDGEMENTS IX

CONTENTS XI

INTRODUCTION 1

PART I. MODERN ARABIC AS A STANDARD LANGUAGE: LITERATURE REVIEW

1. The Standard Language 11
   1.1. Characteristics of standardization 13
      1.1.1. Selection 13
      1.1.2. Codification 14
      1.1.3. Normalization 15
      1.1.4. Elaboration 18
      1.1.5. Propagation 19
   1.2. Functions of standard languages 20
      1.2.1. Unification function 20
      1.2.2. International function 21
      1.2.3. Status function 21

2. The Arabic language situation 22
   2.1. The Arabic dialects 22
   2.2. Classical Arabic 23
   2.3. Modern Standard Arabic 25
      2.3.1. Origin 25
      2.3.2. Reforms of the classical language 27
      2.3.3. Modern Arabic as a new language variant . . . 30
      2.3.4. A new Arabic language variant with a lot of names. 34
      2.3.5. Modern Standard Arabic: a standard language?. . 36
      2.3.6. Modern Standard Arabic and the dialects. . . . 39

3. Diglossia 41
   3.1. Characteristics of Diglossia 42

3.2. Comments on Ferguson's Concept of Diglossia 46

4. Multi-layered Diglossia 50
4.1. Division on five levels 50
4.2. Triglossia 54
4.3. ESA 56
4.3.1. Specific characteristics of ESA 58
4.3.2. Critical remarks on the notion of ESA 59
4.3.2.1. Contradictory definitions 60
4.3.2.2. Indistinct grammatical difference between ESA and the dialects 61
4.3.2.3. Indistinctly defined categories of investigation 63
4.3.2.4. Indistinctly defined geographical categories 66
4.3.2.5. ESA as Educated speech is too limited. . 67
4.4. Quadriglossia 70

5. Coalescing Language varieties 76
5.1. Influence of MSA on dialects 77
5.2. Influence of dialects on MSA 79
5.3. European influence on Arabic dialects 81
5.4. European influence on MSA 82
5.5. Influence of Classical Arabic on MSA 84
5.6. Vagueness of the influences 85
5.7. Code-switching 86
5.8. Hybrid versus symbiotic forms 89

6. Propagation of MSA 91
6.1. Propagation of MSA by the media 92
6.2. Propagation of MSA by education 97
6.3.1. Productive linguistic skills 98
6.3.2. Receptive linguistic skills 100
6.4. Impediments to linguistic skills 101

PART II. METHODOLOGY

7. Methods of investigation. 107
7.1. Introspection 107
7.2. Experimental investigation 111

7.3. Participant observation 113
7.4. Importance of statistics 115
7.5. Corpus linguistics 116
7.6. Function of modern corpus linguistics 120

8. External structure 122
8.1. Definition of the size of the corpus 122
8.2. Contents of the corpus 125
8.3. Definition of the places of investigation 128
8.4. Composition 130
8.5. Corpus organization 131

9. Internal structure 133
9.1. Types of corpora 133
9.2. Transcription problems 134
9.2.1. Choice of transcription 135
9.2.2. Slips of the tongue and misinterpretations . . . 138
9.2.3. Orthography 140
9.2.4. Punctuation 141
9.3. The tagging of textual material 143
9.3.1. Identification of words 146
9.3.2. Attribution of grammatical categories, a problem . 149
9.3.3. Attribution of grammatical categories and the problem of ambiguity 157

10. Operationalisation of the corpus 161
10.1. Encoding 161
10.2. Software 164
10.2.1. Spelling- and Code-checker 164
10.2.2. Software to define sentences 166
10.2.3. Kwic-sentence software 168
10.2.4. Software for frequency counts 169
10.2.5. Decoding software 175
10.3 Exploration of corpora: The testing of hypothesies . . 176
10.3.1. Distribution of the plural forms *'ašḫāṣ* and *šuḫūṣ* 176
10.3.2. Distribution of the substantive *najā's* 176
10.3.3. The use of the preposition *'an* after *badalan* . 177
10.3.4. The gender of some substantive ending in *alif-maqṣūra* 177
10.3.5. The passive form and the mentioning of the agent 178

10.3.6. The use of a particle after the verb *qāla* . . . 179
10.3.7. The correspondence with *'ayy* 182
10.3.8. The cardinals from 11 to 19 183

PART III EMPIRICAL INVESTIGATION

11. Investigation of variation in Broadcast MSA 189
11.1. The particle as grammatical category 190
11.2. The concept of complementary particle 191

12. The complementary particles *wa* and *fa* 193
12.1. The Arabic approach 193
12.1.1. The particle *fa* as conjunction according to Yaʿqūb abd Al-ʿUmarī 194
12.1.1.1. General division 194
12.1.1.2. al-fā' as-sababīya (the causative fa) . 196
12.1.1.3. al-fā' al faṣīḥa (the space-creating fa) . 196
12.1.1.4. al-fā' al-isti'nāfīya (the resumptive-fa) 197
12.1.1.5. al-fā' ar-rābiṭa li-jawāb aš-šarṭ 'aw fā' al-jazā' (the apodosis fa). 197
12.1.1.6. al-fā' az-zā'ida (the added fa) . . . 197
12.1.1.7. al-fā' az-zā'īda li-tazyīn al-lafẓ. (the fa added to embellish a word) 198
12.1.2. The particle wa as conjunction according to Yaʿqūb and Al-ʿUmarī 198
12.1.2.1. al-wāw al-ʿāṭifa (the conjunction wa) . 198
12.1.2.2. al wāw al-ʿāṭifa an-nāṣiba al-fiʿl al-muḍāriʿ bi-'an muḍmira. (the subjunctivising wa) 199
12.1.2.3. al-wāw al-isti'nāfīya 'aw al-ibtidā'īya (the recommencing-wa) 199
12.1.2.4. al-wāw al-ḥālīya (the circumstantial wa) 199
12.1.2.5. wāw al-qasam (the wa of oaths) . . 199
12.1.2.6. al-wāw allatī bi-maʿnā maʿa (the comitative wa). 199
12.1.2.7. wāw rubba (the wa in the meaning of 'many') 199
12.1.2.8. wāw al-luṣūq (the attachment-wa). . 200

12.2. The western approach 200
12.3. Evolution in the use of the particles fa and wa . . . 203
12.4. Quantitative analysis 204
12.5. Qualitative analysis 206
12.5.1. Comparison of the use of the particle wa in the three countries 207
12.5.1.2. Syntactic uniformity 209
12.5.1.3. Syntactic variety 211
12.5.2. Shift in the use of the particle wa in the three countries in relation to the description in the Classical grammar 213
12.5.3. The use of the particle fa 222
12.6. Conclusion 230

13. The complementary particles *'iḏā, 'in* and *law* 232
13.1. The Arabic approach 232
13.1.1. The particle 'iḏā 232
13.1.1.1. 'iḏā with conditional meaning . . . 232
13.1.1.2. 'iḏā referring to the future 233
13.1.1.3. 'iḏā with past meaning 233
13.1.1.4. 'iḏā as nominal phrase (*ism*) . . . 233
13.1.1.5. 'iḏā al-fujā'īya ('iḏā of surprise) . . 233
13.1.2. The particle 'in 234
13.1.2.1. 'in aš-šarṭīya ('in with conditional meaning) 234
13.1.2.2. The 'in at-tafṣīlīya aš-šarṭīya (the separating conditional 'in). 235
13.1.2.3. 'in al muḫaffafa 235
13.1.2.4. The particle 'in with the meaning of laysa (not to be) 235
13.1.2.5. 'in an-nāfiya (negative 'in) 235
13.1.2.6. 'in az-zā'ida al-kāffa (added negative 'in) 236
13.1.2.7. 'in az-zā'ida ġayr al-kāffa (added non-negative 'in) 236
13.1.2.8. Other functions 236
13.1.3. The particle law 236
13.1.3.1. al-law al-imtināʿīya (irrealis law, the law of the impossible) 237
13.1.3.2. al-law aš-šarṭīya (the conditional law) 237

13.1.3.3. al-law al-maṣdarīya (the nominalizing law) 237
13.1.3.4. law li-t-tamannī (the law of wishing). 237
13.1.3.5. law li-t-taqlīl (the limitating law) . . 238
13.2. The western approach 238
13.3. Shift in the use of the particles 'iḏā, 'in and law . . . 240
13.4. Quantitative analysis. 242
13.5. Qualitative analysis 245
13.5.1. Function of the particle 'in 245
13.5.2. Function of the particle 'iḏā. 248
13.5.2.1. 'iḏā as introduction to indirect questions 248
13.5.2.2. 'iḏā as conditional particle 249
13.5.3. Function of the particle law 254
13.6. Conclusion 256

14. The complementary particles of negation *mā* and *lam* . . . 258
14.1. The Arabic approach 258
14.1.1. The particle mā 258
14.1.2. The particle lam 259
14.2. The western approach 259
14.3. Evolution in the use of the particles of negation mā and lam 260
14.4. Quantitative analysis. 264
14.5. Qualitative analysis 265
14.6. Conclusion 272

15. Other complementary particles 273
15.1. The complementary particles sawfa and sa 273
15.1.1. The Arabic approach 273
15.1.2. The western approach. 274
15.1.3. Quantitative analysis 274
15.1.4. Qualitative analysis 277
15.1.5. Conclusion 281
15.2. The complementary particles 'aw and 'am 281
15.2.1. The Arabic approach 281
15.2.2. The western approach. 284
15.2.3. Quantitative analysis 285
15.2.4. Qualitative analysis 286
15.2.5. Conclusion 290

15.3. The complementary particles 'a and hal 290
15.3.1. The Arabic approach 290
15.3.2. The western approach. 292
15.3.3. Quantitative analysis 293
15.3.4. Qualitative analysis 294
15.3.5. Conclusion 295

16. General conclusion 296

17. Bibliography 302

INTRODUCTION

To what extent is Modern Standard Arabic (hereafter MSA), as it is used nowadays in the spoken media, uniform on a syntactic level? Is there within MSA a certain degree of variation? This is the central topic of this study. Modern Standard Arabic is the official and national language in nineteen member states of the Arabic League.[1] In all these states MSA is used daily in the media and in official documents. MSA is not a 'dead' language, but a living language that is used daily by a large number of people. We agree completely with the proposition of Stetkevych (1970: 116), viz.: "MSA has become a usable functional language." In the different countries of the Arab League, books are published as regularly as clockwork, newspapers and magazines are being published, and also on radio and television a lot of programs use MSA.

The question arises whether the language in such a large area is likely to show a quite large degree of variation, even if it concerns a standard language.[2] Until now there are, as far as we know, no empirical studies that prove the possible uniformity or regional variation within MSA. What we do know is that there exists an important variation between the Arabic dialects.[3] There are different impressions and assumptions about

[1] Except Somalia (Abuhamdia 1988: 1239)

[2] There seems to exist a clear variation between the 'standard' English language as it is used in the US and the UK. El Hassan points out that there is variation in spelling, phonology, lexicon and syntax where he writes: "Similarly, lexical variation is exemplified by the occurrence of pairs of items like 'side-walk' (USA) and 'pavement' (Britain), 'fall' and 'autumn' and so on. (...) The above are only a few illustrative examples of variability in Modern Standard English. Some of them are regionally bound, others cut across regional boundaries." (El Hassan 1977: 118). Within the spoken language that variation is even bigger. "Now, regional and social heterogeneity in speech exists in all languages. Take English as an example; within the same country (Britain) Quirk observes 'The divergence between one man's English and another is great enough to be striking... and is growing seriously wide.'" (1982: 37). A stronger assertion comes from Bandes and Brewer (1977: xvi) "English is a set of languages distinguished from other sets, e.g. the Russian (set). (...) The point to emphasize here is that speech is universally heterogeneous. Heterogeneity is the norm... its absence would be pathological" (Abuhamdia 1988: 1241).

[3] A difference can be made between variation within dialects and variation between different dialects. The investigation of variation in dialects is concentrated for the greater part on Egypt. "Almost all of the work done in this area was done on variation in Egyptian Arabic" (Eid 1990: 23).

the Modern Arabic Standard language that have never been based on a detailed empirical investigation. Versteegh (1984) e.g. describes MSA as a "highly uniform language that is essentially identical with classical Arabic."[4] We find the same opinion in Cowan (1970).[5]

El-Ezabi (1967: 175) writes about MSA: "The importance of written Arabic is indicated by the position it occupies in the Arabic-speaking countries. It is the language of books and newspapers and, when read, of broadcasting stations, as for example in news broadcasts. (...) It is, therefore, the only language which all educated Arabs have in common. Its structure has been kept *intact* throughout the centuries, and *uniform* throughout the Arabic-speaking world, due mainly to the conservative influence of the Qur'an, the Moslems' Holy Book." (*my italics*).

In this way, El-Ezabi expresses the opinion of a large group of Arabs, but also of Arab grammarians, that the Arabic language is in fact, synchronically as well as diachronically, completely uniform. A large number of contemporary Arab descriptions of the 'Arabic language' are entirely based on corpora of classical Arabic texts, with the *Qur'ān* occupying the most important place. It is assumed that the language is only correctly used when it is completely in agreement with the grammatical rules as they were deduced from 'traditional' writings. According to these grammarians the grammatical rules that were deduced out of the *Qur'ān* and other earlier writings are still applicable to MSA. Such researchers refuse to take the language as it is actually used nowadays as a basis for their investigations, because in their opinion there is only one correct grammar that is considered to be the norm in all circumstances. It therefore seems interesting to compare our findings in this study with the norm as it is postulated in a few traditional Arabic grammars to check whether and where precisely we can determine a possible diachronic variation.[6]

When we consider language as a dynamic fact and investigate other text corpora we are likely to discover new regularities that offer another

[4] Ditters (1992: 4).

[5] On the other hand, Gully (1993) observes certain developments in Modern Arabic of which the importance is not quite clear to him: "We would suggest that the compilation of a comprehensive description of modern Arabic would constitute a sound beginning in the attempt to establish exactly how significant these developments are." (1993: 56)

[6] We will only indicate whether there is a deviation of the norm, which might be an indication of evolution. We are aware that a possible diachronic variation can not be determined this way with a 100% certainty. There is a possibility that certain classical texts also show deviations with regard to the norm. Only when we compare classical corpora with modern corpora can we obtain a greater certainty about possible evolution and diachronic variation.

view on the linguistic reality and lead to a more balanced judgment. As Blau writes: "The theoretical notion of a uniform and invariable Standard Arabic obtains till our day, and this is factually true as to spelling and morphology, with only a few changes in syntax" (Blau 1981: 17), but he also adds that, in case of a diachronic analysis of the classical Arabic language, this language variety does not seem to be completely uniform: "Even Classical (Literary, Standard) Arabic is not completely uniform. Important differences obtain between pre-Classical Arabic and the classic secular prose of the early Abbassid age" (Blau 1981: 148).

It is quite obvious that native speakers of Arabic have a strong desire for a uniform united language. Monteil (1960: 26) pointed out the need of the masses for a common international language 'qui est normalisée et unifiée'. In this context he referred to the statement of *Al-Ḥusrī* (1957) that the 'standard language' ought to be *muwaḥḥida and muwaḥḥada*, that is "unificatrice et unifiée". As a matter of fact, language is often seen as a homogenic unity. "Most of the linguistic research done so far tends to treat language and varieties thereof as if they were coherent, homogeneous static systems, with a minimum of variation or none at all" (Meiseles 1980: 121).[7]

However, not everybody shares the view that MSA is indeed a *reasonably* uniform language. Tarrier, for instance, takes the view that MSA shows a large regional differentiation due to the influence of the dialects. "Présenter un MSA comme homogène pour tous les pays arabes revient à nier l'influence des différents dialectes dont les différences mêmes devraient faire varier le MSA" (Tarrier 1991: 6-7). According to Diem (1974: 2) there are big differences between the MSA of the East and the MSA of North Africa. Without further pursuing the matter, Diem states that the *impression* of unity of the Arabic language is caused by the great difference between the different Arabic dialects. Farhat (1989: 7) feels the same. "MSA is continuing to evolve along two major lines, the North African and the Eastern. Although both use basically the same grammar and word set, some words have different meanings, fre-

[7] According to Blau this is to a great extent true for Arabic. "For the majority of Arab linguists, with few exceptions, only one uniform Classical Arabic exists, which alone is worthy of imitation. And this claim of uniformity and invariability is even to a great extent true in the fields of spelling and morphology, and to a lesser degree, also in the domain of syntax" (Blau 1981: 150). The uniformity of MSA is also stressed by Parkinson (1990: 289) who writes: "It is admitted that Standard Arabic has many variable aspects, although a fair observer must also admit that it also has an enormous number of invariable aspects as well."

quency and contexts of usage."[8] According to Harrell (1960: 3) 'Classical Arabic' is relatively uniform throughout the Arab world. About the spoken form he writes: "We may assume a priori, however, that spoken 'Classical Arabic' is not entirely uniform from one set of cultural conditions to another or from one geographical area to another."

Also Ditters (1991: 200) holds the view that there is *strong* variation in MSA. He even talks about a few new versions of MSA. "Since the 19th century onwards we believe to have been confronted with a number of new versions of MSA. In any case, we witness variation in the use of MSA depending on factors as the progress in time and the geographical spreading by way of interference with colloquial varieties. We also assume factors of variation based on differences in subject-matter, register, genre, style, target-group, frequency of appearance and a few more."

And in a later work he adds: "However, on the other hand the mention of regional varieties suggests that MSA deviates from the Classical norm and is less uniform than presumed. This observation tallies with the observation of Arab and Arabic linguists that the language of a Moroccan newspaper is different from one from Somalia (!) or Kuwait. It is, however, not (yet) clear in what respect these regional varieties of MSA exactly differ from each other and to what extent they differ as a group from *their common origin*, Classical Arabic" (my italics) (Ditters 1992: 5). These quotations clearly show that contradictory *impressions* exist about the uniformity of MSA. Moreover, in none of these works is it clearly specified why one has the *impression* that there may or may not be variation within MSA. The authors limit themselves to non-quantifiable concepts such as *big* or *small* variation without indicating on what basis their findings are based.

Investigation into variation within a language demands a few specifications, however. In the first place one has to know what exactly is meant by the concept of variation and in the second place one has to know which variety is to be investigated. Even in this short introduction it appears that not everybody uses the same terminology for one and the same variety. What is called MSA by one person is called Classical Arabic by another person (cf. infra 2.3.5.). First of all it is incumbent that we obtain a very clear insight in the big unity that is indicated by 'Ara-

[8] As the only (!) example to sustain his claim he quotes the words *najā'a* (*benefit*) and *'aḥṣaru* (*shorter*) which are, according to his view, used less (!) in the Middle-East. In any case, the question can be raised whether these two examples alone can suffice as an indication of regional diversity in MSA. Both words are extremely rare. The word *'aḥṣaru* is not even in Wehr's dictionary (1971). The word is in Abdel-Nour's dictionary (1983) which was published in the Middle-East (Beirut).

bic', and to define and name the different varieties that might exist. This big unity, that is indicated by the word 'Arabic', is in itself already very varied.[9]

Further on, a distinction has to be made between the (possibly spontaneous) spoken language and the written language. Probably the variation in the (spontaneous) spoken language is much greater than in the written language. When authors talk about variation, it is not always clear whether they mean dialects or standard language.[10]

Finally, one has to specify in which domain variation is to be investigated. One can investigate variation in spelling, morphology, lexicon, phonology, pronunciation or syntax.[11] It is quite possible that variation is abundantly found on the phonological level, but that it occurs much more limited on the lexical level, and even more limited on the syntax level.

It is important to limit the investigation to only one aspect, because in the investigation of variation, uniformity also matters. If we do not take into account the common features of the language and if we only want to demonstrate variation, we run the risk of erroneously stressing variation in a one-sided fashion, which will produce a very biased view of the language. Geerts rightly remarks that "in such contexts all attention is drawn to the differences and not to the common aspects, which in a variation linguistical approach seems to be essential. Without common features no statistical correlation is possible." (Geerts 1992: 62).

[9] Schippers writes (1987: 80): "Every language community knows variation. Besides the regional variations (the dialects) and the social variations that are characteristic for some classes in the society (the sociolects), every speaker has different registers (language levels) to adapt his language to the circumstances, the mood, the person one is speaking to, etc. In language communities where more than one language exists, the speaker can make use of the different languages to create variation."

[10] This is, for instance, the case in the study by Bentahila: "Further divergence results from the fact that in different parts of the Arab world borrowings are likely to be drawn from different sources. (...) These differences of background and viewpoint mean that quite frequently there is no agreement even between two of the language academies on the term they recommend for a particular purpose; it is then hardly surprising if no uniformity is achieved among actual users of the language" (Bentahila 1991: 77).

[11] Some people claim that even technical terminology in MSA is not uniform. "La lexicologie juridique, par exemple, n'est pas encore unifiée. Le terme utilisé en Egypte pour désigner le Procureur général (an nâ'eb el 'âm)(sic) est considérablement différent de celui employé au Liban et en Syrie (al mudda'i el 'âm)(sic). Il en est de même pour le "conseil d'Etat" appelé en Egypte (Majless ed dawlat)(sic) et au Liban et en Syrie (Majless el Choura) (sic)" (Mattar 1986: 257). In my opinion, difference in terminology takes nothing away from the unity of the language, certainly when it concerns collocations. Both collocations fit completely within the lexicon of MSA, and can be understood in the whole area without problems.

As far as the investigation of variation within language is concerned, a distinction can be made between *vertical variation*, namely, the variation between different styles or levels of speech within one area; and *horizontal variation,* namely the variety within one speech level over a vaster area. We can also make a distinction between *diachronic variation*, where we compare the previous use of the language with the contemporary language use and *synchronic variation*, where we exclusively investigate the language use during one period of time.[12]

There are a few investigations into vertical variation within one area that have been conducted, especially in Egypt (cf. infra 4.1.). In the domain of horizontal variation different investigations have been conducted on a dialectical level. As far as I know, there are no investigations of MSA that deal with the horizontal variation of this variety. What we do know is that there exists within MSA a *normative variation* (cf. infra 1.1.4.), which means that the language user has a choice of several possibilities for a given structure. He can, for instance, choose between the particle *lam* + jussive or *mā* + past tense for past events.[13] We do not know whether there exists some regional variation in these items.

It is clear, however, that regional variation can emerge out of contacts between different varieties or other languages.[14] Not all scholars, however, consider such differences in the standard language as variation. According to Geerts (1992: 61), in that case we do not talk anymore about variation, but about code-switching and interference, this in contrast with van Marle (1992: 5) who assumes that variation within the standard language is precisely caused by the influence of the dialects. MSA of the media can also be influenced through translations from French or English. In this work we will not go deeper into this aspect because it requires another methodological approach.

In this first investigation, we want to keep the concept of variation as open as possible. Indeed, it is not obvious to identify the elements that influence a language with a 100 % certainty, because different factors together can exert an influence on the language (cf. infra 5.6.). It is im-

[12] We also remark here that variation can also exist in the language use of one speaker. This variation, which Labov called 'inherent variation', also exists in the speech of native speakers of Arabic (cf. El-Hassan 1977: 122).

[13] Of course, this choice is conditional by syntax and semantics. True 'free variation' is probably very rare.

[14] Cf. Ditters (1992: 5): "Regional varieties of MSA could be explained by different forms of language contact (Arabic with non-Arabic and written Arabic with spoken Arabic)".

portant first of all to define the concept *standard language*, to know how it functions and then to investigate its variability. Before conducting an investigation into the syntactical variation within the MSA of radio news broadcasts (hereafter MSA-RN) we have to know what is understood by *standard language* in general and MSA more in particular.

In the first chapter we pursue the notion of standard language in greater depth and we investigate what the characteristics of a standard language are. Because of the fact that the Arabic linguistic reality is very complex on the one hand, and because a lot of scholars use different terminologies to describe elements of this Arabic linguistic reality on the other hand, it is also necessary to give a short description of the Arabic language situation and the place of MSA. In the second chapter we describe the Arabic language situation as it has developed during its long history. The stress in this chapter will be put on diachronic variation.

In the third and the fourth chapters we discuss the vertical variation within the Arabic language, and the different approaches about this topic. Next we try to show in the fifth chapter that these varieties do not stand alone, but influence each other, and finally, in the sixth chapter, we examine the importance and the propagation of MSA as a standard language in the Arab world.

PART I

MODERN ARABIC AS A STANDARD LANGUAGE: LITERATURE REVIEW

1. THE STANDARD LANGUAGE

The notion of a standard language is a relatively young concept in general linguistics. The process by which a standard language emerges is called standardization. Often the concepts underlying the definition of standardization are used without a precise description of the substance.

It is not very easy to define the concept of standard language. Often the term is used in two ways. On the one hand standard language is seen as the *result* of language engineering and language planning. In that case standard language indicates the norm of how the language ought to be used. On the other hand the concept of standard language is defined as the sociolect of a certain group in society (Vries 1987: 130). In the first case standard language is seen prescriptively as an abstraction, in the second case descriptively as a reality.

An additional problem which is closely related to this concept is that in a lot of cases scholars do not mention explicitly whether oral or written language use is meant (Vries 1987: 132). As a matter of fact the standardization of oral language use is often closely intertwined with written language use.[1] It is, however, much more difficult to describe the oral realization of the standard language than the written realization of it. In the definition of the oral standard language the written standard language is often taken as a frame of reference (Al 1987: 38). In this way Owens (1991: 17) sees standardization as "the degree to which speech is characterized by the use of Standard Arabic (SA) forms." Owens presumes that there already is a standard language, in this case the written norm. According to Owens standardization is the gradation with which one can express how far the spoken language approaches the written norm.

[1] In the 18th and 19th century, the dictum about the spoken language in German was "*Sprich wie du schreibst.*" *(talk as you write)* (Beersmans 1987: 44). Conversely Vooys (1914: 33) claimed about Dutch: "The difference between writing and talking can no longer exist: from now on the motto is: 'write as you talk!' (p. 15). Joseph (1987: 39) remarks that the written language exerts a great influence on the spoken word: "It seems to be a very 'natural' development for literate people to take to planning formal spoken utterances by means of writing. Indeed, much of what we think of as 'standard spoken' language entails complete or partial retransferral from the visual channel." Also in Dutch, the grammatical norms for the polished standard speech are borrowed from the written standard language (Vries 1987: 135)

Specifically with regard to Arabic, we find that there are two different approaches as far as the notion of *standardization* is concerned. In the first approach it is assumed a standardized written language already exists, namely Standard Arabic, of which the grammatical rules have been known for centuries. Thus Ditters argues (1991: 200): "The rules governing this language system have their origin in the language spoken at the beginning of the Islamic era and were formulated during the standardization of this language in what we now call Classical Arabic."[2] In this context Standard Language would be a clear example of the *result* of language policy. In this case standardization means a conscious policy which was adhered to in the past.

On the other side we note the observation by Ferguson (1990: 49) who writes that a process of standardization is taking place *nowadays*.[3] By standardization he means the process by which it is generally accepted that one variety of the language is better than the others. If we assume with Ditters and Owens (cf. supra) that a standardized form of the language already exists, then there is no doubt that Ferguson, although he does not mention it explicitly, means the spoken language with respect to standardization.

Ferguson describes standardization as a spontaneous process that is experienced and that can lead to two possible situations.[4] Standardization as a spontaneous process can result in one single center of which the standard language sets the pace. The other possibility "is for the language eventually to split into several different standards, as happened with the Latin and Romance languages."[5]

It is clear that the notion standardization has different meanings. The lack of clarity and the vagueness of this concept is also manifest for Mitchell (1982: 151) who puts standardization on one line with koinization. This contrary to, for instance, Gillaerts (1986: 7), who puts standardization on the same level as normalization. Nevertheless there is a clear distinction between the two processes. The process by which one variety obtains a greater prestige , and as a result of that will function as a general *Umgangssprache* or *koine* can be called koinization. So we observe that in the Flemish part of Belgium, migrant workers from dif-

[2] See also Fischer and Jastrow (1980: 16).

[3] Ferguson (1990: 49) writes: "Standardization is taking place in various parts of the world, a fascinating process not at all well understood either from the social networking side or from the linguistic structure side."

[4] "Arabic is *undergoing* standardization on a vast scale." (my italics). (Ferguson 1990: 49)

[5] Bentahila (1991) does not exclude this possibility for "Arabic".

ferent countries use a special kind of French as a common *Umgangssprache* or *koine*. The fact that a 'koine' is subjected to certain regularities does not mean that it is *officially* normalized.

As a matter of fact, there is a vagueness about the standard language. Therefore, it seems to me essential first of all to define what we mean exactly by the notions *standard language* and *standardization* for this particular investigation. In this way we will be able to examine variation within a standard language

1.1. Characteristics of standardization

One basic characteristic of standardization is that influence is consciously exerted on a specific language situation.[6] According to Haugen (1977: 137) this human intervention has four aspects, namely: selection, codification, elaboration and propagation. Next to codification we add *normalization* as a fifth aspect.

1.1.1. *Selection*

In the first place, a conscious *selection* was and is made between dialectical variants. Sometimes this conscious choice can be fixed in a law.[7] One example is the *Ordonnance de Villers-Cotterets* which was signed by François I on the 15th of August 1539 turning the dialect of Paris at that time into the official language (Al 1987: 36).[8] This gave the Parisian dialect an official character.[9] It is clear that also for the Arabic language a selection took place in the past. Although the pre-Islamic poetry had a very high prestige as a language variant, we think that the choice has been influenced historically by the revelation and writing of the *Qur'ān*.[10]

[6] Cf. Joseph (1987:15): "Direct human intervention is not only possible, but essential, in the establishment of a standard language."

[7] "Selection involves the decision among various dialects or preexisting written traditions or the creation of an entirely new norm. This is essentially a political decision" (Haugen 1977: 137).

[8] Especially in the Flemish part of Belgium people are aware of the importance of language laws. Cf. Goossens (1986: 11) and Verrept (1986: 83-84). The decision about the new spelling of the Dutch language, for instance, could only be taken on a political level.

[9] Also Deprez (1987: 224) mentions Standard Dutch in terms of *official* Dutch.

[10] Feitsma (1987: 57) points out that the selection can be influenced by the literary character of a variant.

1.1.2. *Codification*

A second aspect of standardization is *codification*. The alphabet, orthography, lexicon and structure of the language have been laid down in dictionaries and grammars.[11] The sources on which the codification is based are often merely descriptive scientific descriptions of a language which thereby unintentionally obtain a prescriptive character.[12] According to Joseph (1987: 115) we certainly should not underestimate the influence of editors on the standard language: "Planning Boards, Academicians, and grammarians may discuss the abstract nature of things *ad infinitum*, but the editor must decide *hic et nunc* whether a given word or syntactic device is acceptable. (...) All these considerations make it very likely that editors play the single most substantial and direct role in linguistic control at the present time."[13] Therefore a standard language often considerably bears the hallmark of those groups in society that set the pace. (Haeseryn 1987: 21).[14]

The question is whether these remarks are also applicable to the Arabic language situation. In this respect it is not unimportant to remark that a certain codification of the Arabic language had already taken place centuries ago. Descriptions of the Arabic language were made in very early times. The first more or less complete extant description of the Arabic language dates from the eighth century with the book *Al-kitāb* of *Sībawayhi*.[15]

[11] Shorrab (1984: 212) points out that this codification happens according to two norms: "1) the establishment of grammatical rules and stylistic devices that govern the language; and 2) these rules and the use of the language must be administered by a certain body of authority or agency. This ruling power can be a governmental agent, a private agency, or a public authority." According to Beersmans (1987: 51), the norm for the German language is essentially given by a private agency, namely the *Dudenverlag*.

[12] Cf. Haas (1987: 2): "Whether they like it or not, phoneticians, grammarians and lexicographers exert a decisive influence on what eventually counts as 'received' or 'accepted'; and there is no reason why linguists should ignore these consequences of their work".

[13] Also radio and television play an important role in the spreading of a language norm. The BBC has a team of four men in the *Pronunciation Unit* whose principal task it is to determine the pronunciation of foreign names. According to Gussenhoven (1987: 28) the BBC is seen as a normative institute everywhere. This does not mean that every expression in the media conforms to the current language norm.

[14] Also Rebhan (1986) points out that at the end of the 19th century the press played a crucial role in the spreading of certain political terms in Arabic. Newly created words which were not used by the press disappeared, whereas others which were frequently used were generally accepted.

[15] Ditters (1992: 16) writes about him: "His *kitāb* represents an accurate, detailed and precise elaboration and systematization of what he heard from his teachers and it is illus-

His *kitāb* was based on the daily language use of the Arabs, the text of the *Qur'ān* and the language use of the literature of that time, of which poetry took the most prominent place (Cf. Ditters 1992: 18). Of all these sources the *Qur'ān* was the most weighty. "Le Coran s'imposait comme l'oeuvre de langue arabe parfaite et inimitable. Il devenait la référence centrale et fixe de la langue arabe, le facteur le plus considérable et le plus constant de sa stabilité" (Roman 1987: 133).

One can ask whether the first Arab grammarians only had descriptive purposes with the description of their language. According to Suleiman (1996: 102) this was not completely the case. Early descriptions of the Arabic language already had a prescriptive character.[16]

Moreover the question can be raised whether the codification of the language in the Arab world today is based on current descriptions of the language. We have the impression that contemporary Arab grammarians mainly base their work on older grammars, which they consider to be the norm for correct language use (cf. infra 2.3.3.). Indeed, a lot of contemporary Arabic grammars take the *Qur'ān* as basis.[17]

1.1.3. *Normalization*

The codification of the language gives it a normative character. Al (1987: 35) defines standard language as follows: "the language variant that is seen by the members of a community as model. In this way it is an example worth imitating. In short it is the variant which is considered to be the prescriptive norm." Shorrab (1984: 218) states about the Arabic language: "The standard language must serve as a norm for the correct usage of speech in a speech community."[18]

trated by numerous language examples. It became a reference work to the extent that it was called *Qur'ān an-naḥw* (the Koran of Arabic Grammar)".

[16] "From its very inception, grammar in the Arabic intellectual tradition is characterized by a duality of function, encompassing the descriptive *objective* of accounting for the facts of the language with a view to understanding the primary source texts upon which it is based, as well as the utilitarian and prescriptive *end* of 'regulating' the speech of the Arabs and non-Arab learners of the language. (...) The descriptive objective and the pedagogic-cum-prescriptive end are fully intertwined in the earliest formulations of Arabic grammar." Suleiman (1996: 102).

[17] This is not only the case for the grammars of *Shalaby* (1985) and *Ad-Daḥdāḥ* (1990), but also in the most recent series of Arabic teaching manuals for the primary school in Jordan, *luġatunā al-'arabīya* (1996), mainly Koranic verses are given as illustration for grammatical rules.

[18] Suleiman (1996: 103) points out that the element of correctness (*ṣawāb*) versus flaw (*ḫaṭa'*) played its role from the very beginning, but even for specialists it is not always easy to determine whether a certain construction is correct or not. For a deeper analysis of the notion *correctness* see Suleiman (1996: 103-113).

However, not everybody within a certain language community masters the standard language in the same way. Pauwels (1986: 78) makes a distinction between passive knowledge and active knowledge of a language. He observes that, for instance, in Belgium, almost all Flemish people have a thorough passive knowledge of the standard language, but only a minority have an active knowledge of it. Martin (1988: 96) observes the same discrepancy in the mastery of a language where he defines the Dutch standard language as the supraregional language norm which is not spoken by everybody but which is understood by everyone.

When the norm of the standard is not attainable for very large groups within a language community, this may cause a lot of frustration (Koefoed 1987: 115). In the Arab world the Standard language is only mastered by a minority. Nevertheless, it still exerts a great attraction on the masses.

When the norm is not attainable, an intermediate form can emerge, that is to say, a language intermediate between the standard language and the dialect. When this intermediate language becomes the *Umgangssprache* of a community in a certain area, then, we can use the term *koine*. A *koine* as a common *Umgangssprache* can be a standard language or an intermediate language. In this aspect the difference between standardization and koinization is essential. In the first case it means the conscious introduction of a standard language according to specific norms. In the second case we observe a spontaneous process. An intermediate language is used which is not necessarily normalized nor codified by a higher authority. Its usage may be, however, widespread.

On the other hand this does not mean that a koine does not comply with certain regularities. Even hybrid language forms and code-switching in intermediate languages are submitted to certain *rules* or regularities (cf. infra 5.7.). The difference with the standard language is that these are not institutionalized and that they are not being transmitted in an educational system.

Moreover, language norms are not always strictly applied to every element of the language. Pronunciation, for example, is probably the most problematic aspect of language norms. There are different views about the pronunciation norms of the standard language. Vries (1987: 131) for instance considers the ideal speaker of a standard language to be the person who uses the unmarked pronunciation variants at the maximum level, which means that nobody can precisely determine which region he is from.[19] According to Gussenhoven (1987: 13) the pronunciation norms for the English language are completely varied. It is the least institutionalized element of that language.[20] In Germany before the sixties, the artificial norm of the 'Bühnenaussprache' was accepted as rule. Nowadays Beersmans (1987: 52) observes a much greater tolerance towards the possible variations in pronunciation. It is even chic to betray one's origin by using regionalism in the spoken language.

For the Dutch language pronunciation norms are even more difficult, as a phonetic normative study about the pronunciation of the Dutch standard language does not exist (Vries 1987: 137). Dutch language experts do stress, however, that the pronunciation over the whole area of Belgium and Holland ought to be as uniform as possible. Here too we notice a conscious influence which some want to exert on the standard language.

As for the Arabic language, we already pointed out that it has had a long tradition and history as far as codification and normalization are concerned. The question that can be raised, however, is whether these norms determined centuries ago are still applicable. Or are we, on the contrary, witnessing a renovation process of normalization, in which old norms are substituted by new ones, or adapted. It is very well possible that these new norms are generally accepted and applied without being explicitly depicted in a grammar. In other words, does a dynamic view on the notion of standard language exist in the Arab world, a view in which norms are possibly adapted and changed? Or should we assume a static view in which norms bave been fixed once and for all? It is certainly clear that the last view is absolutely prominent.[21]

19 This conviction is, according to Geerts (1987: 168), not new. Already in 1841 the conviction existed that pronunciation is considered to be purer the less the regional origin of the speaker is identifiable. This idea existed already in antiquity in the terms of Atticismus (with the Greeks) and Urbanitas (with the Romans).

20 The standard pronunciation of England is called RP, an abbreviation of *Received Pronunciation* (received in the meaning of *generally accepted*). In England however there are a lot of cultivated speakers that do not speak RP. According to Gussenhoven (1987: 24) persons that have had an academic education, but that do not belong to a traditional RP-speaking group, probably have a certain regional coloring in their pronunciation.

21 This has been crisply expressed by Shorrab (1984: 213): "The grammatical rules of Arabic were set a long time ago. Changing them, or even deviating from these rules, is considered a grammatical flaw." In the Arab world the resistance against the adaptation of the grammatical rules is, according to Suleiman, due to the *sacred* character of the language. He also states that "any change or modification in the grammar, no matter how slight, will inevitably be regarded as a change in the language itself" (1996: 115).

Still, we do observe some regional variation here and there. As an illustration of regional variation on the orthographiuc level I would only like to mention the generally known phenomenon that the Arabic long final vowel /ī/ (for instance in the particle /fī/) is written without dots in Egypt whereas in most other Arab countries it is always written with dots. Also in school manuals, where this norm is being propagated, this regional difference is present. This simple example indicates that, albeit on a limited scale, a certain new process of codification can take place. It is not very easy to find out how this variation has come into being. Is it under the influence of the Arab academies or is it rather an influence of the local publishers in Egypt? It is beyond the scope of this investigation to look into the causes of these differences.

1.1.4. *Elaboration*

Notwithstanding the normative character of a standard language, it can indeed be the subject of evolution. According to Haugen, another characteristic of the standard language is that it is constantly adapted to the changing social and cultural circumstances (*Elaboration*).[22] A standard language is adapted to certain needs but always within certain restrictions. Contrary to dialects or an intermediate language, which can adapt new words in their vocabulary without any restrictions, the emphasis in the standard language lies more on the purity of the language. This means evolution, but within certain limits.[23]

The fact that the development of a standard language is steered causes a standard language to lose its casualness to a certain degree. A standard language has to be learned over and over again by all kinds of people (dialect speakers and foreigners). But also those who use the standard language more or less daily and spontaneously do sometimes doubt the correctness of their own language use and that of others. In all these situ-

[22] Haugen writes on *Elaboration:* "A language that has not previously been used for the expression of complex scientific and sophisticated prose needs first of all a great new vocabulary, which can be created in various ways, by borrowing, by calquing or by original creation. The language may even need to develop a more complex syntax to cope with the concentrated expression of complex ideas." This saying is completely applicable to the Arabic language situation (cf. infra 2.3.2. en 2.3.3.).

[23] In this respect we mention the fact that Anglicisms in France are officially opposed (by among others the ministerial decree of 12th January 1973). For each of the loanwords a French equivalent was proposed and promoted by a special commission (Al 1987: 41). In the Arab world as well the authorities take measures to counteract the use of foreign words. Holes (1995: 257) mentions an interesting example from Saudi Arabia: "The word *bāṣ* for example, which originally seems to have come into MSA via the dialects, was replaced on street signs and other forms of public writing in the 1970s by the neologism *ḥāfila,* as was on telephone booths, *tilifūn* 'telephone' by *hātif.*"

ations people have a need for explicit norms which can be consulted. When doubt arises people expect decisive answers from authorized agencies (Haeseryn 1987: 19).[24] Within the Arab world, traditional Arab grammars are no doubt considered as the most authoritative sources.

On the other hand, this does not mean that variation cannot exist within a standard language. In this respect we have to make a distinction between *variation,* i.e. variation which is generally recognized to be a language norm, and *non-institutionalized variation*, i.e. the variation that might occur in the functioning of the language but which is not generally accepted. The difference between these two concepts is not easy to define. In the first case there are options that are possible in a standard language. In the second case, from a strictly normative view, variation might be considered faulty.

In general there is an equilibrium between keeping the norm and accepting variation.[25] The gradation of this equilibrium can differ from country to country. According to Suleiman the tendency in the Arab world to limit the variation is more prominent than in other countries because of the *sacred* character of the language.[26]

1.1.5. *Propagation*

Apart from exceptions, in general a standard language has no native speakers. As the mother tongue is never a pure standard language in any

[24] In this respect the Council for Language Recommendation (Raad voor Taaladvies) was installed in the Flemish part of the country. The task of this council was to aid citizens in using their language correctly. Radio and television but also newspapers and magazines engaged language specialists to guide the staff in the use of correct language. The influence of these people cannot be underestimated, because they played a very important and influential role (Willemyns 1987: 153).

[25] Cf. Joseph (1987: 127): "Every standard language, by virtue of continuous change and conscious elaboration, contains a minimum level of variation. Every standard language, by virtue of inherent stability and conscious control imposes a maximum limit on variation". Or as Haas (1982: 19) puts it: "At any particular stage in the development of language its variability is balanced by standards. The inherent variability of language would be a threat to communication if it were not held in check by an equally inherent normative tendency to maintain rule-governed standards of usage. Without the former, language would lose its adaptability to changing conditions, without the latter it would disintegrate." In that sense Shorrab (1984: 211) refers to a flexible stability: "The language, in order to function appropriately, must be stabilized by the correct norms; it must at the same time, allow for new changes and developments according to the cultural alternation of the speech community."

[26] "It may even be argued that, because of the 'sacred' nature of the language through its organic association with Islam's revealed text, the drive to achieve uniformity and remove, or at least arrest, variability may be judged to be culturally more rooted in the Arabic context than what might be the case in other linguistic environments" (Suleiman 1996: 112).

country (Vries 1987: 137) the standard language has an artificial character in one way or another. The standard language has to be *learned* by everybody. The norm of the standard language is also spread by education and the media (i.e. *propagation*).

In my opinion the next observation of Joseph's is completely justifiable: "If the standard language were 'native' to a given person, he or she would not need to study it. Native Anglophone students all through their education take courses in 'English,' Hispanophones in 'espanol,' and so on." (Joseph 1987: 17). And further: "Standard languages are acquired largely, even primarily, through instruction, correction, imitation, assimilation, acculturation — precisely the ways in which one's native dialect is not acquired" (Joseph 1987: 19). In fact, we might conclude, according to Joseph, that the education of the standard language always ought to be seen as second-language acquisition (Joseph 1987: 80).[27]

1.2. Functions of standard languages

1.2.1. *Unification function*

In the first place standard languages have a unification function. A standard language has no local character. In other words it does not belong to a certain area or to a certain group but to a region as a whole (Joseph 1987: 129). The stress lies mainly on *uniformity*. A resolute attempt is made to attain this uniformity. In the strive for a standard language, it is considered correct to strive for a situation in which variation is as limited as possible in order to obtain the highest possible unity in the language area and the language community (Haeseryn 1987: 21).

Uniformity of the language is stressed. Also in education, the standard language is presented as a completely homogeneous phenomenon. (Al 1987: 38). This does not mean, however, that the uniformity is complete

[27] Also the authorities can take measures to propagate the standard language. In the Flemish part of Belgium a magazine to promote the standard language has been published since 1951. For years Radio and television have had a special program to spread the *good* Dutch (Goossens 1987: 13). There are also the pedagogical books about language purity that aim at counteracting the use of Belgicisms. The most famous are the books of Penninckx W. and Buyse P. (1988, 1991) and more recently the *Woordenboek voor correct taalgebruik* (dictionary for correct language usage) of Theissen e.a. (1995). The same kind of books is found in the Arabic world (for instance: Al-'Adnānī: 1989)

on all levels of the language; on one level this uniformity can be greater than on another level. According to Gussenhoven (1987: 13) there exists a far-reaching uniformity in the English language as far as syntax, lexicon and spelling is concerned (cf. introduction p. 1 note 2), but less so in pronunciation.

1.2.2. *International function*

The tendency to uniformity is directly linked with the international character of standard languages. Standard languages ought to be tools that can easily be translated from one standard language to another (Joseph 1987: 6), which is called the *function of participation* by Garvin.[28]

1.2.3. *Status function*

In the third place a standard language has a prestige function. It is the language that is the model of erudition and civilization. A standard language, however, does not exist in isolation but exists within a certain area where other languages exist. The consequence is that a standard language can undergo different influences. A standard language is constantly exposed to interaction with all kinds of other varieties within this language as well as with foreign languages (Cf. Van Marle 1992: 19). This influence can be exposed on different levels of the language and in different degrees. Joseph (1987: 94-95) makes a difference between 'minimal adjustment', to which he counts loans from a foreign language and 'maximal adjustment', to which he counts the calques. It is however not very easy to determine where influences in a certain language come from.

In the next chapter we will give a description of the Arabic language situation. We will try to define the standard variant within the Arabic language on the basis of the characteristics that we defined previously, and also to define the standard variant with respect to the other language varieties. By standard language we mean the codified and normalized language variety that has been selected as such by society, and which is propagated in education and by the media with its possible adaptations.

[28] Cf. also Shorrab (1984: 217): "The standard language enables the members of the speech community to have access to the cultural developments of other nations, either directly or through translation. "

2. THE ARABIC LANGUAGE SITUATION

2.1. The Arabic dialects

The Arabic language has many representations. Every Arab uses his own dialect in his daily contacts. Moroccans speak in their community a Moroccan dialect (or some of them also Berber dialects) while Egyptians speak the Egyptian dialect. The dialects that are spoken in the Gulf region also differ in turn from the other dialects.[1]

The current Arab world can be divided in different dialectal areas. The dialects sometimes differ a lot and sometimes a little bit from each other. The regional variations between the dialects seem to be very old. They were first described in the middle of the tenth century by the geographer *al-Muqaddasī* (Bateson 1967: 102). On the basis of morphological and syntactical similarities and differences a classification can be made of the dialects in different groups. Bateson (see also Abboud 1970: 439) divides the Arabic dialects into two large groups. Her division is exclusively based on the variation of one single grammatical element, i.e. the contrast between the prefixes of the verbs of the present time.[2] In this way she makes a difference between the Eastern Arabic dialects, spoken in the whole Arabic East from Egypt and beyond, and Western Arabic dialects limited to the Maghreb area and some regions in West-Africa (Bateson 1967: 103).

Abuhamdia (1988: 1240) distinguishes between the dialects of the Arabic peninsula, of Mesopotamia, the Eastern Arabic and the Arabic of the Maghreb. Fischer & Jastrow (1980) make an even finer division. They divide the contemporary Arabic dialectical regions into five large groups. Besides the dialects of the Arabian peninsula, Mesopotamia and

[1] The study of the Arabic dialects has a large tradition. The most detailed contemporary descriptions of the Arabic dialects, in which different existing dialects are compared, are by Fischer & Jastrow (1980). Behnstedt & Woidich (1985) composed a detailed dialectical atlas of Egypt. The most recent study of the dialects of the Gulf is the study of Holes (1990). In the Dutch area we have the teaching manual and lexicon Moroccan Arabic by Van Mol (1981 en 1983), the dictionary Moroccan Arabic - Dutch by Otten (1983) and the recent manual by Hoogland (1996).

[2] There are of course other elements of comparison. Another *horizontal* investigation about language variety was conducted by Fischer (1959), who examined all the demonstratives of the whole area and by Van Mol (1980), who examined the difference between the verb forms in the dialects of Rabat and Cairo.

the dialects of the Maghreb they distinguish between Egyptian Arabic and Syro-Palestinian Arabic.

Most differences concern phonology, morphology and lexicon. Cadora (1966) examined the compatibility of the different Arabic dialects in the whole area with reference to vocabulary. For some of the words he observed a similarity of 96 %.[3] According to Becker (1964: 161)[4] there is a correspondence for the 200 most frequent words of the Lebanese and Egyptian dialects of 78%. Between the Moroccan and the Lebanese dialects he observes a correspondence of 65.8% and between the Egyptian and the Moroccan dialects a correspondence of 62.2 %.[5]

In spite of the fact that there are many similarities between the dialects of the Eastern and the Western region, it is not possible for people from different regions to understand each other (Kaye 1987: 676; Bentahila 1991: 69). Mattar (1986: 263) observes that: "Lorsqu'un Nord-africain veut se faire comprendre, dans un des pays du Machrek arabe, il lui faut soit recourir à la langue classique, soit renoncer pratiquement à tout dialogue".

2.2. CLASSICAL ARABIC

The Arabic language variety that was codified and normalized centuries ago is called Classical Arabic. The works of the Arab grammarians have been considered as normative works form the early beginning.[6] The adherents of Arabic-Islamic education considered Classical Arabic, as it was described by the philologists and the grammarians of the 8th and 9th centuries, to be the only *true* Arabic. "Schon seit dem 2. Jahrhundert d. H. traten Sprachkritiker auf, die sich mit den volkstümlichen Abweichungen des Sprachgebrauchs von der als Norm angesehenen Sprache befassten" (Wehr 1943: 17). In that period books were compiled to aid language users in avoiding language errors. These books, like for instance the *'Adab al-kātib* by *Ibn Qutayba,* belonging to the *laḥn*-literature, were widely circulated (Fischer 1982: 91).

[3] Cadora (1966: 310) describes this compatibility as follows: "Compatibility is a synchronic dialectological concept that operates on the lexical level. It assesses the degree of lexical relationship that exists between two or more varieties of a given language at a given time irrespective of geography."

[4] Cited in Diem (1974: 1)

[5] It is not clear how Becker was able to select the *most important* words. Neither is it clear which criterion he uses to demonstrate the correspondence between words in different dialects.

[6] Although Sībawayhi described a good deal of linguistic variation in his kitāb. See Owens (2001). For variation in Classical Arabic see Bohas and Aḥmad al-Qādirī (1998).

For many centuries the profound knowledge of Classical Arabic was the privilege of a small minority of scholars. There were also users of the Arabic language that did not master the language completely and people that did not attach a great value to the exact application of the grammatical norm. This was noticeable with some Jews and Christians, who did not participate to the same degree in the Classical Arabic educational tradition.[7] The Arabic from the Classical period (ca. 600-1200 and later) that does not completely comply with the norms of the Classical Arabic language and that reveals rather an influence from the spoken language, is called Middle Arabic.[8]

Given the fact that the norm was not always respected by language users, it has never been adapted. Possibly also because of the fact that within the Sunni community the conviction was widespread that the language of the *Qur'ān* was not a human language, but the language of God himself, "une langue dont Dieu serait l'Auteur, une langue en conséquence nécessairement une et immuable" (Roman 1987: 133).[9] This conviction is still widespread among Muslims.

In general the dogma of the *'Arabīya* was accepted, viz.: "the doctrine that the classical language as codified by the Arabic philologists, the language in which are written the sacred *Qur'ān* and the classical works of Arabic literature is unchangeable and is the only one to be used when writing" (Blau 1981: 7).

In this Classical language a very vast amount of literature came into being.[10] Arabic literature was flourishing up to the 11th century. All secondary school manuals in the Arab countries pay a lot of attention to this classical literature, offering students access to a rich cultural past.[11]

[7] Cf. Blau (1981: 181): "The last period of the Arab Middle Ages, in many fields was dominated by a careless style, which stemmed from the indifference of many authors toward correct language".

[8] For a more extensive discussion on Middle Arabic see Schippers (1987: 58-65), Blau (1969), and Larcher (2001). Versteegh (1997: 114) defines it as "The collective name for all texts with deviations from Classical grammar. On the problems concerning the intrinsic definition of the term Middle Arabic and the confusion about it in literature see Hary (1989).

[9] Bentahila (1991: 70) writes: "The Koran is in fact considered to be the word of God Himself. (..) This profound respect for the high variety (Classical Arabic) is reflected in many traditional customs still to be observed in Arabic-speaking communities". See also Ditters (1992: 51).

[10] Cf. Tapiéro (1976: 24): "Cette langue devient le moyen d'expression de toute une littérature classique, brillante parfois, présentant une certaine diversité, durant tout le moyen-âge, mais faute de renouvellement, cette littérature parvient assoufflée à la période moderne".

[11] Cf. Cachia (1969: 21): "Above all, the classical is the key to the immense treasure-chests of the past. This is both the justification and the guarantee of its retention as the language of literature. Its stability has seldom been paralleled in other languages, and to-

From the 12th century onwards the Arab-Islamic world goes through a less productive period on a cultural and scientific level. No important literary works were produced and the use of classical Arabic became very limited. This *silent* period lasted till the 19th century.

2.3. Modern Standard Arabic

2.3.1. *Origin*

Although in the 18th and 19th centuries a few local centers emerged in which the literary and philological revival (*nahḍa*) came into being, as for instance in Aleppo (Syria) under the influence of Mgr. Germanos Farhat (Monteil 1960: 32), Napoleon Bonaparte's expedition to Egypt in the year 1798 is generally considered to be the starting point of the modern period (Monteil 1960: 32-35; Tapiéro 1976: 74; Ditters 1992: 2; Suleiman 1994: 5). This expedition marked the beginning of a period in which more and more intensive contacts would take place between the Western world and the centuries-old Arabic culture.

From 1809 onwards the sovereign in Egypt at that time, *Muḥammad ʻAlī*, started to send small groups of students to Italy, France and England, in order to study applied and military sciences. (Cf.: Abdulaziz 1986: 12). Later on, in 1826, there was a mission under the leadership of *aṭ-Ṭahṭāwī*, who gave an interesting and detailed description of life in France in those days, in his book *Taḫlīṣ al-'ibrīz fī talḫīṣ bārīs* (Tapiéro 1976: 106 and Le Gassick 1979: 7). In 1835 *aṭ-Ṭahṭāwī* became the head of the school of translators in Cairo. With his school he exerted an important influence on the translation of European concepts into Arabic.[12]

In 1830, France conquered Algeria and started colonizing the country. Later on Morocco and Tunisia also came under French influence. Arabic

day any Arab with a secondary education can, if he is interested and prepared to go to a little trouble, gain access to the entire record of the past 1300 years."

[12] "*aṭ-Ṭahṭāwī* und seine Schüler, die sich intensiv mit dem Westen befassten, spielten eine beträchtliche Rolle bei der Einführung neuer Begriffe" (cf. Rebhan 1986: 128). See also Ayalon (1987: 12; 37 en 40). Ayalon points out that the 19th century can be seen as an experimental period: "It comprises the important formative stages of the process of linguistic change: initial unawareness; early piecemeal lexical experimentation; intensified but still unorganized innovation; and the beginning of orderly adjustment. (...) By the last decade of the century this initial phase of adaptation seems to have run its course" (Ayalon 1987: 9).

as a cultural language was completely ousted by the language of the colonizer. By 1848 Algeria had become formally a part of France and the French language became the official language. Later, in 1938, Arabic was declared a foreign language by decree (Holt 1994: 29). A reaction that would consider Arabic as a cultural language of paramount importance would soon make itself felt.

Modern technological printing techniques gave the Arabic language more importance and influence. The first Arabic printing press was put into use in 1610 in the *Quzhayyā* convent in Lebanon.[13] In Aleppo (Syria) the first printing press was imported in 1702 (Hanam 1984: 25). The first Arabic printing press in Egypt was introduced by Bonaparte in 1798 (Cf. Tapiéro 1976: 74). However, it was no longer used after the departure of the French in 1801. A few years later *Muḥammad ʻAlī* started a printing press in Bulaq (Cairo). The first work that was printed on this press was an Italian-Arabic dictionary. From then on all kinds of books were printed on the printing presses of Bulaq.[14]

The Arabic press made its first appearance in Cairo in 1828 with the publication of the bilingual Turkish-Arabic newspaper *al-Waqā'iʻ al-Miṣrīya* (Ayalon 1987: 13). Barbot (1983: 130) writes about this newspaper: "Elle éduqua politiquement les lecteurs, et son language fut important pour l'élaboration de l'arabe littéral moderne." According to Tapiéro this brought about a real upheaval in the Arabic world that might be compared to a cultural revolution: "car, jusqu'au premier quart du XIXe siècle, tout est encore manuscrit et cette langue savante ne connaît qu'une très faible diffusion, réservée à une poignée d'aristocrates qui ne virent peut-être pas d'un bon œil l'introduction de l'imprimerie" (Tapiéro 1976: 74-5).

The evolution cannot be stopped anymore. The modern press in Egypt goes back to 1875 when *Sālīm Taqlā*, a Lebanese Greek Catholic from Kfar Shima (near Beirut), migrated to Egypt where he founded the weekly *al-'Ahrām*.[15] In 1889 *Sarrūf an-Nimr* launched the newspaper *al-Muqaṭṭam*, that became the most important rival of *al-'Ahrām*. The latter will later on be published daily and is at present the most important newspaper of Egypt.

[13] Tapiéro writes about it: "Une machine à imprimer existait déjà au Liban dans un monastère, mais ne servait pratiquement à aucune publication" (Tapiéro 1976: 74).

[14] For a detailed survey of the history of the Arabic printing press, see Hanan (1984).

[15] The development of the press started in Beirut and Istanbul as early as 1860 (Cf. Rebhan 1986: 6). In 1855 the first newspaper was published in Istanbul (*Mir'at al-aḥwāl*) but it only appeared for a short period. In Beirut the newspaper *Ḥadīqat al-aḫbār* was published in 1858 and it lasted more than half a century (Ayalon 1987: 13).

The contacts with the Western world and the resulting technological developments were indirectly the cause for the revival of the Arabic literature, especially in the *Mašriq*. This revival encompassed both a conservative and a progressive current (Cf. Barbot 1983: 129). The modernistic current can be situated with the Syrian-Lebanese Christians, and more in particular the Jesuits of Beirut.[16]

Although Christians played a decisive role in the revival of the Arabic language, their influence compared to the Muslims' remains marginal.[17] The revival of Arabic literature (the *nahḍa*) in the beginning of the 20th century and the development of the newspaper industry have given a very important stimulus to a renewed use of a reformed or renewed Classical Arabic.[18] Actually, some considered this new language variety as the language of the (written) press, because of the great influence that newspapers have exerted on the development of the language (Monteil 1960: 27).[19]

However, the efforts made in the field of education have also been meaningful. These were in the first place a reaction against the Turkification that had been forced through in the East. In 1913 the first conference of Arab activists took place in Paris; they called for the use of Arabic as an educational language in all primary schools of the provinces of the fertile crescent instead of Turkish. They also demanded the foundation of new secondary schools, in addition to the Turkish state schools, where the education would be completely in Arabic. Moreover, numerous cultural associations came into being, aimed at the promotion of the Arabic language (Suleiman 1994: 8).

2.3.2. *Reforms of the classical language*

By the 'Arabic language' these cultural associations meant the Classical Arabic as it is written in the *Qur'ān* and in old writings, and of which

[16] This does not alter the fact that there were modernistic tendencies in other countries too. In Egypt, for instance, Ṭāhā Ḥusayn even argued for opening the doors of the linguistic *ijtihād*, parallel to the religious reforms, to adapt the classical language to the modern era (Cachia 1967: 16).

[17] Cf. Blau (1981: 27): "Christian writers played a prominent role in the awakening of modern Arab literature, but even so the old slogan *al-'arabīya lā tatanaṣṣaru*, "the Arabic language cannot be 'christianized' still looms large in the conscience of many Arabs and may manifest itself when a Muslim author writes, unaware of the implication, that only Muslims master Arabic properly".

[18] The development of the literature got into its stride only in the beginning of the 20th century: "The first five decades of this century saw beginnings of the development of Arabic literature as a modern world literature" (Abdulaziz 1986: 17).

[19] On the decisive influence of the press on the development of the language see also Ayalon (1987: 13 and 78).

the grammar had been laid down by the Arab grammarians in the first centuries of the Islamic era. However, the Classical language had now to be adapted to the demands of modern life (cf. supra 1.1.4. note 18).[20] In the 19th century, the school of translators in Cairo run by *aṭ-Ṭahṭāwī* in particular made a valuable contribution to the research to find adequate translations of new European concepts.

Later on in the years 1880-1890 (Blau 1981: 159) there emerged the idea of founding an Arabic language academy based on the French academy. The first Arabic language academy was founded thirty years later in Damascus at the end of World War I in 1918.[21] These different Arab academies dealt with the renovation of the Arabic language.[22] They mainly tried to limit the influence of foreign languages on Classical Arabic. "Language academies in the *Mašriq* have concentrated on the preservation and renovation of Classical Arabic as the standard, unifying language of all the Arabic-speaking peoples and have rejected the incursion into it of foreign borrowings and colloquialisms" (Benabdi 1986: 65).[23]

Cooperation between the academies was not always easy, all the more because the different Arab countries found themselves in unequal situations. Of course, the countries that had already gained their independence had more freedom of action than the other ones.[24]

[20] Cf. Abdulaziz (1986: 16): "Ancient classical Arabic, which further developed in the Middle Ages, was not equipped to cope with the new conceptual demands. It was now a question of developing within a few decades, in response to the various socio-cultural and psychological stimuli, a new and refined Arabic capable of expressing a material and intellectual civilization that had evolved over centuries in Europe".

[21] The foundation of the academy of Cairo followed in 1932, the Academy of Baghdad in 1947 and finally in 1976 the foundation of the academy in Jordan. Due to the fact that the countries of the Maghreb obtained their independence much later, these countries had by no means the possibility of founding an academy. But in 1961 the authoritative *Institut d'Arabisation* was founded in Rabat.

[22] For a thorough discussion of the development and the activities of the Arab academies see: Hamzaoui (1965 en 1975) and Schippers (1984: 147-150). The work of the academies is hampered by the fact that there are different language academies, about which Barbot (1983: 126) writes: "Le monde arabe actuel ne dispose pas encore d'institutions assez homogènes et efficaces pour que la réforme voulue par tous se soit déjà généralisée."

[23] Not all the propositions of reform were accepted (cf. Bateson 1967: 93-94 and Bentahila 1991: 78). All propositions in relation to the Latinizing of the Arabic script were rejected by all five academies. This is easily understandable considering the great religious importance of the Arabic writing (Monteil 1960: 50; Shorrab 1984: 212). Europeans also have tried to reform the Arabic language. On these and other reformers see Diem (1974: 130-142). On attempts to simplify the grammar see Stetkevych (1970: 79-94), Barbot (1983: 137) and Suleiman (1996).

[24] Talmoudi (1984: 27) writes about this subject: "Despite the establishment of the coordinating committees at the Conference of the Academies of Language (1956) which

After the independence achieved in the period of 1945-1972 Arabic as a cultural language gained many more opportunities to develop completely.[25] It is clear that this is a very recent phenomenon. Arabic became the official language of Egypt as late as 1943 (!) (Tapiéro 1976: 115). The other Arab countries followed even later.

"Tous les pays arabes, ayant réalisé leur indépendance, mais à des dates échelonnées, après la deuxième guerre mondiale, ont fait suivre cette accession du même acte: l'adoption de l'arabe comme langue officielle, ce qui entraînait automatiquement trois conséquences importantes sur le plan socio-culturel: 1) effort considerable pour développer la scolarisation 2) développement important du livre arabe et 3) développement important de tous les 'media' en arabe" (Tapiéro 1976: 115). Tapiéro also adds: "Il est très important de remarquer que depuis l'accession à l'indépendance, tout usager de la langue arabe dans ces pays, aspire à l'employer oralement, même s'il est d'abord incité à l'écrire et à la lire." This means that in most Arab countries the Arabic language has been the official language for less than fifty years,[26] but this does not alter the fact that it was used previously in administration.[27]

Only in the second half of the 20th century did the knowledge of written Arabic become more generally spread through education and the mass media (Diem 1974: 23).[28] Also Monteil (1960: 35) observes espe-

were meant to establish contact with existing academies for a better Pan-Arab cooperation facilitating the coining, improvement and simplification of the language, the effects were rather negative. This was due to the political rivalries in the Arab world but also to cultural factors. The task of simplification was never meant for example, to take into consideration the linguistic and cultural interests of the North-African countries which were then colonized, attention being only paid to the problems of the leading countries, i.e., Egypt, Iraq and Syria".

[25] According to the writer Nakhla (1938) cited in Mattar (1986: 254) the Arabic language was in a pitiful state before the second World War: "Cette langue que l'on a qualifiée comme étant la plus riche de toutes, en fait de vocabulaire, et la plus souple pour l'expression des idées, se trouve réduite de nos jours, à un tel état de pauvreté que si un écrivain voulait décrire sa chambre à coucher, il trouverait à peine dans cette langue de quoi suffire à cette tâche insignifiante."

[26] See also Schulz (1981: 127).

[27] In Egypt Turkish was the language of administration since the 16th century. From 1845 on, Turkish was replaced gradually by Arabic. In 1870 not more than one fifth of the official correspondence was conducted in Turkish (Rebhan 1986: 11).

[28] Ferguson describes the Arab world of forty years ago as follows: "In the first place, there was what has been called 'restricted literacy' or 'elite literacy' or even 'Oriental literacy'. That is, the Arab world was then a society like many others in Asia, where there had been literacy and works of literature for centuries in the society but where the society was overwhelmingly non-literate: there was only a thin layer of traditional scholars and people who used literacy in their own language in their daily lives. Forty years ago that was still a salient characteristic of the Arab world" (Ferguson 1990: 42).

cially after the end of World War II a new revival of Arabic as a cultural language, particularly by the development of press, radio and television and the activities of the intelligentsia to find new technical terms.[29] As a matter of fact, the wide-spread use of MSA as a means of communication is of a very recent date.

2.3.3. *Modern Arabic as a new language variety*

Lecomte's thesis (Meiseles 1980: 138) that Modern Arabic is nothing else but Classical Arabic is clearly out of date. Blau (1981: 145; 177) remarks correctly that "Neither Hebrew nor Arabic intellectuals should ignore the basic fact that Modern Hebrew and Modern Standard Arabic are new layers in the development of their respective languages". It is commonly known that languages do evolve, albeit very slowly.

Roman points out that besides the external factors (cf. supra) there are also internal ones: "Il y a à l'évolution des langues non seulement des causes externes, des causes historiques, mais aussi des causes internes, des causes linguistiques, qui empêchent qu'elles soient stables jamais" (Roman 1987: 135). It seems to me extremely important to examine the evolution of the language and to discover on which points contemporary MSA differs from previous language use, in this case Classical or Middle Arabic.[30]

According to Stetkevych Modern Standard Arabic deviates strongly from Classical Arabic. "Modern Arabic is moving away from both the classical and the colloquial languages. While retaining the morphological structure of classical Arabic, syntactically and above all, stylistically it is coming ever closer to the form and spirit of the large, suprageneaological family of Western culture bearing languages" (Stetkevych 1970: 121).

To what extent and in what way Modern Arabic deviates from Classical Arabic is not always clear. According to Bateson (1967: 84) and

[29] Abdulaziz (1986: 16) points out that only after World War II did the influence of the Arabic *nahḍa* became more general: "Another movement that greatly contributed to the shaping of MSA was the modern Arabic literary renaissance that began in the last half of the last century and gained momentum after the Second World War. (...) In the 1950s and 1960s other genres unknown in classical times developed, including the modern novel, short stories and drama" (Abdulaziz 1986: 17).

[30] Cf. also Fehri (1981: 302) who writes: "Par ailleurs, on gardera présent à l'esprit le fait que la langue évolue (même si l'évolution est quelquefois timide) et qu'on doit s'attendre à ce que des données authentiques à un certain stade de l'histoire de la langue arabe soient différentes de celles qu'on rencontre aujourd'hui".

Nofal (1980: 12) it involves only 'acceptable simplifications'. It is however not further specified what these acceptable simplifications precisely are about. Ditters (1992: 42) correctly remarks that there does not yet exist a profound study about the differences between these two language varieties.[31]

The only clear observation is that there are indeed differences. According to Mitchell those are limited in number. "MSA shares most of its morphology and syntax with the classical language of the Qur'ân and canonical literature of Islam" (Mitchell 1982: 124 and 1986: 9).[32] According to Morsly they are on the contrary very numerous. "Cette variété ne correspond plus à la langue coranique, elle a subi de nombreux changements tant au niveau morpho-syntaxique qu'au niveau lexical et même phonologique" (Morsly 1990: 164).

There are very few investigations in this field. Kästner conducted an important investigation of the phonology and phonetics. He concludes: "Die Unterschiede zwischen klassischem Arabisch und modernem Arabisch auf diesem Gebiet sind minimal" (Kästner 1980: 5).[33] Thiry (1985: 97) and Mattar (1986: 272) are of the same view, but they add that the rare differences are caused by dialectal influences. In the field of morphology it is generally accepted that Modern Standard Arabic has kept the same morphology as the Classical language (Mattar 1986: 272-3).[34]

Also on the syntactic level the differences seem to be limited. According to Kropfitsch (1980: 124-125) there are some shifts in the use of the prepositions, probably under the influence of dialects and European languages. Bateson (1967: 85) makes the same observation. She writes that "many particles have undergone a slight shift in meaning". Stetkevych (1970: 87) points at the differences in the correspondence between the

[31] Ditters writes further on (1992: 39) "There does not exist a single exhaustive study of the two language varieties. To our knowledge there does not exist a single exhaustive description of MSA based on authentic language data". One can now make the claim, however, that, for instance, Cantarino's Syntax (1974) is indeed based on a thorough study of the Arabic literature.

[32] Monteil (1960: 26) is of the same opinion: "En principe l'arabe moderne ne connaît pas, avec le classique, de différence fondamentale sur ce point (syntaxe)." Thiry (1985: 107-8) talks about 'faibles differences entre MSA et langue classique'.

[33] Abdulaziz remarks correctly that it is very difficult to verify this: "The phonological structure of MSA is assumed to be the same as that of the classical language. It is doubtful that the phonetic values of phonemes and morphophonemes have truly remained the same. We may never be in a position to check this because nobody knows the actual phonetics of classical Arabic during pre-Islamic and medieval times" (Abdulaziz 1986: 20).

[34] This is also confirmed by Larcher (1990: 137): "L'arabe moderne se caractérise par une absolue continuité morphologique".

particle *'ayy* and the substantive that follows it and at the fact that in MSA word order has changed. The subject precedes the verb more frequently.[35]

Yet another modern development is the frequent use of *yūjadu* 'there is' (Stetkevych 1970: 98). Stetkevych also mentions new possibilities in the construct state. The construct state where two substantives are in relation to a third one seems to be the most characteristic difference with Classical Arabic[36] (Monteil 1960: 231; Cachia 1967: 16; Tapiéro 1976: 91; Thiry 1985: 107; Gully 1993: 23 et seq.). Another element mentioned is the fact that with a passive form the agent is not used in Classical Arabic, whereas this may be the case in Modern Arabic[37] (Mc Loughin 1972: 60; cf. infra 5.6. note 25).

Wehr underlines the fact that it involves not only changes in the language but also constructions that disappear and are no longer used. "Wir dürfen also zusammenfassend sagen, dass die formalen, in Regeln fassbaren Elemente der heutigen Sprache keine wesentlichen Abweichungen aufweisen, es sei denn, dass viele syntaktische Erscheinungen in Vergessenheit geraten sind und syntaktische Neuerungen in beschränkten Umfang auftreten" (Wehr 1943: 43). Blohm (1991: 90) observes the almost complete disappearance in language use of Modern Standard Arabic of the *modus energicus*.

Beeston points out that the use of the feminine form of adjectives to indicate a plural is a neologism. "In pre-Islamic poetry, it is virtually a universal rule that adjectives, no matter whether color terms or otherwise, show plural forms when referring to pluralities. (...) The use of the feminine singular concord with 'irrational' substantives is a neologism in Arabic which only gradually won its way to becoming the norm" (Beeston 1975: 66). This is confirmed by Belnap's more extensive examination who concludes: "It may be that plural agreement is dying out and is restricted to regular use in a few collocations only" (Belnap 1992: 260). Further on, he points out that this evolution has taken place very slowly. "The pre-modern materials in the corpus show considerable variation. There is much more broken and feminine plural agreement with non-human controllers in the earliest sample, pre-Islamic poetry, than in the later works, medieval and modern" (Belnap 1992: 255).[38]

[35] See also Monteil (1960: 227) and Tapiéro (1976: 90).

[36] Such as, for instance, the phrase *kitāb wa qalam aṭ-ṭālib* in stead of *kitāb aṭ-ṭālib wa qalamuhu* (the book and the pencil of the student).

[37] Such as, for example the construction *rufiḍa min qibali* (it was rejected by).

[38] Blau (1973: 209) also mentions this tendency but he also remarks that the knowledge of Classical and Middle Arabic is too restricted to jump to conclusions. "Moreover,

The most important modernizations, however, are situated in the lexicon, phraseology and style (Wehr 1943: 43; Blau 1981: 30; Mattar 1986: 272-3; Larcher 1990: 137; Bentahila 1991: 72).[39] The new lexicon does not exclude the use of words of the old classical lexicon (Thiry 1985: 97). "With few exceptions, nothing contained in the numerous ancient sources of Standard Arabic has, in principle become obsolete and authors draw freely from them, including the huge vocabulary of Arabic as codified in native lexicons" (Blau 1981: 29).[40]

This has been confirmed by Parkinson (1991: 36): "There are language columns in Egyptian newspapers and magazines that continually blur the line between classical *fuṣḥā* and modern *fuṣḥā*, on the assumption that any word, form, or structure sanctioned long ago is also fine today." Parkinson also blames the Arabic Academy of Egypt for their lack in compiling their new dictionary empirically, when he writes: "Even the Arabic Language Academy, whose mission is to modernize *fuṣḥā*, has published a dictionary recently with an absolutely confusing mixture of archaic, classical, and modern meanings under almost every

because of our limited knowledge of various layers of Arabic, especially of Middle Arabic, both as to grammar and vocabulary, many of the conclusions reached may prove inaccurate" (Blau 1973: 172). Belnap's study (1992) is probably the only one that is based on corpora from different periods of the history of the Arabic language, which makes the conclusions more reliable. However Blau also observes that all tendencies still can evolve in another direction. "Besides, the trends noted are still opposed by strong factors, which may eventually overcome them. Effective opposition of puristic tendencies may revert the direction of development, whereas lenient decisions of the language academies may accelerate changes" (Blau 1973: 173). See also for adaptations in the correspondence between substantives and adjectives: Tapiéro (1976: 93).

[39] The most profound studies about a renewed lexicon and changes in phraseology are by Monteil (1960) and Stetkevych (1970). See Rebhan (1986) and Ayalon (1987) about the introduction of new political concepts.

[40] Many authors refer to the vast lexicon of Classical Arabic and in particular they note the abundance of synonyms (Mattar 1986: 256-7; Nofal 1980: 8). "Il faut y ajouter la surabondance du vocabulaire. (...) A côté de cette synonymie redoutable, se rencontre une polysémie peut-être plus redoutable encore. On parle toujours des 200 mots arabes qui signifient 'serpent'" (Marçais 1930: 403). The same has been observed for the dialects (Benabdi 1986: 67). Although Stetkevych observes that this is still the case in MSA "We observe that the modern Arabic lexicon sometimes suffers as much from a superabundance of synonymous terms as it does from the lack of new vocabulary" (Stetkevych 1970: 28). The question can be raised whether elements of the Classical lexicon are still operational in MSA (with maybe exception of poetry). It is not difficult at all to compose lists of Arabic synonyms (cf. Justice 1987: 20; Bentahila 1991: 78). When talking about the large quantity of synonyms, one often forgets that only few of them are frequently used. "In practice, only a very small portion of this vast accumulated vocabulary is used" (Bateson 1967: 87). This does not alter the fact that there are almost no empirical data about vocabulary use. There are only a few frequency lists, most of which are obsolete or limited. See, for instance, Brill (1940); Landau (1959); Pellat (1971); Bobzin (1980) and Kouloughli (1991).

entry, with no marking whatsoever on which are likely to be understood by modern readers, and which are entirely out of date, as if the unity of classical and modern *fuṣḥā* was a political imperative to be enforced, rather than an empirical question, to be decided by observation" (Parkinson 1991: 36). Without a corpus analysis it seems to me however very difficult to show that words included by the Arab Academy of Egypt in its dictionary are obsolete or are not any more used. One has to take into account that apparently obsolete words can be quite current for Muslims, maybe only because of the fact that they do often occur in Islamic traditions (cf. infra 5.6. note 25).

2.3.4. *A new Arabic language variety with many names*

In the course of this century a new language variety has come into being that is based to a great extent on Classical Arabic, but that can be seen as a separate language variety. In the beginning many names were created to name this variety. Monteil (1960: 25) wrote in this respect about a Neo-Arabic that was, according to him, a modern written or literary form of Classical Arabic. Wehr (1943: 44) proposed to use the term Neoclassical. "Es würde sich empfehlen, mit Lecerf, vom neuklassischen Arabisch (l'arabe néo-classique) zu reden, um nicht die Fiktion der Unveränderlichkeit des Arabischen zu pflegen."

Others called it *Arabe Vivant* (Pellat 1971) or *Arabe Médian* (Berque 1974). In England, France and Italy also the term Literary Arabic was used, a term often used in Dutch too. However, it was not always clear what was meant by this term. Did it only refer to the language of literature or did it also include other language registers? It is, for example, clear that the manuals of Lecomte and Ghedira (1970) and Borrmans and Müller (1977) aimed at introducing the students into the language of contemporary Arabic literature. Gully (1993: 20) too makes a clear distinction between *Modern Literary Arabic*, which exclusively comprises the contemporary Arabic literature, and *Modern Standard Arabic*, including the Arabic of the journalists. As a matter of fact the gap between these two, according to Gully, becomes wider and wider.

According to Ziadeh (1957), Meiseles (1977: 173) and Killean (1980: 177) the term Modern Literary Arabic covers journalistic language and the language of the media. With Cowan (1970), the term Literary Arabic also covers a much vaster language use than pure literary. Often the term *literary* was used in contrast with the dialects. Another less frequently used term is Contemporary Arabic.[41] Thiry (1985: 102-103) does not consider this term to be appropriate at all to designate this language variety, because also dialects are *contemporary*.

Initially in Germany this new language variety was called *Hocharabisch*,[42] and later on *Modern Hocharabisch* (Kästner 1981: 26). This term does not exclusively involve the language of literature but on the contrary all contemporary Arabic language usage that is clearly distinct from the Arabic dialects. Nevertheless, this language variety was gradually and in more and more publications called Modern Arabic.[43] Also the authors of a lot of manuals that treat contemporary Arabic talk about *Modern Arabic*.[44]

[41] Especially in the Arab world this denomination is often used. See, for instance, the Arabic translation of Abboud (1983) and further on also Badawī (1973), Meiseles (1980), Al-ʿAdnānī (1989) and Al-Warrāqī (1994).

[42] In German there is no equivalent for the term 'standard language'. Keller (cited in Joseph 1987: 5) writes: "There is no single completely satisfactory expression in German for the notion of standard language. *Schriftsprache* puts the stress one-sidedly on writing but is the current popular term for the NHG standard language. *Hochsprache* has definite cultural, literary and social connotations, while *Gemeinsprache* would appear to need further definition since forms which are definitely not standard are nevertheless *Gemeinsprache*. The English word *standard*, in contrast to these German terms, places the stress exactly on the most essential features, namely on *norm*." The term *Hochsprache* was first used by Wehr, H. (1934) in relation to Arabic in his article "Die Besonderheit des heutigen Hocharabischen. Mit Berücksichtigung der Einwirkung der europäischen Sprachen", *Mitteilungen des Seminars für Orientalische Sprachen* 37. Later on it was also used by Diem (1974), and also by Reuschel, W. (1978) in the article: "Die Grammatik des modernen Hocharabisch. Stand und Tendenzen internationaler Forschung". *AALS* 6, pp. 958-978. Although this term is still used in Germany [e.g. Forkel (1987)] on other occasions also the term 'modernes Arabisch' (Krahl 1974) is used.

[43] The term Modern Arabic was already used at the end of the 19th century (Serruys 1897). In the 20th century Modern Arabic was often seen in narrow relationship to the written language. We have e.g. the manual of Smith, H.L., *Modern Written Arabic*, Washington, D.C.: Department of State, Foreign Service Institute, 1969; Vol I, xiv, 419 pp.; the studies of Snow, J.A., *A Grammar of Modern Written Arabic Clauses*. Ph D, University of Michigan at Ann Arbor, 1965; 214 pp.; Speers, P.C., *Development and Present State of Modern Written Arabic*. Ph D, University of London, 1959; 287 pp.; B Killean, M.C.G., *The Deep Structure of the Noun Phrase in Modern Written Arabic*. Ph D, University of Michigan at Ann Arbor, 1966; 148 pp. and El-Ezabi, Y.A., *A Sector Analysis of Modern Written Arabic with Implications for Teaching English to Arab Students*, Ph D, Columbia University, 1967, 183 pp. and finally the dictionary of Wehr, H., *A Dictionary of Modern Written Arabic*. Ed. J. Milton Cowan, Wiesbaden: Otto Harrassowitz, 1971; xvii, 1110 pp.

[44] The term Modern Arabic occurs in all European languages. Examples of German publications: Ambros, A., *Einführung in die Moderne Arabische Schriftsprache*, Max Hueber Verlag, München, 1969, 428 p.; Klopfer, H., *Modernes Arabisch. Eine Einführung ins heutige Zeitungsschriftarabisch*. Heidelberg: Julius Groos Verlag, 2nd revised edn, 1970, 136 pp. and also the three-volume manual of Blohm, D., e.a. *Lehrbuch des Modernen Arabisch*, Leipzig, 1981, 3 volumes. In the French area there is the book of Pellat, Ch., *Introduction à l'Arabe Moderne*, Paris, 1970; 248 pp. More recently the

The notion 'modern' is not always clearly characterized. This concept too can cover different contents. Does it cover the period from 1789 until now, the period since the turn of the century, or the period after World War II (Ditters 1992: 2-3)? Tapiéro (1976: 9 en 69) holds the view that it covers the period 1875 till now. Bathurst (1971: 187) and Blohm (1991: 90) see the modern period as the period after World War II.

It is clear, however, that the current use of *Modern Arabic* only became possible after the sizable adaptations to the lexicon. Ayalon (1987) clearly demonstrated that the period of the 19th century was characterized by experiments as far as language is concerned. He also observed a strong evolution of the language in that period so that "An Arab intellectual in 1900 examining a political text from 1800, or even an account from the early years of the press in the mid-1860s, would have found many ideas to have been ambiguously presented and numerous expressions to be obsolete, if not altogether unrecognizable" (Ayalon 1987: 130-131). Given the important evolution on the lexical level, *Modern Arabic* can not simply be defined on the basis of the period from 1789 until now.

2.3.5. *Modern Arabic: a standard language*

Beeston (1970: 12) calls Modern Arabic "Standard Arabic, in default of a more satisfactory term." *In my opinion, however, this language variety is correctly looked upon as a standard language. Indeed this language variety meets the four characteristics of standard languages* (cf. supra 1.1.). A certain language variety (namely Classical Arabic) was selected as a basis (selection); it has been codified and normalized, by the work of the different language academies, adapted to the evolution of time (elaboration) and specifically spread through education and media. As it meets these four characteristics, it is proper to call this variety Modern Standard Arabic in contrast with the Arabic dialects and Classical Arabic. MSA also fulfils the different functions of standard languages. It is the status form of the language and within the Arab world it

manuals of Reich, D., *Manuel d'Arabe Moderne*, Paris, 1984, who 'wrongly' translates the term Modern Arabic into German by Neu-Arabisch: in fact the term Neu-Arabisch in German is used for the dialects (cf. Fischer 1980: 12). For the English area there is the well-known book of Ziadeh, F.J., e.a. *An Introduction to Modern Arabic*, Princeton, N.J.: Princeton University Duplicating Bureau, 1955; x, 331 pp. For the Dutch area there is the manual by Van Mol, M., *Handboek Modern Arabisch*, Orientalia Lovaniensia Analecta 17, Leuven, Peeters, 1984, 422 p.

fulfils a function of unification.[45] Moreover, it is one of the official languages in international organizations as e.g. the United Nations.[46]

Modern Standard Arabic then, includes both contemporary literature and journalistic language. This is the way Mitchell (1982: 123-4) defines MSA: "The label 'Modern Standard Arabic' (MSA) has been applied to the written language of, say, contemporary literature, journalism, TV and radio newscasting, scientific and technological writing, administration and diplomacy". Similar definitions are given by Abdulaziz (1986: 17) and Bentahila (1991: 72). The stress in these definitions lies on the written character of MSA. Mc Loughin (1972: 58); Diem (1974: 52); Kästner (1981: 26) and also Ditters (1992: 128) also point at the oral use of MSA. Emphasis then lies on the formal kind of discussion. Mc Loughin completes the definition of MSA with "and that is used orally in formal speeches, public lectures, learned debates and in religious ceremonials."

However the term Modern Standard Arabic has not been widely accepted. Both Arab and European researchers still disagree about the appropriate terminology. Larcher (1990: 137), for example writes: "Chez les linguistes arabisants d'expression française, 'classique' s'oppose à 'dialectal'. Chez ceux d'expression anglaise, 'classique' se réécrit souvent 'standard', 'classical' prenant alors le sens 'd'ancien', par opposition à 'moderne'. Parler en français d'arabe standard' constitue un anglicisme inutile, et, qui plus est, source de confusion, dans la mesure où francophones et anglophones ne donnent pas le même sens à 'standard'".

Initially Morsly used the term Classical Arabic for this new language variety (1986: 254-255), but later on she holds the view that this term is no longer appropriate when she writes: "le terme d'arabe classique semble dorénavant impropre et l'on parle pour mieux désigner ce nouvel état de langue (...) d'arabe *moderne* ou *standard* (en français!) de *Classical* ou *Modern Arabic* ou de *Modern Standard Arabic* (en anglais)" (1990: 164). However she still keeps using the term *Arabe Classique* in her article (169 et seq.).

Other researchers, such as, e.g. Bateson (1967 75-81); Palva (1969: 3); Mattar (1986: 253) and Tarrier (1991: 1 and 1993: 116-117) stick to the term Classical Arabic. Talmoudi (1984: 26) prefers to talk about semi-classical. Moreover, a lot of researchers mix up the different terms.

[45] Cf. Abu-Absi (1990: 35): "It was argued that MSA was the language of education and culture and functioned as a bond that symbolized and fostered Arab unity".

[46] Cf. (Nofal 1980: 6) and also Hussein (1989).

Kaye (1987: 377) is convinced that Modern Standard Arabic is not the same as Classical Arabic. "The fact is, however, that MSA is not the language of the purists, nor of the language academy in Cairo, nor of Wright's grammar of Classical Arabic, etc." However, in the same article he uses the term Classical Arabic to refer to MSA (1987: 387). Later he keeps using the different terms (1987: 664-675) and even he uses the term "Modern Classical Arabic". Justice (1987: 12) proposes to reserve the term for "the period between Muhammad and any of the various eclipses and hard times that succeeded each other beginning around the eleventh century", but further on (p. 19) he talks about the contemporary use of Classical Arabic.

In the Arab world it seems to be even more difficult to make a distinction between Modern Standard Arabic and Classical Arabic. For both the 'literati' and the unlettered people Classical Arabic is the symbol of an uninterrupted tradition. Both culturally as well as politically Classical Arabic has been of great importance in the Arab world. Arab nationalism and panarabism have from the very beginning been based on Classical Arabic as an element that would advance unity in the Arab world. In this respect Parkinson (1993: 47) remarks that: "Although scholars have no trouble (?) distinguishing MSA from Classical Arabic on formal grounds, native speakers in Egypt do not typically distinguish between the two, using the term *fuṣḥā* for both" (see also Meiseles 1980: 124 and Forkel 1980: 51).

Modern Standard Arabic and Classical Arabic are often seen as one unity, viz. *al-luġa al-fuṣḥā* or simply *al-fuṣḥā*. The distinction is sometimes hard to make because old texts in the Arab world, and especially Koranic texts and traditions, do remain of current interest.[47] This also emerges from the fact that in contemporary Arabic grammars no distinction is made between both language varieties. *Ad-Daḥdāḥ* (1990) uses the term "universal grammatical rules".[48] In his examples there is an abundance of Koranic verses. Koranic Arabic is still considered to be the sublime norm (cf. Diem 1974: 8; Blau 1981: 8 and Kaye 1987: 666).

Nevertheless, attempts are being made to label the language varieties separately. Parkinson (1991: 33) reports that some scholars of the *Dār*

[47] Cf. Forkel (1980: 51): "Da das klassische und das moderne Hocharabisch im Bewusstsein der Marokkaner nur eine Sprache, die fusha darstellen, ist das moderne Hocharabisch gegenüber Wörtern, Formen und Ausdrücken aus der klassischen weitgehend offen".

[48] *Ad-Daḥdāḥ, Anṭwān* (1990). *Mu'jam qawā'id al-'arabīya al-'ālamīya*, Beirut, 249 p. (Subtitle: A Dictionary of Universal Arabic Grammar)

al-ʿUlūm, the Arabic department of the training college for teachers at the University of Cairo, have started using the term *faṣīḥ* (*pure Arabic*) for translation Modern Standard Arabic, whereas they keep the term *fuṣḥā* for Classical Arabic.[49] Scholars of *Al-Azhar* disagree. In their view the Arabic language is one. As a matter of fact, both for Arabic speakers and others *Fuṣḥā* is clearly distinct from the dialects.

In this work Classical Arabic means the language that has been laid down in the traditional Arabic grammars. *By Modern Standard Arabic we understand the standard language, such as it continued to develop in the 20th century and such as it is used in literature, media and in formal conversation, and such as it has been described in modern Western grammars.* Indeed it does not suffice to link MSA to a certain period, nor to a certain language use, because in literature dialectal language also occurs.

2.3.6. *Modern Standard Arabic and the dialects*

There have been some investigations about the differences between Modern Standard Arabic and Arabic dialects. According to Forkel, the most important difference is the omission of the *'iʿrāb* in the dialects.[50] "Das wichtigste Kenzeichen des Hocharabischen gegenüber dem Dialekt ist der Iʿrāb, die "Arabisierung", das Kasus- und Modussystem. Ein Arabisch ohne Iʿrāb ist deswegen per definitionem kein Hocharabisch mehr" (Forkel 1980: 52)[51]. All dialects still have a number of features in common with Standard Arabic. Ferguson (1959) selected 14 elements that Arabic dialects have in common as opposed to

[49] Such a tendency is confirmed by Badawī (1973: 83), who recalls a meeting in the Arabic Academy of Cairo using the term *fuṣḥā*. Classical Arabic was called *al-fuṣḥā al-qadīma* and Modern Arabic *al-fuṣḥā al-jadīda* or *al-fuṣḥā al-ḥadīṯa*. إن لدينا الآن فصحى جديدة لها صفاتها الخاصة بها والتي هي أقرب الى صفات العامية المحلية منها الى صفات الفصحى القديمة (...) إن لدينا لغة فصحى حديثة لا تكاد تمت الى الفصحى القديمة إلا بصلة قليلة. (*Nowadays we have to do with a new fuṣḥā, that has its own characteristics, much closer to the characteristics of the local colloquial language than to the characteristics of the old fuṣḥā. We have to deal with a modern fuṣḥā, that has only a slight link with the old fuṣḥā.*)

[50] On the rules in the use of the *'iʿrāb* in standard language see Atioui (1979: 3-4).

[51] See also Bateson (1967: 97) "The most striking feature of colloquial Arabic is that it has completely abandoned the system of nominal inflection for cases and verbal inflection." (see also Monteil 1960: 57). It is a phenomenon that all dialects have in common (Cowan 1968: 30) and that is probably very old (Fischer 1982: 83). Also *Ibn Ḫaldūn* reports omission of the *'iʿrāb* (Thiry 1985:108). It is worthwhile noting here that the word *'iʿrāb* in Arabic has two meanings: It refers to the case vowels, but also to the grammatical rules that underlie these adaptations of the vowels (ISESCO 1989: 830). All writers mentioning *'iʿrāb* have only the first meaning in mind.

Classical Arabic, among which are the loss of the dual and the morphology and syntax of the cardinal numbers.

In general it is assumed that one dialect cannot be alleged to be closer to Standard Arabic than another one. A limited investigation of the verbs in the dialects of Rabat and Cairo, however, demonstrated that the verbs in Cairo do bear more resemblance to Standard Arabic than the verbs of Rabat as far as morphology is concerned (Van Mol 1980: 12). The verbs in themselves, however, are not sufficient to measure the 'distance' between a dialect and a standard language.

The only complete study about this problem is Altoma (1969) who compared Modern Standard Arabic with the Iraqi dialect. "His findings show that the two varieties of Arabic differ considerably in every respect including phonology, morphology, syntax, lexicon, semantics, and contexts of use" (Ibrahim 1983: 509). This, however, does not mean that there are no similarities that might facilitate the learning of MSA by a native speaker of an Arabic dialect. Nevertheless there are considerable differences between the dialect and the standard language.

The fact that two strongly different language varieties exist side by side is called diglossia. In the next chapter we will deal with the problem of diglossia in the Arab world in more detail.

3. DIGLOSSIA

The linguistic situation, in which, by and large, a literary language coexists with a dialect in one single community, was described in terms of diglossia for the first time by Marçais in 1930. Marçais found in Algeria two language varieties occurring side by side, viz. a written literary variety and the spoken dialects which were not written at all.[1] The description by Marçais of the language situation in Algeria of that time was, however, very general and impressionistic. In the first place he did not give an exhaustive description of the language situation in Algeria. The presence and the influence of the French language was at that time still quite great.[2] Moreover in his series of articles he does not mention the Berber language at all.

According to Marçais diglossia clearly marks the duality of spoken language versus written language: The written language had never been spoken and is never spoken and the spoken language had never been written and is never written. Later investigations (cf. infra 3.1.) revealed that dialectal language was, indeed, also written from time to time. Diglossia certainly does not coincide with the duality of written language versus spoken language. Without doubt, in particular personal letters are often written in dialectical form.[3] Eventually Marçais' aim was

[1] About the situation of that time Marçais wrote: "La langue arabe se présente à nous sous deux aspects sensiblement différents: 1° une langue littéraire dite arabe écrit ou régulier, ou littéral, ou classique qui seule a été partout et toujours écrite dans le passé, dans laquelle seule aujourd'hui encore sont rédigés les ouvrages littéraires ou scientifiques, les articles de presse, les actes judiciaires, les lettres privées, bref tout ce qui est écrit, mais qui, exactement telle qu'elle se présente à nous, n'a peut-être jamais été parlée nulle part, et qui dans tous les cas ne se parle aujourd'hui nulle part. 2° des idiomes parlés (...) dont aucun n'a jamais été écrit, dont la fixation scripturale a valu aux orientalistes qui l'ont tentée des sarcasmes indignés du monde arabe, (...) et qui partout est la seule langue de la conversation dans tous les milieux, populaires et cultivés" (Marçais 1930: 401). And he concludes: "Disons deux états d'une même langue, assez différents pour que la connaissance de l'un n'implique pas la connaissance de l'autre; assez semblables pour que la connaissance de l'un facilite considérablement l'acquisition de l'autre" (Marçais 1930: 409).

[2] In the following article *'la langue arabe dans l'Afrique du Nord'* he wrote: "*le deuxième responsable de la crise de l'arabe, c'est le français*" (Marçais 1930: 39).

[3] Even at present a lot of personal letters are written, albeit partially in dialect. In Moroccan letters the preposition *diyāl* (of) and many dialect words as, for instance, *ṣīfet* (to send) often occur. Meiseles (1977) classifies this form of written Arabic as IWA, Informal Written Arabic. Meiseles is inclined to classify this Arabic variety as

to give a general description on behalf of policy officials in the domain of education in a situation where two language varieties coexisted.

Later on Ferguson (1960) tried to give a broader scientific basis to the concept of diglossia, by refining its definition and in testing it in other language situations. After examining the language situation in Greece, the Arab countries, Haiti and Switzerland he comes up with the following definition of diglossia: "Diglossia is a relatively stable language situation in which, in addition to the primary dialects of the language (which may include a standard or regional dialects), there is a very divergent, highly codified (often grammatically more complex) superposed variety, the vehicle of a large and respected body of written literature, either of an earlier period or in another speech community, which is learned largely by formal education and is used for most written and formal spoken purposes, but is not used by any sector of the community for ordinary conversation" (Ferguson 1960: 336).

3.1. Characteristics of diglossia

In Ferguson's notion of diglossia, the high variety H is in all cases a language with great prestige and a rich literary tradition, which is used as a written language, and also orally on formal occasions, whereas the low variety L is exclusively used in informal situations.[4] Ferguson's concept of diglossia does not coincide anymore with the duality of written language versus spoken language. It is however clear that in the

substandard. "It is the extemporaneous writing the social circumstances of whose production do not pressure the writer into closely observing the language quality of his writing, and which includes private correspondence, drafts, personal records, and the like. In these cases, the manner of the writer is free; his writing is generally spontaneous, unedited and free to amendation from the language point of view" (Meiseles 1980: 125). Parkinson (1991: 39) remarks correctly that it is premature to classify this variety as substandard. More empirical investigations should reveal whether writers of these letters would not have corrected these faults themselves in other circumstances. In any event the Ditters' proposition (1992: 8) that "No native speaker uses colloquial Arabic for written communication" is only partially correct. See also Cachia (1967: 13).

[4] Often the notion diglossia is mixed up with bilingualism. According to Kaye (1987: 675) diglossia refers to a situation in which two varieties of the same language function side by side, in contrast with bilingualism which supposes the existence of two different languages. Nevertheless, Diem (1974) describes the Arabic language situation in terms of *Zweisprachigkeit*. About the difference between diglossia and bilingualism see also Schippers (1987: 80) and Wilmsen (1995: 14-16).

Arabic language community MSA is the prestigious variety par excellence.[5]

In a diglossic situation the dialects are seen as inferior to the High language variety (Abu-Absi 1990: 34; Bentahila 1991: 71). In this sense Nagīb Maḥfūẓ wrote: "The colloquial is one of the diseases from which the people are suffering, and of which they are bound to rid themselves as they progress. I consider the colloquial one of the failings of our society, exactly like ignorance, poverty, and disease" (Cachia 1967: 20).[6]

Moreover, within a language community there are many prejudices against the dialects. The grammar of the High variety, e.g., is considered to be more complex than the grammar of the dialect. It goes without saying that this impression is very subjective. From the point of view of dialect speakers the *High variety* is, indeed, more complex because it is not learnt in a spontaneous 'natural' manner (see also Tarrier 1991: 4; and cf. infra 6.4. note 33). Only the High variety has a long tradition of grammatical study and a fixed norm for pronunciation, grammar and lexicon, whereas there are almost no descriptive or normative studies of the Low varieties.[7]

[5] According to Mahmoud (1986: 241) this is due to the close connection between MSA and Koranic Arabic: "The prestige assigned to MSA stems from its close association with Classical Arabic eminently represented by the Quran". In this respect Ibrahim (1986: 115) observes that a language with great prestige is not necessarily a standard language. In a given community also dialects which are not standard languages can enjoy great prestige (cf. Diem 1974: 4 and Wilmsen 1995 about the dialect of Cairo).

[6] Blau (1981: 22) comes to the same conclusion: "Since, in their subconscious mind, the Arab elite are well aware of the dangers of "diglossia" and yet want to stick to the use of Standard Arabic, they react with extreme enmity toward the dialects". As example he cites a book by *Nafūsa Zakarīya* condemning in 1964 the use of dialects in literature as an imperialistic conspiracy.

[7] Whether the language situation in the Arab world has always been characterized by diglossia is not quite certain. According to Ferguson (1959: 616-617) this has always been the case: "It is widely accepted that the Classical language, the *'Arabīya* of the grammarians, was based on a standard poetic language not necessarily identical with any one dialect, but in oral use by poets and orators of many dialects and known to us fairly directly from the remnants of pre-Islamic poetry and from the *Qur'ān*." And Ferguson (1960: 327): "Arabic diglossia seems to reach as far back as our knowledge of Arabic goes." Eid (1990: 7) shares that view: "Diglossia has been characteristic of the Arabic speech communities since our earliest records of Arabic." Also Bateson (1967: 76-77), El Hassan (1978: 113) and Nofal (1980: 5) hold the same view. On the contrary Schippers (1987: 46) and Ditters (1992: 13) remark that Nöldeke, Fück and Blau hold the view that in the pre-Islamic period such a thing as diglossia did not exist. According to Versteegh (1984) the literary language in the pre-Islamic period was only another register of the spoken languages. See also Fischer & Jastrow (1980: 20-24) and Badawī (1973: 60).

It is claimed that dialects would have 'no grammatical rules'.[8] As a matter of fact, in the Arab world there is some resistance against conducting investigations into the dialect.[9] Almost no investigations have been conducted into the dialects by Arab scholars.[10] In this respect Blau (1981: 22) observes that most studies about Arabic dialects have been conducted at European and American universities. Moreover not everybody fully appreciates this scientific work.[11]

One of the fundamental characteristics of diglossia is that each variety has a specific function. In the High variety it is not always possible to say what can be said in the dialect. According to *Kamāl Yūsuf al-Ḥājj* (Monteil 1960: 71) the dialect expresses the sentiment, whereas Classical Arabic expresses the intellect. The main importance of the dialect lies in its ability to express sentiments and emotional feelings. According to Diem (1974: 20) dialectal words also often have a symbolic meaning. My own investigation has shown that, indeed, the Moroccan dialect has a very strong communicative value within the community (Van Mol 1980a, 1986).

Moreover, there is also what Diem (1974: 23) calls grammatical pressure. Circumstances define to a large extent which language variety is chosen. In one's own group it is not appropriate to use the High variety because one might be looked upon as pretentious. On the other hand it is not appropriate either to use dialect in certain circumstances because one might be looked upon as inferior. The language which is used is not defined by linguistic necessity, nor by one's knowledge of the High variety, but rather by rules of conformity.[12]

[8] In this respect Diem (1971: 12) observes: "Typisch für diese abschätzige Haltung ist auch die häufig anzutreffende Meinung, die Dialekte hätten im Gegensatz zur *fuṣḥā* keine festen Regeln". This is confirmed by Badawī (1973: 54): اما العامية فهي عندهم ليست ذات نظام خاص بها وليس لها قواعد وقوانين. *(But the colloquial has according to them no structure peculiar to it and does not know any rules or laws.)*

[9] Mitchell (1980: 93) has the same impression: "The 'high flown' style is the one deemed by Arab academies, the Arab League, and most Arabists to be alone worthy of study."

[10] One and probably the only exception is the two-volume work of *'Abd al-Mun'am Sayyid 'Abd al-'Āl* about the dialects of *Tiṭwān* (Northern-Morocco) and environment (1968) viz.: *Lahjat šamāl al-Maġrib, Tiṭwān wa-mā ḥawlahā* and *Mu'jam šamāl al-maġrib, Tiṭwān wa-mā ḥawlahā (The language of Northern-Morocco, Tetwan and environment)*, both published in Cairo. In any case, the Arabic alphabet is not suitable for a solid phonemic transcription.

[11] Cf. Ibrahim (1983: 513-4): "Anyone who deals with spoken Arabic, including Arab linguists who have studied certain aspects of their dialects, is looked upon with suspicion".

[12] See further also Diem (1974: 54 e.v.)

Diglossia in the Arab world is not restricted to the spoken language. Diglossia also occurs in the written language. The investigations of Diem (1974: 88-105) and Tapiéro (1976: 76 et seq.) in particular have revealed that on some occasions, such as film and theater, the High variety alternates with the Low variety. Further, speeches and reports of debates are often not written down in MSA but in dialectal form, probably to reflect the spoken words as truthfully as possible.[13] Some poems, especially songs, and also some novels have been written completely in dialect (Bateson 1967: 113-114).[14] The same still happens in magazines when dialogues are reproduced and in cartoons or some comics.[15] It is also found in manuals which are intended for a larger public.[16]

The use of dialectal Arabic in literature, however, is unmistakably subject to criticism. Although Cachia (1967: 17) ascertains that the dialect takes root in literature here and there, he otherwise has to admit that "furthermore, works in the colloquial receive no recognition from the Egyptian Academy, and do not qualify for State prizes." Diem has the same impression: "Die Beschäftigung mit den Dialekten galt seit jeher als eines adīb unwürdig" (Diem 1974: 12).[17]

Diem (1974: 3), who conducted the most extensive investigation based on Ferguson's concept of diglossia, which he defined as bilingualism, stresses the fact that the Low varieties also strongly differ from each

[13] See also Meiseles (1980: 126).

[14] Here too the emotional value of the dialect seems to play. According to Diem (1974: 21) lettered Arabs, asked in which language variety they would write a letter to their mother, answer that they would do so in dialect. He also quotes (p. 94) the example of a journalist who wrote a report about a lawsuit in MSA, but who switches to dialect when he allows the mother of the murdered child to speak, because otherwise he cannot adequately express the deep feelings of the mother.

[15] Recently also, for instance, in an interview with Sheik *aš-Ša'rāwī* in the Egyptian magazine *al-muṣawwar* (18th of April 1997) that was transcribed partially in dialectal Arabic. For a thorough study of the emergence and the spread of comics and cartoons in the Arab world see Douglas, Allen & Malti-Douglas, Fedwa (1994): *Arab Comic Strips*, Indiana University Press, Bloomington, 263 p.

[16] For example, a booklet that recently has been published in Rabat (Morocco) viz. *Kūdlārūt maġrib 2000*, a manual of the traffic regulations which is completely written in Moroccan dialect.

[17] Meiseles (1980: 124) writes: "In practice, the use of the vernaculars in (written) literature is *quite* acceptable to the literary norm of Modern Arabic Literature, generally for artistic reasons." Whether the use of the dialect in the written language will continue is not quite certain. Tapiéro (1976: 264) observes: "De grands écrivains comme Maḥmūd Taymūr et M. Ḥusayn Haykal qui avaient employé l'arabe dialectal égyptien pour les conversations de leurs premiers romans, ont présenté les dialogues de leurs ouvrages postérieurs en langue savante." Badawī (1973: 51) compared the two versions of Taymūr, but he concludes that other Arabs experience great difficulty in understanding the dialectal version.

other geographically, whereas in the High variety regional differences seem to be much smaller. Tapiéro (1976: 68) too observes this difference and defines diglossia as follows: "la coexistance d'une langue commune qui est l'arabe classique et d'une langue de communication courante qui est l'arabe dialectal, variable d'un pays à l'autre, voire d'une région à l'autre dans un même pays" (Tapiéro 1976: 68). Basically, the High variety is likely to be more eligible to function as a common koine between the different Arab countries than the Low variety.

3.2. Comments on Ferguson's Concept of Diglossia

This section deals with the concept of diglossia such as it has been introduced by Ferguson. First of all, the underlying concepts, and particularly the notion of standard language, are not clearly defined. Ferguson regards the whole process of two different language varieties which coexist as a kind of standardization, viz. "the kind of standardization where two varieties of a language exist side by side throughout the community, with each having a definite role to play" (Ferguson, 1960: 325). Ferguson still uses the term standardization when a Low variety fulfils a higher function. As as example, Ferguson (1960: 332) mentions the dialect of Cairo, which functions as standard L in Egypt.

However, this dialect is not codified, nor is it taught in Cairene schools. In this way Ferguson places the notion of standard language in a wider context. According to him dialects also can be standardized. In applying one and the same term to two very different language varieties some confusion is created. This prompts Ibrahim (1986: 115) to use the term non-standard standard language. It also leads Haery (quoted in Eid 1990: 25) to conclude that there are two types of standard: "an 'organic' standard developing out of the colloquials and the 'classical' Arabic as a standard." However, it is clear that no dialect can meet the criteria of a standard language (cf. supra 1.1.). It, therefore, seems more reasonable to use the term supra-regional dialect or supra-regional koine for such a language variety.[18]

A second problem, related to Ferguson's concept of diglossia, is that other language situations have been described in terms of 'nondiglossic speech communities' (Belnap 1992: 245, Wilmsen 1995: 154). Ibrahim (1991: 45) describes this situation as follows: *'des langues allergiques à*

[18] Ibrahim (1986) too points out that such a supra-regional dialect can not be identified by the notion of standard language, even if it possesses a greater prestige than the other dialects.

la diglossie comme le français.' However, this definition starts from the faulty assumption that there are language communities where the standard language is equal to the mother tongue. A standard language such as we have defined it is, however, seldom a mother tongue. It always is a more or less artificial language which is taught at school. This language can be related to the mother tongue.

The lack of clarity is partly due to the fact that the notion of mother tongue is ambiguous. On the one hand the mother tongue is the language which a child learns and uses at home. It is the language of the *mother*. On the other hand, 'mother tongue' is a subject at school. Children are taught their 'mother tongue' which refers to standard language. As a matter of fact, every Fleming is convinced that Dutch is his mother tongue. The same goes for Arabs. Every Arab is also convinced that (standard) Arabic is his mother tongue.[19]

Ferguson himself never used the term "nondiglossic speech communities". However, he had in mind language communities where the High language variety is used by its members in a more or less natural way. "As characterized here, diglossia differs from the more widespread standard-with-dialects in that no segment of the speech community in diglossia regularly uses H (the prestigious variety) as a medium of ordinary conversation, and any attempt to do so is felt to be either pedantic or artificial. In the more usual standard-with-dialects situation the standard is often similar to the variety of a certain region or social group which is used in ordinary conversation more or less naturally by members of the group and as a superposed variety by others." (Ferguson 1960: 337).[20]

However carefully this characterization may be phrased, it does not hold true completely. After all, the question remains how this distinction can be made. Parkinson (1990: 292) e.g. writes about English as follows: "Only a few people speak literary English at home, as any linguist who has worked with transcripts of natural conversation can demonstrate, but this does not mean no one is a native user of literary English."

According to Abuhamdia this is confirmed by sociolinguistic investigations. "Recent sociolinguistic research has proved as false the long

[19] Blau points out that especially Muslim Arabs consider Classical Arabic as their 'own' language.. "One cannot compare the status of the Christian priest, whose Latin prayer was not felt to be connected with the language of the worshippers, with that of the Jewish rabbi or the Muslim imam, whose language of prayer was considered by the worshippers as their own, even though they did not always understand it" (Blau 1981: 13).

[20] Ferguson (1996: 52) emphasizes once more, in his last article on this issue, that in the case of diglossia the High variety cannot be spoken without effort.

held assumption that the standard is native to a certain regional or social group. One quote should suffice, taking English as the illustration. 'Standard American English' is an idealization, no one speaks this dialect natively" (Abuhamdia 1988: 1241). And Abuhamdia (1968: 1242) winds up with: "The upshot is that diglossia is a universal phenomenon of all living languages."

Ditters described MSA within the Arab world as a second language[21]. This description is correct only if we take into account that every standard language is taught at school.[22] In that way MSA as a standard language does not differ from Dutch or English. This context puts into perspective the proposition of e.g. Kaye (1970: 377) and Ibrahim (1983: 514) that Modern Standard Arabic has no 'native speakers'. Parkinson (1990: 292 and 1991: 39), therefore, prefers to use the term 'native users': "The author strongly believes that Standard Arabic is a full-fledged language, and that it has native users, with native intuitions about its use: people who read it fluently and listen to it with ease and understanding every day, and who occasionally use it in speaking and writing as well. Some of these native users should also be considered native writers of the form, since they use it effortlessly and skillfully." This brings us back to the characterization of Marçais that 'la connaissance de l'un facilite considérablement l'acquisition de l'autre.' (cf. supra 3. note 1.). The native speaker of an Arabic dialect stands, as a matter of fact, much closer to the standard language than a non-native speaker.

A last observation is that Ferguson does not make a distinction between written and spoken Modern Standard Arabic. He assumes that the spoken form of MSA is realized in the same way as the written form, which is not really the case. It seems clear to me that MSA is spoken nowadays more than it used to be. Forkel e.g. points at the increasing importance of spoken MSA in the Arab world. "Von grosser Bedeutung ist weiter, dass die Gelegenheiten, bei denen Hocharabisch *gesprochen* wird, im Vergleich zu früher stark zugenommen haben. Der gebildete Marokkaner spricht und hört Hocharabisch in der Schule und an der Universität, er spricht es in öffentlichen Diskussionen und mit Arabern aus anderen arabischen Ländern. Politiker sprechen es im Parlament, bei Interviews, in öffentlichen Erklärungen und Reden" (1981: 42). This

[21] "This language is taught at school as a secondary language to people whose native tongue is one of the regional dialects" (Ditters: 1986: 47 and 1988: 32).

[22] According to Parkinson (1993: 70) native speakers do not consider MSA as a second language: "At least in the case of high school graduates and higher, subjects do not appear to experience MSA as a foreign or 'second' language." (cf. supra note 19).

still does not make clear whether the spoken realization of MSA is identical to the written form. Close observation reveals that most Arabs experience difficulties in maintaining this High variety in its spoken form.[23] Spoken MSA is not identical to the written form.[24]

The dichotomic division between a High variety and a Low variety only gives a very general view of the Arabic language situation. Nevertheless, the notion of diglossia has found acceptance.[25] *However, we take the view that the notion of diglossia is not fine enough to conduct empirical investigations into the spoken language varieties.*[26]

Kaye (1970: 391), Mitchell (1980: 104; 1982: 155 and 1986: 11), Mahmoud (1982: 83 and 1986: 239) and Holes (1993: 14) also hold the view that Ferguson's definition of diglossia, as it has been applied to the Arabic language situation, is too impressionistic and too categorical.[27] Later researchers used more precise diversity within the spoken Arabic language in defining different language and style levels. This variationalistic approach is quite new.[28] These researchers do not describe the Arabic language situation in terms of diglossia, but in terms of a continuum (Eid 1990: 21). In the next chapter we go into more detail into the variationalistical approach of Arabic.

[23] Cf. Abdulaziz (1986: 21): "MSA is basically literary, used in formal writing and, in certain cases, in formal speech, as in religious lectures or highly official written speeches. Speakers experience difficulty in maintaining it in unwritten speech, apart from the artificiality of its use in spontaneous delivery. This is true of members of parliament, government workers, and intellectuals alike". This has also clearly been demonstrated by the investigation of Schulz (1981: 156-158).

[24] This has been confirmed by Cowan (1968: 29): "MSA has two manifestations: a written manifestation and a spoken manifestation. These two manifestations differ significantly in the amounts and type of information they convey about the language. For example, the spoken manifestation ideally indicates case and mood inflections; the written manifestation does not."

[25] Cf. Winford (in Eid: 1990: 7): "Although the nature of diglossia is still not fully understood, yet it is now taken for granted that the label diglossia should be part of any attempt at typological classification of sociolinguistic situations."

[26] Moreover, not everybody interprets the notion of diglossia in the same way. Mattar (1986: 249), for instance, writes: "la diglossie de la langue arabe: la réalité d'une langue coranique immuable et source indispensable de toute évolution de la langue (...) et d'au moins une langue profane." (cf. also note 4 this chapter).

[27] Willemyns (1987: 145) holds the same view about the linguistic situation in Flanders. Ferguson, conscious of this criticism, in a more recent article, confirms again that intermediate forms exist but he justifies the notion of diglossia again in the following words: "I felt then and I still feel that in the diglossia case the analyst finds two poles in terms of which the intermediate varieties can be described; there is no third pole" (Ferguson 1996: 59).

[28] The linguistic reality is in some countries even more complex because of other languages. Morsly (1996: 254) e.g. remarks: "Four languages are presently in conflict in Algeria, in the various fields of communication: the so-called Classical or Modern Arabic, dialectal Arabic, Berber and French."

4. MULTI-LAYERED DIGLOSSIA

4.1. Division on five levels

The first study devoted to different forms and levels of spoken Arabic was Blanc's (1960) investigation about interdialectal conversation. Blanc asked four Arab native-speakers, who worked at the Army Language Institute in California, to have a conversation. Two of them came from Baghdad, one of them from Jerusalem and the fourth from Aleppo. Their conversation, which treated the future of common Arabic language use, was completely transcribed and analyzed.

Blanc investigated what strategies were followed by these Arabs to come to genuine interdialectal communication in Arabic through modification of their own dialect. He distinguished two strategies: The 'leveling' strategy and the 'classicizing' strategy. The leveling strategies consisted of adaptations of the language using higher dialectal forms which did not necessarily belong to the dialect of the speaker. He observed that the aim of the leveling was to suppress local dialectal expressions and characteristics in favor of characteristics that were more common cross-dialectally.

The 'classicising' strategies consisted mainly of borrowings from Classical Arabic. Such elements were found by all speakers and in all kinds of stylistic varieties. Blanc observed that his subjects switched from one language level to another when they treated a non-daily subject. These stylistic changes depended on a whole range of factors, e.g. the personality of the speaker, the subject of conversation, his attitude toward the interlocutor or the topic of discussion, his mood, etc. Blanc summarizes his observations by setting up the following distinctions (1960: 85):

(1) "plain colloquial" refers to any local dialect within which the speaker may select 'informal' or 'mildly formal' features; (2) "koineized colloquial" is any plain colloquial into which leveling devices have been more or less liberally introduced; (3) "semiliterary" or "elevated" colloquial is any plain or koineized colloquial that is classicized beyond the "mildly formal" range; (4) "modified classical" is Classical Arabic with dialectal mixtures; and (5) "standard classical" is any of a variety of Classical Arabic styles essentially without dialectal admixtures.[1]

[1] It is remarkable that Willemyns (1987: 144-5), who analyzed the spoken language in Flanders, comes to an 'arbitrary' division in five groups; viz. (1) dialect (2) transliter-

It was, however, clear that these five levels can not be rigorously separated from each other. Many phonological, morphological and syntactic elements are common to more than one level. In other words there is a whole range of language choices, from "plain colloquial" to "standard classical", using phonemic changes [e.g. */bilād/* (*land*) in stead of */blād/*].

It is rather strange that Blanc distinguishes five levels on the basis of his very limited investigation, which was not only experimental, but also not completely representative (viz.: Arab native-speakers who live in the US). Nothing of his investigation demonstrates that the upper language type, viz.: standard classical, is also found in reality. Blanc's division is based on intuition rather than on empirical investigation. El-Hassan (1977: 119) points out that it is very difficult for Arabs to accept this division: "Perhaps level 5 and 1, e.g., 'standard classical' and plain 'colloquial' respectively, are fairly easy to establish in formal linguistic features; but the other three levels can hardly, if at all, be verified." As a matter of fact, Blanc's language sample seems to be a mixture (cf. infra 4.4.).

Analyzing the situation in Egypt, Badawī (1973) too makes a division into five levels.[2] Albeit limited, Badawī, uses a few purely linguistic criteria.[3] Moreover, he links the use of the different language levels to socio-economic classes or the degree of formal education (Badawī 1985: 16).[4] The five levels he distinguishes are[5]: (1) *fuṣḥā at-turāṯ*, purely traditional Classical Arabic, which has undergone almost no foreign influences, and which is exclusively written[6]; (2) *fuṣḥā al-ʿaṣr*, Modern Standard Arabic, which has been influenced by modern civilization and which is mostly written; (3) *ʿāmmīyat al-muṯaqqafīn*, Educated

ated dialect (3) regional colloquial (4) cultivated Belgian and (5) general Dutch. He remarks, though, that boundaries are drawn between different systems which in reality overlap each other. Researchers of other languages have also set up a system of five levels. Wilmsen (1995: 133-136) refers to a study by Browning (1982), who distinguished five language levels for Greek, and to a study by Barbour (1987), who distinguished five levels for German.

[2] In this connection Badawī uses the term of *language ladder*: *sullam luġawīy* (Badawī 1973: 97).

[3] The two linguistic characteristics which *Badawī* uses to discriminate the five different language levels are, on the one hand, the distribution of the letter *qāf* on the different levels as compared to *hamza* and on the other hand the proportion of nominal phrases and verbal phrases in the different levels.

[4] In a later investigation Schulz demonstrates that social-economic class in Egypt is not a parameter for the type of language use: "I do not think we can predict, given a type of person and a type of situation, exactly what kind of style will emerge" (Schulz 1981: 183).

[5] The English terminology is from Badawī (1985: 17).

[6] According to Badawī (1985: 19) this level is time-bound so that there is no question of its being related to contemporary life.

Spoken Arabic, colloquial which has undergone the influence both of contemporary civilization and of Classical Arabic; (4) *'āmmīyat al-mutanawwirīn*, Semi-literate spoken Arabic and (5) *'āmmīyat al-'ummīyīn*, illiterate spoken Arabic, which is influenced neither by contemporary civilization nor by Classical Arabic (Badawī 1973: 89). These five varieties each exhibit their own distinctive linguistic properties (phonological, morphological, etc.), coupled with parallel social functions (locutors, topic, place, etc.) (Badawī 1985: 16).

"These levels are not segregated entities; a certain amount of overlapping exists between them, thus blurring their lines of demarcation and creating a graded continuum of features either as we go from level 1 to level 5 or vice versa (Badawī 1985: 17)." To exemplify the language varieties, which Badawī observes in Egyptian society, he quotes examples of such language use from different radio and television programs. Badawī regards the first two levels as literary languages, of which the first can be compared with Classical Arabic and the second with Modern Standard Arabic. The three last levels belong to the dialect.[7] Every classification has its own function. In the two highest levels written preparation is always involved. The first level is used by scholars of the Azhar for their sermons or for programs in which they answer questions from listeners. News broadcasts, commentaries and documentary programs belong to the second highest level. Spontaneous unprepared speech always involves the three lowest levels.

The highest of the three lowest levels, viz. the *'āmmīyat al-muṭaqqafīn* or the colloquial of the educated, is used in discussions about contemporary subjects, such as conversations about science, politics, culture and social issues. The fourth level is used by educated people in their daily lives and in their families. The lowest level is the language of the farmers in the country side. However, a person can shift from one level to the other depending on the circumstances.[8]

[7] Schulz (1981: 6), in my opinion correctly, remarks that it would have been better to place the break between MSA and the dialect between Badawī's third and fourth level. This means that Schulz would reckon the level *'āmmīyat al-muṭaqqafīn* as *fuṣḥā*.

[8] كل فرد من افراد المجتمع المصري (...) يستطيع استخدام أكثر من مستوى. والمثقف الذي أكمل تعليمه الجامعي من شأنه أن يكون قادرا على استخدام المستويات الثلاثة: الثاني والثالث والرابع كل فيما يناسبه. [*Every person in Egyptian society can (...) use more than one level. The educated person who has finished his university studies is able to use three levels according to the situation, the second, the third and the fourth*] A person might use two or more language levels in the same conversation, going up and down from one sentence to the other: الشخص الواحد قد يستخدم مستويين او أكثر في نفس المحادثة، بل وينتقل بين المستويات صعودا وهبوطا من جملة الى اخرى. (Badawī 1973: 93). (cf. infra 5.7.)

After all, the dialect is everybody's mother tongue and the Classical language is a language that is learned at school. And of course the educated have much more knowledge of Classical Arabic than the large masses of illiterate people who know nothing about this variety. But educated people also use the common informal dialect in their daily life. As a result a person is able to use different language levels in different situations, except the illiterate who are by definition limited to one language use (Holes 1993: 15).

Still, there is an important difference between the studies by Blanc and Badawī. Blanc conducted an investigation into the different styles of speech in interdialectal contact, viz. the language which is used by Arabs of different regions when they want to talk with each other, whereas *Badawī*'s investigation is about intradialectal contact, namely the different levels of spoken language by users of one region.

Different comments can be given on Badawī's study. First of all Badawī, being a native speaker, came to this classification exclusively on the basis of participant observation. "Although Badawī suggests some correlation between these levels and the social backgrounds of speakers within each, he does not establish this correlation on the basis of actual recordings of speakers" (Eid 1990: 22). We have to do with Badawī's *impressions* rather than de facto analyzed empirical material.[9]

In the second place, Badawī's observations are not always scientifically firmly grounded. Tarrier (1991: 9) rightly observes that it is unjustified to take the examples of level 5, *'āmmīyat al-'ummīyīn*, the colloquial of the illiterate, from stage plays. "Badawī étaye sa description sur une pièce de théâtre radiodiffusée, or n'y a-t-il pas quelque chose de fallacieux à representer le langage des "illetrés" par un genre extrêmement "lettré" comme l'est la pièce de théâtre ? L'auteur de la pièce et les acteurs peuvent-ils être considérés comme des représentants pertinents d'illettrés?" Tarrier concludes as follows: "Insistons sur le fait que cette étude illustre une tentation commune à de nombreux linguistes, tentation qui est de décrire les variations linguistiques en les rapportant simplement à leur distribution sociale, et en négligeant toute description linguistique approfondie" (Tarrier 1991: 9).[10] Nevertheless, Badawī him-

[9] Badawī (1985: 21-22) prefers to talk about his intuition, and he warns: "Arab intuition concerning their language should not be scoffed at or taken lightly."

[10] Yet, social boundaries can be used to define language use. Ibrahim (1991) discovered in his investigation about the spoken Arabic of Egypt that "il existe bien une frontière, généralement plus sociale que proprement linguistique, entre des mots et tournures que certaines personnes utilisent plus ou moins spontanément alors que d'autres ne les utilisent jamais ou se refusent à les utiliser." As example he quotes three different terms which are used for Mercedes. "Ainsi ces trois termes relativement récents désignant trois

self also mentions that radio programs are not suited to illustrate all the language situations that he observes in daily life.[11]

Both Blanc and Badawī clearly argue that the boundaries between the varieties they distinguished are vague and that they overlap each other.[12] To illustrate this, Badawī (1973: 94-95) uses the metaphor of the rainbow whose colors merge gently.[13]

4.2. Triglossia

Ferguson (1960: 332) has already mentioned intermediate forms in a diglossia situation: "The communicative tensions, which arise in the diglossia situation may be resolved by the use of relatively uncodified, unstable, intermediate forms of the language (Arabic: al luġah al-wuṣṭâ)." Ferguson mentions intermediate forms (plural!), which he describes in Arabic as one single variety, viz.: "This kind of spoken Arabic has a highly classical vocabulary with few or no inflectional endings, with certain features of classical syntax, but with a fundamentally colloquial base in morphology and syntax, and a generous admixture of colloquial vocabulary." Ferguson, however, does not come up with empirical evidence to verify his allegation.

Bishai (1966: 320), on the other hand, remarks that speakers of Arabic will be forced to adapt themselves to be able to talk with each other, given the increasing international contacts within the Arab world. He expected "the emergence in the Arab world of what may be called 'A Modern Inter-Arabic Language.' Some scholars refer to this language, still in the making, as 'colloquial Arabic of the Intellectuals', while oth-

modèles successifs de voitures "Mercedes": *temsāḥa*, *ḥanzira*, *zalamokko*, sont-ils compris de la quasi totalité de la population mais ne sont pas utilisés par tous" (p. 39).

[11] About the fifth and lowest level he writes: ولهذا السبب لا يوجد بين برامج الإذاعة برامج معين تيتخذ منه لغة اساسية له على العكس المستويات الاربع الاخرى، ومع ذلك يسمع المرء نماذج منه في البرنامج التي تقوم على الاتصال بالجمهور خارج الاستوديوهات مثل برمانج «على الناصية» الشهير. ولو لا أن المذيعين – بكل اسف – يتبعون اسلوب «إعداد الحوار» قبل تسجيله لكان من الممكن الحصول على مادة لغوية طيبة من هذا النوع. (*For this reason there are no specific programs on the radio that use this 'basic' language, contrary to the four other language levels. Examples of this language use can, however, be heard in programs outside the studios, where contacts are made with the public. If radio producers did not prepare the conversations before the recording, it still could be possible to obtain such a language sample. Unfortunately this is not the case.*) (Badawī 1973: 91).

[12] See especially Badawī's diagram (1985: 17).

[13] Holes (1987: 5) also remarks about the Blanc's investigation: "No inventory of the variants which belong to each bloc can be given, since some of the variables (e.g. vowel quality) are continuous rather than discrete."

ers call it 'Substandard Arabic'. However, I would like to refer to it simply as 'Modern Inter Arabic', chiefly because at the present time it is used in various inter-Arab meetings, which include representatives from different countries of the Arab Middle East."

Diem (1974: 26) too observes the existence of such a language. He says that there is a mixed speech of which it is impossible to say whether it is "Hocharabisch", or dialect.[14] In this respect Badawī refers to a language which is neither *fuṣḥā* nor dialectal. This third language or intermediate language, according to Badawī (1973: 68), is hermaphroditic (*al-luġa al-ḫunṯā*).[15]

When it is assumed that there are three language levels: a High variety, a Low variety and an Intermediate variety, the term triglossia is used.[16] Researchers, however, do not always give the same interpretation to the notion of triglossia. According to Ferguson, triglossia involves an intermediate form between Classical Arabic (which corresponds to Modern Standard Arabic) and the dialects.[17]

Blau (1981: 145) holds the view that the intermediate language is made up of Modern Standard Arabic with Classical Arabic at one end of the continuum and one of the dialects at the other. But between brackets he added: "(without taking various mixed forms between dialects and Modern Standard Arabic into consideration)." According to Nofal (1980: 7; 9) the intermediate language is Modern Standard Arabic. "The emergent 'third' or "middle" language (between Classical Arabic and the dialects) as some native speakers of Arabic call it; MSA they

[14] See also Eid (1982: 55)

[15] Badawī also points out that Tawfīq al-Ḥakīm once tried to write plays in such an intermediate language. These plays could be read in two ways, as dialect or as *fuṣḥā*. He also points out that this intermediate form was initially intended to reflect feminine language (!) (Badawī 1973: 69).

[16] The division of the Arabic language in three levels is not new, however. According to Badawī the orientalist Karl Vollers had already made a division of Arabic into three levels as early as 1895: أشار الى وجود مستويات ثلاثة فيها تقوم على اسس اجتماعية هي ما أسماه بلهجة الطبقة الدنيا ولهجة الطبقة الوسطى ولهجة الطبقة العليا. وإن لم يقم ببيان الفروق العلمية بين هذه اللهجات. (*He pointed at the existence of three language levels, which he based on social grounds, and which he called the language of the lowest class, the language of the middle class and the language of the high class. However, he did not demonstrate in a scientific way what were the differences between these different languages.*) (1973: 77).

[17] According to Tarrier (1991: 6), the concept of intermediate language is empirically very difficult to define: "La notion d'un arabe moyen reste très imprécise dans la mesure où elle s'applique, selon les auteurs, à des objets souvent différents: elle est ainsi tant appliquée à ce que certains décrivent comme du dialectal auquel serait ajouté du vocabulaire classique, qu'à la langue écrite de la presse". Hereby we can remark that also in the written language efforts have been undertaken to simplify the language. Badawī mentions in this respect *al-luġa al-ḫafīfa* (the light language) (cf. also this chapter note 10).

mean, which in many cases varies according to the ability of the particular user to absorb as much as he can of Arab culture."[18] But, if we consider Modern Standard Arabic to be an intermediate language, then we deny the problem of variation such as is apparent from the investigations of Blanc (1960) and Badawī (1973).

Morsly defines the intermediate language as "l'arabe marocain médian, qui est essentiellement le fait des élites marocaines, la langue de l'oral formel ou officiel" which she identifies as a real mixed language. "Il ressort de la description que l'arabe marocain median tire vers l'arabe marocain dialectal pour ce qui est du système phonologique et de la prosodie et vers l'arabe classique pour ce qui est du lexique" (Morsly 1990: 167). This corresponds to Schulz's findings (1981) in Egypt. Schulz, who conducted a thorough investigation into what he considers to be the third level within Badawī's model, arrives at the conclusion that language use at that level is a mixture. He writes (1981: 19): "I have found that we get a very broad spectrum of speech, ranging from what is almost "pure" colloquial to what is almost "pure" classical" and further on (183): "formal spoken Arabic, as spoken by educated people in formal situations, which traditionally require classical Arabic, is realized in actual fact by a type of speech, which is, as a rule, neither classical nor colloquial, e.g., which always has some classical elements and some colloquial elements in it."

4.3. ESA

Mitchell was the first to consider this 'intermediate language' as an independent variety which differs thoroughly from Modern Standard Arabic. He called this variety Educated Spoken Arabic (ESA). According to him, the difference from MSA is, among others that ESA "qua 'spoken language' may not be any more freely written than the regional vernaculars of Arabic" (Mitchell 1978: 227). Later on he writes: (1986: 8) "Proof of the distance between the written language and ESA is in the great amount of lexico-grammatical editing currently necessary for publication in written form of, say, a radio discussion program with educated participants."[19]

[18] The same view is found at Suleiman (1986) who describes the situation in Jordan (Tarrier 1991: 6).

[19] We can remark here that the same can be said of a dialectal text. The difference between ESA and MSA can be characterized this way but not necessarily the difference between ESA and the dialects.

El-Hassan, one of Mitchell's collaborators, regards ESA as the variety that lies between 'written' MSA, which also encompasses spoken 'prose' (read texts), and dialects. "Educated speakers in the Arab world use the variety of Arabic, which we here call Educated Spoken Arabic (ESA), which draws upon both MSA and Colloquial Arabic. MSA, ESA and Colloquial Arabic constitute a continuum. These varieties of Arabic are neither discrete nor homogeneous; rather they are characterized by gradation and variation" (El-Hassan 1978: 32). The highest form (MSA) is looked upon by El-Hassan as the acrolect, the lowest, the dialects, as the basilect and ESA as the mesolect (1978: 54).[20]

Initially Mitchell considered this language variety as a separate language. "Generally speaking, it has been found that ESA is its own kind of language, neither the written so-called Modern Standard Arabic (MSA) of contemporary literature or journalism, nor any given regional vernacular, nor a straight mixture of the two" (Mitchell 1982: 155). According to him even Arabs could recognize this variety as an independent whole. "Palestinians of several regional origins continue to have clear ideas as to what they would or would not accept as ESA" (Mitchell 1980: 90).

This view contrasts sharply with Ferguson's opinion that the Arabs have no clear view about the oral use of their language. "Speakers of Arabic often do not have clear-cut intuitions for oral use of the language, and the prevalence of intermediate and fluctuating variants between MSA and pure dialect makes grammaticality judgments problematic in any case" (Ferguson 1990: 49).[21] Morsly too remarks that when Arabs intend to speak 'Classical Arabic' this speech contains a lot of dialectal elements. "However, in the great majority of oral situations we notice that Dialectal Arabic is ever present, even when the speakers believe or assert that they are speaking Classical Arabic. As a matter of fact, the phonology and the syntax they use are those of the dialect. It is, doubtlessly, at the lexical level that they borrow most from the classical language" (Morsly 1986: 255).

[20] For some critical remarks about the use of these terms by El-Hassan see Tarrier (1991: 10).

[21] This has been confirmed by Meiseles' finding (1980) that 'informants' not always know themselves which language variety they use. "Informants I have on occasion asked whether they speak *fuṣḥā* or *'ammīya* could not reply. Their reaction was that they 'sometimes speak more nicely and sometimes less'. But they could not make a sharp distinction between OLA (cf. infra 4.4.) and ESA." Parkinson also points out that Egyptians have no unanimous view about what *fuṣḥā* is and what it is not. "It is clear from observation and experiment that Egyptian native speakers of Arabic are not of one mind when it comes to their formal language" (Parkinson 1991: 60).

Later on Mitchell alters his view when he writes: "It is the interplay between written Arabic and vernacular Arabic(s) that creates and maintains Educated Spoken Arabic (ESA) both nationally and internationally" (Mitchell 1986: 8). And: "We do not see it as one of a series of separate varieties, on a par with MSA and the vernaculars, but rather as created and maintained by the constant interplay of written and vernacular Arabic" (Mitchell 1986: 12-13). But, in the end he considers it to be a mixture: "ESA, both within and across national boundaries, is a mixture of the shared written language and regional varied vernaculars or mother-tongues" (Mitchell 1994: 2).[22]

4.3.1. *Specific characteristics of ESA*

When Mitchell (1986: 9) compares the Arabic language situation to the German one, he considers MSA to be the *Schriftsprache* and ESA to be the *Umgangssprache*, "that is, to the colloquial language of educated people which lies between or, better, comprises a mixture of the *Schriftsprache* and regional vernaculars." Mitchell (1986: 10) distinguishes five characteristic differences between ESA and MSA.These differences are: (1) the disappearance of the *'i'rāb* in verb forms and (2) nouns, which in ESA makes analytical constructions likely to be used; (3) the typical passive verb forms of MSA are realized otherwise in ESA, "though some reflexes of MSA passive verb form do occur in Formal-style ESA"; (4) MSA negation particles, *lam, lan, lā* en *mā* are *replaced* by dialectal particles and (5) for the numbers *preferably* dialectal forms are used (*my italics*).

However, two statements by Mitchell make us believe that the above-mentioned elements do occur in Mitchell's corpus. In fact, he wrote earlier: "It is thus a mistake to think, as some do, that the *'i'rāb* do not occur in ESA. It seems that there are observable regularities in respect of what may and may not occur, and that these regularities do not conform to the rules of either CA or MSA" (Mitchell 1980: 102). By the way, Mitchell places great weight on *'i'rāb* as the characteristic element to distinguish MSA from ESA.[23] "Perhaps the only really well established

[22] Further, Badawī (1985: 16) points out that, "the very label itself, ESA, is variously applied to (a) spoken Arabic used by an educated Arab while conversing with an Arab from a different country, (b) spoken Arabic used by educated nationals of the same Arab country on subjects pertaining to their level of education and culture, and (c) the variety used by educated Arabic speakers coming from different Arab countries or from the same country to communicate with one another."

[23] More than once *'i'rāb* is taken as a point of reference to distinguish one language variety from another one. It is well known that the omission of *'i'rāb* is considered to be

fact of spoken standard Arabic is that it lacks the case and mood endings of MSA and the Classical language as well as the indefinite mark of so-called nunation" (Mitchell 1982: 145-6).

Indeed, later on Mitchell contends that the *'i'rāb* does on no account belong to ESA. "The case and mood endings of MSA (the so-called *'i'rāb*) form no part of ESA. Certain individuals may be more emotionally committed than others to a greater use of MSA forms but, if they use the *'i'rāb*, then by definition they are not speaking ESA" (Mitchell 1986: 19). The same goes for the negation particles of MSA, which, in spite of the fact that they do occur, can on no account be counted to be a part of ESA. "Sentences containing *lam* and *lan*, for example, will be heard, but are too 'high-flown' for inclusion in ESA" (Mitchell 1986: 11). And further: "Excluded from ESA (...) are, the high-flown Arabic appropriate to reading aloud, otherwise termed 'spoken prose'" (Mitchell 1994: 2).

4.3.2. *Critical remarks on the notion of ESA*

Some critical remarks can be made about the notion of ESA. In the first place, the definition of ESA is not unambiguous. Furthermore the grammatical difference between ESA and the dialects is indistinct. The categories of investigation also are not distinctly defined. Furthermore, ESA is not distinctly defined geographically and, finally, we hold the view that ESA as Educated speech is too limited. We will go into more detail on each of these five points.

4.3.2.1. Contradictory definitions

The problem with the concept of ESA is that it is not unambiguously defined. Indeed, on the basis of the same corpus El-Hassan comes to other findings. As a matter of fact, it becomes clear from a previous

one of the most important characteristics of the difference between Classical Arabic and the dialects (cf. supra 2.3.6.). Tarrier too regards *'i'rāb* as a typical characteristic of 'Classical Arabic': "L'absence de marques casuelles sera considerée comme un état neutre; en revanche, la présence d'une marque casuelle sera considerée comme un élément marqué du classique." Arabic speakers also take *'i'rāb* as a point of reference. Bishai (1966: 320) e.g. writes: "They maintain, rather emphatically, that what they speak at the intellectual level in their own gatherings is actually classical Arabic without the complexity of its case and state endings." This is confirmed by Meiseles (1977: 176): "The *'i'rāb*, and with it all the 'word-endings' are identified by Arab speakers as the most distinctive feature of CA." However, in my opinion, *'i'rāb* in itself is not sufficient to characterize 'Classical Arabic'. See also Badawī (1985: 20) and McLoughin (1972: 72): "As Fück says, it is, en soi trop superficielle pour servir, à elle seule, de marque distinctive de la langue classique".

study by El-Hassan that the five characteristic elements (cf. supra 4.3.1.), which Mitchell quotes, do occur in ESA (El-Hassan 1977: 120-125). As Mitchell's corpus has, as far as we know, never been transcribed completely, it is impossible to define precisely to what extent the preference is given in ESA to dialectal forms instead of MSA forms. Nevertheless, according to El-Hassan the five above-mentioned characteristics do belong to ESA.

In reaction to Blanc's study (cf. supra 4.1.) El-Hassan writes about *'i'rāb*: "The conclusion to be drawn from the above illustrations of educated usage is that, although a good deal of educated spoken Arabic exhibits no case endings, it is nonetheless wrong to claim that, quoting Blanc: 'There are no occurrences of classical *'i'rāb* other than such as also occur in plain colloquial.' A fairly large proportion of educated spoken Arabic does carry fully marks of Classical *'i'rāb* which in no sense can be said to be restricted to what Blanc calls 'set phrases' and 'proverbs'. It also is worth noting that speakers who know the 'rules' of Classical *'i'rāb* are not consistent in applying these rules to their speech" (El-Hassan 1977: 121).

The same goes for the negation particles of MSA. According to El-Hassan (1977: 129) these certainly belong to ESA. In a critical remark on the study by Ezzat (1974)[24] e.g. he writes: "There are other relevant negative particles in ESA which should have been mentioned under this category, e.g. *lam*, *lā*, *lan*, etc." (El-Hassan 1977: 129). However, if we drop these elements, the difference between the dialects and ESA becomes completely vague. El-Hassan, for instance, reproaches Ezzat for confusing ESA with the dialects. "The author sets out to describe the intelligibility of ESA, but he seems to have confused ESA with the colloquials" (El-Hassan 1977: 129). However, if we follow this course of reasoning, we arrive at the same conclusion about Mitchell. El-Hassan's critical remarks (1977: 129) about Ezzat (1974), on this point, can also be applied to Mitchell. Moreover, in his investigation El-Hassan gives a few examples of MSA passive forms and numbers to demonstrate that those also belong to ESA. As a matter of fact, this means that within the team researchers of the Leeds corpus there is no consensus about the grammatical characteristics of ESA.

[24] In his study 'Intelligibility among Arabic Dialects' Ezzat investigates the use of negation particles in the ESA of a few countries in the *Mašriq*. According to him MSA particles do not occur in ESA. The title of Ezzat's work clearly illustrates that ESA, in his view, has more to do with interdialectal language use than with the use of MSA as a spoken language.

4.3.2.2. Indistinct grammatical difference between ESA and the dialects

The characteristics which Mitchell quotes do not make the distinction between ESA and the dialects clear. Indeed, the Arabic dialects do not have *'i'rāb* either nor do they have the negation particles typical of MSA. Dialects often have their own passive forms and use numbers in a different way from MSA. This means that the criteria which Mitchell enumerates prevail just as well for the Arabic dialects. Moreover, in my view, Mitchell is in error in presenting ESA as if it were an adaptation of MSA. The dialects are the mother tongue of the Arabs. Only in formal education do children become intensively acquainted with Modern Standard Arabic. It is possible that in a later phase of their lives, when they try to talk MSA, they use a kind of higher language variety, which might be called ESA for convenience's sake. When people in that phase do not use certain MSA forms, then it cannot be said that ESA is an adaptation of MSA but, rather, that ESA (such as it has been defined by Mitchell) should be considered a development of the dialect.[25]

When we observe that in ESA no MSA negation particles are used, then, in my opinion, this is not a valid criterion for calling it a separate variety of Arabic. At best, it can be argued that ESA stands much closer to the dialects than to MSA, and that even 'Educated Arab Speakers' are not yet able to express themselves spontaneously in MSA. The same misrepresentation can be found in the article by Abu Absi (1990: 34) when he writes: "One characteristic of ESA is the simplification of grammar along lines that bring linguistic structures closer to the colloquial, an instance of which is a tendency to ignore MSA case endings." In my opinion, there is no simplification whatsoever of MSA, since already in the dialects the case endings are omitted, and in fact, nothing has been adapted.

As a matter of fact, most researchers recognize that the basis of ESA is, indeed, the dialect, of which the lexicon consists of quite a lot of words out of MSA (Abu Absi 1986: 342; Abdulaziz 1986: 22). Tapiéro (1976: 124) too describes the emergence of a new language variety in that sense. "Aussi fleurit depuis quelques années un arabe dialectal moderne, que certains qualifient 'd'arabe moyen' ou de 'voie moyenne', ce qui est une erreur fondamentale du point de vue linguistique. En réalité, chaque dialecte garde tous ses caractères diversifiés et divergents et ne fait que, par moments, un pas ou plusieurs, selon les pays et les

[25] Owens (2001) too holds the view that the dialects serve as the basic imput for ESA.

individus, vers la langue 'savante' en lui faisant de véritables emprunts de vocabulaire et de tournures."[26]

According to Mitchell the difference between ESA and the dialects lies in the fact that in ESA certain words are 'stigmatized' (Mitchell 1994: 3).[27] In his view a lot of 'vulgar speech' is stigmatized (1986: 14) and as such it does not, ipso facto, belong to ESA. The term 'stigmatization' must not be confused with taboo forms (Mitchell 1980: 91). Nothing, however, indicates that the words which Mitchell regards as 'unstigmatized' have simply been included into the dialect because of the evolution of the language.

Moreover, in the investigation by El-Hassan (1978: 36), who was a member of the Leeds team, it is clearly demonstrated that 'stigmatized' forms are still used: "Some speakers are (or seem to be) invariable users of stigmatized forms (e.g. Speakers 25 and 28 [both teacher and 'Islamic religion specialist']), others seem to alternate stigmatized and prestigious forms, while others still are (or seem to be) invariable users of prestigious forms."

How and who decides which forms are stigmatized and which are not, is not clear. If we take language use as a basis, and the educated language user as a norm, then we find immediately a stigmatized form in El-Hassan's work, which ought to be de-stigmatized, unless we take situational variables into account. According to Mitchell (1986: 15) the nationality of the speaker has something to do with it. Syrian people, e.g. don't use certain forms in conversations with Egyptians and Jordanians.[28]

But even then it still remains extremely difficult to make out what forms can be considered to be stigmatized and what forms can not. Mit-

[26] Tarrier (1993: 104) too arrives at this conclusion: "Nous résumerons la situation ainsi:

– dans les mots lexicalement ou morphologiquement classiques apparaissent (très souvent) des "dialectalismes";

– dans les mots lexicalement ou morphologiquement neutres apparaissent des "dialectalismes" et des "classicismes";

– dans les mots lexicalement ou morphologiquement dialectaux il ne se passe rien.

[27] This phenomenon is also known in Dutch. Willemyns points out that in Dutch too, there are words which educated people will try to avoid in circumstances where their use does not seem appropriate to them (1987: 147). A comparable concept is Diem's negative interference (1974: 44; See also Schippers 1987: 83). Negative interference implies that the speaker tries to avoid MSA words which also occur in the dialect. According to Diem, Maḥmūd Taymūr and Al-Māzinī have composed entire lists of words which are avoided because they also occur in dialect. In particular speakers who do not master MSA are inclined to avoid MSA words which also occur in their dialect. See also Schulz (1981: 131).

[28] Abu-Melhim's investigation (1991) confirms that Jordanians who converse with Egyptians replace certain Jordanian dialectal words by Egyptian words.

chell is obviously conscious of this problem when he writes: "Analysis is not made easier by the fact that a given form may be stigmatized in one area, but not in another, as when, for example, *katbat* 'she wrote', is stigmatized in Syria but not in Palestine." (Mitchell 1986: 15). Neither the investigations by El-Hassan or by Mitchell, moreover, demonstrate whether the situational variable exerts any influence on language use.

The notion of ESA does not present clear-cut criteria to distinguish it from the dialect. The fact that certain words are 'stigmatized' is not a sufficient indication. It might just involve the natural development of a dialect. As a matter of fact, it is a generally known phenomenon, in all the countries of the world, that dialects are being leveled out in competition with more prestigious dialects on the lexicographical level.[29] Besides, ESA also seems to be understood by people who received no formal education (Mahmoud 1986: 245; Abu Absi 1990: 41), which demonstrates that the difference between ESA and the dialects is very small.

According to Mahmoud the interregional migration of labour has played a great role in the emergence of an intermediate language. According to him this is a consequence of the fact that the intelligibility of the dialects has increased: "Another important factor in the development of ESA is the dramatic increase in inter-Arab worker migration as well as bilateral and multi-lateral meetings. As a result of these contacts the intelligibility between dialects has increased and so has the viability of ESA as an effective and versatile means of oral communication between Arabs of different countries both in formal and informal meetings and discussions" (Mahmoud 1986: 246). All these conclusions show that ESA should be considered as a kind of 'interdialectal Arabic' and should not necessarily be associated with 'educated Arabic'.[30] In my view the term Educated Spoken Arabic is misleading for three reasons, which will be discussed below.

4.3.2.3. Indistinctly-defined categories of investigation

First of all, the category of ESA-speakers is not clearly defined. Mitchell considers ESA to be the language that educated people use. Never-

[29] The important dialectological evolutionary investigation by Belemans (1995) has demonstrated that lots of dialectal words are disappearing in the Flemish part of Belgium. Prof. Woidich (University of Amsterdam), who constantly follows the development of Egyptian dialects, confirmed to me in a personal communication that also in Egypt many dialectal words are disappearing and are being replaced by words from the Cairene dialect.

[30] For Holes too the distinction between ESA and interdialectal Arabic is not very clear. The question that Holes (1993: 17) asks, "What is ESA?" and "what linguistic features characterize interdialectal Arabic?", has not yet been thoroughly answered.

theless, 'specialists' do not belong to this category (Mitchell 1980: 89; 104). "ESA is better defined ostensibly by reference to the practice of the overwhelming majority of the professional classes whose representatives have provided the extensive corpus of data on which the Leeds project is based" (Mitchell 1980: 90). Who these educated persons are is not clearly specified. Reference is made to the article by El-Hassan (1978). In his description of the investigated testees he gives a whole variety of occupations, from different specialists in the Arabic language (13 op 90) to clerks, but also housewives and even an 'Egyptian Lady' (1978: 55-57). This means that the notion of Educated speaker is very wide and ill-defined.[31]

Furthermore, the investigations by Badawī (1973) and Diem (1974) have demonstrated that educated people adapt their language depending on the situation in which they find themselves. This means that an educated Arab can feel compelled to speak a dialect in certain circumstances and in other situations he might be likely to avoid certain dialectal forms. This also means that the situational component is essential in the description of language use.[32] The language investigation by the university of Leeds, however, only provides information about the occupation of the testee and the nationality of the person with whom he is conversing. This can be a person of the same nationality, or a person of one of the neighboring countries (mainly Egyptians, Lebanese, Syrians or Jordanians, and in one single case Kuwaitis) (El-Hassan 1978: 55-57).[33]

[31] Wilmsen (1995: 4) remarks that the 'Educated speakers' of the 'upper class' are not necessarily the most proficient Arabic-speakers: "Indeed, often ordinary Egyptians will have had better educations in literary Arabic than will their upper class compatriots. This is because the upper classes often send their children abroad for schooling, or they send them to foreign language schools within Egypt, neither of which avenues will provide them with a thorough preparation in literary Arabic. Meanwhile the middle and lower classes send their children to Egyptian public schools, at which the study of literary Arabic is a curriculum requirement at all levels". See also Schulz (1981: 9).

[32] This has been repeatedly emphasized by Badawī (1973: 52, 85) also. فإذا ما قارنا بين اللغة تالتي استخدمها ذلك الشخص في هذه المواقف الثلاثة فسنجد انها تترتب ترتبا تنازليا حسب الدرجة التي تحتلها كل واحدة من السلم اللغوي. ففي الموقف الاول يغلب ان يكون كلامه بالفصحى وفي الثالث بالعامية وفي الثاني بلغة «بين بين». (*If we want to make a comparison between language varieties which this person uses in these three situations, then we see that they are ordered in descending order, according to the level that every one of them occupies on the language ladder. In the first situation the language will be most probably fuṣḥā,* in the third colloquial, and in the second a language in between) (Badawī: 14).

[33] According to Mitchell (1986: 13), the nationality and the status of the interlocutor and the politeness forms that are being used clearly influence the language use. "The grammarian, and indeed the user of a language, needs to be aware not only of the cultural context of speech but also of the range of functions that speech may fulfill, including such as the indication of role and status relations between collocutors."

Less is known about the situation in which these conversations took place, except the fact that it involved rather experimental conversations. "The speakers were encouraged to speak as freely as they desired, and more often than not, were aware that the conversation was being recorded" (Mitchell 1994: 1). Emphasis was put on 'relaxed conversation' (Mitchell 1994: 2). Moreover, Mitchell also made use of conversations on the radio and of debates, where it was known that they could not have been written beforehand. For the evaluation of the data Mitchell relied on the intuitions of Arab research fellows (Mitchell 1994: 1).

Because the situational data are unknown, it is possible that sometimes conversations have been held which are entirely dialectal. In my view, quite a number of the sample sentences from Mitchell's last study (1994) can be classified as dialectal as well. Almost all sample sentences quoted by Mitchell (1994) in his last work on ESA testify to very simple everyday language use. The sentences are taken from conversations about the simplest subjects and the lexicon comprises the simplest everyday words. Besides some everyday sentences, there are no examples of serious debate in Arabic; the level of conversation alone points out that it might well be that the testees saw themselves obliged to use dialectal language.[34]

But maybe Mitchell only wanted to make a selection of the simplest everyday sentences. Since no complete corpus is available, it is impossible to determine whether Mitchell's sample sentences (1994) are representative of the whole. As the negation particles of MSA do not occur at all, we have the *impression* that the sample is not representative.[35] Tarrier too points out that ESA is a very large category. In his description of the Arabic language situation, he wants to take into account the nationality of the speaker as well as the situational variable. He prefers to talk about: 'arabe parlé formel' or APF (Tarrier 1993: 94-95). "Cependant, alors que l'appellation de l'un ne se réfère qu'à la nature contextuelle du discours, l'autre ne prend en compte que la nature du locuteur. De fait, l'ESA recouvre un champ beaucoup plus vaste de discours, ces derniers pouvant être de nature surveillée ou pas."

[34] We refer to the study by Abu-Melhim about everyday conversation between a Jordanian and an Egyptian couple. Abu-Melhim confirms that, in most cases, speakers switch to the dialect of the other party, mostly the Egyptian dialect. However, he also states that "In some cases, speakers use their own dialects" (1991: 249).

[35] It is remarkable that in the Arabic translation of Mitchell's book (1994) the term *al-luġa l-dārija* is used instead of *al-luġa l-'āmmīya* which, in my view, might indicate that it involves *dialectal* language use.

4.3.2.4. Indistinctly-defined geographical categories

The term ESA is misleading in the second place because it is 'geographically' too widely defined. It is misleading to talk about *one* Educated Spoken Arabic, as if it were a single language variety used all over the Arab territory.[36] In spite of the fact that there are almost no corpora of ESA except the non-transcribed corpus at Leeds,[37] many people have the *impression* that ESA is a language variety that exists everywhere. "ESA is assumed to be readily understood by most speakers regardless of their degree of education and it serves as a convenient tool among bilinguals who may not share the same foreign language and who find it cumbersome and unnatural to communicate in MSA. The frequent use of ESA by politicians, religious leaders, and educators has brought this variety closer to the people and made it a viable means of communication among all Arabs" (Abu-Absi 1990: 41). In this way Abu-Absi, and also Abdulaziz (Abdulaziz 1986: 22) create the *impression* that one and the same intermediate language is used in the entire Arab world.

Ferguson (1990: 49) too has the *impression* that ESA is a genuine language variety, which prevails in the entire territory, when he contrasts ESA with the option of different regional standard languages: "A number of observers have claimed that a new supradialectal norm of educated spoken Arabic (ESA) is coming into existence, and other observers have documented unmistakable trends toward diverse regional standards."

As far as ESA is concerned, Mitchell's findings can not be generalized to the entire Arab world. Lots of sentences from Mitchell's material (1994) will inevitably be categorized as Eastern dialectal language by Arabic speakers from the Maghreb. Moreover, in his investigation Mitchell (1980: 89; 1982: 131-3) consciously chose to limit himself to 'the middle region, comprising Egypt, Jordan (Palestine), Lebanon and Syria'. He did not want to include the countries of the Maghreb in his investigation because, in his view, French is 'probably' still, de facto, the working language![38]

[36] Badawī (1985: 20) too seems to be conscious of this when he writes: "To attempt a grammar and a lexicon for level 3, or ESA as it is universally known, of one particular community is one thing, but to attempt a grammar and a lexicon for ESA on the pan-Arab scale is another."

[37] El Hassan (1977: 112), e.g. writes: "Very little is known about educated spoken Arabic (ESA) as it is used in particular Arab countries and 'inter-nationally' between them. There are, to be sure, allusions to ESA in a number of works, but these are little more than skin deep." According to him, the best on this subject are the studies of Blanc (1960), Badawī (1973) and Ali Ezzat (1974).

[38] On the contrary, to us it seems interesting to investigate the language use of speakers of very remote regions when they have to talk to each other. Abu Melhim (1991: 249)

This means that the investigation of ESA is limited to that region. Even if Mitchell is interested in "The Arab 'experiment', the creation of a single educated spoken language" (Mitchell 1982: 147), which he previously called 'spoken Standard Arabic' (145), then it still is clear that this 'single educated Arabic' based on his investigations is limited to Egypt and the Levant. Mitchell's ESA (1978: 254; 257) contains many pure dialectal forms, such as, for instance, the negation particle *miš*, which for Arabs of other regions makes it unacceptable to talk about 'educated language'.[39]

It might be more appropriate to talk of, for instance, 'Educated Levantine Arabic'. Holes (1990), who describes the spoken Arabic of the Gulf states, including the Eastern territory (al Hasa) of Saudi-Arabia, follows these lines of thinking by calling the investigated language variety: Educated Gulf Arabic. In this way the local character of this language variety is underlined.

4.3.2.5. ESA as Educated speech is too limited

Finally, Mitchell's notion of Educated Spoken Arabic is misleading because it is too limited in its definition. Forms which are supposed not to occur in ESA are in fact used by Educated Arabs, even those who are not language specialists. The typical negation particles of MSA, for instance, were not included by Mitchell in ESA. On the contrary, it is just typical of Educated speakers to avoid dialectal negation particles such as *mā*. Both Diem (1974: 46) and Schippers (1987: 84) point out that negation by means of the particle *lam* has spread largely at the cost of *mā*. Palva (1969: 37), on the other hand, points out that the negation system is one of the most inalienable characteristics of the dialect. As a consequence, the occurrence of the negation particles of MSA with 'Educated speakers' is a very important indication of a higher language level.

My own analysis of thirty interviews from the Algerian radio (Van Mol 1992) proved that all interviewed Arabic speakers, as well as from other nationalities including even Egyptians, abundantly make use of the

too raises the question: "What accommodation strategies would be used by speakers of geographically distant and diverse Arabic dialects, i.e., Iraqi and Moroccan?"

[39] In the Arab world there is a lot of resistance to accept another, even cultivated, dialect as any kind of inter-regional standard. "At present it seems to us highly unlikely that the idea of adopting one particular colloquial would be acceptable to speakers of the other colloquials" (Bentahila 1991: 83). Fleisch had the same view: "Un dialecte ne peut se développer en langue commune par-dessus les autres dialectes que par des circonstances spéciales. Les circonstances lui sont opposées: l'immense prestige de l'arabe classique lui barre la route et même la vie moderne, d'une manière générale, défavorise les dialectes" (in Tarrier 1991: 2).

negation particles of MSA. The contention by Mitchell (1982: 124) that "the man who wants to talk at all times like a book or a newspaper is a decided oddity" is only correct when we take the limitation 'at all times' seriously.[40] As a matter of fact, it seems that 'Educated Arabs', certainly in formal situations, will try to approach the written language even in the spontaneously spoken language. ESA might well be the language of the 'Educated Arabs', but this possibly only demonstrates that 'Educated Arabs' in relaxed situations still often talk in a dialect with lexical MSA interference. This still does not prove that , in other, more formal situations, educated Arab speakers do not speak MSA or a language variety that comes much closer to MSA.

Moreover, there are a few elements that point out the increasing importance of MSA as a spoken language. In the first place, Mitchell himself reports that not all Arabs accept the language that he describes as 'educated Arabic', especially when he writes about the "continuing circumstances of hostility in influential circles towards its (ESA) systematic study" (Mitchell 1980: 105). Abu-Absi too reports that speakers of Arabic do not attach great value to ESA as 'educated language'. The

[40] Nevertheless, although mention is made within the Arab world of people who devote themselves to talking MSA in everyday circumstances this phenomenon still seems to be marginal. Different cultural societies made attempts to do so in the beginning of last century. In Beirut, e.g. the *'Ifṣāḥ* was founded. "This society required its members to use the standard at all times and in all places in their speech" (Suleiman 1994: 9). Forkel also reports of such attempts: "Um einen Sonderfall handelt es sich bei einem Marokkaner, der den Muslimbrüdern angehört. Er spricht bewusst mit voller Absicht fast mit jedermann Hocharabisch. Er sagte mir dazu: '*Nurīdu 'an nanzila bi-l-'arabīyati min al-kutubi 'ilā š-šāri'*.' (Wir möchten das Hocharabische von einer Buchsprache wieder zum Umgangssprache machen)" (Forkel 1980: 17). A similar case has been reported by Blau: "In very unusual cases and in quite abnormal circumstances a few people did use Standard Arabic as their exclusive means of oral communication. This was true for three or four boys whose families emigrated from one Arabic-speaking country to another. In order not to make themselves conspicuous as immigrants of low status, they decided to utilize Standard Arabic even in oral communication and succeeded" (Blau 1981: 24). According to Ibrahim (1983: 513) Muslims are incited by their religion to use the 'standard language' when they speak. On the contrary, Parkinson (1991: 40) reports of heavy social control and pressure in Egypt which makes the use of *fuṣḥā* in everyday speech almost impossible. That does not alter the fact that MSA can gain influence in the future (cf. infra 6.1.). After all, for some European languages it took a long time before the written language was used as spoken standard in everyday situations. Forkel, e.g. writes about German: "Das Hochdeutsche — in der Schweiz nicht zufällig Schriftdeutsch genannt — gehörte bis vor nicht allzu langer Zeit ebenfalls zu den traditionellen Sprachen gemäss obiger Definition, denn bevor es Ende des 19. Jahrhunderts zu einer gesprochenen Sprache wurde, war es mit keiner im täglichen Umgang benutzten Form der deutschen Sprache identisch" (Forkel 1987: 289). Furthermore, Blau points out that this is also the case for Hebrew: "Hebrew, the common cultural language of all these communities, thus became not only a cultural language, but a spoken tongue as well."

producers of the television series *iftaḥ yā simsim*, e.g., an educational program for children based on the American PBS children's program "Sesame Street", did not decide in favor of ESA as the language for the program. "Nonetheless, the deliberate and successful choice of a 'simplified' MSA as the language of *iftaḥ yā Simsim* seems to go against the trend to the use of ESA, an option that was not considered as a viable alternative" (Abu-Absi 190: 41).

For all these reasons, it seems more sensible to talk about ESA in terms of a supra-regional dialect or koine.[41] We can conclude with Abu-Absi (1986: 342) and Bentahila (1991: 80) that at this moment ESA cannot be considered as a standard language.[42] At best, ESA can be seen as a supra-regional koine. Meiseles also holds the view that ESA belongs to the dialect: "Circumstantial factors (...) have led to the development of a vernacular type characterized by the aspirations of its speakers to get rid of local features peculiar to their dialects through a process of koineization and/or borrowings from MSA, especially on the lexical and morphophonemic levels" (Meiseles 1980a).[43] Wilmsen (1995: 153) arrives at the same conclusion: "At least insofar as it is manifested in the conversational speech of theatrical practitioners in Cairo, it (ESA) is colloquial Arabic".

ESA, such as it has been defined by Mitchell, is limited to interdialectal communication. In this respect, Mahmoud's contention: "This medium is now a reality and it is gradually becoming a viable, communicative tool" (Mahmoud 1986: 246), seems to us premature. Only a statistical study, based on the entirely transcribed Leeds corpus, or other well-defined corpora of contemporary spoken (standard) Arabic in which all

[41] Ferguson (1990: 49) uses the term 'supradialectical norm'.

[42] We do not agree with Mahmoud's proposition (1986: 247) that the impact of ESA is the most noticeable in education: "It is perhaps in the teaching and learning of Arabic that the impact of ESA has been most noticeable. There have been commendable efforts to tap the flexibility and spontaneity of ESA in bringing Arabic closer to the Arabic child. The compilation of lexicons and word lists that cut across dialects, as well as grammar books which take into account the commonalities between the home language and MSA are now a reality." As an example Mahmoud quotes Baccouche (1973). Baccouche's manual, however, runs counter to the trend to accept ESA as means of communication; Baccouche refuses to regard MSA as a 'dead' language. He does not agree with the argumentation that the use of MSA is artificial and unnatural. With respect to the compilation of word lists, Mahmoud refers to the compilation of the functional word list in Morocco. However, the aim of the compilers of this word list was to classisize widespread dialectal words and to include them into the basic word list of MSA school manuals in the Maghreb countries. (cf. Benabdi 1986: 68 and infra 5.2.)

[43] See also Meiseles (1980b: 79) where he calls this language variety *luġa ʿāmmīya ʿulyā (Elevated colloquial).*

the relevant variables (situational, professional, etc.) are taken into consideration can give decisive answers about the precise characteristics of the intermediate varieties.

4.4. Quadriglossia

Meiseles, who investigated spoken Arabic on the radio, holds the view that there is another spontaneously spoken variety, which approaches MSA to a high degree. According to Meiseles, this language variety is quite new. "Recently, particularly in the last ten years or so, MLA (Modern Literary Arabic) which was (and still is) considered as a written variety of Arabic *par excellence*, has been developing into an oral medium as well, not only in reading aloud or recitation, but in speech, too. We term this variety of MLA, Oral Literary Arabic (OLA)" (Meiseles 1975). This language variety would be reserved for formal and semi-formal language use only.

Precisely because the ESA category in the triglossia option is not clearly defined, and because the confusion with the dialects is very big, Meiseles (1980a) proposes to talk of quadriglossia: "distinguishing two varieties in the 'in-between' range of the Literary Arabic — Vernacular Arabic dichotomy: ESA and Sub-standard Arabic" (Meiseles 1980a: 118). After the transcription of the radio material of spontaneously spoken Arabic he arrives at the conclusion that there are two intermediate varieties: "This classification work has finally driven me to conclude the independent existence of two coherent varieties: one basically vernacular-oriented (confirming Ferguson's 1959 tacit assumption that such a variety should be regarded as [structurally] belonging to an L form) — ESA, and another, reflecting a steady LA orientation - OLA" (Meiseles 1980: 120).[44]

The highest category in Meiseles's model is Literary Arabic. "This is the language Arabs learn in the course of their formal education, and the one they aspire to follow in writing and, at times, in their speech as well" (Meiseles 1980a: 123). This language is considered to be 'standard'. In our opinion this variety matches with MSA.

Completely at the bottom in his model are the dialects, with ESA just above them. "Apparently, among speakers who have 'widened their ho-

[44] Further on, in the same article (p. 132), however, he claims that the linguistic situation of Arabic nowadays can not guarantee that even the slightest (spoken) passage is linguistically uniform and coherent.

rizons', there is a visible tendency to abandon them in favor of any 'higher' variety of Arabic, and first of all ESA, which is most readily accessible" (Meiseles 1980a: 124). In my opinion Meiseles gives here a very clear and thorough description of ESA such as Mitchell (1994) describes it.

The highest variety in between (OLA) is regarded upon by Meiseles as substandard:[45] "The variety termed Sub-standard Arabic (= SsA) is defined exactly as an 'Arab's attempt to speak 'classical Arabic'. The reconstruction of the prescriptive LA model is the goal" (Meiseles 1980a: 125). This variety is characterized by many (!) deviations compared to the LA norm and a mixture of dialectal elements: "It is the language generally used for oral expression in the mass media of communication, on all formal occasions, and many a time also on semi-formal ones" (Meiseles 1980a: 125).[46]

In this respect, Meiseles makes two important methodological remarks. The first is that, as a spoken variety, OLA is not identical with the variety which is used when reading aloud or reciting. Structurally these are "manifestations of the written language, its audial actualization" (125). Killean, who conducted a limited investigation into variation of the demonstratives in spontaneously spoken Arabic (OMA: Oral Media Arabic) on the Egyptian radio, arrives at the same conclusion: "Any spoken media Arabic material that is read aloud or repeated from memory from original written material is always literary Arabic (LA) in its form" (Killean 1980: 177).[47]

The lowest intermediate variety (ESA), however, can not always be sharply demarcated from the highest intermediate variety (OLA). "In the reality of Arabic, these two are so closely intertwined that, at first glance,

[45] Mitchell (1986: 12) finds this term infelicitous "since 'substandard' has unintended pejorative connotations." This observation seems to me correct. The question can be raised why Meiseles creates two designations for this variety, viz.: OLA and SsA. In an Arabic article Meiseles (1980b: 79) calls this variety *al-luġa al-fuṣḥā ad-dūn qawā'idīya*. (This could be translated as '*standard language without rules*'). This designation seems to be a little bit exaggerated because every language variety is subject to certain regularities (cf. infra 5.7.).

[46] With certain reservations, this variety might be regarded equally as Tarrier's *arabe parlé formel* (1993), especially since Meiseles observes that in OLA too there is a large mixture with the dialect: "The most remarkable characteristic of OLA is the blending of linguistic systems of LA and those of the colloquial varieties of Arabic" (Meiseles 1975). This corresponds, in my opinion, to the language layer investigated by Schulz (1981).

[47] Morsly too is convinced that the language of the news broadcasts is, in its essence, written language: "In other words, it appears essentially as the language of writing" (Morsly 1986: 255). According to Tarrier this remains to be seen: "Rien n'est moins sûr que le langage des écrits contemporains soit le même que celui de la radio ou de la télévision" (Tarrier 1991: 7).

the impression they produce is that of an obvious continuum" (Meiseles 1980: 128). According to Meiseles, the boundary between these two varieties is extremely vague. In order to distinguish an OLA text methodologically from an ESA text Meiseles bases himself on the structure of the sentence: "A text can be said to belong to OLA when the general structure of its sentences has an LA character; a text belongs to the colloquial variety when the general structure of its sentences is of a colloquial character" (Meiseles 1975: 3). In a later article, he adds that this criterion is, moreover, not very stable. "It is certainly not the most stable and unequivocal criterion, and — we should point out — it is no less 'impressionistically' based than others" (Meiseles 1980: 129). To demonstrate the OLA character of a text, Meiseles selects a number of syntactic, morphological, lexicographical and phonological elements.

Meiseles's aim is to make a distinction between OLA and 'spontaneous spoken interdialectal language' (ESA), which contains no MSA characteristics. In this way he considers the limited text sample of interdialectal conversation of Blanc's (1960) as typical ESA.[48] Meiseles considers a language variety to be OLA or Oral Literary Arabic when the spontaneously spoken Arabic sentences of that language sample contain certain MSA characteristics (which have been preselected by Meiseles). These characteristics are: the use of *'i'rāb*, MSA negation particles, MSA passive verb forms, MSA numbers, MSA dual forms, abundant use of the particles *'an* and *'anna*, and, on the phonological level, the reintroduction of *qāf* as a uvular stop (in a whole range of Arabic dialects *qāf*, however, does occur in the local dialect too) and of *hamza* (Meiseles 1980: 129-132).

On a lexicographic level OLA is defined by the choice of words. In an OLA text, for instance, the verb *ra'ā* is likely to occur instead of the dialectal *šāf* (*to see*), and instead of the dialectal relative pronoun *illi* the MSA relative pronoun *allaḏī* (*who*), is likely to occur. Yet, according to Meiseles purely dialectal elements can also belong to OLA. When a complete sentence has a LA (Literary Arabic) character but also contains one dialectal element, then this sentence still belongs to OLA. As an example Meiseles quotes the verb prefix *bi,* which indeed occurs in certain countries in the Middle-East in spoken texts with a literary character. On the basis of his criteria Meiseles categorizes the (ESA) text samples of El-Hassan (1977) as OLA.[49]

[48] This is tantamount to Ezzat's view of ESA. However, El-Hassan, on the other hand, holds the view that Ezzat confuses ESA with dialect (cf. supra 4.3.2.1.).

[49] "The examples El-Hassan (1977) has recourse to belong to another variety, which I have termed OLA" (Meiseles 1980: 118).

A first element that strikes one in Meiseles' quadriglossia option is that his classes are not very strict. His proposition, that there is beside ESA as described by Mitchell still another higher spoken language variety, is correct.[50] However, Meiseles also counts certain purely dialectal elements as OLA. At a certain moment he refers to the 'lower levels' of OLA. In these lower levels of OLA *qāf* is pronounced like *hamza*, and the relative pronoun *illi* is used. By referring to lower levels between OLA, it becomes even more difficult to determine precisely the difference between OLA and ESA. Moreover Schulz's investigation (1981) demonstrates that it is very difficult to obtain 'pure' language samples.

Schulz's investigation confirms that Meiseles's OLA characteristics do not occur 100% in any language sample. There always is a certain proportion in the use of, e.g., MSA negation particles and dialectal particles. This proportion can be higher depending on the speaker group. Further on, the investigation by Schulz (1981: 161) also demonstrates that there is a kind of hierarchy in the use of 'classical' elements. Some, such as *qāf* and *hāḏā*, occur with every speaker. Other 'classical' elements occur with many speakers, but *'i'rāb*, for instance, did not occur at all.

As a matter of fact, this also appears from the examples that Meiseles gives. Owens (1991: 20) too remarks that Meiseles does not apply his criteria strictly enough. Meiseles takes *'i'rāb* as the fundamental distinction for ESA, but in an OLA example *yajib 'an yata'allam 'aw 'an yukmil ad-dirāsa* (1980: 131) *i'rāb* does not occur at all.[51] However, the

[50] Despite Mitchell's (1986: 9) claim that, for the sake of convenience it is better to omit the distinction ESA - OLA. "It seems to us that much of OLA can be regarded as belonging to a formal style of ESA." Mitchell prefers to stick to three varieties MSA/CA (Classical Arabic), the dialects and a mixed intermediate language ESA. Nevertheless in the sample sentences of ESA in Mitchell's last work (1994) mixed forms do not occur. According to Mitchell, ESA is, theoretically, a mixed form, but in practice it turns out to be a higher form of the dialect.

[51] In my view, this sentence of Meiseles' indeed belongs to a higher (OLA) language level. In my opinion the occurrence of *'i'rāb*, however, is not a good criterion, because every Arabic speaker is free to use *i'rāb*, or not. Forkel too points out that people who talk MSA use more pausal forms: "Nach der klassischen Regel wird der Teil des *i'rābs*, der aus kurzen Endvokalen, '*ḥarakāt*' besteht, in Pausa eliminiert. Viele Sprecher benutzen Pausalformen jedoch öfter auch im Kontext" (Forkel 1980: 52). The omission of the *'i'rāb* does not harm at all the literary character of the language. If you say *'urīdu 'an 'aḏhaba 'ilā l-madīnati* (*I want to go to the town*) or *'urīd 'an 'aḏhab 'ilā l-madīna* or *'urīdu 'an 'aḏhab 'ilā l-madīna* or *'urīd 'an 'aḏhaba ilā l-madīnati*, all these examples are unmistakablely of a higher level, contrary to ESA or dialects. The investigations by Parkinson also show that *'i'rāb* does not have to be the distinctive characteristic to define whether or not a variety belongs to MSA. In 1991 Parkinson writes about the Egyptians: "When I asked two assistants (both with advanced training in Arabic) to conduct oral interviews entirely in *fuṣḥā*, they both spontaneously produced a completely vowelless variety" (Parkinson 1991: 37). During a later experiment Parkinson observed the opposite:

definition of OLA by Meiseles is not solely based on the *'iʿrāb*. Meiseles only states that the occurrence of *'iʿrāb* is an indication of an OLA text. When the *'iʿrāb* does not occur, this alone does not mean that it cannot be an OLA text, because of other elements. The above-mentioned sample sentence is considered by Meiseles as an OLA sentence, and this on the basis of other elements, viz. the abundant occurrence of the particle *'an*.

Problematic, however, is the fact that Meiseles' text material is not clearly categorized. The examples on page 130 create the impression that, at least for this part, it involves texts read aloud.[52] The only indication in the texts is the radio station and the date. It is, however, extremely important to mention the type of program. Is it an interview, about what, with whom, or is it a prepared text? Also in his original work, Meiseles (1975) only gives fragments, and not complete texts. Besides the importance of the context in which sentences are produced, it also is important to analyze the context as a whole.

Indeed, it might well be that certain persons use different styles of speech in one conversation. Meiseles too observes that the identification of the Arabic varieties is often problematic: "The identification of varieties of contemporary Arabic and their description (impressionistic to a large extent) on the basis of the predominance of specific features in a text or excerpt, does not — in the linguistic situation of Arabic today — ensure that such passages, even the shortest, are linguistically uniform and coherent, the reality of contemporary Arabic is such that every text (except perhaps certain LA printed ones) embodies an incommensurable amount of variation and shifts alternating between one variety and another even within the frame of a sentence" (Meiseles 1980: 132). And page 142: "In such receptive languages as OLA and ESA, switching from one to the other is a central feature."[53]

According to Holes, precisely one of the conclusions that can be drawn from the investigations by Meiseles, Mitchell and El-Hassan is that all efforts to divide the Arabic style spectrum into clearly distinguished levels are doomed to fail (Holes 1993: 16). Tarrier (1991:12)

"It is clear that all speakers, when they decide to do *fuṣḥā*, whether for just a part of a sentence or for a whole exchange, use the ending vowels along with other *fuṣḥā* markers to indicate what they are doing" (Parkinson 1994: 207). In a previous study (Parkinson 1991: 38) he demonstrates that Arabic speakers themselves do not consider the *'iʿrāb* to be an essential characteristic to categorize language use as *fuṣḥā*.

[52] It is remarkable that in an earlier article Meiseles (1977: 179) puts OLA on the same level as the language use analyzed by Harrell (1960), viz. broadcast news.

[53] This has been confirmed by Schulz (1981).

supports him in his opinion: "Nous insisterons donc tout d'abord sur la nécessité, pour toute étude efficiente, de considérer l'inanité d'un découpage par lequel la langue arabe serait disséqué en plusieurs variétés ou états, car rien n'empêcherait alors, sans l'hypothèse d'un tel découpage, de la segmenter à l'infini, sans pour autant la saisir dans sa réalité propre; rien n'indique, en outre, que chaque niveau corresponde à un code linguistique cohérent, homogène et spécifique."

Indeed, Hary (1996) arrives at the term multiglossia, dividing the Arabic language continuum in even more levels.[54] On the basis of one sentence *I saw him*, he arrives at a division into 9 (11) levels. The question remains, however, whether the analysis of one simple sentence can suffice to describe a complete language, and then to divide a complete language into a multitude of levels.

With Meiseles (1980: 141), we have the impression, though, that the division ESA-OLA corresponds to the boundary between *al-luġa al-'āmmīya* and *al-luġa al-fuṣḥā*.[55] As a matter of fact, in the Arabic introduction of his last book (1994), Mitchell translates ESA by the term which Badawī uses as the third highest dialectal level, viz. *'āmmīyat al-muṯaqqafīn* or the colloquial of the educated.[56]

Due to the lack of transcribed corpora, we have to content ourselves with impressions. When we want to investigate the Arabic language on different levels, we first have to compile sufficiently large corpora of texts which can form the basis of empirical investigations, whose hypothesis can then be verified by other researchers. As a matter of fact, these corpora ought to be thoroughly structured and all situational data ought to be taken into account. Only then is it likely to be possible to make scientific, reliable pronouncements about linguistic characteristics of language varieties. And even then it will be very difficult to define pure language varieties because in a given community language varieties do not stand alone but influence each other.

[54] For multiglossia see also Dichy (1994).
[55] Cf. also Diem (1974: 3). See also Schulz (1981: 6).
[56] Cf. also supra 4.3.2.2. note 29.

5. COALESCING LANGUAGE VARIETIES

The different language varieties do not stand alone but melt into one another. Children are familiar with the dialect at home, but are confronted with MSA in school and through the mass media. From an early age on, Muslim children also are confronted with Classical Arabic by way of instruction in the *Qur'ān*. The emphasis lies on the memorization of the Koranic verses. Although some verses are not easily understandable for a small child, there are many other verses that can be easily understood, even with the limited knowledge of the local dialect.

Moreover, there also are indirect influences, because of the contacts between different cultures, giving lots of objects unusual names which are first introduced in the dialect, and sometimes later on also in the standard language. "No doubt, some of the foreign importations gain currency in the spoken language before they find their way into writing so that they may be said to have come in not directly but *via* the colloquial" (Cachia 1967: 16). In particular the educated language user is exposed to different influences which, in turn, can play a role in personal language use, either in the dialect or in MSA.

Every language sample which is distilled and analyzed by a researcher has been produced by one or more language users, who are exposed to different influences. When the use of the standard language is involved, then the user is not always conscious of the foreign influences. Since the standard language was taught at school and, consequently, the language user may doubt whether certain constructions are correct, it is possible for him/her to start applying foreign constructions unconsciously.

According to Kropfitsch, the European languages in particular, on the one hand, and the Arabic dialects, on the other hand, exert an important influence on MSA. "Einflüsse auf die semantische Ausformung des Neuhocharabisch (MSA) kommen im wesentlichen von drei Gruppen von Sprachen, mit denen eine mehr oder weniger enge Symbiose besteht: von den Fremdsprachen, den Umgangssprachen bzw. Dialekten und dem klassischen Arabisch. Besonders bedeutsam sind die beiden erstgenannten" (Kropfitsch 1980: 136). Mc Loughin holds the view that three factors exert a negative influence on the accuracy of MSA, viz.: "Arab intellectual's education abroad; the existence of numerous foreign educational establishments in Arab countries; the need to adapt Arabic vocabulary to the pressing demands of modern scientific technology etc." (Mc Loughin 1972: 72).

The influencing is a mutual one. In producing MSA, the language user is influenced by both his dialect and the foreign languages he is familiar with but, in turn, expressing himself in his own dialect, he probably is more or less influenced by the language varieties he is familiar with. "l'arabe dialectal existe toujours et continue d'être soumis a l'influence du français, il est également soumis à celle de l'arabe moderne, surtout depuis ces vingt dernières années où l'arabe moderne, devenue langue officielle à l'indépendance nationale du pays, voit son champ s'étendre grâce à la scolarisation, aux médias, à l'arabisation de l'administration, etc." (Bouchérit 1987: 118-9).

There are a few studies about these influences. Since some researchers also use the term Classical Arabic for MSA, it is not always clear whether they do not mean MSA when they refer to the influence of Classical Arabic. As we suppose that they do mean MSA instead of Classical Arabic, we classify these influences with MSA.

5.1. Influence of MSA on dialects

The evolution of language is a function of use and consequently is subject to the needs and wishes of the language users.[1] "Si les langues évoluent, et elles le font, c'est parce que les besoins de leurs usagers se modifient" (Tapiéro 1976: 17). Because dialects are not codified, this is the area that is particularly subject to change. "Arabic vernaculars — Cairene included — cannot be considered as homogeneous and static varieties of language. They are, and always have been, undergoing change — albeit slow change — and a number of factors like education, urbanization, the mass media, the mosque and so on are, and have been for some time, contributory to this change" (El-Hassan 1977: 117).

[1] Both conservative and progressive tendencies play their roles. According to Diem, the Arab socialists were more dialect-oriented because they wanted to write for the people and because they did not attach great importance to the religious and cultural dimension of their language. Others considered the use of the dialect in literature as literary communism. The degree of conservatism can exert an influence on language use (Diem 1974: 138). Given the revival of the Islam, it may well be that in the beginning of the 21th century more conservative (classical) tendencies might be expected.

Because of the inadequacy of the dialect, an educated speaker, may, in certain circumstances, have to resort to higher language varieties, thereby using a non-normated mixed language.[2]

The educated speaker seems, then, not only to be influenced by MSA, but also by other Arabic dialects. "Among the author's observations are two, by now familiar ones, namely, that educated Arabs use 'hosts of classical words and expressions', and make adjustments whereby a speaker replaces some of his own dialectal features with their equivalents in the dialect of another speaker in a particular situation" (El-Hassan 1977: 128).

According to Bateson (1967: 110), these 'classical' expressions are mostly used in set phrases, such as for instance, daily greetings and appropriate wishes for every time of the day. Classical interference was found both in interdialectal conversation (Blanc 1960: 83), elevated dialect (Palva 1969: 31 en 41) and 'the most colloquial style' (Killean 1980: 166). This interference, sometimes, consists of a classical pronunciation, which can be no more than a stylistic device, but more in particular it consists of borrowings from the MSA lexicon.[3] "A great majority of the classicisms in the 'elevated' colloquial are lexical, or at least indirectly due to lexical loans. This is only natural, because modern concepts usually have no equivalents in the dialect but must be borrowed from literary language" (Palva 1969: 40).[4]

Diem (1974: 26) considers these borrowings to be borrowings of necessity. As the elevated vocabulary of MSA is lacking in the dialect, people have to resort to the vocabulary of MSA when discussing an 'elevated' topic.[5] This view corresponds to the observation by Owens. "Borrowing of (M)SA words is motivated to a great extent by need. For example the founding of Yarmouk University in Irbid, NW Jordan in 1976 has given (M)SA words like *muʿaddal 'average', masāq 'course'*,

[2] Al-Ḥakīm declared in 1967: "It is enough, that one listens to the farmers or the workers in Parliament or on the board of Directors; and one would then realize that the language of normal speech has been 'classicized' to a high degree" (quoted in Nofal 1980: 4).

[3] Referring to Diem (1974), Owens (1991: 18) argues that it is quite problematic to use the term interference with respect to MSA and the dialects: "The idea that SA (Standard Arabic) interferes with dialectal speech is problematic. SA influence on dialect implies a population who have SA as a native language, what self-evidently is not the case." However, MSA is a language variety which is daily used in newspapers and books, and which is spoken and can be heard in news broadcasts, radio plays, documentaries, etc. It is clear that because of intensive contacts with MSA, interference in the dialect can take place. (cf. Parkinson 1991: 39).

[4] See also Tapiéro 1976: 124.

qāʿa '*classroom*', etc. greater prominence and currency in the area than they had before the university's opening" (Owens 1991: 25).

Diem (1974: 46) also points out that borrowings, because of their frequent use, can become a 'natural' part of the dialect. This has been confirmed by the investigations of Schmidt (1974), Abu-Haidar (1992) and Wilmsen (1995: 60-61). Wilmsen emphasizes that such words are completely assimilated in the dialect. Moreover, Arabs consider these words to be a real part of the dialect. On the other hand, Abu-Haidar found that some words keep their 'literary' pronunciation. "In the past twenty years or so a number of MSA terms conveying more abstract ideas have been incorporated into Muslim Bagdadi and Christian Bagdadi word inventories, without being assimilated to the sound system of their dialect. Forms like *taʾaṯṯur* 'influence', *muṯaqqaf* 'educated', *talawwuṯ* 'pollution', *taqaddum* 'progress', *ratīb* 'monotonous', *riʾāsa* 'leadership', are now part of MB and CB speakers' everyday experiences" (Abu-Haidar 1992: 104).[6] Schmidt (1974: 73) recorded this in the spoken language, especially for the political terminology.

5.2. Influence of dialects on MSA

When studying the influence of the dialects on MSA, we have to distinguish between written and 'spoken' MSA. Almost no investigations are available of 'spoken' MSA, except the investigations by Diem (1974), Schulz (1981), the very limited observation by Kaye (1991) and the ex

[5] Borrowings often are necessary because the dialects do not get the chance to develop their own terms because of the fast evolution. "Phénomène sociolinguistique, l'emprunt répond à un besoin en ce sens que, dans la plupart des cas, le contact brutal avec les réalités nouvelles n'a pas permis à la langue d'accueil de se forger ses propres termes" (Bouchérit 1987: 120).

[6] Bouchérit distinguishes between borrowings and mixtures. In the former case the words are completely adapted to the language, but in the latter case they maintain their original character. "Emprunt et mélange ne sont cependant pas à placer sur le même plan. L'emprunt, à plus ou moins long terme, est intégré à la langue d'accueil et se coule en principe régulièrement dans les moules offerts par cette langue. Ainsi, "l'école" à été emprunté sous la forme [*līkūl*] avec les voyelles [i] et [u] plus proches de ce que connaît l'arabe.(...) En générale, l'emprunt se plie aux contraintes structurelles de la langue." (Bouchérit 1987: 119). Holes too holds the view that it is sometimes better not to speak of interference, certainly when the words are completely integrated into the dialect. "Variation in dialectal Arabic, should not be discussed, for example, as 'interference' from the standard, but incorporated into dialectological description, since from the speaker's point of view it is every bit as much a part of his speech behaviour as 'the dialect'" (Holes 1987: 7). When a word is not completely assimilated, Wilmsen (1995) uses the term code-mixing. (cf. infra 5.7.)

perimental investigation by Parkinson (1994). Owens doubts whether the investigations of Diem deal with MSA, because 'spoken' MSA is very difficult to define as an independent variety.[7]

There are some data available on interference in MSA. Bishai (1966) conducted an investigation into the reports of the debates of the United Arab Republic. Probably these were written reports of the 'spoken' interventions, which might explain a bigger interference from the dialect on the written language. He concluded that "out of about 4000 words in the 20 columns examined, there were 188 colloquialisms representing only 26 separate items." *ḥa*, *mā — š*, *miš*, etc., which corresponds to 4,7 %.[8] Mc Loughin examined the same kind of text, viz. a recording of a conference, which later was written down for the newspaper. Here too, it was a written report of speech acts. He concludes that, in addition to foreign words, also dialectical words (local vocabulary) and dialectical expressions were used (Mc Loughin 1972: 58-9).[9] Mc Loughin, however, did not count the number of words.

In an investigation of newspapers Tomiche states that "l'insertion du dialecte dans l'écriture s'effectue sur le plan du vocabulaire, certes, mais aussi et plus en profondeur, sur celui de la syntaxe" (Tomiche 1969: 185). She gives an enumeration of a number of foreign words which occur in the press. As far as syntax is concerned she points at the dialectical word order which is subject + verb (NP + VP) instead of verb + subject (VP + NP). She concludes that: "Les caractéristiques du parler infléchissent donc les structures de la langue écrite" (Tomiche 1969: 186).

But, sometimes, conscious efforts are also made to include dialectical words into the vocabulary of MSA.[10] The most sizable initiative was the

[7] "Secondly, the notion of dialect interfering in SA, though an obvious one, nonetheless runs afoul the question, what variety it is, when educated Arabs speak, that they are trying to speak" (Owens 1991: 18). The same goes for the investigation by Schultz (1981) who does not categorize his language samples as MSA, but as an intermediate language, viz.: the third level of *Badawī*'s. Ditto for the experimental investigation by Schmidt (1974), who does not conduct an investigation into MSA, but rather into 'spontaneously spoken Arabic in Egypt'.

[8] Mind: Bishai did not call this language variety MSA, but Modern Inter-Arabic. For a detailed survey see Bishai (1966: 321).

[9] Somekh (1993) observes the same in the works of some Arab writers. In this case, however, we have to do with conscious adaptations to MSA in order to render the dialogues as lifelike as possible.

[10] Dialectical words have been included in MSA as early as the end of the 19th century. Monteil (1960) observed that many words, which are still described in the dictionary of Belot as dialectical, are described as MSA in the Hans Wehr dictionary. We have, however, to be cautious. It is not because a word is included in the Wehr dictionary that it is recognized as a fully MSA word (cf. Diem 1974: 44).

compilation by three Maghreb countries of the 'Functional Linguistic Corpus'. Researchers have compiled a word list of dialectical words, common to those three Maghreb countries.[11] "Words taken from spoken Arabic have been altered phonologically and morphologically to fit patterns acceptable in written Arabic. (...) It is an attempt at leveling, at drawing together elements common to the dialects of three contiguous Arab countries, but at the same time maintaining continuity with the Arabic of other periods and of other Arab countries" (Benabdi 1986: 68).[12] These originally 'dialectical' words have been included in the latest series of school manuals from the Maghreb countries.[13]

5.3. European influence on Arabic dialects

Monteil (1960: 90), Badawī (1973: 109 et seq.), Mattar (1986: 264), Bouchérit (1987: 118) and Wilmsen (1995: 67-74) point out that foreign words are most easily integrated in the Arabic dialects. Mattar too observes: "Dans les grandes villes égyptiennes, il faut également signaler l'apport considérable des langues européennes modernes qui ont fourni une quantité impressionante de termes aux populations urbaines, surtout à celles des ports comme Alexandrie, Port-Saïd et autres" (Mattar 1986: 264). In the Lebanese dialects and in the dialects of the Maghreb countries in particular many borrowings from European languages are to be found.[14]

11 A similar initiative took place in Syria in 1956 when the Arabic Academy proposed to examine which words could be easily integrated into the vocabulary of MSA (Monteil 1960: 73-75). For a critical review of the Functional Linguistic Corpus see Mahmoud (1982). See Benjelloun (1990: 359) for interesting critical comments on the application of the FLC in education.

12 Also in the 'classical' period dialectical words found their way into the classical vocabulary. "As in any literary language in use over such a large span of space and time, Classical Arabic has coined new words and has absorbed and 'classicized" words from the spoken dialects" (Ferguson 1959: 628). Mc Loughin (1972: 68) too emphasizes that "some of the most respected 'literary' vocabulary is of dialectal origin." As an example he quotes the word *māl* (money). Owens' proposition (1991: 25) that "Borrowing goes from the prestige to the non-prestige variety" is consequently not completely proper and certainly not in the case of language planning. About the insertion of foreign words in Classical Arabic see Schall (1982: 143 and 148).

13 See, for instance, the new series of school manuals *al-qirā'a* (Jārī 1992) for primary schools in Algeria, in which a number of dialectical words have been included, such as, for instance, the verb *na'asa* (to sleep), whereas in previous manuals the word *nāma* would have been used.

14 Bouchérit points out that the dialects also influence each other. "En outre, dans une ville comme Alger, les variétés dialectales représentées — variétés régionales et sociales — s'influencent les unes les autres et cette interaction peut donner naissance (cela

5.4. European influence on MSA

It is beyond dispute that the European languages have exerted an influence on MSA. It also is beyond question that this influence still prevails. "Die starke Wirkung der Fremdsprachen auf die Entwicklung des Neuhocharabisch darf als bekannt gelten" (Kropfitsch 1980: 136). The influence of European languages on MSA is noticeable on both the lexical level and syntactic level, and also on the style level. "MSA borrows heavily from European styles of discourse. Thus Arabic discourse styles (...) tend to have the same syntactic and logical structures as those of English and French" (Abdulaziz 1986: 18-19).[15]

A number of modern words derive from French and English and others from Italian and Turkish. The most important influence seems to be exerted by French.[16] "Its most formidable rival among European languages was undoubtedly French, which exerted a strong influence in most Arab countries and was the language of government of Lebanon, Syria, and for quite a long time, northwest Africa (the Maghreb)" (Blau 1981: 20-21). New concepts especially are adopted literally.[17] Further, according to Monteil (1960: 306) there is a large amount of European

semble dessiner) à une sorte de koiné dialectale, variété commune à la population algéroise" (Bouchérit 1987: 128). Whether the influence of the dialects on each other is larger than the influence of MSA on the dialect is not so easy to determine. Tarrier, for instance, comments on Palva's investigation (1982) as follows: "Palva conclut que les dialectes ont plus d'influence les uns sur les autres que n'en a le classique sur eux.. Une telle conclusion ne peut manquer d'être abusive dans la mesure où, si effectivement les faits évoqués laissent entendre une influence de tel dialecte sur tel autre, on ne peut pourtant pas en déduire, a contrario, le rôle qu'a ou n'a pas le classique. De plus, si ces faits rapportés concernent des situations de discours où seul le recours au dialecte est motivé, il y a effectivement peu de chance que l'influence du classique se fait sentir..." (Tarrier 1991: 11) But also on the level of a standard language a certain region can influence another one. Forkel, for instance, highlights the influence of the Mashreq on the Maghreb among others because the overwhelming majority of the Arabic books have been published in Lebanon or Egypt and because many teachers got their training in the East. Further on he writes: "Ein äusseres Zeichen des ostarabischen Einflusses ist darin zu sehen, dass heute in Marokko allgemein der ostarabische Duktus der arabischen Schrift verwandt wird. Der traditionelle maghrebinische Duktus is fast nur noch bei Koranausgaben üblich" (Forkel 1980: 9).

[15] See also Bateson (1967: 91-92) and Morsly (1990: 165).

[16] Cf. Rebhan (1986: 11-13). Ayalon (1987: 5) mainly refers to the influence of Turkish.

[17] For instance, the linguistic terms: *funīm* (phoneme), *funuluzyā* (phonology) (El Sayed 1984: 333). Both Al Sayed (1984: 338) and Altoma (1980: 51) point out that there is a great resistance against the use of loan words and that Arabic words are preferred. See also Wehr (1943: 29) and Rebhan (1986: 121), who writes about the introduction of new political concepts: "Die meisten politischen Begriffe, die im Arabischen des 19. Jahrhunderts als äquivalente Ausdrücke für die europäischen Vorbilder fungierten, wurden mit eigenen sprachlichen Mitteln geschaffen."

phrases (Anglicisms as well as Gallicisms) which have been translated literally.[18] Monteil supposes that these are highly accepted because even the best writers use them, which means that this phraseology escapes, to a large extent, from the criticisms of language purists.

The influence of European languages has been exerted, in the first place and mainly, in the press (Monteil 1960: 306-7; Gully 1993: 21; Abdelfattah 1996: 131). Via the press these influences penetrate into the literature. "As expected, European influence was especially strong on journalistic style, which is exposed to the pressure of time when journalists are translating from European languages. (...) Journalistic phraseology penetrates even higher literary language, since authors, reading newspapers, are influenced by their style" (Blau 1981: 60-61).[19] A number of foreign words have conquered their place within MSA. For instance, 1% of the words which occur in the Functional Linguistic Corpus originally are foreign words (Benabdi 1986: 75).

The editors of Arab magazines and newspapers, especially those published in Europe, who use a European language day in day out are under heavy pressure to use European phraseology when they write their articles in Arabic. When reading these articles, it sometimes can be doubted whether such constructions are generally accepted in the 'Arab world'. However, the extent of the European influence is difficult to determine. Most researchers only investigated limited 'language samples', and almost never check the extent to which these samples are representative. Moreover, in these investigations, European phraseology is searched for, which then of course is highlighted. According to Thiry (1985), as far as we know the only author who conducted a statistical analysis of neologisms in MSA, the influence of European languages on MSA should not be exaggerated.

Thiry (1985: 115) reports that there are fewer loan translations in Arabic than in French. He writes: "Quand aux calques, ils sont infiniment moins nombreux en arabe q'en français ou en espagnol". Thiry selected a number of pages from five Arabic books and counted the number of neologisms. When we add up Thiry's result (1985: 116) we get 14 neologisms out of 4285 words, which is, 0.3 percent.[20] Besides it

[18] See Mc Loughin (1972: 69).

[19] Belnap too emphasizes that the language of the press exerts great influence: "Although the press is often criticized as being substandard, almost all Arabs are exposed to it on a daily basis" (Belnap 1992: 252). For examples of stylistic influences in literature, see Wehr (1943: 25 and 26).

[20] Among the words that have been classified as neologisms by Thiry, there are some which seem to be completely integrated in MSA, such as: meter and kilometer.

is not completely certain whether these influences will have a permanent character.[21]

On the other hand, efforts are made in the Arab world to urge the population to avoid the use of foreign words. A study which got a lot of attention in the Arab world in this respect is the work by Baybars (1990), who gives a long list of alternatives to counter the use of foreign words in Arabic. We should not forget that the standard language is consciously promoted and adjusted. (cf. infra 1.1.4.). It is striking that also in radio news broadcasts, some foreign words are omitted after a while.[22]

5.5. Influence of Classical Arabic on MSA

On the other hand, MSA keeps being influenced by Classical Arabic. In the first place, because all the Arabic grammatical works, both the scientific ones and the textbooks, are entirely based on the Classical language. Koranic texts and pre-Islamic poetry remain the pre-eminent sources of the Arab grammarians. "The *Qur'ān*, of course, ranks high among religious books influencing modern Arabic phraseology" (Blau 1981: 27). Lately, we have even witnessed an increase in the number of classical texts in education. Previous manuals for the secondary schools had a more or less secular character. The number of Koranic texts has increased in the manuals used in schools today.[23]

But in literature also phraseologies based on old texts do occur. Blau (1981: 27) gives a few examples of phraseology he found in the works of modern authors, which find their origin in certain Koranic verses. Even though MSA has developed its own vocabulary, old classical words, though used less frequently, do not lose their attraction. In poetry especially the possibilities of this huge classical vocabulary are keenly exploited to make verses rhyme. As a matter of fact, it is never considered faulty to reintroduce classical elements, on the contrary. "There is even detectable in some modern writers an archaizing tendency towards re-introducing some features of ancient Arabic which had

[21] It also is remarkable that Schulz did not find many European borrowings in his spoken language samples: "There was a surprising lack of borrowing from European languages" (Schulz 1981: 83). This appears also in the study by Ayalon (1987).

[22] The word بروتوكول (*protocol*), for instance, which could be heard repeatedly in the eighties on the Egyptian news broadcasts, has disappeared completely in the news broadcasts of the nineties. Maybe this is due to the influence of professional correctors (cf. supra 1.1.4. note 24).

[23] See, for instance, the series *al-nuṣūṣ al-muḫtāra* (Rabat 1984) for the secondary schools in Morocco.

virtually disappeared from the language of the golden age" (Beeston 1970: 15).[24]

In the second place too, Classical Arabic continues to influence MSA because Arabic Academies mainly have drawn words from the classical vocabulary in order to create new words by means of derivations and adaptations. (cf. Stetkevych 1970).

5.6. Vagueness of the influences

It is, however, not always possible to discover with 100 % certainty precisely where all these influences come from. Sometimes an Arabic phrase seems to be drawn from a European language, whereas this is not always the case. According to Blau, other influences also may be prevalent.[25] He mainly points at the importance of Middle Arabic as a point of reference. "Sometimes one wonders whether a MSA phrase came into being through parallel development or through direct or indirect influence of the Old Testament (and, therefore, indirect influence of Hebrew). It was *pānīm el pānīm* (from Genesis xxxii 31) which gave rise to face to face, Fr. face à face., etc. The question is whether Modern Arabic *wajhan li-wajhin* arose independently or is influenced by European usage" (Blau 1981: 53-4). Further on, Blau gives a lot of MSA examples which, according to him, do not stem from European influence, but are due to direct influences of the Scripture (Blau 1981: 54-59).

We should not forget that also from the 8th to the 10th centuries, Greek and Syriac exerted an influence on the Arabic language, especially in the translations of philosophy. Blau emphasizes, however, that "Neither classical Arabic nor classical Hebrew has been sufficiently analyzed to enable us to know their phraseology in a sufficient matter. (...) Therefore, it is not beyond the realm of possibility that a feature occurring in MSA and at first glance accurately modeled on Standard Average European, is attested in classical literature and has arisen through

[24] Blau (1981: 47; also 50, 51 and 53) also observes that Biblical influences can be traced in MSA, especially under the influence of Christian writers. See also Schippers (1987: 46).

[25] The most detailed study on the different influences on MSA are the two articles by Blau (1973 and 1976) and the reaction on these by Beeston (1975). The study by Blau is especially interesting because it shows that the often one-sided emphasized European influence on MSA is inaccurate. According to Blau some influences can be due to different language varieties together.

parallel development" (Blau 1981: 61).[26] Beeston (1975: 66-67) too, observes that the influences on MSA can not always be determined with 100 % certainty.

Monteil concludes, correctly, that the affinity between English and French makes it difficult to determine whether we have to do with a gallicism or an anglicism (Monteil 1960: 310).[27] As a matter of fact, all this shows that MSA is not an independent isolated language variety, but that the language users of this variety are influenced in their language use by their dialect, the Arab cultural heritage and modern European languages.

5.7. Code-switching

It is not amazing then, that, also due to the inadequate linguistic skills (cf. infra 6.3.1.), and because of these different influences, a mixed variety can emerge in which several language forms are mixed. Blanc (1960: 85), had early pointed out that his testees spontaneously switched

[26] Blau gives, for instance, the example of *hunāka*. "Similarly, Arabic *laysa hunāka 'amalun* 'there is no hope' is considered to exhibit *hunāka* through the influence of 'there'. The situation is much more complicated. (...) Accordingly, one need not consider that English 'there' gave rise to a feature completely alien to Arabic, but rather that among the contesting words it made *hunāka* prevail, as well as *hunālika*" (Blau 1981: 118). Further on, Blau mentions the often quoted example of the passive construction, of which the agent is marked. "In both Classical Hebrew and Arabic, as a rule, the passive is not used when the agent is marked. Yet this construction, which has already become quite usual in Middle Arabic, is very frequent in both Modern Hebrew and Modern Arabic" (Blau 1981: 128). Consequently, according to Blau, it is not evident that this construction is due to European influences and he concludes as follows: "MSA, being open to all its preceding layers, has been influenced by all of them, including Substandard Middle Arabic, as exhibited for example in popular literature and Christian Arabic texts. Since modern authors, including journalists, read ancient texts written not only in Classical Arabic but also in Standard and Substandard Middle Arabic, they are liable to transfer Middle Arabic elements into their writings (Blau 1981: 149). This also means that the identification of which words belong to the modern vocabulary and which words do not, remains a problem. Monteil (1960: 30), for instance, holds the view that the old language has not sufficiently been examined to determine whether 'neologisms' did not yet exist in the 17th or 18th centuries. This has been confirmed by Beeston (1970: 116): "In fact, easily the most difficult problem confronting research into modern vocabulary is that of identifying what is a 'modern' usage. I myself have time and time again discovered that a word which I had thought to have a characteristically modern sense has turned up in that sense somewhere in medieval literature. The problem arises in part from the deficiencies of Arabic lexicography."

[27] Monteil (1960: 311) also observes American influences. It is clear that both English and French still independently exert their influence on Arabic. Take, for instance, the Arabic word for AIDS. In the Gulf region the word AIDS (English origin) is used, whereas in the Maghreb countries the word SIDA (French origin) is used.

from one style level to another one. El-Hassan (1977: 114-5) too points at the occurrence of code-switching or style shifts in spontaneously spoken ESA.[28] The term code-switching is used when mixing between two different languages, for instance, French or English and Arabic (Bouchérit 1987); two different language levels within one area (e.g. Egypt) (Schmidt 1974; Schulz 1981 and Eid 1982) or two different Arabic dialects (Abu-Melhim 1991).

In the Arabic language situation, code-switching is most manifest in Algeria and in Lebanon, where French words and constructions are mixed with dialectal constructions. This mixing occurs within one sentence or within subsequent sentences.[29] Code-switching differs from interference, because in the first case the two language systems are used in their totality. "On constate que les segments qui alternent répondent aux règles structurelles de la langue dans laquelle ils sont produits; il s'agit donc bien d'alternance de deux langues en non d'interférence du français sur l'arabe" (Bouchérit 1987: 124).

On the basis of an analysis of grammatical elements, Eid (1988) arrives at the conclusion that code-switching does not happen at random. It seems to be subject to certain regularities. Bouchérit observed the same, but he based himself on what informants considered to be correct or not. "L'existence des formes considérées comme aberrantes par ses locuteurs laisse supposer qu'il existe une grammaire propre au mélange. Les segments qui alternent sont soumis aux règles structurelles de l'arabe et du français, mais les énoncés ainsi produits ne sont pas la somme de l'application des règles structurelles des langues en présence. Ils sont régis par d'autres règles, spécifiques au mélange" (Bouchérit 1987: 127).[30]

Owens (1991: 26), on the other hand, holds the view that the concept code-switching is very difficult to define when applied to the (internal) Arabic reality, because, in his view, the material switched has to maintain all the characteristics of the original code so that it remains very clearly recognizable. When this is not the case, we ought to use the term

[28] See also Holes (1993), who investigated code-switching and style shifts in the speeches of Nasser from 1956-65, Mitchell (1980: 100) and Kaye (1987: 677).

[29] Eid (1982: 55) too observes that code-switching takes place within a sentence. "Speakers switched from one variety to the other not only across sentence boundaries, but also within the same sentence."

[30] Owens (1991: 27), who based himself on Bentahila's investigation (1983), writes of Arabic-French code-switching thus: "For example, * cette *l-ḫubza* 'this the bread' is not allowed because the French demonstrative does not co-occur with an article. Cette *ḫubza* on the other hand is allowed." For critical remarks on this point see Wilmsen (1995: 116).

"borrowing". According to this view, we have to use the term "borrowing" (and not "code-switching") when in a dialectal conversation a completely assimilated MSA word occurs (cf. supra 5.1.)[31]

Consequently the study of inter-Arabic code-switching is not made any easier. There are ambiguous words and there are words which have a neutral character (Schmidt 1974: 55; Schulz 1981: 63; Eid 1982: 56), but there also are MSA words which are realized in a dialectal manner. When code-switching occurs within a certain language, a mixture of two different language levels is involved.[32] The most difficult point, here too, seems to be the precise demarcation of the different language levels.

Eid (1982; 1988) starts from the diglossia option; there are two basic varieties: Standard Arabic and dialectal Arabic. Given the fact that speakers use both language varieties, a kind of mixed language emerges between dialectal Arabic and Standard Arabic. "But despite the high level of education of the participants and despite the high level of formality of the situation, all participants without exception mixed the two varieties of Arabic — Standard Arabic (SA), Ferguson's 'superposed variety', and colloquial Egyptian Arabic (EA)" (Eid 1982: 55).

The problem of the code-switching investigation by Eid results from her subdividing every word in an SA form or a dialectal form. Words with a dialectal pronunciation may considered to be Standard Arabic for pragmatic reasons, viz.: 'speakers view them as belonging to SA although they are given EA pronunciation (Eid 1982: 57).[33] As an example she takes the word *ra'ēt* which is *ra'aytu* in SA, and in EA *šuft*.[34] In

[31] It is not always possible to maintain the difference between these two concepts in actual practice. Abu-Melhim (1991: 236), for instance, precisely uses the term code-switching when a Jordanian borrows an Egyptian word. Neither does Mitchell (1986: 19) always find the term 'borrowing' not appropriate. "Nor do we find it necessary or helpful to refer to *borrowings* from the written language into ESA, though in passing it may be said that *interference* or, better, *influence* of the vernacular is properly spoken of as characterizing quasi-orthopedic renderings of MSA."

[32] Which is called 'diglossic code-switching' by Eid (1988: 53).

[33] Elsewhere Eid (1988: 56) writes: "Such intermediate forms were treated as SA on the basis that EA has an alternative lexical item *šuft* with identical meaning 'I saw'."

[34] The word *ra'ēt* can easily be considered as an intermediate form which might be classified under ESA. There are also, however, intermediate forms which are much less easy to classify. Tarrier (1993: 104), for instance, could not identify intermediate forms in the spoken language which he investigated: "Un autre fait général qu'il nous paraît important de mentionner est qu'à aucun moment nous n'avons rencontré de formes qui ne pourraient pas être caractérisées comme 'classiques' ou bien 'dialectales', la seule exception étant la présence des réalisations [ey], réalisations susceptibles d'être qualifiées 'd'intermédiaires'". Schulz (1981: 63, 136), who can even give a precise percentage of the number of 'classical'" verb forms and the number of dialectal verb forms, reaches the same conclusion. This contrasts sharply with the findings of Wilmsen, who identifies certain intermediate forms and who considers these to be characteristic for ESA. "It is pre-

Owens' view this is not a case of code-switching, but of borrowing. An MSA word, which obtains a pronunciation which is adapted to the dialect has to be considered of as a borrowing. According to Owens we can not use the term code-switching in this case.[35] Owens (1991: 27) points out that the material which Eid shows can hardly always be considered as SA. "Case endings, for example, are lacking, *qāf* is pronounced as Egyptian *g*, and many stretches of speech apparently fall within the colloquial spectrum."

The same goes for the code-switching investigation by Abu-Melhim (1991). There too, code-switching is mentioned between MSA and the dialects, whereas *ḫamista'š tis'a* (15 September) can hardly be considered MSA. In its essence, code-switching is based on a dichotomic language system. We only can use the term code-switching when we can clearly distinguish two language varieties from each other. Consequently, the problem of an intermediate language between higher and lower varieties remains.

5.8. Hybrid versus symbiotic forms

When within one word a mixture occurs of two language levels, we can talk about hybrid forms.[36] These forms too, do occur in Arabic. As an example Mitchell quotes the combination between a dialectal prefix (of the future) *ḥa* and a completely conjugated MSA verb, for instance: *ḥayuwāfiqu* (*he will agree*).[37] These forms are seen by Meiseles as symbiotic forms. "Symbiotic forms and constructions are those produced in language contact situations by the linking together of elements belonging to every one of the languages involved, with each retaining its identity" (Meiseles 1981: 1083).

We only can use the term "hybrid forms" when mixtures are involved in a 'hypo-correct' MSA word with a dialectal word. As an example Meiseles quotes the case of *ra'ētu* 'I saw him'. "It is a sure instance of Hybrid form occurring as a result of interference" (Meiseles 1981:

cisely this employment of intermediate forms that characterizes educated Arabic" (Wilmsen 1995: 91 en 124). See also Schmidt (1974: 55), who arrives at the conclusion that many words (min. 37,8 %) are common to MSA and the dialect of Cairo.

[35] Note that Mitchell characterizes the form *ra'ēt* as MSA (Mitchell 1986: 19).

[36] Owens (1991: 27), though, uses in these cases the term code-switching.

[37] Several examples can also be found in Schmidt (1974: 116, 158) and Schulz (1981: 87 and 164 et seq). According to Schmidt hybrid forms are not formed arbitrarily but are subject to certain rules (174).

1082). According to Meiseles, such combinations often occur in contemporary spoken Arabic.[38]

This brings us to the conclusion that Arabic spontaneous language use does not always involve two or more clearly distinguished varieties (discrete varieties). "Modern *fuṣḥā* is really there; it is a named form which people think they use on a daily basis. Many of our problems in describing it stem from the fact that it forms a relatively broad but indeterminate section of a much bigger continuum, and while there is general agreement about the continuum, there is little agreement about where the natural breaks in that continuum lie" (Parkinson 1991: 60). However, in my view, there is a relationship between the development of education, the "secondary exposure" by the mass media, especially television, and the development of language skills which accompany these, and the way in which contemporary and future generations of Arabic-speakers will realize the spoken standard language, in this case MSA.

[38] For several examples see Meiseles (1980a and 1981).

6. PROPAGATION OF MSA

As we all know, a dialect can evolve spontaneously. This is less the case for a standard language, which is subjected to a much more severe control (cf. supra 1.1.4.).[1] However, a standard language can gain influence at the expense of the other language varieties. Language evolution also can be related to the degree to which the use of one language variety loses its influence in favor of other language varieties.[2] The language policy of the different Arab countries aims at stimulating the use of MSA as much as possible and in as many fields as possible.[3]

It is not very easy to estimate to what extent the Arab world gives priority to the use of MSA compared to the dialects. MSA, as a language variety occupies a more and more prominent place also in its oral version. "The most common form of speech in rural areas is the local dia-

[1] Even so, in the 'oral' realization of MSA as well a certain evolution is noticeable. Forkel (1980: 60), for instance, writes: "Die von Diem vermerkte Zunahme des *I'rābs* beim Ablesen im Hocharabischen des Mashriq in den letzten Jahrzehnten hängt ohne Zweifel mit der Einführung des Rundfunks zusammen — in Ägypten im Jahre 1928 —. Man vergleiche demgegenüber die Texte bei Gairdner, The Phonetics of Arabic, aus dem Jahre 1925, vor Einführung des Rundfunks. Danach war es damals üblich, ohne *I'rāb* zu lesen." According to an article in the magazine *al-muqtaṭaf* (1927) the *'i'rāb* was not pronounced, either by authors or by professors. As far as reading is concerned, Meiseles observes that the *'i'rāb* is used more and more in pausal forms. Comparing his 'read aloud' material with the material of Harrell he concludes: "It seems that in the present-day OLA the occurrence of contextual forms before a pause no more represents 'a sort of hyperurbanism'. The extension of this phenomenon underlines its being a living feature of the language and not (anymore) a kind of pseudo-correction. Statistical data corroborate this fact: in comparison to the findings of Harrell (1960: 39) who found in the Egyptian Radio Arabic 10 contextual forms before a pause in a count of 1000 cases, I have counted in OLA in a similar number of cases, 183 contextual forms, among them 24 at the end of sentences" (Meiseles 1977: 179). The same has been observed by Diem (1974: 37), who writes that, when reading aloud, the contextual forms have increased during the last ten years.

[2] This prevailed also for the situation of Dutch in Flanders. Van Marle (1992: 24), for instance, writes: "40 years ago, Kloeke observed that the standard language only was spoken by some 3% of the population. It is indisputable that this is no longer the case. Whichever way you look at it, Standard-Dutch is spoken by a much larger part of the population nowadays."

[3] In 1952 it still was permitted at the writers' congress in Damascus to choose between dialect or MSA, but in 1956 the use of MSA was obligatory. This evolution continued in the following writers' conferences. The Academy congress in Damascus also proposed (1) to make MSA compulsory for teachers, (2) and also for plays on the radio, and, moreover (3) the dialect ought to approach MSA more and more (Diem 1974: 137). On the importance of MSA in the media see also Al-Shabbab (1986: 32).

lect, although because of the influence of the mass media, literacy programs, and all forms of contact with modernizing agencies, MSA also prevails, exposing, to a varying degree, the rural population to modern standard forms of usage" (Abdulaziz 1986: 14).[4] The propagation of MSA mainly takes place via education and the mass media. "Needless to say, in many Arab countries MSA is becoming more readily available to a large number of speakers of Arabic through the spread of education and mass media, especially television" (Abu-Haidar 1992: 93).

6.1. Propagation of MSA by the media

It is generally known, from the investigation by Diem, that in the media, both standard language and dialect are given a chance. This also has been confirmed by Thiry: "A la radio et à la télévision, les présentations de programmes, les nouvelles, les bulletins du temps, les émissions culturelles et certains débats sont en MSA, le reste est en dialecte" (Thiry 1986: 106). It also is generally known that the dialect is mostly used in spontaneous speech. "Many speech samples from the oral media showed various style shifts but remained within the limits of strictly Egyptian colloquial (ECA) usage" (Killean 1980: 165). A few domains, however, seem to be reserved for the standard language, in most cases monologues (Diem 1974: 60). "Monologe im Rundfunk und im Fernsehen wie Nachrichten, Kommentare, Vorträge und Einleitungen zu Interviews werden fast ausschliesslich auf Hocharabisch gesendet" (Forkel 1980: 70). Mainly thanks to the media, MSA has been able to develop as a separate variety compared to Classical Arabic (Kästner 1981: 25).

My own experience is, however, that dialect can also be used in news broadcasts. This is mainly the case for those countries, such as, for example, Algeria or Jordan, where people from all the sections of society are interviewed. The news itself, however, is always in MSA. This is also the case in Algeria: "Le journal télévisé algérien remplit donc apparamment toutes les conditions pour qu'apparaisse la variété la plus formelle d'arabe: l'arabe classique" (Morsly 1990: 169).[5] As a

[4] We must not lose sight of the fact that in some Arab countries, such as, for instance, Egypt, the rural population precisely through the media, is influenced by the dialect of the capital, which probably exerts an even greater influence on the local dialects.

[5] So 'classical', that, given the many language faults, Morsly finds it ridiculous: "En ce sens, la langue du journal télévisé algérien a un aspect archaïsant indéniable et quelque peu dérisoire du fait des nombreuses "ratées" (fautes) que ne manquent pas de relever les cerbères de la langue" (Morsly 1990: 173). We should, however, not forget the pressure

matter of fact, if all the Arab countries have to be covered, the use of the standard language remains maybe the only possibility.[6] It is agreed upon, though, that the propagation of MSA happens, chiefly, through the 'oral' media: "La radio et la télévision sont de loin les deux moyens les plus répandus d'utilisation de la langue savante dans l'expression orale, car ce sont les deux instruments de la communication de masse ou 'mass-media'" (Tapiéro 1976: 83).

In order to establish clearly whether MSA is gaining influence in general as well as in the media, we ought to have comparable material, which is hardly available. We might, for instance, examine, whether the use of MSA increases under certain circumstances, and whether in certain domains MSA has taken over the place of the dialect.

We only have three indications. A first indication of the propagation of the standard language can be found by comparing the data of Diem with the contemporary situation. This comparison partly falls short, because in reality the situations can differ a lot. Diem observed that for illiterate people MSA remains an obscure language, which they can hardly understand.[7] As an example, he quotes that in Algeria films about hygiene had to be remade in dialect because they were not understood. According to Diem some illiterate Lebanese people do not understand

of time, in which journalists have to work, which might increase the risk of 'faults': "The pressures of preparing news for broadcasting and of broadcasting life give rise to some special features, such as impoverished and ephemeral coinages and the occasional misreading or mispronunciation" (Ashtiany 1993: xi; cf. also Bateson 1967: 93). According to Witteboon (1972: 240), who conducted an investigation into the use of Dutch in news broadcasts, the style of the written text often is adapted for understandability, even when the style is correct. He also reports that journalists receive about 18,000 lines of text each day of which only 1,000 may be uttered (Witteboon 1972: 237).

[6] The importance of MSA as language of communication also appears from the number of short wave broadcasting stations that use MSA as a medium of communication. In 1979 Arabic featured in third place in world rankings with 67 broadcasting stations. The BBC started its broadcasts in Arabic as early as 1936. Wood mentions some of the reasons that might explain the importance of Arabic on the radio (1979: 117-8): "— There is high appreciation for oral culture in the Arab world. — Radio surmounts both the physical and political barriers which hamper the distribution of printed matter, and the obstacle of illiteracy. — There is a saturation of short-wave receivers in most Arab countries. — In sharp contrast to countries where the cultural elites have inherited the ex-colonial languages, there is a comparative lack of such linguistically alienated elites in most Arab countries. Spain, for example, which uses only three languages, selects Arabic as one."

[7] See also Monteil (1960: 32) and Mattar (1986: 273): "Cette langue est absolument incompréhensible pour un public arabe illetré." Abdulaziz nuances this: "These different forms of mass media have greatly helped to spread the knowledge of MSA and the urban forms of spoken Arabic to such an extent that it is claimed that even the peasants in places like Egypt, Syria, and Iraq can 'comprehend' news in MSA, although this can hardly be true in all of its ramifications" (Abdulaziz 1986: 15-6).

MSA news broadcasts and others buy a television set in order to understand at least something through the images. (Diem 1974: 11).

Twenty years after Diem's study, however, we observe that in different Arab countries important announcements to the population are made in MSA. These announcements go from simple calls to the population to watch for the appearance of the new moon at the end of the month Ramadan (Saudi-Arabia), to reports on conferences, developments in the Gulf War and military announcements (Algeria after the coup), in which the population is summoned to stay at home and to avoid visiting certain mosques. In Algeria too, for instance, advertising often is in MSA (Van Mol 1992: 68-69). This is certainly an important indication, because, as far as advertising is concerned, the advertiser wants to make sure that the message is very well understood.

A second, clearer indication can be found when comparing the news comments, described by Diem (1974), with the contemporary news comments, which we have recorded 20 years later. According to Diem (1974: 64), the comments on the radio in Egypt were strongly interlaced with dialect.[8] The starting point usually is an MSA text, which has been transposed into the dialect. Sometimes in one program there is a switch from one language variety to another variety. The radio comments which I have recorded and transcribed are completely in MSA. This is only one example of the propagation of MSA as compared to the dialect.

A third and last indication, which shows a larger influence of the standard language in the general language use, can be found by comparing the analyses by Bishai (1966) with those by El-Hassan (1978) and Schulz (1981). Bishai wanted to investigate what inter-Arabic language use would look like in the future. He therefore investigated the discussions which were held about the Arab Union by delegations form Syria, Iraq and Egypt .

Since El-Hassan in the Leeds corpus only investigated the use of the demonstratives, only this element can be taken as a point of comparison. It is remarkable that Bishai observed that the 'classical' demonstrative *hāḏā* was not used at all in the discussions, whereas the dialectal demonstrative *hādā* did occur (Bishai 1966: 321).[9] In El-Hassan's corpus the

[8] We notice here that Badawī (1973: 90), in his study which was published the year before Diem's study, classified the news comments as *fuṣḥā al-ʿaṣr*, which can be compared to MSA. Without quoting examples, Wilmsen (1995: 142) reports that "in radio commentaries, colloquial Arabic is encroaching upon the preserve of literary Arabic." This conclusion clearly is only an impression, since our completely transcribed corpus of radio comments reveals the contrary!

[9] In Schulz' corpus (1981: 153) the form *hādā* did not occur at all!

'standard form', indeed, does occur and even to a large extent. Of the total of demonstratives examined El-Hassan (1978: 53) recorded the following percentages of the use of *hāḏā*: Jordan 67%, Egypt 6.7% (In Egypt the dialectal demonstrative *dā* abundantly occurs viz.: 70.6%)[10], Syria 49.5% and Lebanon 14.2%. Even though the situational data do not completely match, the use of the MSA demonstrative is remarkable.[11]

Since the situations of the three above-mentioned indications are not 100% comparable, we have to be careful not to jump to conclusions. Nevertheless, we take the view that previous data show that in the Arabic language landscape, there is a stronger movement in the spoken language towards the use of MSA features.[12]

But, even if MSA were not to occupy a broader place in the media, it still does occupy a strategic position. Thorough knowledge of MSA is required in order to participate fully in the social life.[13] Newspapers and magazines, professional journals and others are spread on a large scale all over the Arab world. Thorough understanding of MSA is imperative in order to follow the television or the radio news broadcasts transmitted by any Arab radio or television station. Also many documentaries, radio-plays, etc. are in MSA.

Also the new Arab television station from London, Middle-East Broadcasting Corporation (MBC), has many programs in Modern Standard Arabic.[14] In the future the importance of Modern Standard Arabic will increase in the entire Arab world. Also traditional tendencies can consolidate the importance of the standard language as a culturally binding element. Consequently, every day the population in the Arab world is confronted with MSA in the media. Those who want to follow what is said will have to take pains to understand MSA: "Modern education and

[10] This again contrasts with the data of Schulz (1981: 153), who reaches a percentage of 85% for *hāḏā* and *hāza* together as demonstratives, and as pronomomina a percentage of 38%. A number of speakers in his corpus always used the dialectal forms.

[11] In Killean's investigation of the use of demonstratives on the Egyptian radio, the MSA form *hāḏā* does not even occur. In her comparison, Killean takes *hāzā* as a literary form and *dā* as a dialectal form (Killean 1980: 166). When we consider *hāzā* in the investigation of El-Hassan also as a MSA form, then we obtain a percentage of 30%.

[12] Beware: only thoroughly controlled longitudinal investigations can bear serious conclusions about such a tendency. Such an investigation ought to be conducted in different countries, because this tendency, of course, can differ from country to country.

[13] See also Diem (1974: 24).

[14] As a matter of fact Meiseles points at the uniform character of MSA on the radio: "The language of the broadcasts also has a unifying effect: the tendency is to broadcast in a language that is familiar, understood and uniform as much as possible throughout the Arab world" (Meiseles 1980: 139).

participation in the intellectual, literary, and sociopolitical life of the urban milieu required knowledge of MSA and one or more of the two languages, English and French" (Abdulaziz 1986: 13).

According to Tapiéro (1976: 85), the fact that large sections of the population are exposed to MSA every day might influence the language skills of the listeners: "L'auditeur ou le téléspectateur, même le plus passif, est agressé par une succession de signes linguistiques qui finissent par imprégner son "moi". (...) Signes nouveaux, qui répétés, finissent par être mémorisés; d'où production d'un changement d'attitude linguistique."[15] MSA, such as it is spoken on radio and on television holds a great prestige.[16] This language use, thus gradually becomes the model for many listeners of pronunciation also.[17] In this way Meiseles (1980: 139) writes: "Because of the great influence of these media in Arab society, the language of broadcasts, in large measure Arabic read aloud or OLA, is becoming the model of the spoken language for the entire Arabic-speaking audience."[18]

The influence of the media on language use has been confirmed by different researchers.[19] Forkel reports of a number of Arabs who claim that their language skills have improved by listening to MSA broadcasts on the radio: "Eine wichtige Rolle bei der Ausbreitung des Hocharabischen spielen neben den Schulen der Rundfunk und das Fernsehen. (...) Er spricht ein recht und flieszendes und korrektes Hocharabisch, das er

[15] Abdulaziz holds the same view: "The radio reaches the deepest parts of the rural areas and introduces listeners to wider linguistic habits" (Abdulaziz 1986: 15). This influence does not necessarily have to be exerted by MSA. It also can be exerted on the dialects by a greater supra-regional koine, such as, for instance, the Cairene dialect in Egypt.

[16] Cf. the investigation of El-Dash and Tucker (1975) which revealed that standard language is considered to be more appropriate for use in the media than other language varieties: "Classical Arabic was considered significantly more appropriate for use on radio and television than any other language variety" (El-Dash and Tucker 1975: 49).

[17] We should not lose sight of the fact that on the different channels there are also language programmes which are broadcast precisely to influence language use (cf. Jernudd 1986: 267).

[18] See also Meiseles (1977: 176). This contrary to Owens (1991: 25), who writes: "There is no independent group of speakers of the prestige variety to dictate what the spoken norm should be." However, journalists working at the radio station form an independent group of speakers. In my view, it is wrong to depart always, as far as standard language is concerned, from a group in the society who speaks this language variety as its mother tongue. I agree with Meiseles (1980: 139) that the radio unmistakably plays here a normatizing role.

[19] According to Meiseles this is even the most characteristic feature of the linguistic situation in the contemporary Arab society. "Through listening to radio and television Arabic speakers (even the little educated and the entirely educated) acquire a partial passive knowledge of LA: and that is one of the most characteristic features of the linguistic situation of contemporary society" (Meiseles 1980: 139).

nach eigenen Angaben durch Radio und Fernsehen gelernt hat" (Forkel 1980: 16). Other important results of investigations are reported by Abu-Absi, who observed that the use of MSA in the media exerts an influence on the language use of children: "The results point to a tendency on the part of these children to modify their language phonologically, morphologically, and lexically in the direction of MSA" (Abu-Absi 1990: 45). The question remains whether these changes in language use also will maintain in the long run.

6.2. Propagation of MSA by education

However, MSA can only be used efficiently when large parts of the population speak it and understand it. The propagation of MSA depends to a large extent on the receptive and productive skills of the language users. Next to the indirect influence of the media, the competence of MSA mainly depends on the education: "Competence in MSA is also an indicator of one's level of education. The more educated a person is the better he/she is at using MSA" (Abu-Haidar 1992: 93).[20] Important investments have been made in education and here too an evolution can be found.

MSA remains, of course, a very difficult language for the illiterate people, but their number has decreased to a great extent after World War II. More and more young people go to secondary school. Their knowledge of MSA, and their understanding of this variety is, therefore, much greater than the knowledge of their parents.

The number of comparable data available on illiteracy in the Arab world is limited. Yet, an evolution is noticeable. According to Bateson, the degree of illiteracy in the fifties was between 85 and 90% in Northern Africa, 95% in the Arab peninsula, 70-75% in Jordan and 50-55% in Lebanon (Bateson 1967: 83-4). According to Talmoudi the number of literates increased respectively from 2%, 7% and 15% for Algeria, Morocco and Tunisia in 1964 to 22%, 27% and 38% in 1974. (Talmoudi 1984: 18)[21]

[20] See also Parkinson (1993: 67) and (1994: 183).

[21] Anyhow, illiteracy in the Arab world is steadily decreasing. According to Parkinson more than 50% of the (predominantly rural) population is illiterate: "It is important to keep in mind that literacy rates in Egypt as a whole are still less than 50%" (Parkinson 1994: 207). According to Diem the literacy rate in Egypt in 1974 was only 25% (Diem 1974: 10). Anyhow, the percentage of the population which buys a newspaper has increased: "Circulation of daily newspapers rose form 310,000 (1.6 percent of the population) in 1949 to 2,475,000 (5.9 percent of the population) in 1979" (Abdelfattah 1996: 133).

On the other hand, the Unesco statistical yearbook of 1992 clearly shows that, especially the last 15 years, in the period from 1975 to 1990, education in the Arab world increased substantially. Although the percentage of illiterate people is still very high (year 1990) in certain countries, viz.: in Egypt + 50% and Saudi Arabia 37.6%, it is extremely low in other countries, such as, for example, in Syria only 7% (3.9% of the men and 10.1% of the women). In a period of fifteen years the number of teachers and the number of students in the Arab world has almost trebbled.[22]

Of course, there still remains a large difference between elementary language skills, such as the ability to read and the ability to write simple sentences, and full language proficiency, which always remains an ideal goal as far as the standard language is concerned.[23] However, the large number of students in education clearly is an indication that language proficiency with regard to the standard language can hardly be compared with language proficiency such as it was 20 or 30 years ago. Undoubtedly more people have access to MSA via education. However, with regard to language skills a distinction must be made between productive and receptive linguistic skills.

6.3.1. *Productive linguistic skills*

The productive linguistic skills concern both the written and the spoken language. These skills go from the production of simple announcements to the writing of literary texts. The oral linguistic skills go from simply reading aloud a text to spontaneous conversation in correct MSA. It is logical that there also are different levels in language proficiency. Not everybody has the proficiency to produce literary texts.[24]

[22] In 1975 there were 820,000 teachers at work in the Arab world against 2,199,000 in the year 1990. The total number of registered students increased from 23,197,000 in 1975 to 46,159,000 students in 1990 of which respectively 5,645,000 and 15,351,000 in the secondary schools and 896,000 and 2,433,000 in high schools or university. (Unesco statistic yearbook 1992: 2-10 and 2-14).

[23] One of the most eminent writers of the 19th century, viz.: 'Aḥmad Fāris aš-Šidyāq reported, when he was 85 years old, that after 70 years of study of Classical Arabic, he still was not certain whether he made errors when writing (Monteil 1960: 350).

[24] Tomiche (1969: 183-4) writes on these language skills: "En 1960, M. Muḥammad Mandūr, chargé de lire les nouveaux romans susceptibles de recevoir un prix littéraire, notait: 'la faiblesse de la langue écrite actuellement est un phénomène général'. Pendant vingt ans d'enseignement dans les Universités et Instituts supérieurs, ajoutait-il, il avait eu le loisir de se convaincre de l'incapacité des étudiants à s'exprimer correctement et clairement: 'corriger les copies aboutissait souvent à résoudre une série d'énigmes'."

In all probability, there are more people able to write simple announcements than there are people who can write literary texts. But, here too, the linguistic skills in European countries must not be overestimated.[25] According to Ibrahim, the (productive) linguistic skills, even of graduate students of universities still leaves a lot to be desired: "Dissatisfaction with the students' proficiency in Arabic, even at the university level, is universal throughout the vast Arab region. It is a rare thing, extremely rare indeed, to read or hear any document read in Arabic these days, whether it is a personal letter, a newspaper, or a work of art, without encountering mistakes due to interference from the spoken language" (Ibrahim 1983: 512).[26] Although Parkinson too observes deficiencies in the productive linguistic skills of Egyptians, his judgment is more clement: "The average Egyptian with a college education could be described as a competent user of MSA."

Measuring productive skills, however, does not always involve the registration of mistakes. Every standard language contains elements which are difficult for many language users.[27] The registration of mistakes against correct language use only gives a limited idea of the language skills of the 'testees'. Kaye (1970: 387), for instance, conducted an investigation into the reading proficiency of Arabic texts. He observed that many mistakes were made in case and voweling.[28]

[25] One of the characteristics of standard language is that its skills have to be developed at school. This is also the case with respect to Dutch. Productive and receptive skills are to be developed in education (Cf. also Vries 1987: 137).

[26] Thiry is much more optimistic: "L'avenir n'est cependant pas aussi sombre qu'il y paraît. L'arabisation que connaissent les pays arabes dans tous les domaines, surtout celui de l'enseignement, permet aux jeunes dès l'âge de douze ans de s'exprimer correctement en MSA" (Thiry 1985: 119).

[27] In general, only very proficient people take part in a dictation contest of Dutch. Nevertheless mistakes are always made. Compare Parkinson (1990) on the writing of the *hamza*.

[28] "I have taken the first fifty pages of 'Aḥmad 'Amīn's autobiography, My life (*ḥayātī*), and recorded 'educated' Arabs from several parts of the Arab world reading this text. (...) I have noticed many so-called errors" (Kaye 1970: 387). One of the examples that Kaye gives is the reading of *fī madārisin* instead of *fī madārisa* (*in schools*). However, every language has its problematic grammatical issues. The correct reading with *nunation* in Arabic is one of these. Stetkevych quotes an Arab author who found the *'i'rāb* the most difficult element in the teaching of Arabic. "We have failed to teach it [the *i'rāb*] even to the educated minority" (Stetkevych 1970: 85). Monteil (1960: 45) observes that it is one of the two fundamental difficulties of the literary language. He quotes different Arab writers who witness that they have problems with the Arabic script. "We try to read a text correctly, but this way the meaning of the sentences escapes." (Kafūrī, 1948, 26). "We are the only people that have to understand in order to read. All other peoples of the earth read to understand" (A. Furayha, 1955, 26). Ṭaha Ḥusayn holds the view that you first have to learn to read and write in order to understand. These quotations go back to the period right after World War II. We have to be conscious that

It seems, however, that a lot of people still experience problems expressing themselves in MSA. Bishai, for instance, observed in 1966 that "It is no secret that, relatively speaking, very few Arabs can really master classical Arabic in such a way as to be able to engage extemporaneously in literary activities or participate in public formal discourses" (Bishai 1966: 319). According to Benjelloun the situation, since then, has not improved. "Bon nombre d'artistes, de pédagogues, de psychologues, etc. refusent de se produire à la télévision chaque fois qu'ils sont invités à des émissions en langue arabe. Quant à ceux qui maîtrisent la langue, ils préfèrent lire leur texte" (Benjelloun 1990: 355).

Nevertheless, I have the impression that there is some improvement in this field. To my utter amazement, I heard children of 12-13 years old expressing themselves fluently in MSA. We lack a sufficiently large number of investigations, which made a thorough evaluation. In most cases the evaluations are not more than personal impressions.[29] Parkinson (1994) experimentally tested the skills of a few Egyptians to talk *fuṣḥā*. He concluded that all speakers mainly emphasize the pronunciation of the *'i'rāb*. The results of the investigation of Parkinson show a thorough productive linguistic skill, as far as the use of oral MSA is concerned.[30]

6.3.2. *Receptive linguistic skills*

As for any language, the receptive linguistic skills of MSA are larger than the productive skills. "Moreover, the receptive awareness of speakers is much greater than their productive performances suggest" (Mitchell 1986: 10). This has been confirmed by the investigation which has

there were, at that time, no campaigns to eliminate illiteracy nor Arabization campaigns. Moreover, Arabic had not yet completely developed in education at that time. The problem of the *i'rāb,* though, remains, even today, a difficult topic: "I will claim that the system of *i'rāb* (grammar vowels at the ends of words) is not a viable part of most Egyptians' MSA" (Parkinson 1993: 48). But, even when somebody reads *fī madārisin* instead of *fī madārisa*, this fact alone gives but a limited idea about the language skills and proficiency, because the grammar vowels at the ends of words are not essential to understand an Arabic text. See for mistakes in reading also Meiseles (1977: 181-185).

[29] According to Parkinson children, indeed, have, both orally and in writing, a high productive language skill: "By the time they finish school they are using it constantly and consistently to perform real communicative functions: writing papers and exams, writing letters and notes to friends, etc. They are also very proficient at using spoken forms of Standard, or spoken forms of colloquial that have been heavy influenced by Standard" (Parkinson 1990: 288).

[30] The dialectal interference which has been observed by Parkinson (1994: 180) in some vowels, does not, in my view, harm the MSA character of the spoken samples.

been conducted as a result of the MSA children series on television *Iftaḥ yā Simsim*. Abu-Absi writes about this program: "One of the problems facing the researchers associated with the project was the question whether or not preschool children understood MSA. A second issue was related to how unnatural it would be to use MSA, a formal written medium, in spoken everyday-type situations. The third area of concern had to do with the ability of actors, including child actors, to use MSA correctly and comfortably. (...) The result of the pilot studies, which were carried out in four centers (Kuwait, Cairo, Amman and Tunis) representing the four main dialect areas, left no doubt regarding the ability of children to comprehend the contents of the program and the receptivity and enthousiasm of the adults" (Abu-Absi 1990: 35).

Abdulaziz also, without referring to investigations, points at the large receptive language skills as far as MSA is concerned. "It is, however, remarkable that MSA is understood by almost all Arabic-speaking peoples possessing a minimum of formal education" (Abdulaziz 1986: 18).[31]

6.4. Impediments to linguistic skills

According to many scholars, the complexity of the Arabic language is an impediment for the full-fledged mastery of the language. Often it is reported (Monteil 1960: 42) that one of the biggest impediments seems to be the omission of the vowels, which makes it difficult to define the precise word. According to Mattar, due to the Arabic (consonantal) script, children in the Arab world experience many more difficulties to read than western children: "L'enfant occidental, dès l'âge de 9 ou 10 ans, est capable de lire et de comprendre à peu près tout ce qu'il lit. L'enfant arabe du même âge ne peut lire et comprendre que des livres entièrement 'vocabilisés', imprimés à l'usage des enfants ou des débutants; et encore faut-il qu'il ait atteint un certain niveau de savoir" (Mattar 1986: 259).[32] Others point at the deficiencies in the educational system (Diem 1974: 13; Abdulaziz 1986: 21; Mahmoud 1986: 243; Benjelloun 1990).[33]

[31] This has, more or less, been contradicted by Mattar who argues: "Un message exclusivement codé sur la base de l'arabe classique est entièrement décodé et assimilé par une minime partie seulement des récepteurs (3% à 6%) selon le degré de culture et d'instruction. Cette proportion peut atteindre 8% à 10% pour un décodage partiel" (Mattar 1986: 253). Mattar, however, does not refer to any investigations to support his claim.

[32] For a discussion on the problems with the Arabic (consonantal) script see also Diem (1974: 15).

[33] Children can also experience difficulties in the dialect in the learning process. Ferguson and Eid (1990: 17) refer to an investigation by Kassem (1987) which demon-

It is also argued that MSA is not always necessary to communicate. Arabs from neighbouring countries, in most cases, speak a related dialect, allowing them to understand each other. The necessity to express oneself in MSA is not everywhere equally great. This fact, certainly, has an influence on the productive language skills, explaining why they may be better in one country than another one. Egyptians, in particular, are known to be devoted to their dialect. This is illustrated by El-Hassan, who reports: "It seems that in general, there are two main forces which operate on an educated Egyptian speaker: the desire to sound like an Egyptian and the desire to sound educated" (1978: 42). Both at home and abroad an Egyptian does not feel the same need to speak MSA as other Arabs do.[34]

The situation in Morocco appears different. A Moroccan can use his dialect in the entire Moroccan area, but his dialect will be of no use when contacting somebody from the Mashreq: "Von besonderer Wichtigkeit ist das Hocharabische für Marokko, da der marokkanische Dialekt ausserhalb des Maghreb völlig unverständlich ist" (Forkel 1980: 27). This too might be of importance in the development of productive language skills. Forkel (1980: 16), for instance, continues: "Ein ägyptischer Dozent, der in Fes Jura lehrt, wies mich sogar im Gegenteil darauf hin, dass seine marokkanischen Studenten das Hocharabische im Durschnitt besser beherrschen als ägyptische Hochschüler."

Finally, we have to notice that in no country do all citizens fully master the standard language. Nevertheless, it is always possible for the dialects to lose their influence and for the standard language to be used in more and more circumstances. Abu-Absi rightly concludes: "This does not necessarily mean that in 2010 Arabic-speaking children will be using MSA in their everyday interaction. It could mean, however, that there will be a generation of educated Arabs who possess the facility to

strates that it is not always easy for children to learn their dialect: "A recent M.A. thesis in Austria studied colloquial Arabic plurals and how children acquire them. At age 11 the children still were not producing them the way the adults did. They had their own patterns, which in some cases the adults found complicated" (Ferguson 1990: 47). The same observation can be made about Dutch. Even for children who live in a Dutch environment, it easily takes several years before they can correctly use the past tense for the strong verbs.

[34] This has been confirmed by Diem, who refers in this respect to language nationalism, which seems to be very strong in Egypt. Apparently more than in, for instance, Syria and Lebanon, dialectal influences are allowed on the radio and in official speeches (Diem 1974: 23). Moreover, Diem observes that another language variety than MSA is allowed and even widespread in monologues in Egypt, probably because of the bigger consciousness of nationality in Egypt (Diem 1974: 63).

use a form of MSA or ESA or colloquial in a manner analogous to the facility that many educated speakers of English of French have in using their standard language in addition to some regional or social nonstandard dialect" (Abu-Absi 1990: 43).

Nobody can tell what the future will bring. It is, however, clear that under the influence of MSA in education and in the media, other possibly intermediate varieties may lose their importance. Different authors, among them Wehr (1943: 16), believed that MSA would become the koine of the future. Tapiéro too believed that MSA would become the koine of the Arabs and the colloquial language of the future: "Ce koiné qui s'impose à toutes les communautés pour des raisons spirituelles et politiques, a déjà montré ses aptitudes dans l'expression écrite et commence à les montrer dans l'expression orale. Mais grâce à une scolarisation qui se généralise et à l'influence des "mass-media" (surtout radio et télévision), les conditions sont réunies pour que cette langue progresse également dans le domaine de l'expression orale. (...) Dans un avenir plus ou moins lointain, l'arabe moderne, étant donné l'évolution qui s'en dessine depuis la réalisation des indépendances, deviendra cette langue commune écrite et orale véhiculaire entre les citoyens des divers pays arabes" (Tapiéro 1976: 126; 128).

We can conclude that, when variation in the standard language between different countries is to be investigated, the language samples have to be carefully selected. If the language samples are based only on 'media' language, we risk comparing different language varieties. Comparable language samples have to be investigated. Since news broadcasts occupy a central position in society, and since many authors claim (cf. supra.) that standard language is used in news broadcasts, we will here limit our investigation to news broadcasts. Given the extreme importance of deciding which method will be applied in such an investigation, we will elaborate on the methodology in the next part.

PART II

METHODOLOGY

7. METHODS OF INVESTIGATION

It is clear that in general there are different ways to conduct linguistic investigations, but some are particularly pertinent with regard to the Arabic linguistic reality. The different methods of investigation all have their advantages and disadvantages. It goes without saying that it is very important to pay special attention to the way the material is gathered. "If one thing has been learnt from the intense work in socio-linguistics over the last twenty or so years, it is that data collection techniques — what is collected, how it is collected, who it is collected from and who collects it — deserve the greatest attention if an accurate description (let alone explanation) of the vernacular speech forms used by any social group is to be made" (Holes 1987: 1). The same can be argued about investigation into other language layers. The way in which the investigation is conducted is decisive for the representativeness of the results of the investigation with regard to the whole or partial linguistic reality. In this chapter we will discuss successively some methods of investigation and the problem of representativeness.

7.1. Introspection

A method of investigation which finds its origin in the Transformational Generative Grammar (hereafter TGG), of which Chomsky is the founder, is the method called introspection. This method assumes that the native speaker has the competence to express all kinds of language forms correctly. "*Competence* refers to the implicit unconscious or underlying knowledge which every language user has of his language. This knowledge enables him to produce an, in principle, unlimited number of sentences and to interpret these" (Appel a.o. 1979: 18). In this respect the term language capability is sometimes used. This *competence* (or language capability) is opposite to *performance*, viz. the language, such as it is used in reality, or the *language use*.

Central to the method of introspection is the intuition of the language user, who knows best what is possible and what not. "The best way to arrive at a knowledge of competence, it was held, is not by looking at texts but by exploiting the intuitions of the native speaker" (Francis

1979: 110). According to Chomsky language theory ought, in the first place, to deal with the *competence* of the *ideal language user*, e.g., the language user who perfectly masters his language and who is not hampered by his memory, mistakes, etc. A first problem with regard to the TGG is that the ideal language user is an abstraction that does not exist in reality.

Bungarten, for instance, remarks (1979: 29): "Chomsky konstruiert einen idealen Sprecher-Hörer, 'der in einer völlig homogenen Sprachgemeinschaft lebt, seine Sprache ausgezeichnet kennt und bei der Anwendung seiner Sprachkenntnis in der Aktuellen Rede von solchen grammatisch irrelevanten Bedingungen wie — begrenztes Gedächtnis — Zerstreutheit und Verwirrung — Verschiebung in der Aufmerksamkeit und im Interesse — Fehler (zufällige oder typische), nicht affiziert wird'. Dies ist in der Tat ein rein hypothetischer Sprecher-Hörer". And further: "Verschiedene empirische Untersuchungen zum individuellen, schichtenspezifischen, dialektgeografischen, fachsprachlichen und altersspezifischen Sprachgebrauch führen zu der Annahme dass die individuellen Kompetenzen der Sprecher biografisch, sozial und regional determiniert sind und erhebliche Unterschiede aufweisen. Demzufolge ist nicht nur der 'ideale Sprecher-Hörer' ein theoretisches Konstrukt, sondern auch dessen Kompetenz, die keinerlei psychologische Realität in den Köpfen realer Sprecher besitzt" (Bungarten 1979: 31).

A second problem is related to the fact that the main aim of TGG is the production by the language user of grammatically correct sentences based on his intuition. It is assumed that the language user himself is capable of defining what is correct and what is not correct. In other words, the ideal language user is supposed to be intuitively capable of passing judgment on the grammatical correctness of certain sentences.[1]

[1] Ulvestad (1979) remarks that introspection can be based on one or more native speakers. He distinguishes two kinds of method: "However, what I here call the introspectional approach or method should at the outset be divided into two relevantly separate styles: 1. the monointrospectional (MO) method, i.e. the linguist uses his own or somebody else's presumably competential intuition for arriving at statements of (non)grammaticality and the like, and 2. the multiintrospectional (MU) approach, by which the intuition of several native speakers is tapped. (...) In addition it seems to be advisable to distinguish between two different aims of investigation: 1. the establishment of grammaticality and, explicitly or by implication, nongrammaticality; 2. the description of within-class variation in the domain of grammatical constructions." (Ulvestad 1979: 89-90). According to Bausch a distinction also has to be made between the intuitive judgment of the native speaker and the judgment of the researcher, which can be biased: "Demnach ist auch zu unterscheiden zwischen den intuitiven Urteilen des native speaker (informanten), die inkorrekt sein können, und den intuitiven Urteilen des Linguisten, die Auskunft geben sollen über die 'wirkliche' Kenntniss der Sprecher. (...) Diese Auszeich-

This reasoning might hold true for a language community which is very isolated and which has only one language register and which did not undergo influences from other languages. Such a language community probably does not exist. As a matter of fact, as far as Arabic is concerned, its language users not only underwent influences from other languages, but there are even different language registers and grammars to which the language user can appeal.

Moreover the language user, especially for the standard language, has doubts on many points.[2] (cf. supra 1.1.4.). In this respect Schippers correctly argues: "A comment that certainly can be made about the investigation of the TGG, is that this theory supposes a *competence in the mother tongue* of the language user, whereas Modern Standard Arabic, never is a mother tongue (cf. supra 3.2.), but a cultural language which exerts its influence on the speakers of the dialects who try to approach Classical Arabic, when the circumstances demand it" (Schippers & Versteegh 1984: 10).[3]

The recent investigation by Wilmsen (1995) demonstrated that Arab native speakers do not always have a clear-cut judgment of the grammatical correctness of certain sentences. "That native speakers reject a form cannot in itself be an acceptable reason for stating that it is not permitted in a grammar. There clearly are formulations that even native speakers would not care to admit to using or to accept in others that nevertheless occur in speech. There will be others that may be acknowledged as occurring but whose legitimacy is denied" (1995: 100).[4]

nung des Forschers gegenüber den übrigen Mitgliedern der Sprachgemeinschaft ist problematisch, denn auch er ist Teilhaber der Sprachgemeinschaft, und somit unterliegen seine intuitieven Urteile ähnlichen Bedingungen wie die der native speakers" (Bausch 1979: 76). For a discussion on the disadvantages of intuition as method of investigation, see Bungarten (1979: 32-33).

[2] This also means that the proposition of Ditters: "One can only rely on the intuition about language of those educated Arabs who use it as an instrument for written communication", has to be put into perspective (Ditters 1988: 33). Also for Dutch writings people use reference works in order not to make mistakes. We can assume that this is also the case for users of the Arabic standard language.

[3] According to Bausch, it is even not certain whether the descriptions of the 'cultural languages' are reliable: "Der Sprecher lernt Sprache nicht nur in Sprechsituationen, sondern auch aus Sprachbeschreibungen. Sprachbeschreibungen können ein unkorrektes Wissen über Sprachnormen vermitteln, und sie können über Multiplikatoren — wie Bildungswesen und Massenmedien — Sprachnormen verändern" (Bausch 1979: 85). This also has been confirmed by Ulvestad (cf. infra).

[4] Moreover, Wilmsen adds in a footnote: "This is a fine illustration of the inadequacy of transformational grammars that rely for their construction and verification upon introspection and native speaker corroboration. The dichotomy they pose between competence and performance is a false one, in that speaker's competence may include two or more grammars" (1995: 101). See for a similar criticism on the TGG: Meiseles (1980: 137).

Ulvestad's investigations (1979) of German, too, show that investigation by means of introspection with native speakers is of limited value.[5] He concludes as follows: "My general conclusion is that the MO-method has only one advantage: ease of application, but as a fact-producing procedure it must be looked upon as at best a heuristic device, as a way of searching for hypotheses that may be tested by means of MU- and CO-routines. Even the MU-test often leads to questionable results" (Ulvestad 1979: 100). Moreover, Bungarten points out that even TGG, in principle, is thrown back on the analysis of correct language utterances (Bungarten 1979: 30).

A third problem which is related to this method of investigation is the problem of representativeness.[6] When investigations are based on one or more native speakers, even when these are specialists, then we still have but a limited judgment on the whole linguistic reality. Or, as Quirk puts it: "Since native speakers include lawyers, journalists, gynecologists, school teachers, engineers, and a host of other specialists, it follows (a) that no individual can be expected to have an adequate command of the whole 'repertoire': who, for example, could equally well draft a legal statute and broadcast a commentary on a football game? (b) that no grammarian can describe adequately the grammatical and stylistic properties of the whole repertoire from his own unsupplemented resources: 'introspection' as the sole guiding star is clearly ruled out" (Quirk & Svartvik 1979: 204).

This has also been confirmed by Ulvestad: "A national language is always vastly richer than a particular idiolect or local dialect or Umgangssprache, and no linguist, native or not, should assume the competence of deciding what an 'ideal speaker' would consider grammatically acceptable with reference to a given sentence or construction" (Ulvestad 1979: 100). And further: "No speaker and no small group of speakers can reasonably be expected to pass definite judgment with regard to the use of a living language with its truly staggering number of constructional possibilities and impossibilities" (Ulvestad 1979: 106). These observations make us conclude that the method of introspection is em-

[5] According to Ulvestad, the monointrospectional approach holds the risk of premature generalizations. Many German grammars have been compiled that way. A comparison of the results of his corpus investigation of the negation *nicht* with the results of the introspectional methods brings Ulvestad to the following conclusion: "In my corpus I have found close to three hundred examples of the allegibly (sic) ungrammatical type" (Ulvestad 1979: 92).

[6] Cf. Bausch (1979: 75): "Ihr intuitives Urteil muss nicht per se repräsentativ sein für das (identisch sein mit) 'System' des Sprachstadiums."

pirically not sufficiently grounded to make judgments which can be generalized about the language.[7]

7.2. Experimental investigation

A second method of investigation deals more with *performance*. In order to describe current language use, a few testees are placed in an artificial setting to talk with each other and to observe their linguistic behavior. Such investigations have a more or less experimental character.

Examples of such experimental investigations are the investigations of Blanc (1960), Talmoudi (1984), Bakir (1986), Owens & Bani-Yasin (1991), Abu-Melhim (1991), Abu-Haidar (1992) and Parkinson (1993 en 1994). In all these cases, a researcher brought a number of Arabs together and had them talk about a certain topic. Most of these researchers are inspired by the Labovian method.[8]

A first requisite of this investigation method is that the researcher has to remain conscious that (1) the language sample yielded by such an investigation is limited and (2) that such conversations always remain artificial. This is very important for the interpretation of the results. We often observe that conclusions are drawn which are erroneously generalized. We have already mentioned the mysterious way which brings Blanc (1960) to his division into five language levels (cf. supra 4.1.).[9] Incorrect generalizations were also found in Talmoudi's (1984) and Abu-Melhim's (1991) investigations.

The investigation by Talmoudi, for instance, discusses 'The diglossic situation in North-Africa'. Talmoudi brought six (educated) North-Africans together and had them talk 'in an experimental way' about a few topics. "The informants were asked to speak as pure 'Arabic' as possible

[7] This has been more strongly expressed by van de Velde: "Die Norm der empirischen Adäquatheit wird in den Teiltheorien der klassischen TGG-Tradition nicht erreichbar" (van de Velde 1979: 17).

[8] "By using the Labovian method of getting informants to talk about personal issues or subjects they felt strongly about, it was possible to elicit long tracts of spontaneous speech" (Abu-Haidar 1992: 95).

[9] Blanc himself is conscious of the limitations of his investigation where he writes: "The reader may be shocked to discover that the recording was done with all the customary safeguards thrown to the winds: not only are all four of the speakers teachers of Arabic, not only are they well aware of the purpose for which their speech is being recorded, but a good half of their conversation centers upon the 'language of the educated'" (Blanc 1960: 86).

but they produced a semi-formal Maghrebine Arabic which may be characterized as a mixed variety of Arabic" (Talmoudi 1984: 15). Although the investigation aimed at investigating the diglossic situation in North-Africa, the discussions took place in Sweden (Gothenburg). But what is even more important is that the discussions were held by North-African immigrants. Three of those had already lived in Sweden for a longer period (16, 14, and 13 years), and the other three 6, 3 and 2 years. This way it is, of course, not amazing that Talmoudi writes: "Linguistic interference from Swedish on Arabic or traces of linguistic variation has been found in the recorded material." The question can be raised whether the researcher selected the appropriate testees to investigate the 'diglossic situation in North-Africa'.

A similar problem occurred in the investigation by Abu-Melhim. Here too we are confronted with the representativeness of the results of the investigation. Abu-Melhim (1991: 232) asked one Jordanian and one Egyptian couple to talk to each other. They were free to choose the subjects of the conversation themselves. The investigation demonstrated that there was code-switching from Arabic to English. Abu-Melhim, however, used for his investigation persons who had already lived in the US for many years (7).

These two examples show that it is necessary that the testees form a representative sample of the group of speakers whose linguistic habits are to be studied when we want to describe language reality by means of experimental investigations. In both previous investigations this was manifestly not the case. It is clear from Talmoudi's study that she conducted an experiment into the language habits of North-African migrant workers of different nationalities in Sweden. In my view these results can hardly be generalized to the North-African situation.

A second point that has to be kept in mind, when conducting an experimental investigation, is the problem of the bias which might be caused due to the artificial character[10] of these investigations. Certainly when, as in the case of the study by Talmoudi, indications are given to the testees about the language use which is expected from them. This of course produces a bias with regard to natural language use. But also the fact that the testees are aware that their language is being investigated can force them to make adaptations to their language use in one way or another. Tarrier, for example, referring to an investigation by Sallam (1980) writes: "Plus un locuteur se trouve en situation surveillée, plus

[10] Cf. criticism of Holes (1993: 13) on the investigation of Blanc.

ses occurrences classiques sont importantes, et inversement" (Tarrier 1993: 95).

A special kind of experimental investigation is the classroom interview in order to investigate language proficiency. Examples of such investigations are the investigation into reading proficiency by Kaye (1970), the investigation into writing proficiency by Parkinson (1990) and a similar investigation by Van Mol (1990). The results of such investigations have less to do with the observation of language use, and more to do with the testing of the efficiency of language education.

As a matter of fact, the main aim of such experimental linguistic investigations is to obtain data about correct language use. In order to limit the bias which can be caused by these investigations, some appeal to *participant observation* as a method of investigation.

7.3. Participant observation

As far as we know, the only researchers who have made use of participant observation for the investigation of MSA or an Arabic supra-regional koine, are Badawī (1973), Morsly (1990) (the only two native speakers), Kaye (1991), Parkinson (1991) and Wilmsen (1995). The method of participant observation stems from social and cultural anthropology. As it was very difficult to apply the classical survey techniques of sociology, which mainly consist of the direct interviewing of the subjects in non-western cultures, an attempt was made to obtain detailed data about cultures by means of direct participation in the social life.[11]

The big advantage of participant observation is that not only questions can be raised, but also that actual behavior can be observed. As such it was possible to define the discrepancy between the ideas people have of reality and reality itself. This manifests itself clearly in the investigation by Wilmsen (1995) (cf. infra 7.1.). The above-mentioned investigations have one feature in common: no use was made of recorders to make the observations.

This method too has some serious limitations. A first problem is that only a very limited number of elements of the language can be investigated. Kaye (1991), for instance, pays attention, during a conference, to the assimilation of the *alif*. Parkinson (1994: 211) tried to make an inventory of the use of the *'iʿrāb* in a conversation. He observed that his

[11] For a deeper analysis of this method in social and cultural antrophology see: Van Mol (1976).

interlocutor always used the nominative case and no other case endings, which is very difficult to imagine, because there are many fixed forms with the accusative.

As a matter of fact, many questions can be raised on whether the method of participant observation is really adequate and appropriate for linguistic investigations. A first negative indication is speed. Discussions are mostly held at a very high speed (cf. infra 9.2.1.). This demands of the researcher such a high level of concentration that it is extremely difficult not to miss vital elements. In the second place it is very difficult for a researcher not to be distracted by the contents of the discussions he observes or by the topic of investigation itself. When the researcher thinks for one moment of an observation he made, the rest of the sentence or paragraph will be gone. Moreover, the question can be raised whether a non-native speaker is capable of making reliable observations in this way without a recorder. An additional problem is that such observations are very limited and also biased because of the interests of the researcher. In this respect Billiet (1995: 152) uses the term '*over involvement*' of the researcher. Moreover, the researcher must be capable of taking notes. The quality of these investigations depends largely on the quality of the different recordings in the field (cf. Billiet 1995: 302 et seq.).

The most important criticism of the method of participant observation, however, is that this kind of observations is not highly systematized. Often, researchers have a certain impression which does not correspond with reality.[12] Neither is it always possible to concretize these impressions.[13] Wilmsen (1995: 62), for instance, writes that the particle *fa* is frequently used by his testees. "It appears frequently in educated speech, which itself tends to point toward a literary origin". However, it

[12] Personally, I had a similar experience with an investigation into psycho-somatic complaints of Moroccan migrant workers in hospitals. When a researcher investigated the rate of psycho-somatic complaints of Moroccan immigrants, I had the impression that these were at least 60 % of all the complaints. Systematic analysis, however, showed that only 10 % of the complaints had a psycho-somatic character. The big interest of the researcher in psycho-somatic complaints biased his view, which gave him a biased impression of reality.

[13] As far as linguistic research is concerned, it is very important to distinguish between *impressions*, which can be biased, and demonstrable facts. When reading literature, it strikes that some researchers do not separate these two ways of approach in a sufficient way. Forkel (1980: 42), for instance, claims that he has the impression that MSA is more spoken nowadays than it used to be. But Tapiéro (1972: 10) simply claims that Arabs speak MSA among each other. The interesting point about impressions is that they ask, one way or another, for a confirmation. Blau (1982: 104), for instance, writes that he has the impression that the particle *bi* is not more frequently used in MSA than in Classical Arabic. Such statements demand a confirmation by means of empirical investigations.

is not clear at all whether these occurrences were just a coincidental interference or whether they were a real indication of a certain evolution in language use on the level that was investigated by Wilmsen. Moreover, like many other similar concepts the concept *frequently* is too vague for use in empirical investigations. For some an occurrence is frequent with a proportion of one to hundred, whereas others will consider an occurrence frequent with a proportion of one to ten.[14] Many researchers take the view that there is a strong need for statistical analysis of linguistic phenomena. Or as Ulvestad (1979: 103) puts it: "In other words the statistical aspect should not be disregarded."

7.4. Importance of statistics

McLoughlin considers statistics to be the decisive element of linguistic investigations. "Statistical studies are essential to the proper study of usage in such matters" (McLoughlin 1972: 61). Also Kaye (1970: 379), Bobzin (1980: 37), Blau (1981: 141) and Mitchell (1980) point at the importance of statistics in confirming impressions. Mitchell, for instance, writes about his impressions on word order in Arabic: "Before the present hypothesis can be regarded as conclusively proven, at least as far as spoken Arabic is concerned, it should be subjected to rigorous statistical analysis. It could well turn out to be the case that the choice of VS (Verb-Subject) versus SV order is optional at least in some regions with no difference of marking involved" (Mitchell 1980: 100).

The main question, in this respect, is how to measure linguistic reality in a statistical way. "Kaye's suggestion that 'frequency should be our guide in all matters' pertaining to the question of determining what is Cairene and what is not is not very helpful because it says nothing of how to measure 'frequency'" (El-Hassan 1977: 117). In order to make a statistical analysis of the spoken language, the compilation of a representative corpus seems to be an imperative condition.[15] Such a method can be used in corpus linguistics.

[14] We notice here that the example which has been quoted by Wilmsen (1995: 109) comes from an actor who is imitating a news reader (who, of course, is reading an MSA sentence).

[15] See further for the importance of statistics and certain statistical methods in linguistic analyzes: Rieger (1979), Jolivet (1986: 509), Lenoble (1986), Najock (1986) and Briscoe (1994: 101), but especially too Ulvestad (1979: 103) and Bungarten (1979: 43), and for an application to the Arabic alphabet: Mrayati (1990). Hug, correctly, argues that the value of statistics should not be made absolute: "Dans ce qui précède, on peut voir que les observations statistiques ne jouent jamais le rôle d'une preuve, mais celui de l'indice favorable ou défavorable à un type d'explication systématique" (Hug 1986: 490).

7.5. Corpus linguistics

Corpus linguistics is a branch of linguistics in which the relevance of hypotheses about language use are tested on representative corpora.[16] Francis (1979: 110) defines a corpus as: "A collection of texts assumed to be representative of a given language, dialect, or other subset of a language, to be used for linguistic analysis. This takes account of the fact that a corpus may be purposely skewed — toward legal or scientific language, for example — and that it may be used for phonological, graphemic, lexical, or semantic, as well as grammatical analysis."[17]

The central element of corpus investigation is the description and explanation of language use by means of systematic observation (Bausch 1979: 79). The aim is to make statements about the grammar of a language based on current language use.[18] "La valeur d'une analyse grammaticale réside dans la possibilité qu'elle se donne de *décrire* adéquatement les faits de langue et d'en donner une *explication* simple" (Ayoub & Bohas 1981: 267). Both Fehri (1981) and Suleiman (1989: 233) point at the necessity of basing linguistic investigations on empirical facts by means of analysis of texts.[19]

According to Bausch (1979: 78) there are four basic questions related to corpus investigations, viz.: "1. Die Frage des Mindestgrösze, damit verbunden 2. die Frage nach dessen soziokulturellen und kontextuellem

[16] The use of corpora in Arabic linguistics is not new. According to Ditters the first Arab grammarians made use of corpora. "The ancient Arab linguists compiled large corpora for the purpose of studying the *'Arabīya*. (...) There is also frequent reference to language use (*kalām al-'Arab*) of certain Bedouins" (Ditters 1990: 129). Also in the first half of the 20th century elaborated corpora have been compiled, especially of different Arabic dialects. These were written both in transcription and with the Arabic alphabet. Corpora, such as those by Kampffmeyer (1909) Marçais (1911), Lévi-Provençal (1922), Brunot (1931) and Colin (1951), to mention only some of them, are of immense value for the investigation into the influence of MSA on the use of the dialect.

[17] See also Bungarten (1979: 34).

[18] Or, as Ditters (1988: 34) summarizes it: "Here are the keywords: actual occurrence of linguistic phenomena in a certain corpus, their frequency, grammaticality, acceptability, MSA of a certain period, and, I suppose, in a regional version."

[19] Fehri, for instance, is conscious that new corpora have to be compiled in order to describe the new Arabic linguistic situation on an empirical basis. He adds: "La construction d'une théorie (ou d'une grammaire) de la langue est une combinaison d'hypothèses et de moyens descripifs de laquelle on peut déduire des propositions empiriques spécifiques à propos des phénomènes observables" (Fehri 1981: 303). However, especially for oral language use, corpora are scarce. Berens (1979: 268), for instance, observes: "Viele Wissenschaftler jedoch, die sich mit Problemen der gesprochenen Sprache beschäftigen wollen, stehen vor der Schwierigkeit, dass es vergleichsweise wenig und/oder für ihre Zwecke ungeeignete Materialsammlungen gibt."

Bezugsrahmen, mit denen wiederum 3. die Frage nach dessen Repräsentativität für die Sprachverwendung zusammenhängt, und 4; die Frage nach der technischen Aufbereitung für die Auswertung."

The question of the representativeness of the corpus is one of the most important ones. In order to generalize the results of corpus investigation, the sample must be representative. This means that it has to represent the characteristics of the whole that is to be described. In this respect, the problem is not in the first place the magnitude of the population but its heterogeneity, which makes it difficult to define (Martin 1988: 92).[20]

It is almost impossible to compile a corpus which represents the whole linguistic reality.[21] Bungarten, therefore distinguishes between a representative and an exemplary corpus. "Ein Korpus ist repräsentativ, wenn es in spezifischen, zu definierenden statistisch-stochastischen, formalen, semantischen und pragmatischen Konstanten mit bestimmten Varietätentoleranzen des repräsentierten Sprachbereichs übereinstimmt. Ein Korpus ist exemplarisch, wenn seine Repräsentativität nicht nachgewiesen ist, andererseits weniger formale Argumente, wie evidenter Zusammenhang, linguistische Urteile des kompetenten Forschers, fachlicher Konsensus, textuelle und pragmatische Indikatoren, für eine sinnvolle Vertreterfunktion des Korpus plädieren" (Bungarten 1979: 42).[22]

The investigation of corpora bears some advantages compared to other methods of investigation. According to Bungarten, one of the important advantages is the fact that the results of investigation which have been obtained by analyzing a corpus can by verified by other researchers. "Das Korpus bietet empirische, objective und intersubjektiv überprüfbare Datenbasis, die prinzipiell jedem Forscher zu jeder Zeit als statische, d.h. konstante und konservierte Datenmenge zur Verfügung steht und operationalisierenden Verfahren — wie etwa technische Manipulationen in der nichtnumerischen Datenverarbeitung — zugänglich ist." (Bungarten 1979: 36)[23].

Moreover, it is possible to demonstrate the evolution of language in certain areas. Ulvestad (1979: 102) also points at the possibilities of cor-

[20] Martin (1988) gives a very clear description of the heterogeneity of Dutch, and the problems that this heterogeneity causes by the compilation of a representative corpus. See also Lyne (1986: 588).

[21] See also Rieger (1979: 59 et seq.).

[22] Bathurst (1971: 187) makes the same distinction: "There were two alternatives for deciding how to select passages of text for sampling: by random selection or arbitrary stratified selection."

[23] For a thorough discussion see the entire article (Bungarten 1979).

pus analysis in determining the percentage of scarcely used constructions.[24] Another advantage is that corpora often contain constructions which raise questions that can later on be investigated by means of other methods of research.

A disadvantage of corpus investigation, however, is that a corpus always is a snapshot. Since language evolves, new corpora always will have to be compiled. On the other hand, older corpora can be an interesting point of reference for comparative investigations. Another disadvantage is that some scarce grammatical phenomena may be difficult to trace in a corpus. As a matter of fact, the most interesting aspect of corpus investigations is the possibility of verifying empirically whether grammatical rules are indeed applied in current language use. And there is a great need to do so for Arabic.[25]

Often, indeed, grammatical work remains the work of *muqallidūn* or copyists. Rules, such as they have been described and determined by Arab or western grammarians, are often considered to be axioms, which were copied by later grammarians. Two examples of investigations which analyze grammatical regularities based on corpora and which led to new insights are the earlier mentioned investigation of Belnap's (1992) (cf. supra 2.3.3.) and an investigation into the literature by Parkinson (1975) on the substantive *ba'ḍ*.[26] Both researchers demonstrate that the rules,

[24] Also and especially for MSA such an investigation is of great importance. Stetkevych (1970: 28), for instance, writes: "Thus we observe that the modern Arabic lexicon sometimes suffers (...) from a superabundance of synonymous terms." He quotes 11 words for the substantive 'break'. Through corpus investigation we can demonstrate to what extent these eleven synonyms are currently used and possibly also in different countries. The same can be stated about the use of plural forms. "An Arabic noun may have no plurals, one plural, two plurals, three plurals, or some larger number; the various plurals may have differences in meaning or no differences in meaning, they may have certain syntactic preferences or none, and so on" (Ferguson 1990: 47). Here too the question can be raised whether all the plural forms which are mentioned in the dictionaries are still used in MSA, and if so, to what extent. In practice there often seems to be a kind of natural selection in which some words or word forms fall completely out of use. (cf. infra 10.3.1).

[25] Cf., for instance, Frazier (1976: 2): "There is a need for rigorous testing of rules which have long been taken for granted in Arabic." On the basis of corpus analysis, Ulvestad, for instance, observes that the expression *all dem*, which does not occur in the '*intuition based statements*' of the Duden-Grammatik, reached a percentage of 22.8% in his corpus compared to other expressions.

[26] Both corpora are what Bungarten calls 'Belegsammlungen': "Zu unterschieden ist zwischen dem Korpus und der Belegsammlung. Die Belegsammlung orientiert sich in der Suche nach Datenmaterial an einem morphologisch, syntaktisch oder semantisch genau definierten, konkreten Sprachphänomen, für das in der Performanz Exempla gesucht werden" (Bungarten 1979: 35).

such as they have been described and fixed in traditional and modern grammars, not always match with current language use.[27]

This does not mean at all that corpus linguistics is the only responsible way of investigation. Ulvestad correctly points at the complementarity of the different methods of investigation for the compilation of grammars, but in his view analysis of corpora ought to come first. "One may safely conclude that for the time being the primacy sequence with respect to bases for synchronic syntactic description of a historical language like German runs as follows: 1. MO; 2. MU; 3. CO. [28] In my opinion, this procedural sequence should be reversed, in spite of the vast increase in time and labor entailed in my proposal" (Ulvestad 1979: 91); and further: "It is true that even a large corpus will rarely answer all the questions. It will, however, permit the researcher to ask crucial questions the answers to which may subsequently be obtained by means of informant testing" (Ulvestad 1979: 100).[29] Moreover, both Ulvestad (1979: 90) and Ditters (1990: 131) emphasize that the use of corpora is a conditio sine qua non for investigations into variation, because from that point of view the concepts of *frequency* and *probability* are essential.

Without the help of a computer statistical analysis becomes very difficult and time consuming. "Pour être infaillible et absolue, la méthode statistique devrait être basée sur un dépouillement humainement impos-

[27] Belnap, for instance, concludes that although his database is too limited to draw final conclusions, the observations of Reckendorf can not be generalized. "Reckendorf (1895: 8:89), the only orientalist to make detailed observations regarding the relative frequency of different types of agreement, claimed that nonhuman plurals, both broken and feminine sound forms, seldom take plural adjective agreement. This observation appears to be accurate for post-Quranic Arabic only; there are high percentages of feminine singular agreement in the corpus from the *Maqāmāt* on to the present" (Belnap 1992: 255). A similar discrepancy between language use and language descriptions (grammars) can be found in Parkinson (1975). Parkinson based himself on following citation of a grammar, viz.: "it is very common for verb or adjective agreement to be based on the gender and number of the term following *ba'd*", and he concludes: "Harmless as these statements seem (with their 'usually's and 'very common's') it will later be pointed out that my data does not support most of them". And further: "My data does not support the statements in the teaching grammars quoted earlier. MECAS, for example, states that the verb 'always' agrees with the logical subject when it comes after the quantifier phrase" (Parkinson 1975: 54 en 62). Parkinson observed in his corpus that such is only the case in 65%.

[28] Cf. for these concepts supra 7.1. note 1. The abbreviation CO refers to Corpus analysis.

[29] Bungarten (1979: 41) too holds the view that corpus investigations ought to be conducted first and that these investigations can be completed with other methods of investigation, such as interviewing techniques, participant observation, experimental investigations, etc. in order to test the results of corpus analysis.

sible" (Pellat 1971: i).[30] Meanwhile, the technological developments in the field of information technology have created many more possibilities which are being tested out by corpus linguistics. Nowadays corpus linguistics is inextricably bound up with computer linguistics. This form of corpus linguistics is named 'modern corpus linguistics'.

7.6. Function of modern corpus linguistics

The introduction of computers in linguistic sciences brought about a new interest in corpus investigations. "While historically the use of corpora can be traced back to the days before computers were invented, it was with the introduction of the computer into the field that descriptive linguistics became synonymous with computational corpus-based linguistics" (Oostdijk & de Haan 1994: 5). The first machine-readable corpora (e.g. the BROWN corpus 1963/4) go back to the beginning of the sixties. Initially these corpora were 'raw' which means that they were studied in their original form (Janssen 1990: 105).

Initially, the only aim of modern corpus linguistics was to create a database in order to examine the absolute and relative frequency of words. Corpora give the possibility to do extensive lexicographical investigations, such as, for instance, the investigation into collocations. Later on, one of the most important functions of corpora was to test hypotheses about language use. "It should be borne in mind that their function as a testbed for hypotheses about the language under description remains one of the more important uses of language corpora. In this way the analysis of authentic data contained in corpora contributes to the enhancement of existing comprehensive grammars of the language" (Oostdijk & de Haan 1994: 9).

The main aim is to investigate current language use and the variation in language use. "The description, understanding and subsequent generalized representation of language use in its actual communicative situation is the aim of modern corpus linguistics. It studies language varieties including phenomena as time, register, medium, style and genre" (Ditters 1990: 131). Modern corpus linguistics aims at compiling huge databases of linguistic material (Ditters 1992: 421). This way corpus linguistics belongs to the pragmatic branch of descriptive linguistics. "This branch is sometimes referred to as pragmatic descriptive linguistics be-

[30] Cf. Bathurst who writes in the same year "Unfortunately, Arabic is not amenable to being processed by a computer" (Bathurst 1971: 185).

cause it describes what it observes, sometimes as corpus linguistics because the linguistic research is based on the use of factual language material, contained in large corpora of language data" (Ditters 1991: 199).

Our first task was to compile a corpus. Of course, we had to take special care of the structure of the corpus. *The structure of the corpus in modern corpus linguistics confronted us with two main problems. The first main problem concerns the external structure of the corpus. Here questions are raised about the size of the corpus, the way of compilation, the compilation itself and the representativeness of the sample for the whole language layer or language universe which is to be investigated. The second main problem is connected with the internal structure of the corpus. Here questions have to be answered about the definition of words, the definition of the grammatical categories or parts of speech, the encoding or the tagging of the corpus, the transcription, etc. We will further pursue both problems in the next chapter.*

8. EXTERNAL STRUCTURE

8.1. Definition of the size of the corpus

There is no clear norm or indication about the minimal size of corpora. The famous corpus contemporary English, viz. the Lancaster-Oslo-Bergen (LOB) corpus, is a collection of one million words of British-English texts. Just like its American counterpart, the BROWN Corpus, it contains 500 samples of texts of about 2,000 words each divided over 15 kinds of texts (Johansson 1987: 1). Both corpora are collections of written language. There are much less corpora of the spoken language and they are much smaller than corpora of the written language, because of the huge amount of work that it takes to record texts and to transcribe them (Greenbaum 1994: 33).[1]

The existing Arabic corpora are very varied in kind, size and representativeness. The size of most existing corpora is very limited. There are not many data available about the spoken language. Corpora that have been based on language use in the spoken media are limited in size and often very heterogeneous: the corpus by Harrell (1960) contained one news broadcast from radio Cairo (ca. 1,200 words); the corpus by Forkel (1980: 75), which was compiled from "stark gekürzte Ausschnitte aus Sendungen des marokkanischen Rundfunks" (1977/78), contains ca. 2,500 words; the corpus by Diem (1974: 53), which contained 21 selections from 18 hours of recordings from different radio stations (viz. Cairo, Beirut and Damascus) contains ca. 5,000 words, divided in very heterogenous text types, which causes the language samples for each text and country to be very limited (e.g. only 550 words from news broadcasts).

The corpus by Meiseles (1975: 177-207) contains in total 25 texts (30 pages) from four radio stations (Cairo, Damascus, Amman and "the broadcasts of the Israeli broadcasting service in Jerusalem" (!)). Limited

[1] The Spoken English Corpus (SEC), for instance, contains 50,000 words (Taylor 1988: 237). More information on spoken and written English corpora is found in Leech (1992: 118-119). There were until recently no completely transcribed corpora of the Dutch language. There are two frequency lists based on a corpus of ca. 120,000 'words' (De Jong 1977 and Uit den Boogaart 1975). In 1998 there was started a new international project, viz. the Corpus Spoken Dutch, which aims at compiling an extensive corpus of spoken Dutch.

corpora of spoken language use are also the corpora of Blanc (1960), Palva (1969), Talmoudi (1984), Al-Shabbab (1986: 33), Tarrier (1993: 99) and the 'extensive corpus of data' by El-Hassan (1977: 112) which never seems to have been transcribed completely.

There are also a few smaller corpora, but those are no more than a kind of concise reader of Arabic radio transmissions. These are the books by Lecomte (1978: ca. 2,400 words), Lagarde (1981: ca. 3,000 words), Deville & Sekhar (1984: ca. 9,000 words) and Ashtiyani (1993: ca. 3,000 words). The main aim of these works is merely pedagogical. They aim at introducing students to the terminology, used in broadcasts. The texts of these books are no representative sample of MSA as it is used in the media.[2]

The size of the corpora of the written language are larger than the size of the corpora of the spoken language. Some of these corpora are on computer, but they were transcribed, not in Arabic, but in a transcription system. For instance, the corpus by Al-Jubouri (1988) which contains only newspaper excerpts (ca. 250,000 words), by Bathurst (1971) which contains also excerpts from Arabic literature and the corpus by Buckwalter (1994) which contains 1,000,000 words. There also are the corpora by Kouloughli (1991: 200,000 words) and the Nijmegen-corpus by Ditters (1992). The size of the Nijmegen-corpus is not precisely known. According to Aarts (1988: 1), it contains 500,000 words, but according to Ditters (1988: 36) it contains 300,000 words. It seems that for the dictionary project this corpus has been elaborated to millions of words. Through the ELRA agency new corpora have been made available in recent years. These corpora are the An-Nahar newspaper Text Corpus (1995-2000) and the Arabic Data Set. However, none of the above-mentioned corpora is encoded. That is why their value is rather limited (cf. infra 9.3.3.). The analysis of the Ditters corpus (1992: 42), for example, was in the end conducted on a sample of the corpus of only 2,500 words.

According to Francis (1979: 117), the compilation of a corpus of spoken material requires twenty times more effort than the compilation of a similar corpus of written language, because of the intensive work that is involved.[3] The size of the corpus is defined by the aim of the corpus. "Nicht nur die Konstituierung des Korpus in seinen Textsorten, auch sein Umfang ist abhängig vom intendierten Untersuchungsobject

[2] A new project to collect Standard and Colloquial varieties of Arabic is the Oriental project which aims at collecting Arabic speech resources for the IT market. For more details see Siemund (2002).

[3] He even adds: "Transcribing may take anywhere from ten to forty times as much time as written material, depending on the amount of phonetic detail to be preserved" (Francis 1979: 116).

und -ziel. (...) Für eine vergleichsweise seltene sprachliche Struktur ist ein viel grösseres Korpus erforderlich als etwa für statistisch häufige und leicht erfassbare Sachverhalte wie etwa Wort- und Satzeinheiten zur Ermittlung der durchschnittlichen Wort- und Satzlänge" (Bungarten 1979: 48).

If the researcher wants to limit his investigation into the study of the phonology, then a small corpus can suffice. Francis, for example, states: "Similarly, the phonological system, again with relatively few discrete units and fairly simple rules of combination, can be studied on the basis of a quite small sample. The Linguistic Survey of Scotland, for example, used a list of about 1,000 words, which could be pronounced and recorded in a few hours, to establish the phonemic repertories of its informants" (Francis 1979: 113). This way a sample was compiled of model-pronunciation (cf. infra 9.2.1.)

If the corpus has to be used for lexical investigations, then it will have to be considerably larger. "When the purpose of the corpus is lexical, all thought of complete coverage must be abandoned. (...) The lexicon on the other hand is virtually open-ended. No matter how far one extends the sample, one keeps encountering hitherto unrepresented words" (Francis 1979: 115). Farhat (1989: 7), for instance, holds the view that a corpus for lexicographical investigations ought to contain minimum 50 million words.[4]

When the researcher wants to limit himself to the study of grammar, then, according to Ditters, a corpus of 20,000 words may suffice. "This choice is motivated by our conviction that relatively small text samples of about 20,000 running words may be sufficient for an inventory of the basic syntactic sentence and constituent structures in MSA" (Ditters 1991: 205).

On the other hand, Parkinson (1975: 66) in his investigation into the use of the substantive *baʿḍ* found a corpus of ca. 84,000 words not large enough because the word *baʿḍ* did not occur frequently enough in the corpus. He proposes a corpus of ca. 1,000,000 words as ideal size. Quirk correctly observes that no corpus can ever contain all grammatical information. "But, of course, no corpus, however large, could be expected to

[4] Buckwalter finds a corpus of 4,000,000 words insufficient for lexicographic analysis. This has been confirmed by the investigation by Francis (1979: 116). However, we have compiled a learners dictionary Arabic — Dutch, Dutch — Arabic (Van Mol & Berghman: 2000a) based on an Arabic corpus of 3,000,000 words and this dictionary covers 99% of each randomly chosen Arabic text. (cf. also Van Mol 2000b). On the other hand it is not obvious to compile large corpora. The British National Corpus (BNC) aims at a database of 100,000,000 words, which provokes the necessary problems of encoding. According to the estimation by Leech (1994: 50) it would take 41 years to encode such a corpus even with the help of computers.

give information in the requisite degree of detail on all the grammatical structures of English" (Quirk 1984: 114).

In order to define the size of the corpus we postulate the principle of *saturation*. Geeraerts (1989) uses this concept in lexicography to indicate the point where in a certain language layer no new noticeable number of words is found. At that moment the lexicographical investigation reaches a point of saturation. We postulate this principle for the definition of the size of the corpus. We assume that once no new noticeable amount of words appear in a certain context, there will also no longer occur a significant number of new grammatical elements.

In fact, this principle corresponds to the law of diminishing returns. At a certain moment an extension of the corpus will not yield a significant amount of new data. Our investigation reveals that a corpus of news broadcasts yields only 0.3% new words after 200,000 words of text. In my view, this means that for this kind of text material the point of saturation has been reached. That is why we aim at a basic corpus size of ca. 240,000 words or a minimum of 80,000 words for each country.

8.2. Contents of the corpus

The main aim of the compilers of a corpus is the compilation of material of 'real-life example phrases' (Janssen 1990: 105). This means that the kind of language sample has to be defined as well as the way in which it will be collected. In principle, a corpus ought to contain all kinds of texts (cf. Blohm 1991: 90).[5] If, as is the case in our investigation, variation of the standard language within different geographical areas is to be investigated, then it is very important to choose the language samples in such a way that they are mutually comparable.

The discussion of the literature in part one made clear that (1) not only are the boundaries of MSA not very easy to define, but also (2) that the notion of 'educated speaker' is a concept which can stand for diverse contents, which makes it difficult to function as a parameter for comparative linguistic investigations. It is very important to choose language samples which are mutually comparable. It is, for instance, not appropriate to compare monologues from one country with dialogues from another country.

[5] The compilation of the corpus depends on the aim of investigation. It is even possible to exclude certain texts from a corpus. Bathurst (1971: 187) gives an example: "Newspaper Arabic was excluded because of the difficulty of satisfying the criterion of nationality of authorship which was one of the cardinal features of the sample. For the only effective way in which a sample of modern printed Arabic prose can be taken evenly over the entire Arab world is by considering the nationality of the author."

In order to make a sound comparison of the use of the standard language in different countries, we chose to make a comparison between monologues.[6] These monologues encompass the formal language which is used by journalists in the media to inform listeners on certain developments and ongoing facts in the world. Until now, no detailed investigation into Arabic monologues has been done. For example, as far as news broadcasts are concerned, these are always considered to be literary Arabic (cf. supra 4.4.).[7]

Some find the study of news broadcasts less valuable for the investigation of the spoken language. Tarrier, for instance, argues: "Le choix des discours étudiés est tout aussi décisif pour les résultats d'une enquête, celui-ci pouvant en effet aboutir à évacuer la possibilité même de variation. (...) Or, les communiqués d'informations sont préparés et rédigés à l'avance en arabe classique, ce qui a pour effet de fausser au départ l'analyse: le speaker ne fera que lire un texte, n'introduisant que çà et là au cours de sa lecture quelques réalisations phonétiques de son dialecte, et, donc son intervention ne sera pas vraiment représentative d'un arabe parlé" (Tarrier 1991: 11).[8]

However, we can not deny that news broadcasts by the way in which they are presented to the listeners form an essential part of spoken language. It can even exert a certain influence on spoken language. Although news readers on television simply read their texts before the camera they create the impression that they are good 'spontaneous' narrators. Moreover, news bulletins occupy a strategic position in language use and many people, also in the Arab world, listen to these news broadcasts every day. Meiseles correctly observes: "there is no doubt that the influence of the model of the radio/TV speakers' language is considerable indeed on the public in general" (Meiseles 1977: 176).

As Tarrier puts it, news bulletins are not representative of 'un arabe parlé'. This proposition is correct in so far as the fact that news bulletins generally do not contain spontaneous utterances in Arabic. However, news bulletins are an important element in language use. In this case

[6] This way the language sample is clearly defined. In terms of Meiseles (1980: 125) we study MSA read aloud but no OLA, although Meiseles (cf. supra 4.4.) reckons the news broadcasts to be OLA.

[7] However, Diem (1974: 63) points out that in Egypt, for example, the use of a language other than MSA is widespread and permitted in monologues.

[8] Parkinson reasons in a similar way: "It is simply wrong to limit our interest either to the news broadcasters or to the others. Standard Arabic represents a spectrum, a continuum of use, of styles, of functions, of pronunciations, and of forms. To understand and describe it we must look at all of it, in all its variability, across the whole spectrum of the society and people who use it" (Parkinson 1990: 293).

journalists make a short spoken report, which is probably prepared in writing, on the basis of spoken or written messages which they have obtained, for example, via satellite TV, or on the basis of situations they have experienced (cf. supra 1 note 1). As such, the study of this kind of language use seems to us relevant.[9] Besides, Mitchell observes that it can be very instructive to study the language of monologues, even if it were only to contrast it with other language use.[10]

In my view language use in news broadcasts has three interesting characteristics. A first and not unimportant feature is that there is great diversity in the language situation that serves as a basis for news reports. In the first place there is local news, in other words, events which take place in an Arabic language situation. This means that the report about the event is probably based on an Arabic language context. In the second place there is also international news. This news has to be translated from a foreign language into Arabic. There is also a very varied range of topics, going from political news, over local anecdotal news to, for instance, sports news.

The second characteristic is that the information has to be processed very quickly. In literature, the author has a long time to think of the grammatical acceptability of his sentences. He can take his time to choose his words carefully and to think and to carefully consider the style of his writings. This is not the case in news broadcasts. News reports have to be written quite quickly. This means that they give a more accurate image of how people daily treat MSA in a more or less spontaneous way.

A third important characteristic of news broadcasts is that many persons are involved, albeit that they all belong to one category, viz. the journalists.

News broadcasts are, as a matter of fact, a reflection of current language use of the standard language in a certain area and in a certain manner. Moreover, in the investigation into 'spoken language', we are still confronted with the methodological problem of how to define the language sample. When we want to examine variation in standard lan-

[9] In passing we would like to remark that 30.6% of the German Freiburger Korpus gesprochener deutscher Standardsprache (Berens 1979: 271) was made up of monologues from news broadcasts and that Quirk (1979: 207) too, made use of 'broadcast news' for the compilation of his corpus Spoken English.

[10] "But it is often instructive to consider the language of monologue, of speech making, for instance and other 'stilted' types of performance in order to help to define, if negatively, the type of Arabic that really interests us" (in this case ESA) (Mitchell 1986: 22).

guage use a main condition remains that the examined material has to be comparable.

News broadcasts seem to us the most appropriate material, because different language users are using MSA in identical circumstances. In order to keep the comparability as great as possible, the corpus has been limited to news broadcasts. However, there is a certain variety also within news broadcasts. Indeed, news broadcasts contain different kinds of news, such as sports news, local news and international news. In some news broadcasts there are also reports by journalists in the country and abroad. There also are commentaries on the news. This makes it necessary to identify a certain stratification within the news broadcasts itself.

8.3. Definition of the places of investigation

About the investigation of variation in the Dutch standard language Voortman writes: "It is very important to choose the places of investigation in such a way, that they lie in areas which are very remote from dialectological point of view. This makes the chance for regional variation the largest" (Voortman 1992: 24). Also for the investigation into the use of standard Arabic, the geographical delimitation is not unimportant. This also has been emphasized by Tarrier who writes: "Quant au paramètre géographique, il concerne le fait qu'un discours sera différent selon que le locuteur sera syrien, égyptien ou marocain. De ce dernier paramètre découle la nécessité, avant tout, d'établir une enquête pour chaque pays" (Tarrier 1993: 94).

In principle, fifteen Arab countries are eligible for our investigation. It is, however, very important to choose these countries in such a way that they manifest the greatest possible difference on a linguistic level, not only now, but also in the past. For this reason we have chosen the following three countries: Algeria, Egypt and Saudi Arabia. No doubt no Arab country has been so thoroughly influenced by a European language as Algeria. Arabic was almost completely ousted by French during the period of colonization, not only as the language of formal education but also in every day use. Or as Holt puts it: "Algeria suffered a more intense and prolonged attack on its language and culture than any other Arab country. One hundred and thirty years of language and educational policy determined by an outside power have evidently left deep scars" (Holt 1994: 25).

Consequently many parts of the population nowadays use a mixed language, in which French and Arabic elements constantly alternate (cf. Bouchérit 1987). This is also a striking element in the interviews in the news broadcasts. To express themselves, Algerians constantly use French words in Arabic sentences (cf. Benjelloun 1990: 355). Both Nofal (1980: 6) and Mahmoud (1982: 82) hold the view that French is still the de facto second language of Algeria. As a matter of fact, French still occupies an important place in formal education. "The teaching of French begins, as a matter of fact, as early as the 4th primary school year and continues till the end of secondary school" (Morsly 1986: 259). In no other Arab country does a foreign language occupy such an important place. Besides, a large part of the population in Algeria speaks at home not dialectal Arabic but a Berber language.[11] According to Schippers & Versteegh (1987: 52) 35% of the population has Berber as its mother tongue, according to Bateson (1967) only 20%.

On the other hand, it is clear that Egypt has always played a leading role both in the field of the Arabic language and in formal education. This was maybe also due to the prestige and the influence of the scholars of *Al-'Azhar*. Moreover, it is one of the first Arab countries where the press found its way (cf. supra 2.3.1.). Nevertheless, also in its early history, Egypt has undergone strong influences from foreign languages, such as, for instance, Turkish. Schall (1982: 152) observes: "Die Sprache der mamlukischen Geschichtsschreiber wimmelt von türkischen Lehnwörtern". According to Schall those are loan-words which have since disappeared from the Arabic lexicon.

Finally, we chose Saudi Arabia as the third country because of the isolated character of this country. Because of the severe religious doctrine of the Wahhabites, Saudi Arabia was more isolated from the rest of the world than most other Arab countries. The fact that part of this country is one of the most desolate regions of the world has underlined the isolation of Saudi Arabia (cf. Roman 1987: 132). Nature made Saudi Arabia difficult of access for western powers. As a matter of fact, Saudi Arabia has never known a colonial occupation and even the sovereignty of King Saud over Saudi Arabia was recognized in the treaty of Jidda (1927) (cf. Tapiéro 1976: 270).

[11] The first conquests of Northern Africa by the Arabs date from the seventh century. The original languages of the North Africans are the various Berber dialects. Contrary to, for instance, Egypt, Arabic has not ousted the original Berber languages in Algeria (cf. Talmoudi 1984: 21). Except of Siwa Oasis, etc., Arabic did not oust Berber in Egypt but Coptic.

Moreover, everyone who has worked in Saudi Arabia knows how difficult it is to estabnlish contacts with the local population. Most (western) foreigners live in camps, from which they perform short-term projects. Saudi Arabia is also important from a religious point of view. The two holy places Mecca and Medina lie in its territory. This not only means that every year millions of Muslims go to Saudi Arabia on pilgrimage, but also that, especially in earlier days, many of them stay behind to bury themselves in the study of religious sciences, which may also have had its influence on language use.[12] Yet, until recently, Saudi Arabia knew the highest percentage (95%) of illiterates in the Arab world (Bateson 1967: 83).

For the investigation we depart from a corpus which has been compiled on the basis of radio broadcasts of these three countries, which, in our view, are representative of the different regions in the Arabic area and which experienced distinctive linguistic development in the field: Egypt which is known in the whole of the Arab world for its leading role in Arabic literature, Algeria which more than any other Arab country has undergone western, or more precisely French influence, and finally Saudi Arabia, which is the cradle of the Arabic language, and which more than any other Arab country has remained closed and isolated from western influences. We might even say that the Arabic language in Saudi Arabia has preserved its sacral character.

8.4. Composition

A language sample can be composed by random sampling or by spread sampling (Bungarten 1979: 171). In order to obtain the best quality of recordings we chose to make the recordings in the countries themselves. For the compilation of the samples we depended on the possibilities and time of the cooperators in these countries to record news broadcasts. As a matter of fact, the recordings had to be made by Arabists, otherwise the recorder might not be able to 'recognize' news broadcasts.[13] I asked

[12] Forkel (1987: 291) observes that many learned pilgrims from the Maghreb also visited other cities in the East and probably were influenced in their language use: "Der Mašriq übte aber immer, selbst während der Kolonialzeit, einen gewissen Einfluss auf den Maghreb aus. Dabei spielte die Pilgerfahrt nach Mekka keine geringe Rolle. Mit dem Ḥajj verbanden maghrebinische Gelehrte häufig einen Besuch in Kairo und mit einem kleinen Umweg in Damaskus oder Bagdad."

[13] Four excellent Arabists did this job, for which we are very grateful to them. Recordings were made in Saudi Arabia by Mark Mouton, in Algeria by the late father Karel Deckers and in Egypt by Jos Smets and professor Emilio Platti.

the cooperators to make random recordings of news bulletins at short intervals. This way these recordings form a random sample. When I transcribed the radio broadcasts I did not take the quality of the recordings into account. Difficult to understand or bad recordings were not excluded.

All the recordings were transcribed in the order in which they had been recorded. Of course, poor quality recordings provoked more difficulties in the transcription (cf. infra 9.2.). In order not to bias the representativeness, however, all recordings were used. All broadcasts were recorded in the period 1990-1992.

8.5. Corpus organization

In order to make the corpus appropriate for computer analysis, we had to structure it in a way which was recognizable by computer. It was clear from the transcription of the news broadcasts that they were not structured in the same way in the three different countries. In Egypt, for example, the news broadcasts are clearly divided in different sections. First the news bulletin, than usually a news commentary and finally reports with interviews. Furthermore, local news is reserved for a special news broadcast. Sport news also occurs in a special news broadcast at another time.

In Algeria, on the other hand, these different kinds of news sections are mixed in one news broadcast. It is the only country where interviews were mixed in the news itself. (Most of the recordings date from the period of democratization and political renewal, just before the coup of 1991). The news broadcasts also contain reports and commentaries. Moreover, every news broadcast in Algeria also contains a number of reports in which a certain topic is enlarged upon. Every news broadcast in Algeria is concluded with sports news.

In Saudi Arabia there do not occur interviews or reports in the news broadcasts at all. Also sport news is consigned to a special program, just like the news commentaries. The news broadcasts reflect the openness and the political climate of these three countries. For methodological reasons we have divided the news broadcasts into different parts so as to be better able to compare the different parts with each other. When, for instance, an Egyptian gives a report from Moscow by satellite on the situation over there, then this report was separately catalogued. Likewise when an Algerian gave a radio report by telephone from Amman about a certain event then this report was cut from the news broadcast and catalogued under reports.

As a result we have obtained four kinds of texts. The first type are the news broadcasts (from which, if necessary, some parts were left out). The second type are the reports, the third the news commentaries and the fourth sports news. For the different countries we used a three-letter code, viz. ALG, EGY and SAU. This three letter-code was followed by the kind of broadcast, viz. N = news broadcast, R = report, C = news commentary and S = sport news. This information is followed by the number of the cassette and the side and the number of the counter where the recordings of the language samples begin. A language sample could, for example, have following encoding: ALG/S 104a-236. In this case this is sport news from Algeria on cassette 104a, counter 236. This way we obtained a file cataloguing the different kinds of texts. We wanted to keep the name of the files as short as possible. Additional information, such as the date of the recordings, was saved in another file.

The diversity of the news broadcasts meant that we had to transcribe more news broadcasts from Algeria than from, for example, Saudi Arabia. Since the news broadcasts of Saudi Arabia contain no interviews or reports, the target number of 80,000 words was reached much more quickly. The corpus of the news broadcasts alone counts ca. 240,000 words. The news broadcasts together form the main corpus. When we add the other kinds of news broadcasts we attain a corpus of 320,000 words.[13] The other kinds of news broadcasts together form the control corpus, which contains 80,000 words. At this moment the corpus contains 172 news broadcasts (ALG: 53, EGY: 70 and SAU: 49); 94 reports (ALG: 51 and EGY: 43); 49 news commentaries (ALG: 1, EGY: 47 and SAU: 1) and 26 sports news broadcasts (ALG: 22 and SAU: 4).

[14] For a detailed description of what is meant by 'word' see infra (9.3.2.). For the exact number of words in the corpus per kind of texts see infra (10.2.4.)

9. INTERNAL STRUCTURE

As far as the internal structure of the corpus is concerned, different questions emerge. In the first place, we have to decide which kind of corpus we want to compose. Next there is the problem of the transcription. Do I opt for a phonemic or for an orthographic transcription? Another problem is the adaptation of the text by means of encoding in order to make it amenable by computer. Also we have to decide at which level we will work. Do we work at word level or under or above word level (Paulussen 1992: 3). Furthermore, before compiling a corpus for investigations into variation, we have to define which level of investigation we intend to focus on.

Indeed, the investigation can be conducted on a lexical, syntactic, phonological, semantic level, etc. This means that it is very important to structure the corpus as open as possible in order to be able to treat as many levels as possible. And last but not least, we also have to choose which grammatical structure will be the point of reference for the tagging.

9.1. Types of corpora

Internal structure deals with the organization of the text. We can distinguish between three different kinds of corpora. The first kind is the *raw corpus*. Such a corpus consists of a normal text file without any annotation. A specific problem related to the Arabic language is that in Arabic a distinction can be made even between a *raw vocalized corpus* and a *raw unvocalized corpus*. In this respect Ditters mentions "the problem of deficient data representation".

"It only means that an author of a written communication drops all sub- and superimposed short vowel signs and non-consonantal diacritical marks while drafting a consonantal skeleton in the characteristic cursive Arabic script, assuming that a well-trained reader can do without these marks for a (good) general understanding of his message. It also means that 99.9% of all MSA text data is only available in a kind of shorthand form" (Ditters 1992: 417)[1]. As we will see later, the use of a

[1] A raw corpus can be partially vocalized which makes the recognition by computer even more complex. This means that English corpora are more easily amenable by com-

consonantal script imposes specific problems. When a corpus of spoken language is involved, the choice can be made between a *phonemic* and an *orthographic* transcription.

A second kind of corpus is the *tagged corpus*. In order to study the linguistic material more profoundly and in a more efficient way, corpora can be made accessible for computer software. In order to fully use the possibilities of the computer it is necessary to make explicit the linguistic nature of the texts and also to store it in the computer. Thus, codes can be used with respect to morphological, syntactical or semantic characteristics of words or to the characteristics of constituents or sentences (Huber 1988: 61). The implementation of such codes in a text is called *encoding* or *tagging*.

The third kind of corpus is a *parsed corpus*. Souter writes about these: "Parsed corpora are collections of spoken or written natural language text which have been annotated with full syntactic trees according to some particular grammatical description. This definition is intended to distinguish parsed corpora from plain or raw corpora, which have received no annotation, and from tagged corpora, which contain labels for the grammatical categories of each lexical item, but not for non-terminal grammatical categories such as phrases and clauses. Parsed corpora are often referred to as analyzed corpora, treebanks, or syntactic databases" (Souter 1994: 143).[2]

A parsed corpus is in this sense more valuable "since they enable the linguist to search for specific linguistic structures instead of mere sequences of words or labels" (Janssen 1990: 105). It goes without saying that there are many more raw corpora than tagged or parsed corpora. For our investigation we chose to compose a tagged corpus.

9.2. Transcription problems

The composition of a corpus of 'spoken' language involves a few very specific problems which are related to the transcription. In the first

puter than Arabic corpora. The word *school*, for instance, (substantive) exists in English only in this form. In Arabic the word *madrasa* (school) can be written completely vocalized such as: *madrasatun*, unvocalized such as *mdrst*, but also partially vocalized such as *madrst* or *madrast* etc. This poses a problem when we want to treat available electronic corpora (cf. Oostdijk & de Haan 1994: 8). As a matter of fact, in that case only a *raw corpus* is available. Because words have to be recognized by computer, it is very important always to use the same system of vocalization.

[2] Out of an enumeration given by Souter (1994: 143-144) of existing English 'parsed' corpora, it appears that such corpora comprise an average of 130,000 words. Because of the intensive labor involved in the tagging of such corpora they are of limited size. For the parsing of Arabic corpora see Ouersighni (2001).

place, a choice can be made between a *phonemic* or an *orthographic* transcription.[3] When an orthographic transcription is preferred a few orthographic problems which are specific for Arabic need to be solved. For example, general rules have to be deducted about the spelling of the proper names and for the use of punctuation. When composing a corpus of 'spoken' language, the transcriber will encounter 'slips of the tongue'. And of course a risk of misinterpretations by the transcriber remains, especially under the influence of the speed of the spoken text.

9.2.1. *Choice of transcription*

The advantage of a phonemic transcription is that the researcher can make a more thorough phonological investigation. On the other hand, a phonological transcription also imposes serious restrictions on modern corpus linguistics. A short example will make this clear. It is generally known that some consonants in the Dutch language area can be realized in different ways. In Holland, for instance, the *elided* /r/ is used, as in London English. People say, for instance, *ha'd* in stead of *hard*. Moreover, a part of the population in Flanders realizes the /r/ as a French throat /r/.[4]

This means that a phonetic transcription gives great problems for the automatic recognition of words by computer. Indeed, without taking into consideration the variation possibilities of the vowels a word, such as 'redeneren' could be written in three different ways. The same problem occurs in Arabic. It is, for instance, generally known that the pronunciation of the consonant *jīm* differs in different Arabic countries. Even if we were to give a phonetic transcription for the consonant *jīm* alone, this would mean that the comparatibility by computer would become very complex. Kaye (1987: 668-669) also points out that in MSA, under the influence of other letters, among others, the consonant /b/ is often pronounced as /p/ and the /f/ as /v/. The variation in the vowels is even much higher.[5]

[3] By phonetic transcription, we mean a transcription which gives a true reproduction of all the sounds such as they exist in all their variations.

[4] See for other examples Deprez (1985: 216).

[5] Cf. Kaye (1970: 381): "A vowel phoneme may have a tremendous range of phonetic realizations". Moreover Blanc (1960: 88) points out that the phonological variegations of 'spoken Arabic', both dialectical and interdialectical, are insufficiently studied. In corpus linguistics, it is impossible to take into account all the possible phonological variegations that may occur. Phonological investigation requires another approach. Moreover, when phonology has to be investigated also rhythm, intonation and stress have to be dealt with (cf. Willemyns 1987: 151).

Furthermore, it is not always possible to observe the phonemes in the spoken language very clearly and to register them. While recording the phonemic variation of a language, often very clearly registered material is used, in which native speakers talk in a very slow way, articulating very clearly, even pronouncing word after word (cf. supra 8.1.). In the language of the media, however, people speak so fast, that sometimes even complete words can not be recognized, let alone the phonemes.[6] The question is then to what extent the speed exerts an influence on the distortion of sounds. When listening to the tapes, for instance, it is not always possible to find out whether a native speaker realizes the *ṯā* as *tā* or as *ṭā*.[7]

Until now, all authors assume that Arabs are heavily influenced by the phonology of their dialect when reading.[8] Meiseles, for instance, states that MSA read aloud only exists in regional versions. "They occur only in regional performances which are the product of local or regional traditions of reading habits, and as a rule, reflect the local dialectal substratum" (Meiseles 1980: 125).

As a matter of fact, it is certain that speed exerts an influence on the realization of certain vowels. This means that recordings of MSA read aloud quickly can give a decisive answer about which vowels belong to the standard language and which vowels don't. It is not easy to answer such a question, but that does not mean that this question is less important.[9] Finally, we notice here too that even with the same individuals dif-

[6] Kelly (1991: 139) points out that it has been known for years that there is an enormous difference between the pronunciation of isolated words and of words in context. The number of investigations into the speed of the language seems to be rather limited. There is a limited investigation by Vaane (1982) based on syllables. Only Palva (1969: 11; 18) reveals some numbers. He mentions a speed between 110 to 135 words per minute. According to Gran (1990: 64), who conducted an investigation into language speed of interpreters, language speed varied between 106 words per minute to 156 words depending on the language. The counts of our corpus (based on a limited sample) vary depending on the country. The news readers in Saudi-Arabia have the most tranquil tempo: ca. 135 words per minute. In Egypt the speed is more accelerated with an average of 155 words per minute. In Algeria, the average speed is 185 words per minute.

[7] *Badawī* (1973) too observes that the difference often is hardly audible, even for the radio audience. The same applies, for instance, to the pronunciation of the journalists on the Dutch radio. Only a trained ear will hear the difference in the realization of the /a/.

[8] This proposition can be found in Harrell (1960: 14 et seq.), Monteil (1960: 55), Bateson (1967: 86), Diem (1974: 27), Meiseles (1980: 125), Ibrahim (1983: 511), Abdulaziz (1986: 20), Forkel (1987: 289), Morsly (1990: 173), Parkinson (1990: 289) and Wilmsen (1995: 2).

[9] As far as we know, the only one who pays attention to the deformations which may occur in rapid speech, and the necessity to investigate these, is Mitchell, who writes: "The facts of pronunciation in rapid vernacular (...) have in fact never been investigated and would repay close study" (Mitchell 1980: 105).

ferences can be registered in the pronunciation. Kaye (cited in Bentahila 1990: 78) observed this for Arabic, but investigations have proved that this is also the case for other languages.[10] Consequently, this means that a phonetic transcription requires another approach.[11]

An orthographic transcription, on the other hand, has the advantage that every word is written in the same way, even when it is pronounced differently. Whatever way the word 'redeneren', for instance, is pronounced, there only is one transcription. This way the encoding becomes easier. A disadvantage, on the other hand, is that when the word 'redeneren' is pronounced in a dialectical way within a context of a standard language, this variegation does not remain visible. Also hybrid forms become less visible, unless morphological or syntactical hybrid forms are involved.

This is not without importance because in a news coverage, a standard word, for instance, a verb of the second form, can be pronounced in a dialectal way. This means that in the transcribed text the word *ysjjl* could have been pronounced in a standard way as *yusajjil* or in a dialectal way as *isejjel*. For this reason we provided an extra code for dialectical interference, which made us mark in the text when a certain word was realized in a dialectical way.[12] In most cases it involves morphological forms. So we decided to copy out the material of the news broadcasts in orthographic form.[13]

[10] Cf. the investigation of Jolivet (1986: 515) who remarks: "Il y a des prononciations différentes du même informateur d'un texte à l'autre". In this respect he distinguishes between a tight and a loose structure of the language. See also the reference by El-Hassan (1977: 118) to English and Kelly (1991: 137) who argues: "Every individual has his own mode of pronunciation, as the spectrograph has clearly demonstrated". See also for Dutch as standard language Geerts who states that we do not exactly know yet why one variety in pronunciation is accepted and why another variety is not. "In the field of pronunciation Dutch has many varieties which are acceptable while others, for unknown reasons, are not" (Geerts 1987: 167).

[11] Cf. also Francis who states: "Spoken material which is to be used for lexical or grammatical purposes need not be given full phonetic or even phonemic transcription, but can be transcribed in standard orthography" (Francis 1979: 120).

[12] As an illustration we give some examples of the phonological variation which is given by Abu-Absi (1990: 39). He observed that the number *eight* was realized in different ways, viz. as *ṯamāniyah*, also *ṯamānyah* and *ṯmānyah*, and that the particle of negation *lā* also was realized as *la*. In Egypt, children even say *la'a* for emphasis. *la'a* is the normal form for 'no' in Lebanon and Syria. After all, *eight* is pronounced as *tmenya* in some dialects. In my view, there is no question of dialectal interference in the three above-mentioned examples. Only in the case of *tmenya* did we mark the word with a dialectal code which indicates that the pronunciation was realized in a dialectical way. The marking of dialectical interference is the sign #.

[13] Indeed, the same happened with the Freiburger Corpus and the Survey of Spoken English. The compilers of these corpora selected in advance those 'spoken' texts that ap-

9.2.2. *Slips of the tongue and misinterpretations*

A second problem which is related to the composition of corpora of the 'spoken' language is the problem of slips of the tongue and misinterpretations. In the first case a 'mistake' by the speaker is involved. Abdeljawad defines slips of the tongue as follows: "involuntary deviations in performance from the speaker's current phonological, grammatical, or lexical intention" (Abdeljawad 1987: 145). Slips of the tongue can be hyper-corrections, such as, when somebody reads, for instance, *qurqān* in stead of *qur'ān* (Kaye 1970: 386). But slips of the tongue can also consist of a great variety of deformations. These have been described in detail for the 'spoken' language by Abdeljawad (1987) and Safi-Stagni (1990 and 1992).

The study by Safi-Stagni (1990) demonstrates that slips of the tongue can consist of changes of phonemes, for instance, خفت الخرارة (*ḫaffati l-ḫarāra*) instead of الحرارة (*al-ḥarāra*), or حفت الحرارة (*ḥaffati l-ḥarāra*) instead of خفت (*ḫaffat*), transpositions of phonemes, for instance, توالين (*tawālīn*) instead of تلاوين (*talāwīn*), substitutions of words, such as, for instance, في الثلاجة (*fī t-tallāja*) instead of في الغسالة (*fī l-ġassāla*); mixtures of two words such as the word شمين (*šamīn*) as a mixture between شمال (*šamāl*) and يمين (*yamīn*); omission of letters such as in عبة (*'ubba*) in stead of علبة (*'ulba*); wrong plural forms and overcorrections, such as, for instance, in سورة تبارق (*tabāraq*) in stead of تبارك (*tabārak*).[14]

Ashtiany (1993: xi) points out that many slips of the tongue arise because of the high pressure of work in news agencies, which leads to words being easily read in a wrong way or incorrectly pronounced. It is very important for the transcriber to be conscious of this. While transcribing there are two possibilities. When the slip of the tongue is not clear, the transcriber probably will not even notice it. He can transcribe the unclearly pronounced word literally as he hears it, and he can indi-

proached mostly the model pronunciation. This was postulated by the compilers of the corpus: "The speaker should be as close to RP as possible. This excludes the use of, for example, regional dialect or idiosyncratic speech" (Taylor 1988: 237). See also (Quirk 1979: 211) and (Renouf 1988).

[14] Abdeljawad (1987) gives similar examples. Mistakes from texts read aloud, however, are not included in his investigation. He gives the example of substitution from complete words by another word or parts of another word. Among the many examples of slips of the tongue which he gives are slips of the tongue such as تكفير (*takfīr*) instead of تفكير (*tafkīr*); mixtures as, for instance, in قياس (*qiyās*) and تقويم (*taqwīm*) which become قيام (*qiyām*) and تقويس (*taqwīs*). Abdeljawad also points out that slips of the tongue are not always easy to register. "We often know what the speaker intended to say and we often do not pay attention to the full articulation of the message" (Abdeljawad 1987: 147).

cate that the word was pronounced in an unclear way. When it was not possible to identify a word because of its unclear pronunciation, we marked this word by placing an asterisk after the word.[15]

However, there are also many cases where the transcriber clearly hears the slip of the tongue. Harrell (1960) mentions this problem when he clearly heard *qān* instead of *qāl*, whereas it was clear from the context that the word *qāl* was meant. The question whether the transcriber may correct words which he clearly recognizes as slips of the tongue is not very easy to answer. Investigations (a. o. Whitson 1972) have demonstrated that listeners, in order to understand, do not exclusively base themselves on pronunciation. They also make use of cognitive processes by interpreting the spoken utterances. In this respect, Kelly (1991) distinguishes between a bottom-up movement, which he regards as the input of sounds and a top-down movement, which consists of the application of the cognitive capacities. "The mind sets up the expectations and the sound provides confirmation. Perception occurs when sufficient information has been provided from both sources. If the sound signal is weak, obscured or incomplete, the listener will be obliged to make greater use of top-down processing; similarly, in a constrained context, when the following words are highly predictable, he needs only to rely minimally on bottom-up processing" (Kelly 1991: 135).

This means that the listener not only makes use of the sounds which he hears, in order to identify words and contexts, but that he, even more, relies on the prior knowledge which he has about the words he hears.[16] In other words, a word does not have to be pronounced clearly in order to be understood. Listening supposes a constant interpretation, which also means that words can wrongly be interpreted, even by native speakers. "It is often overlooked how often the native speaker does not hear and does not understand what is said. A frequent experience of the author when watching a film or a TV program in his own language is to be asked by a non-native speaker to repeat what was said: his frequent inability to do so is often wrongly interpreted as an unwillingness to do

[15] Sometimes the news reader corrects himself. As an example, we quote a news reader from Algeria who read: *kasb biqātha*, then hesitated, and thereupon corrected himself by reading *ka-sābiqātiha*. It is clear that without the correction by the news reader, it would have been impossible to identify the word correctly as it was read at first.

[16] It is generally known that it is very difficult to make a precise transcription of sounds on a purely auditive basis. An example can illustrate this. In aviation, but also on the telephone, the spelling alphabet is used. When unknown words have to be said on the telephone, such as proper names, the spelling alphabet is used in order to be able to transcribe the proper names correctly.

so! The native speaker also frequently mishears what is said" (Kelly 1991: 137).

As examples of misinterpretations by native speakers (!) of English, while transcribing English 'spoken' texts, Kelly (1991: 140) quotes among others: the "*increasing* vandalism" in stead of "*increase in* vandalism"; "it is very much *a* fault" in stead of "*the* fault of management"; "they can then *mask* their feelings" in stead of "*master* their feelings"; "the effect ... is very *grave*" in stead of "*great*". Cultural factors too play a role. The next example can illustrate this: (Kelly 1991: 141) "at the *Ennis* road service station in stead of *NS* road service station".

Kelly points out that when the acoustic circumstances are reasonable, the non-native speaker is able to transcribe texts as well as a native speaker. When misinterpretations occur, they are mostly due to a too defective prior knowledge which hampers the correct interpretation of the words. For this reason we implemented a safety margin for the transcription of our corpus of investigation. Whenever we were in doubt about the pronunciation of a word, we placed an asterisk behind that word. Such words were later not included in the vocabulary list. The sentences in which those words occurred were also excluded from the investigation. Those words most often occurred in news coverages with very bad radio contact.[17]

9.2.3. *Orthography*

Another problem which has to be solved for the transcription of a corpus is the problem of the precise orthography. Some words in MSA can be written in different ways. In the first place, there is the problem of the *hamza* (Parkinson 1990). Even though there are different possibilities, we stick to the traditional rules, such as they have been described by Atoui (1979) and Van Mol (1984). This means that we don't follow the spelling as it is used in the Egyptian written press. Thus, we write مسؤول instead of مسئول etc. In the Egyptian press, it is also a custom to write the final-*yā'* always without dots.[18] In our orthography we keep the distinction between the final-*yā'* and the *alif-maqṣūra*.

[17] For more detailed information on the percentage of such words in the corpus see infra 10.2.4.

[18] Cf. Meiseles (1979: 279): "It seems that there is a difference in the orthographic tradition between Egypt and the Eastern area: in Egypt, as a rule, the final *yā'* is undotted, while in the Eastern area it is almost always dotted."

Proper names consittute another problem. For the names of countries we based ourselves on the dictionary by Reich (1983: 38 et seq.). However, in news broadcasts small villages sometimes get a lot of attention. We therefore made use of Arabic newspapers and Arabic maps. The same goes for the proper names of personalities. When the persons mentioned were publicly known it was not very difficult to trace the spelling of these names in the different newspapers of the respective countries. Other names were transcribed such as we heard them. All proper names of persons were indicated in the corpus by a code in order to facilitate analysis (cf. infra).

Proper names of non-Arab persons and places create an even more complex problem. Due to the lack of a sound transcription system, proper names are often deformed in Arabic and represented in different ways. In the Arab world there is some resistance to the literary representation of foreign proper names, since additional letters would have to be added to the Arabic alphabet by making use of, for example, three diacritical dots (cf. Monteil 1960: 43). How do you write, for instance, *Shevardnadze*. In one country such foreign proper names are pronounced differently than in another country. In one country they say *slūfīniyā* and in another one *slūfāniyā*. Indeed, there is also within the Arab world no consensus on how these foreign names ought to be written. Bentahila (1991: 76), for instance, writes: "Strikingly, the various countries have not even been able to agree on the symbols to be adopted to represent sounds occurring in borrowed words; for instance, some countries use the symbol ج to represent the sound (g) and others use (sic.) while in Morocco both of these are used interchangeably".

Moreover, different spellings can be found in dictionaries and atlases for one and the same place name. This problem is not strictly limited to Arabic. When Arabic names have to be written in English we encounter the same large variation in transcription (cf. Kaye 1992). As a rule, personal names are not always clearly distinct from common nouns. For this reason we placed personal names between two codes, in this case "=" and "-". This way it will later be clear, when analyzing the text samples by computer, that in these cases we have to do with personal names.

9.2.4. *Punctuation*

A last problem concerns punctuation. For methodological reasons the delimitation of a text in sentences is very valuable. It would lead as too far within the scope of this book to make a thorough analysis and definition of what can be understood by a sentence. As a matter of fact, according to some authors punctuation was not used in Classical Arabic and ought to be considered an innovation under the influence of European languages (cf. Stetkevych 1970: 96; Meiseles 1979: 289; Abdulaziz 1986: 18; Ditters 1991: 213).[19] Others, such as Blau (1981: 138-139), hold another view. They are convinced that punctuation was used in a consistent manner in Classical Arabic. Blau (1981: 139), for instance, writes: "The use of periods is even characteristic of Middle Arabic scientific literature and of belles lettres as exhibited by Jâhiz."

As a matter of fact, punctuation is an important tool in corpus linguistics (cf. Renouf 1988: 204 and Briscoe 1994: 98). But, in this respect, Taylor (1988: 242), correctly points out the danger of overpunctuation. The transcriber often feels inclined to place a comma whenever he hears a pause. On the other hand, Francis (1979: 120) points at the danger of underpunctuation. "Loban's tapes were first transcribed by a typist who followed standard punctuation practice, making her own decisions about sentence boundaries. Some of the material contained passages consisting of long strings of independent clauses linked by *and*. The typist punctuated these as long multiply coordinate sentences. But when a group of linguists listened to the tapes, it became apparent from the intonation patterns that most of the *and*'s were sentence-initial. In fact, for some speakers *and* was the normal way to begin a new sentence in connected narrative" (Francis 1979: 120).

We based ourselves on the intonation in order to define the end of a sentence. The intonation can have different characteristics. Amaireh gives the following scales of intonation for Arabic: "1. Descending positive; 2. Ascending positive; 3. Descending negative; 4. Ascending negative; 5. Ascending relative; 6. Descending relative" (Amaireh 1981: 39). When rereading the transcribed texts, we had the impression that a point might have been placed further on in a text. In other words, we had the impression that sometimes a point cut a sentence in two. Yet, we did not change the place of a point in that case in order to give an

[19] Meiseles (1979: 289), for instance, maintains: "Punctuation, apart of such a paragraphemic element as the paragraph division, is unknown in Arabic writing system. In part, writers of modern literary and journalistic PA make use of punctuation symbols, but — mostly — in such a random way that it makes it impossible to claim for any systematic norm." In this respect, Monteil (1960: 42) uses the expression "les ponctuations fantaisistes". According to Al-Batal, however, punctuation is nowadays consistently applied: "However, in many a modern Arabic text the use of punctuation has become quite common and consistent. This is the case in the text under study in which al-Aqqad uses punctuation in a somewhat consistent way." (Al-Batal 1990: 266).

accurate reproduction of the pronunciation. As a matter of fact, later on we observed the same problem in printed Arabic texts, where, for example, a sentence can begin with the conjunction إلا أنّ. The comma was only used to separate enumerations.

9.3. The tagging of textual material

In corpus linguistics the term 'tagging' is mostly used in the sense of *automatic grammatical tagging*. This means that *tagger* software is developed which is able to define (automatically) the grammatical category of a word in a text , in other words, to *tag* it (Paulussen 1992: 2).[20] Tagging means that the *implicit* information of a word is made *explicit*. The labeling can be carried out on different levels and in different domains. It can, for instance, be done on a phonetical, morphological, semantical or syntactical level.[21] Hlal rightly remarks that the tagging can

[20] Barber (1988: 30), states: "It would be useful to have programs performing automatic word 'tagging' (classification as noun, verb etc.) and analysis (into roots and prefixes, suffixes, and the categories they represent, past, plural and so on)". Previously Cohen (1970: 52) raised two important questions which ought to be answered when automatic analysis of words is intended: "(1) Est-il possible par la simple reconnaissance des formes des graphèmes, et en dehors de tout considération des valeurs sémantiques, d'isoler les radicales d'un mot pour en faire ressortir le schème et les marques flexionnelles? (2) Est-il possible de dresser des listes pratiquement exhaustives des prototypes de ces divers éléments avec le détail des valeurs de chacun?" According to Abi Farah (1986: 17) Arabic, contrary to other languages, is by its structure extremely suited for automatic analysis: "Il faut ajouter que la langue arabe, vu son organisation originale, se prête à l'analyse automatique des mots, et ce grâce aux différents travaux de grammairiens et linguistes arabes. Ces travaux ont permis de révéler des possibilités strictes de classifications des mots selon des classes de mots ou de formes préétablies. A ma connaissance toutes les autres langues ne bénéficient pas de cet avantage". However, in spite of the optimism of Abi Farah there seem to be many practical problems for the automatic analysis which have not been solved yet (cf. Buckwalter 1994). Bathurst (1971: 185) gives an inventory of the possible combinations the Arabic language can yield: "There can be up to 2,300 different combinatory prefixes preceding the first letter of a verb stem and more than 1,600 preceding a substantive stem. The stems themselves are subject to infixion and there are more than 500 patterns for them. Varieties of combinatory suffix are almost as numerous as those of the prefix. In order to write a program for the computer to recognize Arabic word-roots non-intuitively (...) it is necessary to determine the complete range of morphological phenomena occurring in the language." In this respect it is important to notice that, in spite of enormous investments, there does not yet exist an error free tagger for other European languages. "Yet, since 1982, the success rate for automatic grammatical tagging has remained more or less constant at about 96-97 per cent. This appears to be a ceiling difficult to break through" (Leech 1994: 48). Paulussen (1992: 51), Karlsson (1994: 121) and Sampson (1994: 173) arrive at the same conclusion. In Arabic, problems are even bigger because of the consonantal writing (cf. infra 9.3.2.). The automatic analysis of Arabic words, carried out by Ditters (1992: 418) on a corpus of approximately 2500 words, gave a much lesser degree of correctness, viz. 66%. This means that the manual work still remains very important for the tagging.

be phased. He distinguishes four phases in tagging: "1) the morphological analysis which is concerned with the treatment of words without their context; such analysis is by definition ambiguous. 2) the syntactic analysis which is concerned with the words in the context of the phrases. 3) the semantic analysis aims at resolving any ambiguities that are left, taking into account evidence from lexical semantic data. 4) the pragmatic analysis will resolve any remaining ambiguities on the basis of extra-linguistic information" (Hlal 1988: 47).

For the labeling a so-called *tagset* is used, which is described by Leech as follows: "By 'tagset' is meant the set of grammatical tags used for the tagging process, representing the set of grammatical categories which are distinguished by the linguistic model. One could imagine a very simple set of grammatical categories, say 10, representing the major parts of speech, as the crudest possible tagset to be employed. In practice, larger tagsets have been used, varying from c. 30 to c. 240. There is no one 'best tagset', and in practice most tagsets have tended to be a compromise between a desirable degree of linguistic delicacy and what can for practical reasons be required of an automatic tagging system" (Leech 1994: 51).[22]

For the encoding of texts we have to keep in mind that the tagged text ought to be accessible for as many linguistic levels as possible. Butler (cited in Huber 1988: 61) states: "It cannot too strongly be emphasized that it is advisable to include as much information as is practically convenient when coding the text. (...) It should be remembered (...) that the text may be of use to others working on related problems, whose interests in the text may require different information from that which the researcher needs himself. It always is possible to delete information, but information which has not been coded may be very difficult to recover."

[21] Compare for the importance of the encoding on semantic level Abboud (1986: 194).

[22] According to Greenbaum also, it is very difficult to evaluate these tagsets. "To start with we have no general measures for evaluating tagsets or syntactic analyses for corpora, and it is not obvious what evaluation measures we should apply. (...) The larger the corpus, the less detailed the tagging or parsing can be — and also the greater the tolerance for inconsistencies and inaccuracies" (Greenbaum 1994: 33). In this respect, we notice that there are different kinds of tagsets for English. Besides TAGGIT for the Brown corpus and CLAWS for the LOB corpus, there are different other kinds of tagsets, such as the ICE and CLAWS1 who use different grammatical categories (Greenbaum 1994: 34). For European (read English) languages the main aim is to standardize tagsets. "Although encoding standardization is far from obvious, there have been some initiatives which seem to be promising as the Text Encoding Initiative" (Paulussen 1992: 4). About the encoding of the *'Five million word corpus* of the Dutch Institute for Lexicology see Dutilh-Ruitenberg (1994) and Van der Voort van der Kleij a.o. (1994).

This means that it is of primordial importance to encode the corpus in such a way that the encoding remains open enough to cover as many levels of investigation as possible.

In the second place, it is important to work in a way as structured and as consistent as possible. "There is the general point that the information is presented in a structured form, so that it is searchable by computer, and that the conventions proposed form a general coherent system applicable to any text" (Johansson 1994: 25). For Arabic texts, vocalization can be used for the encoding of texts. This does not mean at all that a vocalized text is a *tagged* text. Ditters, for example, assumes that a vocalized text is equal to an encoded text.[23] This is not totally correct.

It is, however, at least possible to disambiguate a text on a morphological level by vocalizing it (Hlal 1988: 45). On the other hand, by vocalizing the word *mas'ūl*, for example, we still do not know whether we have to do with the substantive (*ism ġayr ṣifa*)[24] or an adjective (*ṣifa*). In certain cases, vocalization will give more information about a word. The form *ktbt*, for instance, is very unclear. Sometimes vocalization can be used to disambiguate words up to a certain level (Hlal 1988: 45). In this way *katabat (she wrote)* can be clearly distinguished from *kutibat* (*she was written*). In this form both words are vocalized, but not yet tagged or encoded (See also Cohen 1970: 54).

In the third place, it is necessary to decide on which level the tagging is to be done. "In terms of computational data structuring the following division is most relevant: below word-level, at word-level, and above word-level. Word level structures are the easiest and the most economical in the commonly used format of relational databases. Each word is encoded with a tag. The tagging can be carried out by hand or automatically" (Paulussen 1992: 3). For our corpus we decided to encode the corpus on the word level.

This means that we have to attribute grammatical categories to words. It also means that we can give a suitable description to *every* word in the text (Feat & Kouloughli 1988: 33). "Practically this means that every word is provided with a unique grammatical word label or tag. Such tags are usually encoded next to the word, so that the information is readily available for further linguistic analysis, such as parsing a sentence" (Paulussen 1992: 8).

[23] "Therefore we here discuss the formal description on the 'sentence' in MSA in a 'tagged' (= vocalized) form in preparation of an 'untagged' version" (Ditters 1991: 198 and 221).

[24] See Cachia (1973: 43).

At this level we are confronted with three problems which all have to do with the specific characteristics of the Arabic language. The first problem, which is very specific to Arabic, involves the definition of a word and the delimitation of it in a text. The second problem concerns the attribution of grammatical categories. It has to be decided which grammatical system will form the background for the tagging. And last, but not least, there is the problem of ambiguity, which is an essential problem for all languages, but which obtains an extra dimension in Arabic because of the consonantal writing. We will go more deeply into each of these problems.

9.3.1. *Identification of words*

In English corpora words are often identified as a string of characters between two blanks. This means that in every English, but also Dutch, text, every word is automatically delimited by the author by pressing the space bar. This makes it easier for the programmer and for the computer to define the basic forms of a word. Of course, there are some exceptions. Some lexical units can be made up of more than one word. This is, for instance, the case in the lexical unit 'joint venture'. Sometimes the lexical unit is indicated by a hyphen, making the recognition by computer easier. For instance, the words cash-and-carry, black-out etc.

In Dutch, too, and in similar European languages, words are not always delimited by two blanks.[25] The definition of what is understood by a word always has been a problem, both in Dutch and in other languages. For practical computer technical reasons this problem has been avoided by defining a word as a string of characters between two blanks, although everybody realizes that this is a pseudo solution. In Dutch, for instance there is the problem of the separable verbs such as, for instance, *oplopen* (for instance: De kosten *liepen* hoog *op*). Further on, in Dutch there are word groups such as, for instance: *te werk gaan, tot nog toe* etc. Greenbaum (1994: 39) refers in this respect to what he calls the "complex prepositions" such as, for instance, "in addition to, on behalf

[25] Cf. the definition by Barber (1988: 31): "Words are defined as sequences of characters between spaces or end-of-line markers." Everything, of course, depends on what is understood by 'word'. Owens, for instance, raises the question whether the particle *bi* can be considered as a word. "The traditional formulation, morphological = relation within word, syntactic = relation between words only works so long as 'word' can be unequivocally identified. In the vast majority of cases Bloomfield's (1927) 'word as minimal free form' serves this purpose, though inevitably problematic cases arise. In what sense, for example, is a preposition like *bi* 'by means of' a free form, given that it always occurs with a complement" (Owens 1989: 212).

of" etc. In English there are also many "multi-word items" in the subordinate conjunctions, such as, for instance: let alone, such that, etc.[26] This might seem to confuse word level with phrase level. However, the definition of words and phrases is, in some cases, a matter of degree.

The same problem exists in Arabic. Al-Jubouri (1988: 64), for instance, rightly points at the problems of word groups: "A number of collectives are phrasal in construction, that is to say, they are realized in a word group such as 'on the hand'". For Arabic the problems are even more complex because blanks, in most cases, do not delimit words, but word groups. This means that one word can occur in a text in hundreds of different forms (cf. Hlal 1990: 201).[27] The identification of words in word groups is a first problem which has to be solved. The first author to make a thorough inventory of this problem was Cohen (1970). He distinguished the graphic form of words and the linguistic form: "Mot étant employé (...) dans le sens particulier de 'mot graphique', c'est par forme linguistique qu'on a désigné ici l'unité significative minimale autonome." And further (p. 56): "Dans le mot graphique, défini comme le segment graphique délimité par deux 'blancs' succesifs, sont susceptibles d'entrer divers éléménts en nombre déterminé et dans un ordre fixe" (Cohen 1970: 50).

Cohen tried to foresee what a computer program had to take into consideration. However, Cohen did not arrive at a solution for this problem.[28] Later on, researchers have tried to provide solutions for the identi-

[26] For counting of words Greenbaum (1994: 40) does not object to counting the preposition *of* in *of course* with the preposition *of* in other functions.

[27] This clearly has consequences for the counting of words in Arabic. Until now, not one researcher clearly indicates which method he uses for the counting of words of his corpus. We may assume that the word delimited by two blanks is taken as basis. Only Parkinson (1975: 55) gives an explanation on how he calculated the size of his corpus (expressed in 'words': "To determine the number of words in my corpus, I counted the words from five randomly chosen pages of each work, took the average of these five pages and multiplied by the number of pages that I read from that particular work. My entire corpus, as can be seen from the table below, totaled over 84,000 words." Parkinson too, however, does not clearly indicate what he means by 'word'.

[28] Other researchers, who mention the problem, but who do not provide solutions are: Bathurst (1971: 186), Anwar (1989: 2), Hlal (1990) and Ditters (1992). Buckwalter (1994) tries to solve the problem by compiling a list of certain words which he will reclassify manually. He writes: "A much more serious problem is the lemmatization of the output: i.e., manually reorganizing the data so that the various inflected forms of each lexeme are grouped accordingly. In order to undertake the lexicographic description of the word *taqdīm*, for example, we would need to bring together the concordance lines listing the following" (Buckwalter 1994: 4). Buckwalter then gives a long list of forms in which the word *taqdīm* can occur. This, however, does not solve the problem of the recognition of prefixes and suffixes. Moreover, Buckwalter gives an example of a word (masdar II form) which unmistakably can be recognized. The problem remains complicated for words which consist of three consonants, such as, for example: *ktb*.

fication of words. Abdelkarim (1990: 219) proposed to disintegrate the words by placing a space between the different components of a word. In stead of *liyu'tihim* (*to give them)* the transcriber ought to write *li-yu'ti-him*.

A similar solution has been proposed by Al-Jubouri (1988), who separated the conjunctions *wāw* and *fā'* from the following words. This approach is limited because in this way the computer is only able to recognize those two conjunctions. Moreover, Al-Jubouri used a transcription of Arabic in Latin fonts. Another solution, proposed by Abdelkarim, is to set up word lists in which every word is represented with all the possible prefixes and suffixes, which can be manually removed afterwards. However, Abdelkarim does not consider that many combinations are possible between different prefixes and suffixes, which will yield a very large list which might be difficult to oversee.

What is more, another problem, which is closely linked to the consonantal writing of Arabic, arises with the delimitation of the words. In a word list, it is no problem at all to isolate the prefix *sa* as a particle of the future from the word group *syktb*. What to do, however, with the combination *fhm*. Is it the verb *fahima*, or the prefix *fa* followed by the verb *hamma*, or the prefix *fa* followed by a suffix *hum* (cf. Hlal 1988: 45 and 1990: 201). In other words, identification problems become countless in such a word list. As a matter of fact, Abdelkarim points out that he did not take into consideration the prefixes *fa* and *li* and the article in his scheme. He hopes to identify the definite article in a later stage by sophisticated techniques (Abdelkarim 1990: 221).

We decided to develop an encoding system ourselves which enables the computer to distinguish the prefixes and the suffixes from the word. In advance we laid down two conditions.[29] In the first place the encoding had to be developed in such a way that it could be applied to the Arabic alphabet so that we would not have to compile a corpus in Latin characters. In the second place, the encoding had to be developed in such a way that it would be possible to obtain a normal Arabic text after decoding the corpus with a computer program.[30] Both conditions were met (cf. infra 10.1. and 10.2.5.).

[29] Beside these conditions, there also are the general conditions from modern corpus linguistics, such as they have been formulated by Johansson (1994: 25): "There is the general point that the information is presented in a structured form, so that it is searchable by computer, and that the conventions proposed form a general coherent system applicable to any text." Moreover, the encoding has to be executed very explicitly. "Statistically-based automatic language processing needs data analyzed in a very consistent fashion, and hence requires a very explicit analytic scheme" (Sampson 1994: 172).

[30] This clearly is not the case in the proposal of Abdelkarim (1990). When we use a blank to separate prefixes from the words, it becomes impossible for the computer to con-

Because we typed in the texts in such a way that the computer can distinguish between the 'word' *fhm* as *fa-hum* or *fahima* or *fa-hamma*, we can write a program which analyses prefixes and suffixes automatically from the word. This basic encoding, however, is not sufficient. Isolation of prefixes and suffixes only solves one part of the problem of word recognition. We still have to attribute a grammatical tag to the words which will have been isolated in this way. In Arabic we are confronted with the problem that apart from different modern linguistic approaches to part of speech classification, there is a traditional western approach, as well as an Arabic linguistic approach. Eventually, we will have to make a motivated choice.

9.3.2. *Attribution of grammatical categories, a problem*

Without grammatical terminology, it is impossible to describe a language. The question, however, is which terminology to choose for a language such as Arabic. In the first place we have to take into account that there has been an Arabic grammatical tradition for centuries. In other words Arabs themselves have made a division in their own terms of parts of speech.[31]

Their classification of parts of speech is divided into three large groups. The first group contains the nouns (*ism* plural *'asmā'*). A distinction is made between declinable nouns and indeclinable nouns. The second group contains the verbs (*fi'l* plural *'af'āl*) . All the words which do not belong to the two first groups fall under the third group (*ḥarf* plural *ḥurūf* or *'adā* plural *'adawāt*) which is generally translated by "particle".[32] Within all these groups a detailed distinction is made into different subcategories. On the other hand, in the European traditional grammar a division is made into ten word classes. While describing the Arabic language orientalists have tried to translate the Arabic division into the European one. Arabic categories and subcategories were transposed this way in terms of western categories. It is, however, clear that the

vert such a text into a normal text, because it is almost impossible to distinguish the temporary spaces form the real spaces.

[31] Whether Arab grammarians came independently or under the influence of the Greek thought to their classification into parts of speech is not very clear. (cf. Kouloughli 1987 and Guillaume 1988).

[32] According to Kouloughli, in the oldest writings, there was no question of *ḥarf* but of رباط (*ribāṭ*, 'tie'): "La plus ancienne traduction arabe de La Poétique (*Mattā Ibn Yūnus*) ignore quant à elle le terme de *ḥarf* et parle de *ribāṭ* (littéralement 'ligature')" (Kouloughli 1987: 218).

content of an Arabic category does not always match completely the content of a European category.[33]

Thus Beeston (1968: 4) remarks that it is very difficult to combine both systems: "This is always a difficult problem, and particularly so when one is dealing with a non-European language, for which the conventional European terminology is usually quite unsuitable. So far as Arabic is concerned, almost all of its linguistic phenomena fall into categories which do not correspond happily to European grammatical categories, and the use of conventional European grammatical terminology is consequently liable to mislead."[34]

[33] This reveals itself most clearly in the category of the particles. Particles from the Arabic category of *ḥurūf* (particles), which correspond to the prepositions of foreign languages, are translated as prepositions, whereas the others remain classified in a separate category of particles (cf. infra 11.1). In the enumeration of the *ḥurūf* Wright (1975, volume 1: 278), for instance, distinguishes four groups, prepositions, adverbs, conjunctions and interjections. We find the same division in Blachère who calls these: "des outils linguistiques qui, en arabe, correspondent aux adverbes du français, à ses prépositions, à ses conjonctions etc" (Blachère 1978: 207). Fleisch (1979: 210-211), on the other hand, observes that some of the prepositions are not classified with the *ḥurūf* in traditional Arabic grammar, but with the *ẓurūf* (adverbs of place or time). However, the category of the *ẓurūf* is much wider than prepositions alone. Because some words function as prepositions, such as, for instance, *amāma* and *bayna* (which belong to the *ẓurūf* in Arabic grammar) they are considered by western grammarians to be prepositions. Arab grammarians, for instance, have the category of *ḥurūf al-jarr*. The main characteristic of these particles is that they are followed by a genitive. Most western grammarians classify these under prepositions. However the two divisions do not overlap precisely. For instance, Fu'ād Ni'ma (1973: 105), Ya'qūb (1988: 286,254 and 224) and Ad-Daḥdāḥ (1990: 17) classify *'adā* (عدا), *ḫalā* (خلا) and *ḥāšā* (حاشا) under *ḥurūf al-jarr*. Both Wright (1973 volume 2: 341, 342) and Reckendorf (1921: 75) consider these *ḥurūf* to be verbs (which they initially were). Only Blachère, who states in his introduction that he will make an attempt to classify them according to the role they play in Arabic syntax, classifies those with the particles. He remarks, however, that *'adā* and *ḫalā*: "sont d'anciens verbes figés à la troisième personne masculin de l'accompli" (Blachère 1978: 405). He sees *ḥāšā* as a particle of exclamation (exclamative). In this regard, Cantarino (1974) sees them as merely a formal expression (dl 3: 192), whereas Krahl sees them as particles of exception (dl 1: 454 en dl 3: 717). On the other hand, western grammarians classify certain Arabic words under the particles (especially prepositions), whereas Arab grammarians do not. Both Wright (dl 1: 280) and Blachère (211), for example, classify لدن among *ḥurūf al-jarr*. Wright calls it a separable particle with the function of a preposition and Blachère calls it a prepositional particle. Cantarino (1974) and Krahl (1980) do not mention this word at all. Historically لدن was originally a noun (Fleisch 1979: 487).

[34] Guillaume (1988: 26), for instance, points at the faulty application of the notion 'adverbum' in Arabic. "Il est nécessaire de soulever un point sur lequel il s'est établie depuis fort longtemps, une confusion regrettable; je veux parler de la traduction de *ẓarf* par 'adverbe', dont le premier responsable semble bien être Merx (1889). (...) Dans la mesure où le terme 'adverbe' renvoie, dans la terminologie occidentale traditionnelle, à une catégorie classificatoire, alors que *ẓarf*, dans la tradition grammaticale arabe désigne quant à lui, et sans aucune ambiguité, une catégorie fonctionnelle, à savoir un certain type de complément verbal, affecté de la marque de l'accusatif, et spécifiant les circonstances

Here we touch the heart of the problem. It is, indeed, clear that the application of European grammatical categories to Arabic can be misleading. There seems to be a need to put Arabic categories within its own frame of reference, in order to make it recognizable and to make workable instruments from it.

By stating in the introduction of this paragraph (cf. supra) that in Arabic the second largest group of parts of speech is the verb (*fi'l*), we translated the category of *fi'l* in a western grammatical concept recognizable by every westerner. This, however, does not mean at all that the category *fi'l* has precisely the same contents as the category *verb*. Another possibility is to translate the category in such a way that the emphasis will be put on native Arabic specificity for this category. This, for instance, is Troupeau's method (1976: 164) who translates the category of *fi'l* by *operation*. The disadvantage of this translation is that the category *operation* is not a workable instrument.[35]

From social and cultural anthropology we know that in different cultures similar concepts can have different contents. In social and cultural anthropology it is customary to translate the concepts of another culture, whose contents cover more or less the concepts of one's own culture, by the concept which approaches the concept of the other culture to the highest degree. Only when the contents differ too much from a concept of another culture will no translation be given and the original word will be introduced in the new language. It is, for instance, generally known that the contents of hues differ from culture to culture (Barnouw 1973). In other words the concept *yellow* in Arabic does not comprise the same color shades as the concept *yellow* does in English. However, this does not mean that the Arabic word for *yellow*, viz. *aṣfar*, can not be translated by *yellow*.

spatiales et temporelles de l'action. Tout nom peut donc, en principe, occuper la position de *ẓarf*, dès lors que son sémantisme lexical et celui du verbe s'y prêtent." It is not surprising then that the first orientalists have often been reproached for trying to describe the Arabic language in terms of Latin grammatical terminology and classifications (Killean 1984: 32).

[35] Even when we translate the third category, viz. the *ḥurūf* by the term particle in stead of preposition, we still refer to a known western category. "The term particle stems from the grammar of the classical languages (Latin. particula, literally 'tiny bit'). From the very beginning it served to indicate words (mostly small words, sometimes even morphemes) which were difficult to classify. Negatives, such as the Greek mê, the Latin ne, question markers, such as the Greek and Latin an, enclitiqual forms, such as the Latin -que etc., were classified under this coordinating category" (Van der Auwera, 1984, 7). There were also the *particulae copulativae* (Lat. et, iam, ...), which, according to Van der Auwera (1984) laid the basis for the widespread terminological tradition up to our days to use the term 'particle' also for conjunctions and prepositions.

The word *mosque*, however, is another case. A mosque is, of course, like a *church*, a place of prayer, but the difference in content is so large that it is preferred to adopt the original word. The same method has been applied by many orientalist in linguistics. The Arabic subcategory, *ṣifa*, for instance, was translated by the category *adjective*, because researchers considered it to be the equivalent within European traditional grammar. Arabic categories which had no equivalent within traditional European grammar are generally left untranslated, such as, for instance, the category of the *maṣdar* (the verbal noun) and the *nisba* (relative adjective). This also means that almost all contemporary descriptions use both western and Arabic terms together, so that we might in a certain sense use the term "traditional mixed grammar".[36]

But even when we take into consideration the specificity of every language, and, for instance, apply a specific classification for Arabic, there still seem to remain problems with the exact definition of the different parts of speech. We touch here upon a central problem of both traditional western and traditional Arabic grammar. In *both* 'pure' grammatical systems problems occur with the definition of the different parts of speech.

Both grammars are based on a classification according to parts of speech. Neither grammar, in contrast with what is often assumed, exclusively base this classification on morphology. Owens, for instance, observes: "Among the most famous tenets of Arabic grammar is the division of words into verbs, nouns and particles. What is perhaps given less attention is the fact that the Arabic grammarians defined each of these according to criteria from all levels of linguistic analysis — phonological, morphological, syntactic and semantic/pragmatic. Of these perhaps the two most important are the morphological and the syntactic" (Owens 1989: 211).

Lagarde too has observed that the division into parts of speech in traditional western grammar is not exclusively made on a morphological basis. "Or la partition repose à la fois sur des critères formels (morphologiques), notionnels (sémantiques, ontologiques, psychologiques et logiques, termes souvent confondus) et fonctionnels (syntaxiques)" (Lagarde 1988: 94). According to Guillaume both traditional Arabic and traditional western grammar went through a similar evolution, which brings them to identical results. "Tout semble se passer comme si la tradition

[36] Books which describe the Arabic language in (mixed) traditional terms, are, for instance, the grammars by Reckendorf (1921), Cantarino (1974), Fleisch (1979), Krahl & Reuschel (1980), Brockelman (1992) and also recently in Dutch Stoetzer (1991).

grammaticale arabe d'une part et la tradition grecque de l'autre avaient suivi deux évolutions radicalement symétriques, partant de points de vue opposés pour aboutir à un résultat identique" (Guillaume 1988: 28).

Neither classification system is, however, watertight. Nor is the traditional Arabic system.[37] After all, the problem of classification is closely linked to the problem of the definition of parts of speech. In this respect Lagarde, rightly, refers to a statement of Whorf's: "Si l'on dit que 'frapper, tourner, courir' sont des verbes parce qu'ils expriment un 'événement' temporaire ou de courte durée, autrement dit une action (...) pourquoi les mots 'éclair, étincele (...) sont-ils des noms? Ils expriment des événements temporaires" (Lagarde 1988: 94).

We are confronted with the same problems in Arabic. In the first place, in spite of the large consensus which was reached (cf. Guillaume 1988: 25), there still remain concepts on which Arab grammarians themselves did not always agree (Ditters 1992: 50). Moreover, many a discussion was held about the precise definition of parts of speech. Observations such as those of Whorf for the French language are also found in Arabic.[38] There is in Arabic, for instance, a lack of clarity about the identification of the elative as noun or as a verb. For the Arab grammarians of Basra it is a verb, but for the grammarians of Kufa it is a noun (Kechaoui 1984: 128).

Owens comments on this: "One of the Basran arguments for its verbal status is that it can govern both a definite and indefinite noun in the

[37] According to Briscoe this applies to every grammar. He writes: "The problem of undergeneration relates directly to Sapir's famous observation that 'all grammars leak'. Even if it were possible to develop a totally watertight and comprehensive grammar (which has certainly not proved possible so far), the synchronic idealization underlying all efforts to encode the grammatical rules of a natural language implies that such a grammar would soon be rendered partially obsolete" (Briscoe 1994: 100).

[38] See, for instance, Kouloughli's very interesting conclusion about the definition of the particle in Arabic and the classification of the words which belong to that category. "Pour *Abū 'Alī*, définir la particule comme 'ce qui produit un sens dans un autre mot' c'est être obligé d'admettre que tous les 'noms d'évènements' (c'est-à-dire en pratique tous les prédicats verbaux) sont des particules 'puisqu'ils produisent des significations dans autre chose qu'eux mêmes'. (...) Pour les mêmes raisons, selon lui, on devra reconnaître comme particules tous les adjectifs, ainsi qu'un certain nombre de noms ayant pour fonction de spécifier d'une manière ou d'une autre des termes qui les précèdent, comme les noms en apposition" (Kouloughli 1987: 224). In the light of this new definition even some verbs could be classified by the particles: "En effet certains noms ou verbes fonctionnent souvent, voire toujours, comme purs 'mots outils' et devraient donc, en vertu de la nouvelle définition être considerés comme particules puisqu'ils n'ont alors aucune signification intrinsèque. C'est bien ce que fait *Az-Zajjāji*, qui dans son traité de grammaire intitulé *al-Jumal* qualifie systématiquement de *ḥarf* le verbe *kāna* (être) employé comme auxiliaire ainsi que les autres verbes exprimant diverses modalités d'état" (Kouloughli 1987: 230).

accusative. The Kufan argument rests in part on their analysis of the accusative complement of *'aḥsana* as a specifier, *tamyīz*" (Owens 1989: 221). The same problem arises for the words *niʿma* and *bi'sa*. According to the school of Kufa those are nouns and according to the school of Basra those are 'verbes figés à l'accompli'" (Kechaoui 1984: 128).[39]

One of the main criticisms of the division by both traditional western and traditional Arab grammarians is the fact that grammarians are not able to define the specific and common properties of every word class in such a way that it would be possible to make lists of exclusive categories. This does, however, not mean that in a practical way, at least for European languages, the different parts of speech are not recognizable. "Malgré les définitions qu'on lui propose, l'élève réussit assez bien à reconnaître ce que ni son maître ni les linguistes ne savent définir correctement: les sujets parlants auraient donc engrammé des critères de reconnaissance, qu'il n'a pas encore été possible d'expliciter de façon satisfaisante. Tout se passe comme si, face à une série de mots que, par ex., nous analysons spontanément comme des verbes, malgré notre incapacité d'expliciter le trait qui 'leur serait commun à tous', nous percevions intuitivement un réseau complexe d'analogies qui s'entrecroisent et s'enveloppent les uns les autres" (Lagarde 1988: 105).

Blake too points out that insight into the traditional grammatical categories has so deeply penetrated in the mind that it defines the judgment of a language user about the grammatical acceptableness of a sentence.[40] According to Blake, there is no problem in describing a (European) language in terms of traditional grammar. "It would be perfectly feasible to write a descriptive account of modern English using the terminology of traditional grammar" (Blake 1988: 4). We share this view and it seems to us that, in spite of the deficiencies, it is justified to describe Arabic in traditional (if necessarily mixed) terms.

Another objection which sometimes is raised against traditional (western) grammar is the fact that it is prescriptive. According to Blake this criticism is not correct: "Prescriptivism is not inherent in traditional grammar even if it has frequently been associated with it. (...) Tradi-

[39] Owens also points out the ambiguous statute of the word *rubba.*: "For instance, two of the arguments for the nominal (Kufa) as opposed to particle (genitive particle, Basra) status of *rubba* 'many a' involve syntactic arguments. First *rubba* is a noun because it occurs sentence initially, and nouns but not genitive particles occur in this position. Secondly, *rubba* only governs an indefinite noun, though particles occur with both definite and indefinite nominal dependents" (Owens 1989: 222).

[40] Blake gives different examples, among others the sentence: "Will you cafeteria with me today?" and he comments: "The important point is that we do regard these sentences as aberrant, because we think of cafeteria as a noun and not as any other word class" (Blake 1988: 10).

tional grammar is a method by which it is possible to break the language down into smaller parts so that the make-up of the language can be studied. (...) The methodology of traditional grammar as such cannot be criticized simply because some grammarians have used it as the basis for their rules for standard grammar" (Blake 1988: 2-3).[41] This does not hold true completely for Arabic. All Arabic grammatical works still use the Coranic text and older poetry texts as norm. Within the Arab world, contemporary texts almost never are the subject of grammatical investigations (cf. supra 2.2. and infra 12.1)

The objections which can be raised against the traditional (mixed) grammar, are to be weighed against the possible objections against modern linguistic approaches. When we take a closer look at modern linguistic approaches, we unmistakably can find certain deficiencies there as well (cf. supra note 37). In the first place, these approaches are heavily influenced by the languages in which they originated. Ditters (1992: 62) observes, for instance: "The development of such a descriptive linguistic model is sometimes significantly influenced by characteristics proper to the specific natural language being described (in most cases English) which can make the use of the model for the description of other natural languages less appropriate." In this sense the problem remains that a maladjusted Latin terminology is going to be replaced by an equally maladjusted English terminology.

Moreover, it seems that modern linguistics is not completely independent from concepts of the traditional (western) grammar. In spite of the fact that there is much criticism of the traditional division in parts of speech, they are nevertheless applied in practice in modern linguistics. Lagarde, for instance, observes: "Malgré des déclarations souvent fracassantes sur le peu de valeur scientifique de la partition traditionnelle, la pratique dominante consiste donc à la conserver". And he concludes: "La partition traditionnelle n'est donc pas aussi mauvaise que les critiques pouvaient le laisser supposer: ses auteurs étaient, sans le savoir, des fonctionalistes" (Lagarde 1988: 103).

We observe that in the investigations of Fehri (1981), Oostdijk (1984), Ditters (1992), and many others, the traditional (western) grammatical

[41] Moreover Blake points out that a grammar for a standard language can not be descriptive for a hunderd %. To a certain degree a grammar of a standard language is unmistakably prescriptive: "It may well be that some element of prescriptivism is inevitable in discussions of language, and we deceive ourselves if we pretend otherwise. This applies particularly to the standard language, since that is an artificial written language which can hardly be said to spring directly from any spoken variety. It has developed through the efforts of grammarians who have tried to standardize the usage of this particular variety" (Blake 1988: 6).

categories are preserved along with the addition of some new categories.[42] In modern linguistics the classification is often different. Traditional categories, such as the article and the demonstratives, are grouped together under the determiner, while other classes, such as, for instance, the verbs, are enlarged. "They do however raise questions about the justification for this or that classification" (Quirk 1985: 73).

An additional problem in modern linguistics is, according to different authors the non-transparency of the terminology. In different works objections are raised against the highly specialized terminology of modern linguistics. "Much of the work on Arabic linguistics, especially in the last dozen years, is highly technical and couched in terms that only the initiated can understand (...) This, however, places a burden on Arabic language specialists of other persuasions" (Abboud in Bakalla 1983: xi). According to Ditters it reaches the point that even specialists in linguistics can not oversee the situation anymore: "We refer to this point only to illustrate the detailedness of the discussion, the specificity of the arguments used and the horror of the professional lingo in which abbreviations in capitals live their own lives while the whole discipline has become so vast that it no longer can be overseen let alone mastered in its totality" (Ditters 1992: 76).[43] Precisely because of the 'theoretical burden' of modern grammatical theories, some (for instance, Blohm 1991: 95) prefer the traditional terminology.

The complexity of the terminology of some linguistic systems suffers greatly as a result of the fact that it becomes difficult or impossible to compare the results of the investigations with the existing studies. The disadvantage of some modern linguistic schools is their incompatibility with other linguistic models. As such, a comparison between, for instance, the functional approach by Mutawakkil, the TGG approach by Chomsky and the traditional approach, applied to Arabic grammatical structures, can be valuable and interesting. But this remains a study of its own. It is, of course, more interesting to compare different languages

[42] According to Blake, basic elements of the traditional grammar are still present in modern grammars in spite of the fact that they are not always visible: "There is a clear relationship between the terminology modern grammars use and that in traditional grammar. (...) Many of the bases of traditional grammar have never really been discarded, even if this position is not revealed in modern grammars." (Blake 1988: 12). Lagarde (1988: 99) arrives at the same conclusion: "Même si les nomenclatures ne sont pas nécessairement identiques, le vocabulaire habituel (parties du discours, nom, verbe, etc.) est pour l'essentiel conservé."

[43] Cf. also Wickens (1980: 2) who writes: "Moreover, the linguisticians have created new obfuscations of their own: in particular, a highly specialized terminology in phonetics and syntax, and a reluctance to enunciate principles that may not be universally applicable or ultimately valid, however useful for the study of a particular language or family of languages."

within one linguistic approach. The advantage of the traditional approach is also that the findings can be compared not only synchronically but also diachronically.

Finally, there also is a technical problem. The choice of a linguistic model is in our setting also defined by computer technical possibilities. We assume that for the time being a 'word-based grammar' is the most efficient way to conduct investigations into variation by means of a computer. This means that in our view a 'word-based grammar' offers the most practical approach in the current circumstances. Many modern grammars, however, are 'sentence-based grammars'. From a software point of view this requires another approach.[44] In order to investigate variation in MSA by means of corpus investigation, we opted for the traditional approach, in other words for a 'word-based' grammar. As a matter of fact, according to Paulussen (1992: 7) this seems to be the method which is followed in most cases. This choice, however, does not imply at all a value judgment on the other approaches.

Following the principle of a 'word-based grammar' we will try to encode the words in such a way that they might be categorized both according to the traditional mixed western grammar and the traditional Arabic grammar. First of all, we aspire at making words recognizable in the corpus by means of a primary encoding, so that the computer will be able to recognize prepositions automatically, such as, for example, *bi*. Whether the word *bi* will be classified as a particle of the genitive (*ḥarf al-jarr*) or as a preposition can be decided later on. That doesn't alter the fact that the problem of ambiguity has to be solved as accurately as possible. Here too we depart from both grammatical systems and choose for the largest possible disambiguation. This means that where in Arabic the participle (*ism al-fā'il*) in principle is considered to be a single category, we will make in the encoding a distinction between a participle with the function of a substantive and a participle with the function of an adjective or a verb.

9.3.3. *Attribution of grammatical categories and the problem of ambiguity*

It is generally accepted that the first step in analyzing written texts by means of a computer consists in the attribution of the correct grammatical category to every word in the text (Paulussen 1992: 8). If we obtain

[44] See also Ditters (1992: 106) who for computer technical reasons feels compelled to reject the TGG approach.

a word after isolating the prefixes and the suffixes we can try to attribute a grammatical tag to that word on the basis of morphological characteristics. Morphological characteristics alone, however, are too small a basis to categorize words. Francis describes this problem as follows: "Polysemy presents a problem related to homography. Everybody (but not the computer) knows that *fast* is at least five different words: a verb meaning 'to starve oneself', a noun meaning 'a period of self-starvation', two adjectives meaning respectively 'swift' and 'firm', and an adverb meaning 'swiftly'"(Francis 1979: 122).[45]

The same problem occurs in Arabic. Beeston already demonstrated that it is impossible to determine whether we have to do with an adjective or a substantive solely on a morphological basis. He writes: "I must here stress a terminological point: since substantives and adjectives are distinguishable only by function, not by morphological shape, it may be impossible when quoting a word from context to assert that it is either one or the other, this being determinable only by syntactic context. (...) It is impossible without a sentence context to determine whether *'ādil* represents the English adjective 'just' or a substantive = 'a just man'" (Beeston 1970: 34).[46]

This is also why Branca holds the view that besides a morphological lemmatizing, we ought to provide a lemmatizing based on the syntax. "En gros, on peut avoir une lemmatisation morphologique et une lemmatisation syntaxique. La 1ère considère tout ce qui est vrai d'un mot isolé de tout contexte. La 2ème considère en plus toutes les couches sémantiques que le contexte ajoute ou précise au mot. La 1ère a l'avantage de permettre d'être appliquée aux formes récapitulées graphiques, la dernière exige d'examiner chaque emploi de chaque mot dans son contexte. La dernière demande une concordance déjà faite. La 1ère sert à produire une première concordance. (...) La lemmatisation syntaxique est plus astreignante et demande beaucoup plus de temps; mais elle permet de systématiser aussi des syntagmes composés" (Branca: 1986: 119).

For Arabic the tagging of words on a morphological basis is out of the question. Indeed, the problem for Arabic is not only limited to the dis-

[45] All authors see the ambiguity of isolated words as a very important problem in computer linguistics. See among others: Barber (1988: 34), Feat & Kouloughli (1988: 16), Beesley (1990: 166), Janssen (1990: 106), Comrie (1991: 14), Ditters (1992: 409), Paulussen (1992: 12), Briscoe (1994: 98), Greenbaum (1994: 42), Guthrie (1994, 79), Buckwalter (1994: 4) and Leech (1994: 52).

[46] The same consideration is made by Kechaoui (1982: 149) (who also points out that an adjective can have the function of a present participle).

tinction between adjectives and substantives, but is because of the consonantal writing, even more complex. Since the great majority of the texts are not vocalised, the ambiguity in Arabic is much bigger than in other languages. The letters *ktbt*, for instance, can have different readings. We only can argue with certainty that a verb of the past tense is involved. Other information, such as the finite form (4 possibilities) or whether we have to do with an active or a passive form, can only be defined from the context. The same problem arises, for instance, for the verbs of the IV form, which can not be distinguished from the verbs of the I form in the present tense.[47] If no diacritical signs are placed in a text, which often is the case, then the recognition becomes even more difficult.

But also a syntactical analysis sometimes does not give a decisive answer about the disambiguation of words. In Arabic, for instance, the particles إنّ (*'inna*) and أنّ (*'anna*) are mostly written as ان (*'alif-nūn*). Consequently, on the basis of a written corpus, it is impossible to check in certain circumstances whether the particle *'inna*, *'anna* or even *'an* is used. Thus it is very important for the analysis of Modern Standard Arabic to compile corpora based on oral MSA (cf. infra 10.3.6.).

The problem of the ambiguity has, however, different gradations. As a matter of fact, a minimal disambiguation is necessary. This means that it has to be possible, on the basis of syntactic analysis, to distinguish between the parts of speech and to take into consideration, gender, number and tense, etc. When a word is *homomorphic*, such as the particle *mā*, for instance, then it is necessary to be able to distinguish between the particle *mā* as a negation particle, as a relative pronoun and as an interrogative pronoun. It is, however, also possible to attach semantic variegations. According to Al-Batal (1990: 239), for instance, the particle *fa* can have different meanings, viz.: "causal (because), conclusive (therefore), consequential (accordingly), discourse switch (so then, for instance), succession (in time: subsequent to this) and Topic introduction: *'amma fa* (as for)."[48] This holds also true within the traditional Arabic approach (cf. infra 12.1.1.). It is, however, not very easy to implement such a fine variegation.

In order to carry out the encoding or tagging thoroughly, every word in the entire corpus was translated with reference to the context. This led

[47] According to an investigation by Dobrisan (1985: 290) the verbs of the IV form obtain statistically a very important place compared to the other verb forms, viz. 24,87%!

[48] Al Batal (1990: 266) also refers to the distinction which can be made in English between two types of *and* viz.: "the 'coordinate' *and* and the 'conjunctive' or 'additive' *and*."

to a dictionary file of approximately 9000 words.[49] Every tag was attributed on the basis of a completely translated text and on the basis of the syntactic value of the word in context. This means that we checked in context whether a participle had the function of an adjective, a substantive or a verb. The tagging was executed in such a way that, after the stripping of prefixes, we obtained a word list in which for every word the word class was deducible. This means that it is possible to attribute, at a later stage, semantic values to words as well as the concrete grammatical tags.

[49] This file became the basis for the learners' dictionary Arabic-Dutch and Dutch-Arabic (Van Mol & Berghman, 2000a/b) which has since been developed with support of the Dutch language Union. This dictionary is based entirely on an Arabic corpus of 3,000,000 words which was largely analyzed by computer. More information on both dictionaries in Van Mol: 2000b and 2001c).

10. OPERATIONALIZATION OF THE CORPUS

In this chapter we will discuss three aspects. In the first place we will go more deeply into the tagcodes such as we have designed them. In the second place we will briefly discuss the software which has been developed to explore the corpus; and finally we will demonstrate how certain hypothesies can be tested by applying the software to the corpus.

10.1. Encoding

As far as the encoding is concerned we have to distinguish between a *primary encoding* and a *secondary encoding*. Primary encoding means that every word in the corpus is encoded in such a way that it becomes recognizable and manipulatable by computer. This means that we design an encoding which makes it possible to recognize the different parts of speech, the gender, number, tense, etc., without naming them. As we mentioned before (cf. supra 9.3.2.) there are two possibilities for designing the parts of speech: a western traditional terminology and an Arabic terminology. In certain cases, this does not provoke any problem, but in other cases it does. In Western grammatical terminology, for instance, the words *fī* and *bi* are considered prepositions, whereas they are referred to as genitive particles (*ḥurūf al-jarr*) in Arabic terminology.

Primary encoding has words recognized as independent entities which can be disambiguated and examined in relation to other entities. In other words, the encoding is designed in such a way that the computer knows the difference between the adjective (*ṣifa*) وفي (*wafīy - reliable*) and the conjunction and preposition وفي (*wa-fī - and in*), or, for instance, the difference between the verbal noun (*maṣdar*) وقع (*waq' - the falling*) and the verb وقع (*waqa'a - to fall*).

Before we explain the primary encoding we repeat the extra encoding we have mentioned so far.

Encoding Description	
* after word	Word which is not clearly pronounced and which is not counted
# after word	Refers to dialectal interference
=- before and after word	Proper name
$ after word	Uncommon syntactical construction

The structure of the primary encoding is relatively simple. For the primary encoding we made use of a consistent and systematic selective application of the vowels and the diacritical signs and also of the hyphen (*kašīda*). This was executed according to the following system: All the substantives were written with a vowel on the first consonant whereas all adjectives remained without a vowel on the initial consonant. Substantives which had no counterpart as adjective remained unvowelled. Adjectives which were used as substantives were also vowelled.

Verbs never bear vowels with the exception of the prefixes and the suffixes. The conjunction *wa* always bears a vowel, whereas the conjunction *fa* is made recognizable by placing a hyphen between the conjunction and the following word. The same goes for all the other words that consist of one consonant and that are normally linked to the word, of course with the exception of the *wa*. The prefixed *lām* is also an exception. It is marked by using two hyphens. The combination *lām* + definite article is represented by writing a *lām* twice with an intervening hyphen. Every possessive pronoun (*ḍamīr muttaṣil*) is vowelled. Only in the first person plural is confusion possible between possesive pronoun and the suffix of the first person plural of the verb in the past tense.

After stripping the prefixes the following closed word classes can be defined by means of computer software, viz. words, such as: *ṯumma*, *bal*, *ḥatta*, *baynama*, *lamma*, *am*, *aw* etc. This list is not exhaustive but can be completed at a later stage. Other closed word classes such as the demonstratives can now also be identified, e.g. words such as: *hāḏā*, *ḏālika* etc. Moreover, we can define the interrogative pronouns and particles, the different prepositions or genitive particles, the particles of the vocative, particles with the subjunctive, the particle *'anna* and derivations, the conditional particles, the restrictive particles, the future particle *sawfa* and the negation particles.

We also made a clear distinction between the negation particle *mā*, the interrogative particle and the relative pronoun. Adverbs were made recognizable by vowelizing the last consonant, for instance, *ḥawla*, *dāḫila* etc.

The definite article is indicated by placing a hyphen after the *alif-lām*, except when a word begins with an *'alif* . Then we provided the *'alif* with a *hamza*. This means that the definite article can automatically be removed by computer in order to obtain a word form. The hyphen was not used for proper names such as, for instance, المغرب (*al-maġrib Morocco*). The interrogative particle أ (*'a*) is also written with a *hamza*. The computer program knows that an *'alif-lām* is not removed when a word combination ends after the first consonant of the word, such as, for example, in the combination ألا (*'a-lā*), viz. an interrogative followed by a negative particle. The computer is now able to identify another range of closed categories, such as, the ordinals and the cardinals.

A separate encoding has been provided for some special prefixes, such as the dialectal verbal prefix *bi* of the verbs, the prefix *li* of the subjunctive and the prefix *fal*.

With the prefixes of the verbs an even more refined distinction was made in order to distinguish the different verb forms, by using hyphens in different ways. This made it possible to convert the finite verb forms of the VII, VIII, IX and Xth forms to the basic form.

Passive verb forms in the present and past tenses were marked by inserting a hyphen in the verb. When the use of a hyphen was not possible a letter *p* was placed after the verb. This made it possible to identify all the passive verb forms in the corpus.

Plural and dual forms are also marked by making use of vowel combinations. The same goes for the feminine plural endings. The forms of the *maṣdar* are defined by the consonant-vowel patterns. Since a confusion is only possible between the *maṣdar* of the IVth form and a plural of a substantive (for instance إخطار and اخطار) we decided to mark every *maṣdar* of the IV th form by writing systematically a *hamza* under the *alif*.

Also the feminine form of the adjectives is indicated by writing a *fatḥa* before the *tā' marbūṭa*. When the *tā' marbūṭa* is not preceded by a *fatḥa*, the word is automatically recognized as a feminine substantive.[1] Masculine elatives are recognizable because a *fatḥa* is placed above the *hamza* on the first consonant. We also took into account the fact that in a construct state and before a possessive suffix the ending of a sound plural substantive and of the dual has to be apocopated.

Finally the *nisba* was made recognizable by consistently using a *šadda* above the *yā'*. The ending of an indefinite substantive or adjective in the accusative was marked in the traditional way by using *fatḥa tanwīn*. Weak adjectives, which bear two kasras in the nominative, were marked by placing a vowel before the *yā'*. The entire corpus has been encoded in this way, word by word on the basis of an accurate contextual translation. In other words, the encoding did not take place exclu-

[1] As we already mentioned we describe here the *primary encoding* which by its character is not refined enough on some points. There is for instance the problem of the rare masculine words which end with a *tā' marbūṭa* such as, for instance, the word *ḫalīfa* (*caliph*). By encoding every word separately in the secondary encoding a more precise distinction can be made.

sively on morphological grounds but on a syntactic basis as well. By means of software we are able now to classify the agglutinated word groups in words.

10.2. Software

There are two kinds of programs which have been developed. The first kind of programs was used to structure the corpus and check its correctness. The second kind of software was developed to explore the corpus.[2] In what follows we will give a brief account on the most important programs.

10.2.1. *Spelling- and Code-checker*

Inevitably mistakes happen with the input of spoken text material in the computer. In order to eliminate as many input errors as possible we developed a spelling checker which was also able to check the encoding. On rereading the text striking writing errors are easily detectable, but small ones are, of course, much harder to detect. Even when the human mind will read the word اتنخاب (*itniḫāb*) in context spontaneously as انتخاب (*intiḫāb 'election'*), for the computer these two words are totally different and unrelated. We then have to check whether the encoding has been correctly applied.

The spelling and code-checker is a set of four programs which strip away certain encoded prefixes and thereupon show the remaining word in context. The first program (Make word list 1) makes a unique sorted list of a first text file. This text file was checked thoroughly for errors. The word list (word list 1) which is compiled by this first computer program is compared in a later stage with all the other word lists.

The second program (Make word list 2) checks first of all whether there are any mistakes in the encoding of the proper names. It happens that the transcriber marked the beginning of a proper name by the sign "=", but forgot to mark the end of a proper name by the sign "-". The program assumes that a proper name can not be longer than three words. When the program finds no end-marker three words after the initial

[2] All software was developed by Hans Paulussen, computational linguist, of the university Facultés Universitaires Notre Dame de la Paix in Namur (Belgium). It is clear that without his professional help, the exploration of the corpus would have been impossible.

marker, the program stops and indicates how many proper names have to be checked. It also marks the proper names so that they can be found easily in the text. Once the encoding of the proper names is corrected, we restart the program WL2, which makes a new sorted word list. However, the proper names are not included in WL2. Our intention is to compare the second word list with the first.

The third program (compare WL) checks which and how many words in WL2 do not occur in the basic word list (WL1). These are the words which did not appear in WL1, or words which were wrongly encoded. On the one hand, the output of the program is a word list in a similar format as WL1, and on the other hand, a KWIC (Key Word in Context)-index. The advantage of the KWIC-index is that problems of identification can mostly be solved on the basis of the context. In the KWIC-index format, the complete word is given on the first line, followed by a number which indicates the position of the word in the text. On the next line the same word is shown, but this time within the context of the sentence. This KWIC-index gives an optional number of characters on the left and the right side of the chosen word.

In what follows we give an example of such a WL-DIFF.KWIC output file in order to illustrate our method. A text file of 487 words was compared with WL1 (a word file of 15,867 words). The program indicates that there are 15 new words or errors in the encoding. We limit ourselves here to some typical examples.

بريوني بريوني 120
السلام التي تمّ الاتّفاق عليها في بريوني. غير أنّ بعض قادة القوات السلوف

In this case a new place name is shown, "Brioni". We will have to search back into the text to check the whole context in which the words occur and we also will have to consult an atlas to look for the right spelling.

تباين تباين 742
وا اسلحة تقليدية الى اطراف اخرى إذا تباين أنّ هذه الاسلحة تمسُّب بالاستقرار.

In this case, the context clearly reveals a verb of the VI th form which apparently has not occurred in the corpus. The first step is to check whether there has not been a listening error. It might be that the transcriber heard a verb of the Vth form, and that he wrongly interpreted it as a VIth form. First of all we must translate the sentence, and then check the meaning of this verb form in a dictionary. When the meaning of this verb form fits to the context, then the sentence will be accepted. Otherwise, we must listen to the sentence again in order to determine whether there has been a misinterpretation in transcribing the text.

فيفينا   فيفينا   14

فيفينا صرّحت اليوم عناصر جد

Error in writing. The preposition في was added to the proper name فينا "Vienna". This error has to be corrected in the original text.

مسوول   مسوول   1294

ة تعدّ الاولى من نوعها يقوم بها مَسوول سام سنغاليّ لهذا البلد منذ قط

Error in spelling. The word مسؤول was written without *hamza*. This error has to be corrected in the original text.

The fourth program (Update WL) places all the words in a corrected WL-DIFF and WL1 together and creates a new file which can serve as a basis for further comparison and checking.

The whole corpus was checked by these programs and corrected by the author. All pages were examined. Many ameliorations and corrections have been implemented, resulting in a word list of all the encoded words which can easily be consulted.

10.2.2. *Software to define sentences*

The foregoing clearly shows that a normal KWIC-index offers a lot of possibilities. There are, however, also limitations. The program is very well suited to check words and certain collocations. But when syntactical relations need to be investigated, a normal KWIC-index is very limited in its possibilities. Suppose we want to investigate whether after the verb *qāla* the particle *'anna* is used or the particle *'inna*. In a normal KWIC-index this is only possible when these particles follow closely after the verb. This, however, is rarely the case.

Indeed, in many cases the particle follows after a long parenthesis. In that case it is not useful to adjust the length before and after every searched word. This is why we preferred to implement the analysis on the sentence level. A sentence is simply described as a string of words ending at a full stop. A program was written which converts all texts in sentences. The program also indicates the input errors, e.g. the places where an end of a sentence (full stop) was not indicated. After checking the whole corpus it was converted into a file of sentences.

In what follows we will give an example of the output of the first ten sentences of a Saudi news broadcast. The first three letters refer to the country, the next three numbers to the kind of text which is involved: 001 concerns a commentary, 002 a news broadcast, 003 a reportage and 004 sports news. The last three numbers indicate the place of the sentence in the text.

SAU001001	يقرأها = عبد الله علي عزيري–.
SAU001002	باسم الله الرحمن الرحيم.
SAU001003	في هذه النشرة.
SAU001004	وزير الخارجية الامريكيّ يتوجّه الى المغرب لاستكمال مباحثاته حول عملية السلام في الشرق الاوسط.
SAU001005	اللجنة الشعبية الكويتية تهيب بمنظّمة الصليب الاحمر الدولية العمل على إطلاق سراح الاسرى المحتجزين لدى النظام العراقيّ.
SAU001006	الحكومة اليونانية ترحّب بإعلان الرئيس الامريكيّ عن عقد اجتماع حول قبرص برعاية الامم المتّحدة.
SAU001007	المجاهدون الافغان يعلنون عن سيطرتهِم على مدينة إقليمية هامة شرق افغانستان.
SAU001008	مجلس الرئاسة اليوغسلافيّ يبحث مشروع قرار بوقف فوريّ لإطلاق النار وغير مشروط في جمهورية كرواتيا التي تشهد وضعا خطيرا ومتدهورا.
SAU001009	تفصيلات النشرة.
SAU001010	يعتزم وزير الخارجية الامريكيّ = جيمس بيكر – الذي يسعى الى حشد تأييد لعقد مؤتمر للسلام في الشرق الاوسط توسيع نطاق مهمّته اليوم السبت بإجراء محادثات في المغرب.

This way the whole file was entered in a large file divided along type of program and country. Thereupon a program was developed which uses the sentence as standard unit. In the following table[3] we give a sur-

[3] (cf. Moore 1994: 492).

vey of the number of sentences for each country and for each type of broadcast.

	Algeria	**Egypt**	**Saudi Arabia**	**Total**
News commentary	19	1124	80	1223
News broadcasts	3025	2800	2496	8321
Reportage	624	762	0	1386
Sports news	487	0	28	515
Total	4155	4686	2604	11445

Table 1

10.2.3. *Kwic-sentence software*

The composition of a KWIC-index program for sentences is technically not an easy matter, given that sentences have different lengths. Another problem is that some words have such a high frequency that the output of the KWIC-index program for sentences becomes huge and difficult to control. For this reason we provided options in the program which give the user the possibility of limiting the number of sentences for each country and for each program. When we search for the preposition *'ilā*, for instance, we limit ourselves to 100, 200 or more sentences depending on the requirements.

This KWIC-index has a few interesting characteristics because of the use of a 'similarity-factor'. The 'similarity-factor' indicates which string or substring is being searched. Every search is indicated by an encoding.

The following patterns are possible (as an example we look for the word WORK):

Encoding	example	explanation
0	Work	completely identical
1	WORKable, WORK	identical at the beginning of a word
2	reWORKing	identical in the word
3	overWORK, WORK	identical at the end of a word
4	WORK, WORKable,	
	reWORKing,	
	overWORK	the searched word is a substring

Table 2

We want to point out here that some patterns imply other patterns. Pattern 4, of course, implies all the other patterns, but patterns 1 and 3 also imply pattern 0. Only pattern 2 checks whether there is an additional character before the string searched for, which means that pattern 0 is excluded. On the basis of this KWIC-index program for sentences different analyses can be implemented, as we will show later on (cf. infra 10.3.).

10.2.4. *Software for frequency counts*

Since all the words in the texts have been encoded systematically and consistently, it is now possible to execute detailed counts of the words in the texts. To limit the possibilities we did not include the Arabic suffixes. An example can illustrate this. In the following relatively simple English sentence: "Today I will take you to school in this car," we immediately count, without any problem, 10 words.

For the same sentence in Arabic (*al-yawma sa-'uwaṣṣiluka 'ilā l-madrasati bi-hāḏihi s-sayyārati*) we count, when taking only the blanks into account, only six words. This means that, if we count the words by only taking into account blanks, we obtain in Arabic only half the number of words we obtain in English. However, when we take into account the prefixes, we obtain 11 words. If we also take the suffixes into account, we obtain 12 words.[4] We programmed the counting software in such a way that it took into account all the prefixes. The suffixes, however, were not counted as separate words, which of course is technically possible.[5]

By means of this counting software we can define very precisely how many words the corpus counts. The first part of the following table (3a) gives a survey of the total number of words as well as a few specific characteristics, such as the number of proper names which occur, the number of dialectal words, the number of words which could not be understood and the number of times a grammatical construction was identi-

[4] It depends, of course, on how the concept of 'word' is defined. One might consider a word tobe a string of characters betwen two blanks. In that case we count in this sentence six words. The particles might be considerd of as lexemes. In that case *sa-'uwaṣṣiluka* might be counted as one word and three lexemes. The point I want to stress is that because of the agglutinative character of Arabic word counts differ compared to other languages.

[5] A detail we do not want to withhold is that in our corpus the word اليوم (*today*) is counted as one word because the definite article was seen as forming a whole with the word. Contrary to, for instance هذا اليوم (*this day*) where the definite article was, indeed, counted. اليوم (*today*) was considered of as one word and one lexeme and اليوم (*the day*) as one word and two lexemes.

fied as unusual (cf. supra 10.1.). The second part of the table (3b) shows the division of the total number of words. The definite article and a few particles are also separately counted.

News broadcasts	**Algeria**		**Egypt**		**Saudi Arabia**	
	N	%	N	%	N	%
Total	**80062**	100	**80242**	100	**81127**	100
Proper name:	2997	3.74	2997	3.73	3171	3.9
Dialectal Word:	7	0.008	9	0.011	1	0.001
Unidentifiable Word:	71	0.09	103	0.128	77	0.094
Grammatical Problem:	58	0.07	21	0.026	18	0.02

Table 3a

The basic corpus (= the news broadcasts cf. supra 8.5.) contains in total 241,431 words. We can now check whether there is a relation between the variables of the column (country) and the variables of the row in the occurrence of proper names, dialectal words, etc.) We allege as a hypothesis that there is *no relation* between the variables of the column and the variables of the row. As an alternative hypothesis we allege that there is, indeed, a relationship between both variables. When we apply the chi-square test we can judge whether the observed relation is statistically significant.

We do this by comparing the observed value with the expected value on which we calculate the chi-square. For the proportion of the number of proper names compared to the total number of words we do not obtain a significant difference, viz. a χ^2 value of 4.24, whereas, according to the tables (cf. Neter 1988) we only get a significant difference with a χ^2 value of 10.60 (with a 99.5% certainty). The same goes for the chi-square values of the dialectal interference (χ^2: 6.20) and of the unidentifiable words (χ^2: 7.04). Consequently, this survey shows very clearly that we have chosen a similar language stratum for the three countries.

The percentage of proper nouns does not show a significant difference. Dialectal interference is very low and varies from 0.001% in Saudi Arabia over 0.008% in Algeria to 0.01% in Egypt. However though still low, dialectal interference is the highest in Egypt. Furthermore we can say that an average of one word in a thousand was not identifiable. This percentage is higher for the recordings from Egypt, mainly because of the bad quality of the recordings from Egypt. In all countries the recordings were made directly by cable from the radio, whereas a large number of recordings in Egypt was made by putting the microphone in front of the radio, which means that a lot of disturbing noise was heard on the tape, such as car horns, etc.).

However, as far as unusual grammatical constructions are concerned, we do obtain a significant difference with the chi-square test (χ^2: 31.21). It is striking that we found more sentences with grammatical problematic constructions in Algeria viz. 0.07%, whereas this percentage was the lowest in Saudi Arabia with a percentage of 0.02%.

News broadcasts	**Algeria**		**Egypt**		**Saudi Arabia**	
	N	%	N	%	N	%
Words	56681	70.796	56721	70.687	56040	69.076
wa:	2984	3.727	3834	4.778	4775	5.885
fa:	93	0.116	91	0.113	82	0.101
bi:	1775	2.217	1658	2.066	1642	2.023
ka:	28	0.034	36	0.045	25	0.038
sa:	218	0.272	212	0.264	220	0.271
li (subjunctive):	38	0.047	19	0.024	18	0.022
Definite article:	16529	20.645	15952	19.879	16572	20.427
lām (preposition):	1716	2.143	1719	2.142	1753	2.160
Total:	**80062**	100	**80242**	100	**81127**	100

Table 3b

The application of the chi-square test on this table clearly shows that there are significant differences. Indeed, for this table we get a χ^2-value of 446.51, whereas the χ^2-table value, with a 99.5% certainty, amounts to 34.27. What strikes one most in Table 3b is that the distribution of the different particles is equally spread. The only significant difference is the use of the conjunction *wa* which is used differently: in Algeria relatively seldom (3.7%), in Egypt considerably more (4.8%) and in Saudi Arabia quite a lot (5.9%). This phenomenon will be investigated lateron. Moreover, these numbers teach us something about the minimum size of a corpus (cf. supra 8.1.). It is clear that a corpus of 100,000 words contains a large amount of data, for instance, to investigate the use of the construct state. On the other hand, when we want to investigate the use of the particle *ka,* we will only find an average occurrence of 39 in a corpus of 100,000 words.

The reportages give a similar distribution:

reportage's:	Algeria		Egypt	
	N	%	N	%
Total:	**17622**	100	**23148**	100
Proper names:	545	3.09	900	3.88
Dialectal words:	16	0.09	19	0.08
Unidentifiable Word:	96	0.54	72	0.31
Grammatical Problem:	24	0.14	12	0.05

Table 4a

From this table it is clear that the dialectal interference in the reportages is approximately ten times as high as the dialectal interference in the news broadcasts (respectively 0.09% compared to 0.008% for Algeria and 0.08% compared to 0.01% for Egypt). In the reportages we also observed a higher percentage of unidentifiable words. This is probably due to the fact that reportages are mostly sent by means of a telephone which does not improve the quality of the sound. There are also more grammatical problematic constructions than in the news broadcasts. Here too we observe a lot more problematic constructions in Algeria than in Egypt. The last difference with the news broadcasts (Table 3b) is the more frequent use of the particle *fa* viz. an average of 0.3% compared to 0.1% in the news broadcasts.

reportages:	Algeria		Egypt	
	N	%	N	%
Words:	12263	69.589	16204	70.001
wa:	882	5.005	1300	5.616
fa:	63	0.357	75	0.324
bi:	483	2.740	474	2.047
ka:	16	0.090	12	0.051
sa:	45	0.255	57	0.246
li (conj):	11	0.062	14	0.060
Definite article:	3499	19.855	4650	20.088
lām:	360	2.042	362	1.563
Total:	**17622**	100	**23148**	100

Table 4b

For the news commentaries (Table 5) we only give the Egyptian percentages; the nominal values of the commentaries of other countries are too low to draw conclusions. We will give the nominal values only to illustrate the amount of broadcast time devoted to commentaries in the news.

News commentary:	**Algeria**		**Egypt**		**Saudi Arabia**	
	N	%	N	%	N	%
Total:	652		**32524**	100	2684	
Proper name:	0		654	2.01	42	
Dialectal Word:	0		3	0.009	0	
Unidentifiable Word:	2		69	0.212	10	
Grammatical Problem:	1		6	0.018	1	

Table 5a

Compared to the other types of news we here discover a much lower number of proper nouns. There is also a very low percentage of dialectal interference (0.009%) and an even more frequent use of the particles *fa* and *wa* (Table 5b). For the rest, percentages are strikingly equal to the other types of broadcasts.

News commentary:	**Algeria**		**Egypt**		**Saudi Arabia**	
	N	%	N	%	N	%
Word:	463		22388	68.835	1853	
wa:	32		2208	6.788	178	
fa:	5		184	0.565	5	
bi:	18		678	2.084	66	
ka:	2		12	0.036	0	
sa:	0		60	0.184	3	
li (conj):	0		28	0.086	2	
Definite article:	121		6339	19.490	535	
lām:	11		627	1.927	42	
Total:	652		**32524**	100	2684	

Table 5b

Finally, we will give a survey of the sports news but only of Algeria.

Sports news	**Algeria**		**Saudi Arabia**	
	N	%	N	%
Total:	**13632**	100	731	
Proper name:	853	6.257	67	
Dialectal Word:	33	0.242	0	
Unidentifiable Word:	37	0.271	0	
Grammatical Problem:	20	0.146	0	

Table 6a

The higher percentage of dialectal interference in sports news catches the eye. It is the highest percentage of all the programs, viz. 0.042%. There is also a high percentage of unidentifiable words. This is because of the fact that, in general, reporters read much faster in sports news and that they do not articulate very well when they read.

In the following table (6b) there is a survey of the distribution of the particles in sports news.

Sports news	**Algeria**		**Saudi Arabia**	
	N	%	N	%
Word:	9713	71.251	515	
wa:	553	4.056	28	
fa:	35	0.256	3	
bi:	388	2.846	12	
ka:	1	0.007	0	
sa:	66	0.484	1	
li (conj):	5	0.036	0	
Definite article:	2551	18.713	155	
lām:	320	2.347	17	
Total:	**13632**	100	731	

Table 6b

The main corpus and the control corpus together contain 332,434 words. Overall, we observe that the percentages clearly indicate that we have to do with a similar type of language use. By way of illustration we give the statistical data with regard to a much smaller corpus, interviews of radio Algiers, which were recorded in the same period. In spite of the fact that pure dialectal interviews were excluded from this corpus (Van

Mol 1992), it is more heterogeneous because of the different language levels (cf. Badawī 1973).

Interviews	Algeria	
	N	%
Word:	14244	70.830
wa:	1129	5.614
fa:	132	0.656
bi:	465	2.312
ka:	43	0.213
sa:	40	0.198
li (conj):	13	0.064
Definite article:	3634	18.070
lām:	410	2.038
Total:	20110	100

Table 7

This table clearly illustrates the methodological importance of the precise delimitation of text samples. When we apply the chi-square test on the different kinds of text samples from Algeria we get a χ^2-value of 585.47 compared to a table value of 45.56, with a 99.5% certainty. Indeed, it strikes that within *one* country, in this case Algeria, the use of the conjunction varies significantly depending on the type of broadcast. The vertical variation seems to be very high (cf. supra, introduction p. 5). The occurrence in terms of percentage of the particle *fa* is the lowest in the news broadcasts (0.1%), a little bit higher in sports news (0.256%), still higher in the reportages (0.36%), and still much higher in interviews (0.66%). These statistics clearly show that for the study of horizontal variation within MSA, the delimitation of the text samples is of crucial importance.

10.2.5. *Decoding software*

Finally we also developed a program which transformed all the encoded texts into normal unvocalized texts. In order to increase the readability we preferred to maintain all *šadda's* in the printed text. Here too, however, many alternatives are possible; this depends on the programming. It is clear that, in order to work in a more efficient way, all the previous programs ought to be integrated in one program, which is technically no problem. Furthermore, it is desirable in the future to develop a much more efficient explorer for the corpus, one which attributes, not only the parts of speech to every word (secondary encoding) but which is also able to investigate relationships between words and parts of speech in a sentence. These, however, are technical computational problems which have to be developed in the (near) future. In the following paragraphs we will give a short survey of the possibilities and limitations of the software, such as it has been developed in order to explore the corpus.

10.3. Exploration of corpora: The testing of hypothesies

In the following paragraphs we test a few hypothesies at random in order to show some possibilities of corpus exploration. Some hypothesies are related to lexicon, others to syntax.

10.3.1. *Distribution of the plural forms* 'ašḫāṣ *and* šuḫūṣ

In 7.5. (supra: note 23) we wondered whether certain word forms have disappeared in Arabic. This might be part of language evolution. It should be possible to check whether certain words and word forms are still frequently used in MSA today. We notice that in Arabic dictionaries two plural forms are given for the substantive *šaḫṣ* (person). Analysis of the corpus reveals that in none of the investigated countries is the second plural *šuḫūṣ* (still?) used. The only prevailing plural for the substantive *šaḫṣ* is *'ašḫāṣ*.

10.3.2. *Distribution of the substantive* najā'a

According to Farhat (1989: 7) certain words are exclusively used in North Africa (cf. supra introduction). He does not clarify whether he means by North Africa the whole geographical area or only the Maghreb. The only examples he gives are the words *najā'a* (*benefit*) and *'aḥṣaru*. The second word does not occur in our corpus. Conversely, the word *najā'a* only occurs twice in the Algerian corpus, once in a news commentary, and once in a reportage, in the following sentences:

ALG.001.015

ثالثا إنّ الوزن الدبلوماسيّ الذي تحظى بـهِ دول المغرب الـعربيّ بـفعل العديد من الاعتبارات ونشاطه على الـساحة الـدوليّة والـعربيّة يترك تساؤلا حول ما يمكن أن تقوم بها هذه الدول خاصّة وأنّ الـماضي القريب يشهد على ← نجاعة وساطاتها في العديد من النزاعات.

"The diplomatic weight, which the countries of the Arab Maghreb acquire by means of their considerations and activities on the international and Arabic scene, leaves open the question, about what these countries can do, especially because the near past witnessed the ***benefit*** *of her mediatory efforts in diverse conflicts."*

ALG.003.294

وقد استطعنا من خلال تتبّعنا لاشغال الملتقى، الملتقى أقول، تسجيل قناعة جماعيّة لدى إطارات هذه الشركة وهي أن استقلالية المؤسسات نمط او نمط تسيير له ← نجاعته الاقتصاديّة.

"In following the activities of the conference, we were able to record the common conviction of the senior officials of this firm, which is that the independence of the firms is a style of management which has its ***benefit****."*

Corpus investigation confirms on this point Farhat's proposition.[6]

10.3.3. *The use of the preposition* ʿan *after* badalan

According to Al-Ḥalīm & Al-Fiqīy (1988: 103) and Al-ʿAdnānī (1989: 49) the media often make a mistake using the preposition *ʿan* after *badalan* instead of the preposition *min*. Investigation of the corpus reveals that in every country and in every type of text the correct preposition *min* is used. We were not able to observe regional differences. The division is as follows: ALG/N: 6; ALG/R: 2; ALG/S: 4; EGY/C: 4; EGY/N: 2; SAU/N: 7. In every country, within the news media, on this point the grammatical norm is applied.

10.3.4. *The gender of some substantives ending in* alif-maqṣūra

Substantives with the weak third consonant indefinite ending *-an* and definite *ā*, are masculine. In order to verify this proposition we conduct a limited investigation in the corpus into the gender of the words *(al)-*

[6] See also introduction note 8.

mustawā (*level*), *(al)-mustašfā* (*hospital*) and *(al)-ma'nā* (*meaning*). We want, however, to remark that the gender of these words can not be defined on the basis of the simple occurrence of these words in a text. Indeed, in order to define the gender those words have to be preceded by a demonstrative, or a verb or followed by an adjective.[7] When the substantive is isolated or in construct state, the gender cannot possibly be deduced. The gender of these words is neither given in the dictionaries of Wehr (1979), Al-Munjid (1972), Abdel-Nour (1983), Reig (1983), nor in Doniach (1985). Only Reig gives a few collocations with the words *ma'nā* (m) and *mustawā* (m) which makes it possible to deduce the gender.

Corpus analysis, in the first place, reveals that the substantive *mustawā* (ALG: 11; EGY: 6; SAO: 5) is masculine in the three countries. In the corpus there are only two occurrences of the word *ma'nā*, both in Egypt, but without any indication from which the gender can be deduced. One collocation reveals a masculine gender and the other a feminine gender. This means that we do not have enough evidence to draw conclusions on the gender of the word *ma'nā*. As far as the word *mustašfā* is concerned there is a large diversity. In Algeria, we only registered one occurrence in which *mustašfā* stands in collocation with a masculine adjective. In Saudi Arabia, however, we traced a masculine form five times and a feminine one five times. We may conclude that some substantives ending on *alif-maqṣūra* are masculine whereas for some words, such as, for example, *mustašfā* the choice is free.

10.3.5. *The passive form and the mentioning of the agent*

Cowan (1973: 59) points out that the agent cannot be used in a passive form (cf. supra 2.3.3.). He argues: a sentence, such as: "This book was written by Dickens" ought to be converted into: "Dickens wrote this book". Cantarino (1974, part 2: 53) holds the same view, but more in a descriptive way.[8] Stoetzer (1991: 192) too asserts that "the passive Arabic form is only used when the agent is not mentioned. The origin of the act can be indicated by making use of the construction *min qibali* or

[7] On a total of 152 of these words which occur in the corpus, only 46 give information about the gender of the words through collocation. There are simply not many words ending in *alif-maqṣūra*.

[8] "If the agent has to be mentioned, Arabic repeats the same sentence in the active voice: قد مُدت المائدة مدتها كبرى اخوات الصبي (*The table had been set by the boy's oldest sister*). (Cantarino 1974, dl 1: 53).

min jānib. According to Blohm & Reuschel (1981: dl II/2: 883) the agent can be mentioned in a passive construction.[9]

Investigation of the corpus reveals that the agent is, indeed, mentioned with the use of a passive form. Although the occurrence of the construction *min jānib* is relatively high (ALG: 11; EGY: 38; SAU: 23), it never occurs with a passive form (in contrast with the allegations of Stoetzer and Blohm). It does occur in other circumstances in the meaning of *by* and *on the part of*. The construction *'alā yad* (Reuschel) seems to be semantically limited in the radio news to the connotation of *being murdered by* or *being killed by*. Analysis of the corpus clearly reveals that the agent in a passive form is mentioned by making use of the construction *min qibali* and the construction *min ṭaraf*. We do, however, observe a regional difference. The construction *min ṭaraf* is limited to Algeria. This construction does not occur in Egypt, nor in Saudi Arabia. It clearly is a regionalism.[10]

On the other hand, the construction *min qibali* occurs in all three countries, as well as in Algeria. Further on we observe that the expressions *min qibali* and *min ṭarafi*are not only used after a passive verb but also after a *maṣdar* or after a participle in the meaning of *by* and *on the part of*. We often found expressions such as, for example: *mu'lan min ṭaraf announced by* (ALG/N), *hajamāt min qibali attacked by* (EGY/N) and *taṣrīḥ min qibali a declaration on the part of* (SAU/N). The same goes for the construction *min jānib* which is exclusively used in this meaning. We may conclude by stating that in the modern language use of the Arabic media the agent is, indeed, used and there is even a regional variation.

10.3.6. *The use of a particle after the verb* qāla

According to Blau (1973: 206) the construction *qāla bi-'anna* is used more and more in MSA. In addition to *qāla 'inna* it also occurred in Classical Arabic and the construction *qāla bi-'anna* was also frequently

[9] "Gelegentlich in Zeitungstexten, häufiger in Vertragstexten kommt die Bezeichnung des Urhebers (Agens) durch من جانب ,من قِبَل ,على يد vor. Hierbei handelt es sich offensichtlich um Lehnübersetzungen aus indoeuropäischen Sprachen" (Blohm & Reuschel 1982, II/2: 883-4).

[10] Otten (1983: 25) observes the use of *min ṭaraf* in the Moroccan dialect, but in his opinion it is a loan from Dutch (sic.). He writes: 'In Morocco it is not used frequently, but in Holland it is used frequently in a passive context in order to correspond to the Dutch *door* (*by*)'. In my view the expression *min ṭaraf* is probably a *calque* from French as a translation of *de la part de*.

used in Middle-Arabic. According to Reuschel & Krahl (1980, part 1: 165) the verb *qāla* is always followed by the particle *'inna* to introduce direct speech. In the second volume of the work by Blohm & Reuschel (1981: part 2: 103), however, it is said that the verb *qāla* can be followed by *bi-'anna*, without any further comment.

In the case of an introduction to direct speech, Cantarino (1974, part 3: 128) only mentions the particle *'inna*: "After the verb قال, 'to say,' إنّ is used as if it were introducing a direct speech or quotation. Hence, we find إنّ used after verbs equivalent in meaning to the above with the same implication of direct speech. إنّ is also usually found after قال, even in cases of a clear indirect speech." With reference to indirect speech Cantarino (1974, dl 3: 129) writes: "In indirect speech however, or whenever قال has a meaning equivalent to other verbs of oral communication such as "to narrate", "to express", "to affirm", etc. أنّ can also be used." Cantarino does not mention the construction *qāla bi-'anna*. Although the particle *'inna* is omitted in some sample sentences in the work by Cantarino, this topic is not discussed any further.

On the basis of written texts the use of the particle after *qāla* is difficult to investigate because the *hamza* is hardly ever written (cf. supra 9.3.3.). Even when it is it is not sure it was written so on purpose. By making use of an oral MSA corpus it of course becomes easy to clearly distinguish the use of the particles *'inna* and *'anna* after the verb *qāla*. When investigating the use of the particles after *qāla* in the corpus we get the following results for news broadcasts:

News broadcasts:	**Algeria**		**Egypt**		**Saudi Arabia**		**Total**	
	N	%	N	%	N	%	N	%
'inna	123	67	142	91	176	83	441	80
'anna	12	7	6	4	3	1.5	21	4
bi-'anna	4	2	1	0.5	1	0.5	6	1
elision	19	10	6	4	29	14	54	10
as parenthesis	26	14	1	0.5	2	1	29	5
Total	184	100	156	100	211	100	511	100

Table 8

The calculation of the chi-square on this table gives us (with a 99.5% certainty) an χ^2-value of 66.70 against a table value of 21.96. From this table we deduct that the particle *'inna* is most frequently used after the verb *qāla*, to introduce direct speech. In general, in an important percentage of the cases the particle is concealed and the predicate follows without introductory particle. The construction *qāla bi-'anna* mentioned by Blau occurs in all countries, but to a limited extent. Both in Egypt and Saudi Arabia in only one of the 200 cases, in Algeria a little bit more. More frequent, but still marginal indeed, is the use of the particle *'anna* to introduce direct speech instead of *'inna*, which is more frequently used in Algeria than in the other two countries. The use of the verb *qāla* in a parenthesis is striking. In that case direct speech is started but then interrupted to indicate the source, and then direct speech is completed, such as, for example in the following sentence:

ALG.002.131

الفرق الوحيد بين القطاعين

← **تقول** اللائحة هو أنّ الأوّل ذو رأسمال خاصّ والثاني ذو رأسمال عموميّ.

"The only difference between the two sectors says the statute is that the first originates from private capital and the second from public capital."

This construction occurs very frequently in Algeria. It indicates a more flexible and freer style. In Egypt and Saudi Arabia the parenthesis is always limited to the saying: كما قال. When we compare the results of the main corpus with the control corpus we obtain the following picture:

Other forms	ALG/R		ALG/S		EGY/C		EGY/R	
	N	%	N	%	N	%	N	%
'inna	13	39	0	0	24	80	55	63
'anna	0	3	0	0	1	3	11	13
bi-'anna	1	3	1	25	0	0	1	1
elision	5	15	2	50	4	14	13	15
as parenthesis	13	39	1	25	1	3	7	8
Total	33	100	4	100	30	100	87	100

Table 9

It is striking that the use of *'inna* in EGY/C corresponds to the average of the main corpus. Of course the language type is the same, viz. formal language use. However, we observe much larger differences between the use of *'inna* in the reportages of Egypt and Algeria compared to the main corpus. Furthermore, we observe that in EGY/R *'anna* is significantly more frequent (13%) than in EGY/N (4%) and EGY/C (3%). As far as Egypt is concerned, this might indicate a kind of hypercorrection.[11] Finally, the control corpus also reveals that the use of *bi-'anna* remains marginal.

As a matter of fact the above case very clearly shows the complexity of the vocalizing and tagging of unvocalized written Arabic texts (cf. supra 9.3.3.). Does the unvocalized particle ان after the verb *qāla* always have to be vocalized as *'inna* or do we have to respect the proportion *'anna-'inna* such as it has been demonstrated above. This might mean that, for instance, for Algerian texts, one out of ten ان ought to be encoded as *'anna*.

10.3.7. *The correspondence with* 'ayy

As far as the use of *'ayy* in MSA is concerned, Stetkevych (1970: 90) writes the following: "Another tendency is to differentiate the gender concordance of *'ayy* (which, which one). In classical Arabic *'ayy* is used indiscriminately with nouns of masculine and feminine concordances (where he refers to Reckendorf 1921: 148). In modern Arabic, on the contrary, its use with the feminine ending (*'ayya*) is extremely frequent, and a more systematic concordance of gender tends to become the normal usage in prose as well as in poetry." An investigation of the whole corpus gives us the following picture:

Total Corpus:	**Algeria**		**Egypt**		**Saudi Arabia**		**Total**	
	N	%	N	%	N	%	N	%
'ayy (m) + sub (m)	33		92		32		158	
'ayya (f) + sub (m)	1		0		0		1	
'ayya (f) + sub (f)	14	78	23	55	10	83	47	65
'ayy (m) + sub (f)	4	22	19	45	2	17	25	35
SubTotal 1	18	100	42	100	12	100	72	100
'ayya (f) + sub (pl)	10	83	32	62	11	61	53	65
'ayy (m) + sub (pl)	2	17	20	38	7	39	29	35
SubTotal 2	12	100	52	100	18	100	82	100

Table 10

Analysis of the corpus reveals, indeed, that there certainly is a tendency to adapt the gender of the noun *'ayy* to the gender of the following substantive. The percentage of the cases where the speakers stick to the

[11] Cf. Schulz (1981: 108 and 152).

classical grammar always keeping the form *'ayy* regardless of the gender of the following substantive, is, however, fairly high. In Egypt the division is approximately equal, whereas in Algeria the adaptation to the gender is proportionally much higher. We consider the only case in which a masculine substantive corresponds with a feminine form of *'ayy* as a slip of the tongue.

The correspondence between the noun *'ayy* with a following plural substantive (things) is also interesting. In most cases, the correspondence follows the rules, viz. *'ayy* feminine singular. It is, however, remarkable that in an important number of cases the noun *'ayy* remains masculine singular. This occurs, for instance, with words of the form *fu'ūl*. Such a form is ambiguous. It can be interpreted as a *maṣdar*, for instance, *duḫūl* (*entrance*), and consequently masculine singular, or as a plural, for instance, *burūj* (*tours*). In the case of the word *hujūm* (*attack*) we clearly have to do with a singular form. For the word *ḍuġūṭ* (*pressure*) identification is more complicated because it is a substantive plural.[12] The masculine form of *'ayy* has, among others, been found in collocation with the words: *ḥudūd* (*borders*), *šurūṭ* (*conditions*), *mašākil* (*problems*), *tafāṣīl* (*details*) and *'a'māl* (*activities*).

10.3.8. *The cardinals from 11 to 19*

In order to investigate this element of Arabic grammar, the analysis of 'spoken' corpora is necessary. Indeed, numbers are mostly written in texts as numerals, which makes it impossible to find out how they are pronounced. Harrell's investigations (1960) in particular led to the widespread conviction that Arabs often use dialectical forms of the cardinals above ten in the oral realization of MSA. His investigation, however, was very limited. He transcribed only one short news broadcast from Egypt (approximately 1,200 words) in addition to a short announcement of wave lengths on which the Egyptian radio could be heard. Although Harrell's work is very valuable at the phonological level, his corpus is too limited to draw lexicographical or syntactical conclusions. Moreover, he generalizes his findings to Egyptian Radio Arabic, whereas the Arabic of the Egyptian radio can hardly be limited to one news broadcast.

[12] In Algeria, for instance, also double plurals are found, such as حشودات (*ḥušūdāt* '*masses*'). The word حُشُود (*ḥušūd*) is already a plural of حَشْد (*ḥašd*). It is, however, possible that حشود (*ḥušūd*) is considered a singular form.

Harrell writes: “The category in which ERA (Egyptian Radio Arabic) deviates most sharply from the Classical is the numerals. (...) For the simpler numerals from one to ten, announcers are generally consistent in reproducing the classical forms. For numbers above ten, the pattern is a straightforward use of colloquial numbers without even an attempt at the classical forms” (Harrell 1960: 49). All of the forms from 11 to 19 which Harrell counted in his language sample were dialectal forms except one. This conclusion by Harrell was later adopted by Bateson (1967: 86) and Killean (1970: 423) who argue that the use of dialectal numbers steadily increases in the oral use of Modern Literary Arabic. Palva, referring to Harrell, holds the same view: “It is well known that even in reading a written standard classical Arabic text the simple colloquial numeral system is often used” (Palva 1969: 32). Diem (1974: 48) too points out that dialectal interference is very high especially in the numbers from 11 to 19.[13]

When investigating the main corpus on the use of the cardinals from 11 to 19, we obtain the following result:

News broadcasts:	**Algeria**		**Egypt**		**Saudi Arabia**		**Total**	
	N	%	N	%	N	%	N	%
MSA form	54	91	49	92	73	97	176	94
Dialectal form	5	9	4	8	2	3	11	6
Total	59	100	53	100	75	100	187	100

Table 11

The claim of the above-mentioned authors that in the realization of oral MSA dialectal forms are more frequently used than MSA forms is definitely incorrect. When reading aloud, and we are convinced that the news readers do not write numbers in full, MSA forms are used. Analysis of the corpus reveals that dialectal forms only occur in certain contexts. Four of the five dialectal forms in Algeria occurred in the type number of an American fighter, viz. F-15 etc. The same goes for one of the four dialectal forms in the Egyptian news broadcast. From the other three in Egypt two occurred in the Exchange values and one in a literal citation of the declaration of a politician. When we compare these results with the control corpus we observe interesting shifts.

[13] See also Schulz (1981: 131).

Control corpus:	ALG/R		ALG/S		EGY/C		EGY/R	
	N	%	N	%	N	%	N	%
MSA form	4	67	6	6	6	100	4	29
Dialectal form	2	33	32	84	0	0	10	71
Total	6	100	38	100	6	100	14	100

Table 12

We observe that within the different parts of the news broadcasts a lot of variation becomes visible. In the first place we did not observe dialectal influences in Egyptian news commentaries. As a matter of fact, in contrast with Diem (1974: 64) we found that the news commentaries in Egypt are almost completely free of dialectal influence (cf. supra 10.2.4.). We observe in the reportages of Algeria a larger increase of dialectal forms, but the nominal value is too small to draw conclusions. On the other hand, in the Algerian sports news almost exclusively dialectal forms are used, in contrast with the general news broadcasts. For completeness' sake we have to mention that in four cases the number concerned the proper name of a football stadium.

The above data give an idea of the possibilities which are offered by modern computer linguistics to conduct language investigations. As far as the investigation into language variation is concerned we have to remain cautious. Indeed, in the investigation into variation, the element of uniformity may not be neglected. This is why we will make a more thorough investigation and complete analysis of Arabic particles in which we take into account both variation and uniformity

PART III

EMPIRICAL INVESTIGATION

11. INVESTIGATION OF VARIATION IN BROADCAST MSA

For the empirical study we want, in the first place, to conduct an investigation into variation in MSA in news broadcasts. We have already mentioned that some investigations demonstrate that dialects can exert a certain influence on MSA (cf. supra. 5.2.) and that it is possible that even European languages exert an influence on MSA (cf. supra. 5.4.) The study of such influences requires a specific approach which, however, is out of the scope of our investigation. We also indicated that the differences between MSA and Classical Arabic often are subtle and that in the Arab world often no distinction is made between these two varieties (2.3.3.). Some grammarians assume the existence of a universal Arabic grammar. For this reason we want to contrast our findings with such grammars. The possible contrasts between our findings from the corpus and those grammars can be due to the difference in the kind of texts studied, though, in my view, it also can be an indication of internal language evolution.

If we assume that internal language evolution (cf. Roman 1987: 135) occurs, primarily, in those elements of the language where an option is possible, then it seems advisable to limit the investigation to the already existing institutional variation (cf. supra 1.1.4.).[1] Therefore, when studying Cantarino's three-volume study (1974) and Reuschel (1980) we looked, first of all, for the already existing institutional variation.

Indeed, what strikes one most is that (cf. supra 2.3.3.) certain dissimilarities between MSA and Classical Arabic in the field of syntax have more to do with a *shift* in language use. In other words, constructions which were seldom used in the past come to the fore and gain importance. More specifically, we think about new forms of the construct state, forms which also occurred in Classical Arabic but on a (semantically) more limited scale.[2] This also applies to shift in word order. Indeed, many authors assume that MSA, contrary to Classical Arabic, is characterized by a SVO (Subject-Verb-Object) word order. However,

[1] Cf. Sapir (1921) who demonstrated that a language does not evolve at random, but according to certain patterns which are defined by the structure of the language. See also Martinet (1955).

[2] Cf. Gully (1993: 24) who points out that the double construct state, such as "*sayfu* wa *rimḥu Zayd*", occurs in the works of Wright and Pérès.

we observe that the SVO-structure did occur in Classical Arabic, and even on a not so limited scale (cf. texts of Lyons 1962).[3] In other words, already in Classical Arabic an institutional variation could be found.

When studying the works of Cantarino and Reuschel we were struck by the fact that the institutional variation was most prominent in the particles. For this reason we limit the field of investigation to the particles. As a first step we make an inventory of the definitions of the concept 'particle'.

11.1. The particle as grammatical category

The word *ḥarf* (حَرْف) is polysemic. It means both 'letter' and 'particle'.[4] The original meaning is revealing: originally the word meant 'edge, border'. We may assume that the Arab grammarians named them so because of their functional character at the 'edges' of content words.[5] Indeed, in most cases these words are function words which have no meaning when they are used independently (cf. Al-Batal 1990: 265). In order to clarify the distinction between the two original meanings of the word *ḥarf* it is preferable to use the term *ḥurūf al-mabānī* when indicating letters and the term *ḥurūf al-maʿānī* when indicating particles (Ad-Daḥdāḥ 1990: 7 and Al-ʿUmarī 1993).

The second term which is used for a number of particles is also clarifying. The word أداة (*'adāt*) means 'instrument', 'tool'. These meanings too may point out that Arab grammarians, indeed, considered these words to be function words. From the very beginning Arabs have tried to define the concept of *ḥarf*. In the *al-Jumal* by *Az-Zajjājī* the following definition is found, which, according to Fleisch (1979: 499) is still used by modern Arab grammarians, viz. *al-ḥarf mā dalla ʿalā maʿnā fī ġayrihi*. (*The particle is what indicates (clarifies) the meaning in another word)*. Obviously, every word has a meaning that is related to the

[3] Corpus investigation can give a decisive answer on this point. Only then we can demonstrate the correct proportions of occurrence of certain constructions.

[4] Letter in the sence of grapheme. Cf. Dichy: "On connaît cependant les deux sens concernant notre propos, du mot *ḥarf* (plur. *ḥurūf*): 'son de la langue', 'segment', ou 'lettre d'alphabet.'" (Dichy 1990: 112). See also Fischer (1989) who describes in a very clarifying way the evolution in meaning of the particle *ḥarf*. He also points out that *Sībawayhi* was the first who used the word *ḥarf* in the meaning of particle.

[5] Cf. Dichy who also refers to the word *ḥarf* as reading of the Coran: "C'est ainsi que l'on dit: 'Un tel récite [le Coran] selon le *ḥarf* de *'Abū 'Amr'*, ou d'un autre lecteur, car le *ḥarf* est la limite ou le côté [qui permet de distinguer] entre ces deux lectures" (Dichy 1990: 118).

context. Maybe it is better to define the word 'particle' as a word which in itself is not meaning*ful*. A particle becomes meaningful only in relation with a verb or a noun. If not, it is not completely meaning*less*, but it is not meaning*ful* either.

11.2. THE CONCEPT OF COMPLEMENTARY PARTICLE

The category of the particle is very large. In order to investigate the use of particles, we limit ourselves to those particles which are mutually complementary. Indeed, as far as institutional variation is concerned, we can distinguish between constructions and grammatical elements which are *equivalent*, constructions and grammatical elements which are *similar*, and constructions and grammatical elements which are *unique*. In the first case constructions are involved which are mutually switchable without an occurrence of change in meaning. Pure equivalent constructions are probably rare in a language; nevertheless, some authors do point out that certain constructions are mutually exchangeable.[6] This does not alter the fact that stylistically there still may be differences.

With *similar* constructions and grammatical elements we mean constructions and elements which have a comparable, but not identical function, which means that certain grammatical elements can hold a similar function. This means that they do hold another function, but the difference between their functions is so small that mistakes and also confusions may easily occur. For instance, the two particles of the future, viz. *sa* and *sawfa*, have a similar function. In principle, however, they are not arbitrarily switchable.

In the last case constructions are involved which hold a unique function. This means that the function of those elements is so clearly defined that a shift in use is very unlikely. In other words, we may expect that these constructions are much more stable and are less subject to shifts in use. The difficulty, however, is that in some domains particles hold a similar function, while in other domains they hold a unique function.[7]

[6] Schulz (1981: 104), for instance, writes: "In fact, a verbal noun in Arabic can always be replaced by a clause with */'an/* and the subjunctive of the verb from which the verbal noun was derived". Fischer (1986, II: 117), correctly, expresses this view in a more balanced way: "Der Ersatz des konjunktivischen أَنْ Satzes durch das Verbalsubstantiv ist praktisch unbeschrängt möglich." Further in this work (cf. infra 14.5.) we will, for instance, demonstrate that the different negative forms with the verb *zāla* are mutually exchangeable without provoking a difference in meaning. In that case too we have to do with *similar* constructions.

[7] For instance, *fa* indicating a sequence (*tartīb*) (cf. 12.1.1.1.) holds a similar function with the conjunction *wa*, but the *fa* added to embellish a word (cf. 12.1.1.7.) holds a unique function, viz. فحسب.

Since some particles hold a complementary function, as time goes by the language user may confuse the two functions, which might lead to internal language evolution or shifts in language use. We assume that internal language evolution and shifts in language use most easily occur in particles with a similar function. We suggest to call such particles, *complementary particles*.

On the basis of a thorough study of Cantarino's grammars (1974) and Krahl & Reuschel (1980) we distinguish the following complementary particles: ف (*fa*) and وَ (*wa*), أم (*'am*) and أو (*'aw*), إذا (*'idā*) and إنْ (*'in*) [The discrepancy in function between these two is much smaller then with that of the particle لو (*law*)], the particles of the future سـ (*sa*) and سوف (*sawfa*), the negation particles ما (*mā*) and لم (*lam*), the negation particles لن (*lan*) and the collocation سوف لا (*sawfa lā*), and the interrogative particles هل (*hal*) and أ (*'a*).

For the investigation we want to follow the following procedure: in the first place, we check what is known about each of these complementary particles in contemporary Arabic grammatical studies. We mainly do this on the basis of two very detailed descriptions of the particles by Yaʿqūb (1988) and by Al-ʿUmarī (1993). The first work gives a complete survey of the classical views on the particles, whereas the second work is based on the grammar of Ibn Nūr ad-Dīn, who died in the year 865 of the *hijra*.

Moreover, we also consult three more general contemporary grammatical works, viz. the works of Ad-Daḥdāḥ (1990), Ni'ma (1973) and Shalaby (1985). Further on, we investigate how contemporary western descriptions evaluate the syntax of these particles. For this, we base ourselves on the above mentioned works of Cantarino (1974), Fischer (1982; 1986), Reuschel (1988), Kouloughli (1994) and Holes (1995) and a number of specialized articles. Finally, we investigate the syntax of these particles in the corpus and examine not only the distribution, but also the functions of the particles.

12. THE COMPLEMENTARY PARTICLES *WA* AND *FA*

Although in Arabic grammar much attention is given to the mood of the verb, we will not go into more detail on this point when discussing both particles. Reading a text aloud the final vowels are not always uttered. Thus it is not always possible to identify the mood of the verb used. In general the verb moods were not indicated in the corpus, except for the morphologically clearly recognizable forms. In the discussion on the particles we will mainly devote our attention to the relation between the *equality*, the *similarity* and the *uniqueness* of the functions of the different particles and internal language evolution. In this respect we want to emphasize that the *contrast* between the data of the corpus and the classical Arabic grammars, on the one hand, and the modern western grammars (which are mainly based on Arabic literature), on the other hand, does not necessarily *prove* internal language evolution. However, we do consider it to be a strong *indication* of possible shifts.

Indeed, we assume that, when a particle holds a unique function, the chance is very small that it might be replaced by another particle as time goes by. When the function of the particles is equivalent, then this means that the language user is free to a certain extent to use either of the two particles. But here too there may be tendencies in a particular kind of text in a certain region or period for one particle to be used more than the other one. Real change and evolution in language use, however, probably most frequently occurs in similar functions where the language user, contrary to what the norm dictates, starts using another similar particle. In principle, the similar particles are not mutually exchangeable in those circumstances. The study of Arabic grammar clearly demonstrates that only in exceptional cases do particles have an equivalent function and hence are freely convertible.

12.1. The Arabic approach

In the grammars of Ni'ma (1973), Shalaby (1985) and Ad-Daḥdāḥ (1990) the information given about the particles *wa* and *fa* is very limited. As far as *wa* is concerned a distinction is made between *wāw al-ḥāl*, *wāw al-maʿīya* and *wāw al-ʿāṭifa*. In all these cases the emphasis lies on the mood of the verb required by each of the different particles.[1] The information in the above mentioned works on the particle *fa* is even more scant. The three of them distinguish between *fa* as *ḥarf ʿaṭf* (which refers to a succession viz. *tartīb* or *taʿqīb*), *fa* as *ḥarf naṣb* (in which case [cf. supra 12.1.1.] it is a *fā' as-sababīya*), and *fa* as *ḥarf ibtidā'* (in which case it is a *jawāb aš-šarṭ*) (Ni'ma 1973: 110 and Ad-Daḥdāḥ 1990: 14).

Yaʿqūb (1988) and Al-ʿUmarī (1993) give a much more thorough discussion, which however is exclusively based on the *Qur'ān*, pre-Islamic poetry and some sentences which may be considered to be classical sample sentences, as they are used by both authors. Neither author mentions contemporary or classical Arabic literature. Nor do they refer to newspapers or magazines. Moreover, what strikes one most is that neither author conducted a thorough analysis of the Koranic Arabic, as both refer to the same Koranic verses, which means that these verses too can be considered as classical sample sentences, used only as illustrations. Both works are rather normative works.

12.1.1. *The particle* fa *as conjunction according to Yaʿqūb and Al-ʿUmarī*

12.1.1.1. General division[2]

According to Yaʿqūb (1988: 307) and Al-ʿUmarī (1993: 303) the particle *fa* as conjunction has three functions. In the first place it indicates a sequence (*tartīb*). In that case there are two possibilities. The first one is called *tartīb maʿnawī* by both Yaʿqūb and Al-ʿUmarī. This indicates a succession of acts without break. In this connection Yaʿqūb refers to Koranic verse 82: 6-7,[3] where the particle *fa* is translated by Abdullah Yusuf Ali (1975: 1700) by *and*. Both Yaʿqūb and Al-ʿUmarī give the sentence: قام زيد فعمرو (*Zayd and then ʿAmr stood up*) as an example.[4]

In the second possibility an elucidation of another sentence may be involved. In this respect both Yaʿqūb and Al-ʿUmarī use the term *tartīb*

[1] The description of the *ḥurūf al-ʿaṭf* by *Ni'ma* (1973: 107) is limited to the following sentence: وهذه الحروف تتوسط اسمين او فعلين ويكون الاسم او الفعل الذي يليها نفس حكم الاسم او الفعل الذي يسبقها من حيث الإعراب *"These particles stand in between two nouns or two verbs. The following noun or verb has the same status as the preceding noun or verb, as far as the 'iʿrāb is concerned."*

[2] For the translation of the Koranic verses we refer to Abdullah Yusuf Ali (1975).

[3] Him Who created thee, Fashoned thee in due proportion, And gave thee a just bias.

[4] As both Yaʿqūb and Al-ʿUmarī never vocalize, we too refrain from adding vocalizations.

ḏikrī. As an example both Ya'qūb and Al-'Umarī refer to Koranic verses 2-36[5] and 11-45, and Ya'qūb also refers to Koranic verse 4-58. In the first verse an elucidation of the previous sentence is involved.[6] In the two following verses the particle *fa* introduces the verb *qāla*.[7] Finally Al-'Umarī also points to the use of *fa* in the meaning of *between*, but he adds that not all grammarians agree on this meaning. According to some, in a sentence, such as جلست بين عبد الله فزيد (*I sat between 'Abd Allāh* and *Zayd*) not a *fa* but a *wa* is to be used (Al-'Umarī 1993: 303-305). Here we ascertain a first example of a possible *equivalence* of the particle *wa* and *fa*.

In the second place the particle *fa* can indicate a succession (*ta'qīb*). In this case a succession of events is involved without break. As an example both Ya'qūb (1988: 308) and Al-'Umarī (1993: 305) quote the sentence: تزوّج فلان فولد له: (*so and so married and had a child*). According to Ya'qūb the meaning of the *fa* in this sentence is *identical* to the particle *ṯumma* (*thereupon*). Both Ya'qūb (1988: 308) and Al-'Umarī (1993: 305), for instance, point out that the particle *fa* in Koranic verse 23-14 has the same meaning as the particle *ṯumma*. In this sense we observe here, at least according to these authors, a complete *equivalence* between the particle *fa* and the particle *ṯumma*.[8] Further, Al-'Umarī also points out that in this case the particle *fa* can also have the meaning of the particle *wa*.

In the third place the particle *fa* can indicate a cause (*sabab*). Often in this case a conjunction between sentences is involved. Both Al-'Umarī and Ya'qūb refer to the Koranic verse 28-15: وكزه موسى فقضى عليه (*and Moses struck him with his fist and killed him*). The fact is that he was killed by being struck. The particle *fa* can also be used in an enumeration where a light contrast is pursued, such as, for instance, in the sentence خذ الاكمل فالافضل (*Take the most perfect and the best*).[9] In any case, the *fā' as-sababīya* is, according to Ya'qūb, considered as a conjunction (*'āṭifa*).

[5] We observe that Ad-Daḥdāḥ (1990: 22) quotes the same Koranic verse.

[6] (*sūra* 2-36): "Then did Satan make them slip from the (Garden), and get them out of the state (of felicity) in which they had been." The particle *fa* introduces the sentence which elucidates what the slipping consisted of. Such an elucidation is even more clearly expressed in *sūra* 7-4: "How many towns have We destroyed (for their sins)? Our punishment took them on a sudden by night or while they slept for their afternoon rest."

[7] (*sūra* 11-45): And Noah called upon His Lord and said:

[8] Cantarino (cf. infra 12.2.) does not agree with this view, but his analysis is, of course, based on MSA, not on Koranic Arabic.

[9] In MSA the particle *wa* is also used in this case (cf. infra 12.2.).

12.1.1.2. *al-fā' as-sababīya* (the causative *fa)*

In general we can state that *fā' as-sababīya* is used in circumstances where a wish or a soft order is expressed:

In the first place, after an order (*'amr*). This can also be a recommendation after the *li*, such as, in the sentence: لتكرم زيدا فيحسن لك (*Honor Zayd and he will do good to you*). In this connection Yaʿqūb refers to *sūra* 6, verse 73: كن فيكون (*Be, behold! it is*).[10]

In the second place, after an interdiction (*nahy*). Here Yaʿqūb refers to *sūra* 20-61: لا تفتروا على الله كذبا فيسحتكم بعذاب (*Forge ye not a lie against God, lest He destroy you (at once) utterly by chastisement*).

In the third place, after an interrogative particle (*istifhām*), such as in the sentence: هل يقوم زيد فاكرمه؟ (Is Zayd standing up *so that* I can honor him?)

In the fourth place, as an incitement (*taḥḍīḍ*), for instance: "هلا تكرم زيدا فاكرمه, *(Wouldn't you honor Zayd so that I can honor him*)

In the fifth place, as a wish (*tamannin*), for instance:: ليت زيدا ناجح فاكرمه (*If only Zayd would succeed, So I could honor him)*). Or after the particle لعل. Here Yaʿqūb refers to *sūra* 4, verse 73: يا ليتني كنت معهم فافرز فوزا عظيما (*Oh! I wish I had been with them; A fine thing should I then have made of it*).

In the sixth place, in an invocation (*duʿā'*), for instance, in: اغفر يا رب لزيد فيدخل الجنة (*Forgive Zayd, O Lord, and let him enter paradise*)

In the seventh place, after a negation (*nafy*). For instance: لن تأتينا فتحدّثنا (*You will not come to us so you can talk to us?*).

In the eighth place, with verbs in conditional clauses (*fiʿl aš-šarṭ*). Such as, for instance, in the main clause after *'in*. Yaʿqūb gives as an example: إنْ تَقُمْ فَأَحْسِنَ إِلَيْكَ تُكْرِمْنِي XXX

In the ninth place, as the introduction of the main clause in a conditional construction (*al-jazā'*). Further on Yaʿqūb points out that the *fā' as-sababīya* in all previously mentioned cases can be omitted, except after a negation and a conditional construction. This observation is not without importance, because it leaves the language user a certain liberty allowing for shifts in language use. Yaʿqūb gives as an example: إنْ تَنْجَحْ أُكَافِئْكَ فَأَهَبْكَ مَالا XXX

12.1.1.3. *al-fā' al-faṣīḥa (*the space-creating *fa)*

This is the *fa* which comes in the place of concealed words. As an example Yaʿqūb quotes *sūra* 2: verse 60: وإذ استسقى موسى لقومه، فقلنا

[10] *Ad-Daḥdāḥ* (1990: 22) refers to another Koranic verse (viz. 2-117) where the same verse occurs: viz. كن فيكون.

اضرب بعصاك الحجر، فانفجرت منه اثنتا عشرة عينا. (*And remember Moses prayed for water for his people; We said: "Strike the rock with thy staff." Then gushed forth therefrom twelve springs*). Ya'qūb points out that an act is concealed between the order to strike the rock and the appearance of twelve springs, viz. the striking of Moses on the rock. The function of the *fā' al-faṣīḥa,* which stands before the verb *to gush forth* (انفجر *infajara*), is to express the concealed act.

12.1.1.4. *al-fā' al-isti'nāfīya* (the resumptive *fa*)

This *fa* introduces a sentence, which follows a previous one, but which has no direct relation with it. Literally *al-fā' al-isti'nāfīya* means the recommencing-*fa*. As an example Ya'qūb refers to the Koranic verse 7-190: فلما آتاهم صالحا، جعلا له شركاء فيما آتاهما، فتعالى الله عما يشركون (*But when He giveth them a goodly child, they ascribe to others a share in the gift they had received: But God is exalted high above the partners they ascribe to Him*). Or *sūra* 21-108: أنما الهكم إله واحد. فهل انتم مسلمون (*Your God is One God: Will ye therefore bow to His Will?*). Ya'qūb also observes that not all Arab grammarians agree about the *fā' al-isti'nāfīya*. According to some this *fa* is only a conjunction connecting two sentences.

12.1.1.5. *al-fā' ar-rābiṭa li-jawāb aš-šarṭ 'aw fā' al-jazā'* (the apodosis *fa*)

In this case the *fa* precedes the main clause, such as, for instance, in: من يجتهد فالنجاح ينتظره (*Success is waiting for him who works hard*). The remaining examples quoted by Ya'qūb all are constructions, which are introduced by the particles with a conditional meaning *'in, 'iḏā, law* and the particles *man* or *mā*. In all cases mentioned the *fa* may not be omitted, unless when necessary and in rare cases such as, for instance, poetry. As an uncommon case Ya'qūb quotes a sentence from the traditions by *Al-Buḫārī*. According to Ya'qūb the construction *'ammā ... fa* falls under the *fā' ar-rābiṭa li-jawāb aš-šarṭ 'aw fā' al-jazā'*. Anyhow, the function of the particle *fa* after the particle *'ammā* can be considered unique.[11]

12.1.1.6. *al-fā' az-zā'ida* (the added *fa*)

This *fa* resembles the previous one in that it introduces a main clause after a relative pronoun with the meaning of a condition: الذي يأتي فله

[11] However, in my view, this *fa* can also be considered of as a 'recommencing *fa*"

درهم (*Who comes, gets a dirham*). According to Yaʿqūb this *fa* resembles the *fa* which has the function of introducing a result clause (apodosis). This *fa* is also used after the conjunction *lammā* (*when*). According to Al-ʿUmarī the use of *fa* here is not obligatory; for this construction he uses the term *šibh aš-šarṭ* (*pseudo-condition*).

12.1.1.7. *al-fā' az-zā'ida li-tazyīn al-lafẓ* (the *fa* added to embellish a word)

This *fa* is linked to words in order to embellish them, such as, for instance, with the word قط, which can be written with *fa*, viz.: فقط, and حسب, which is used as فحسب. (cf. Cantarino 1974: vol. 3, 20). Here too the particle *fa* unmistakably has a unique function.

12.1.2. *The particle* wa *as conjunction according to Yaʿqūb and Al-ʿUmarī*

12.1.2.1. *al-wāw al-ʿāṭifa* (the conjunction *wa*)

This *wa* links words to words and sentences to sentences. According to the Kufan grammarians, this *wa* points to an order (*tartīb*). According to Yaʿqūb (503) and Al-ʿUmarī (519), however, this is not the case. The conjunction *wa* only points to a connection which does not elucidate order. In a footnote Yaʿqūb adds that the sentence: "قام زيد وعمرو" (*Zayd and ʿAmr stood up*) contains three possibilities: Either they stood up together, or the first before the second or the second before the first. In other words, contrary to the particle *fa*, this conjunction does not indicate an order in time.[12] The similarity between the particles *wa* and *fa* is reflected here very strongly. As conjunction they hold a slightly different function.

Furthermore, according to Yaʿqūb the particle *wa* can be linked to the particles *'imma, lā* and *lākin*. In some cases the particle *wa* can have the meaning of *or*, such as, for example, in Koranic verse 4-3: فانكحوا ما طاب لكم من النساء مثنى وثلاث ورباع (*Marry women of your choice, two, or three, or four.*) As another example Yaʿqūb also quotes the sentence: الكلمة اسم وفعل وحرف (*The word is a noun, a verb or a particle*).

[12] Yaʿqūb, among others, refers to the Koranic verses 29-15 فانجيناه واصحاب السفينة (*We saved him and the companions of the Ark*) and 57-26 ولقد ارسلنا نوحا وابراهيما (*We sent Noah and Abraham*).

12.1.2.2. *al-wāw al-ʿāṭifa an-nāṣiba al-fiʿl al-muḍāriʿ bi-ʾan muḍmira* (the subjunctivizing *wa*)

In these cases the verb following the particle *wa* is in the subjunctive. These cases are identical with all the previously mentioned ones where *fa* can be used, viz. an order, an interdiction, etc. (cf. the enumeration in 12.1.1.2.). In all these cases the particle *fa* is mutually interchangeable with the particle *fa*. In these cases the particles *wa* and *fa* are completely equivalent and consequently they have an equivalent function. Yaʿqūb gives as an example: زُرْنِي وَأُكْرِمَكَ XXX

12.1.2.3. *al-wāw al-istiʾnāfīya ʾaw al-ibtidāʾīya* (the recommencing-*wa*)

This particle simply connects two sentences which can also occur separately, for instance: جاء صديقي وكافأ المعلم المجتهد (*My friend came and the teacher rewarded the diligent one*). Yaʿqūb gives as an example: حَضَرَ الْمُعَلِّمُ وَقَد طَلَعَت الشَّمْسُ

12.1.2.4. *al-wāw al-ḥālīya* (the circumstantial *wa*)

Only *wa* — and never *fa* — can introduce a circumstancial clause (*jumla ḥālīya*) as in جاء وهو.

12.1.2.5. *wāw al-qasam* (the *wa* of oaths)

The particle *wa* in this function does not occur at all in the text type which we collected. Whereas in the language spoken spontaneously it occurs rather frequently, as for instance in the oath *wa-llāhi* (*By God*). We find examples of *wāw al-qasam* in *sūra* 91-1 (والشمس وضحاها *By the Sun and his (glorious) splendor*) or *sūra* 95-1 (والتين والزيتون: *By the Fig and the Olive*). In this function, too, the particle *wa* is unique.

12.1.2.6. *al-wāw allatī bi maʿnā maʿa* (comitative *wa*)

The noun following this particle always stands in the accusative. This *wa* only seldom occurs in our corpus. When it does occur in the corpus it is marked in a footnote. Yaʿqūb gives as an example: سِرتُ وَالنَّهْرَ

12.1.2.7. *wāw rubba* (the *wa* in meaning of many)

Here the particle *wa* has the meaning of *rubba* (*many*). The question can be raised whether the particle *wa* still holds this function in MSA.

Yaʿqūb gives as an example: وَرُبَّ بَلَدٍ

12.1.2.8. *wāw al-luṣūq* (the adversative *wa*)

This *wa* connects a sentence which holds the function of an adjective with another sentence. As an example Yaʿqūb quotes Koranic verse 2-216: وعسى أن تكرهوا شيئا وهو خير لكم: (*But it is possible that ye dislike a thing which is good for you*). Others consider the *wāw al-luṣūq* as a *al-wāw al-ḥālīya*.

12.2. The western approach

Western researchers emphasize the complementarity between the particles *wa* and *fa*. Fleisch simply adopts the Arab view, such as we find it described, among others, in the grammar of Ni'ma (cf. supra 12.1. note 1). Fleisch confines himself to the observation that both particles "s'emploient pour unir des membres de phrases à l'intérieur d'une même phrase ou des phrases entre elles: *wa* (*et*) et *fa* (*ensuite*)."[13]

All western grammars stress the difference in meaning between both particles, emphasizing especially the temporal or logical sequential character of the particle *fa* contrary to the particle *wa*. Beeston (1970: 97), for instance, writes: "The basic coordinator is *wa* 'and', implying simple structural linkage. *fa* on the other hand has the additional value of implying a sequence from the preceding expression to the following one, whether temporal or logical. (...) In logical sequence, the mind may progress from a cause to its effect, in which case *fa* resembles English 'so'; or from a statement back to its cause or justification, as in 'this must be true, *for* (*fa*) I have seen it with my own eyes."[14]

The same distinction is stressed by Blohm & Reuschel (1981: 2/1: 68-69) who argue: "ف hat zwei Hauptbedeutungen, eine temporale (konsekutive) Bedeutung und eine Kausale Bedeutung." In the first case the particle *fa* is translated by *and then*, and in the last case by *for* or *because*. Both meanings occur after certain turns of phrases meaning

[13] We want to remark here that Kouloughli (1994: 271) too does not translate the particle *fa* by *'and'* but by *'then'*: "Les coordonnants généraux de l'arabe sont: و *et*, ف *puis*, ثمّ *ensuite*, حتّى *même* et لا سيما *surtout*." Stoetzer (1991: 132) does the same by translating *fa* in Dutch by *'en daarna'* (thereupon), *'en bijgevolg' (consequently)*, *'en daardoor'* (and therefore).

[14] Cf. also Cantarino (1974: vol. 2, 497), Fischer (1982, I: 164-165) and Holes (1995: 220).

with regard to, which is placed in the beginning of a sentence, such as, for instance: *'amma, bi-n-nisba, fī-mā yataʿallaq bi*. etc. (Blohm & Reuschel 1981: 2/1: 73). Further on they point out that the particle *fa* can be followed by the particle *qad* before verbs and by the particle *inna* before noun phrases. Finally both the conjunction *fa* and *wa* are used to connect adverbial strings (zweigliederige Adverbialketten), such as, for instance, أكثر فأكثر *more and more* and: كَمًّا وَنَوْعًا *quantitatively and qualitatively* (Blohm & Reuschel 1981: 2/1: 272). According to Yaʿqūb (1988: 310) this function is normally reserved to the particle *fa* (cf. supra 12.1.1.1.). Finally the particle *fa* is also used as an introduction to the apodosis after certain particles with a conditional meaning (Blohm & Reuschel 1981: 2/2: 537).

Al-Batal (1990: 239), in particular, points to the large variegation in meanings of the particle *fa* (cf. supra 9.3.3.). Wittig (1991: 180) too observes the very polysemic character of the particle *fa*. According to her, the particle *fa* is mainly used as 'konklusieve Sprachhandlungen', where the stress lies on the motivating and explanatory function of the particle *fa*, in a way that, in some cases, it is even used in stead of the particle *li-'anna* (*because*). Also Gai (1981: 295) points out that the particle *fa* has rather a 'connective' function than a 'disjunctive' one. He refers to the important function of the conjunction *fa* as *fā' as-sababīya*. He writes: "The function of *fa* is to mark the border-line between two different discourse elements, which occupy different syntactic positions, or to indicate that the discourse continues on another level". That is why he prefers to use the term *ḥarf tartīb* (*particle of order*).

Cantarino (1970: vol. 2, 495) points to the complementarity of both particles, but he also refers to the special complementary function of the particle *ṯumma*. In order to elucidate the difference between those different particles, he refers to 'Arab grammarians', though without mentioning any source.

He writes: "To form syndetical unions, the coordinating conjunction most frequently used is و; ف and ثُمَّ are also common. (...) According to Arab philologists, *there is true equivalence of all members of the coordination* only with و. With ف and ثُمَّ, there is *always* a logical idea of progression of change in the series together with the coordination. *All members with* و *are interchangeable in their order within the sentence, which is not the case with the two other conjunctions*" (Cantarino 1974: vol. 2, 496; *my italics*). Indeed, Cantarino (1974: vol. 3, 20) calls the particle ف a particle of classification. "ف implies an internal — and logical — relationship between the two coordinate sentences." In that case the particle can sometimes be translated by *because* or *thus*.

Contrary to Yaʿqūb (1988: 308) Cantarino holds the view that there is a difference in nuance between the particles *fa* and *ṯumma*. "Although ثمّ may have an effect equivalent to that of ف as a coordinating conjunction in expressing a sequence, its meaning, however, is usually more emphatic". (Cantarino 1974: vol. 2, 498). And further: "ثمّ emphasizes the sequence existing between two structurally independent statements as an interval, contrary to ف, which stresses the connected series; thus before ثمّ, a pause or an interval in the narrative is to be understood" (Cantarino 1974: vol. 3, 35). Sometimes the particle *ṯumma* also loses its temporary aspect and introduces a logically following series (Cantarino 1974: vol. 3, 37).

As far as the particle *wa* is concerned Cantarino (1974: vol. 3, 11) points out that it is the most widespread used conjunction. "The frequency of its use, as well as the manifold meanings that can be expressed with this conjunction, cannot be reproduced in English. Hence, many of the simplest constructions in Arabic require more elaborate ones in their translation." Two adversative sentences, for instance, can be linked by the conjunction *wa* which is then to be translated by *but* or *however*. The conjunction *wa* can often be replaced by the particles *lākinna* and *wa-lākin*. Elsewhere Cantarino (1974: vol. 3, 39) stresses the adversative character of the particle *wa*. But also the conjunction *fa* can have this meaning. "ف, like the conjunction و, may also connect two sentences that are in an adversative relationship; in such sentences, one statement is usually affirmative while the other is negative" (Cantarino 1974: vol. 3, 27). In that case the particle *fa* can also be translated by *but*.

Moreover, both *fa* and *wa* can precede a direct question when it has a logical connection with the preceding situation or statement. It can either precede the interrogative particle or follow it (Cantarino 1974: vol. 3, 29).

One example where the particle *fa* is not mutually exchangeable with the particle *wa* is when it introduces the jussive or the imperfect preceded by the particle *li*, for instance in the expression of an indirect command, such as, for instance, in the sentence: فلنذهب الى عالمنا. (*Let's go to our world!*). Cantarino also pays a lot of attention to the function of the particle *fa* introducing the main clause after particles with a conditional meaning. On this point the findings of Cantarino correspond to the *fāʾ al-jazāʾ* of Yaʿqūb (cf. supra 12.1.1.5.). Cantarino, however, also indicates two other particles which can, in that case, introduce the subordinate clause, viz. the particle *ʾayy* and the particle *mahmā* (Cantarino

1974: vol. 3, 365-366). Moreover, he observes that the particle *fa* is omitted in many cases.

Summarizing we can state that all authors pointedly emphasize the logical sequential character of the particle *fa* in contrast with the particle *wa*. This means that all authors stress the traditional Arab view. There is only one exception. In his third volume Cantarino quotes a number of sentences from modern Arabic literature in which the particle *wa* occurs linking two sentences "occurring in immediate sequence (!) or understood as a natural succession of events" (Cantarino 1974 Vol. 3, 14-15).[15] Given the size of Cantarino's study, it only involves a very small number of sample sentences. Still in our view this might be an indication of a possible shift in the use of the particles *fa* and *wa*.

12.3. Shift in the use of the particles *fa* and *wa*

There is not much information in the literature about a possible shift in the use of the particles *wa* and *fa*. Monteil (1960: 43) observed that many Arab writers often omit *fa's* and *wa's*. Stetkevych too remarks that the use of the *wāw al-ḥāliya* is decreasing. Moreover he observes that, in modern Arabic prose, the use of the particle *fa* is restricted to a pure copulative function. "The conjunction *wa*, which *commonly* introduces the classical Arabic sentence, tends to be used in modern Arabic only where actual copulative clauses exist. No longer is it customary to resort to it as a quasi punctuation device in a narrative sentence-sequence" (Stetkevych 1970: 93-94; *my italics*). He also refers to certain functions of the particle *fa* which are still in use by modern authors. "When the auxiliary *ʿāda* is joined to another verb, this is done by means of the conjunction *fa*, as in *ʿudtu fa šaribtu* (I drank again). Such a use remained a very common stylistic practice even among the present modernists" (Stetkevych 1970: 99-100).

Finally Blau (1973: 177-181 and 1981: 149) observes that in MSA a new tendency has emerged under the influence of Middle-Arabic. Sentences introduced by adverbial constructions are completed by introducing the second part by means of the particle *fa*.

We started form the assumption that when different particles hold a similar function, the odds are that shifts occur in the function and the

[15] One sample sentence from the work of Cantarino is, for example: شكرته وانصرف (*I thanked him and he left*). Another sample sentence is: انت اليوم حبيبي وغدا تكون زوجي (*Today you are my beloved and tomorrow you will be my wife*).

use of such particles. This way a deviation from the traditional norm can originate (cf. supra 11.2.). This is contrary to the unique functions.

This also means that we start from the assumption that the particle *wa* will not easily take over the function of the particle *fa* after the particle *'amma* because the function of *fa* in this construction is unique and clearly delimited. As a matter of fact, Beeston (1970: 66) but also Ya'qūb (1988: 315) point out that the use of the particle *fa* after *'ammaa* is obligatory. It seems clear that the particle *fa* will not easily replace the *wāw al-ḥālīya* or the *wāw al-qasam* because those functions are very clearly defined, which leaves no room for confusion. In the case of equivalent functions it is only a matter of a shift of accent. The previous analysis in this chapter clearly demonstrates that only the copulative function of the particles *fa* and *wa* are similar. Indeed, their use involves a conjunction with a difference in nuance. Our proposition is that shifts can mainly occur in this function. Before examining this topic in the corpus we will first conduct a quantitative analysis.

12.4. Quantitative analysis

In the above paragraphs (cf. supra 10.2.4.) we have already indicated that the particle *wa* occurs much more frequently than the particle *fa* in the corpus of news broadcasts. For the different countries we counted 2984 occurrences of *wa* against 93 occurrences of *fa* in Algeria, 3834 occurrences of *wa* against 91 occurrences of *fa* in Egypt and 4775 occurrences of *wa* against 82 occurrences of *fa* in Saudi Arabia. This means for Algeria a proportion of 1 occurrence of *fa* against 33 occurrences of *wa*. For the other countries this proportion is even higher, viz. 1 *fa* against 43 *wa* (Egypt) and 1 *fa* against 59 *wa* (Saudi Arabia). In Al-Jubouri's corpus of newspaper language (1988: 72) the proportion is completely different. There the particle *wa* occurs 8452 times, whereas the particle *fa* occurs 'merely' 1920 times. This is a proportion of 1 occurrence of *fa* against 4 occurrences of *wa*. We summarize these data in Table 13. [In the table N stands for nominal value and P for proportion].

Newspaper Al-Jubouri			**News broadcast radio**					
			Algeria		**Egypt**		**Saudi Arabia**	
	N	P	N	P	N	P	N	P
wa:	8452	4	2984	33	3834	43	4775	59
fa:	1920	1	93	1	91	1	82	1

Table 13

Application of the chi-square test on this table gives us a value of 1655.40 against a table value of 12.84 (with a 99.5% certainty). This means that the differences observed in this table are significant. A first provisional conclusion to be drawn from these figures is that, compared to the Al-Jubouri corpus (written language, in this case newspaper language) *in News Broadcast-MSA the particle fa is relatively much less frequently used.* Since both corpora involve 'media language' this remarkable difference in relative frequency calls for an explanation.

In his introduction Al-Jubouri reports that he limited the choice of the newspaper articles in his corpus. "The texts are signed articles selected from morning quality newspapers, published during the period of October 1982 and June 1983. Texts that represent telegrams from news agencies, letters from readers, advertisements, anonymous contributions, sports articles, art reviews, light and informal writing, and narrative texts are excluded" (Al Jubouri 1988: 62).[16]

This observation impels us to examine a number of newspapers in order to check whether there is a difference in occurrence of the particles *fa* and *wa* between general articles and signed articles for which we choose the commentaries.[17] A limited investigation yields the following result. Gen. stands for general articles and Com. for commentaries.

Newsp	**Al-Jubouri**	**Algeria**				**Egypt**				**Saudi Arabia**			
	Com.	Gen.		Com.		Gen.		Com.		Gen.		Com.	
	P	N	P	N	P	N	P	N	P	N	P	N	P
wa:	4	21	21	32	4	31	31	33	6	34	34	22	5
fa:	1	0	0	9	1	1	1	7	1	0	0	5	1

Table 14

Application of the chi-square test on the part of the commentaries of this table gives us a value of 0.34 against a table value of 12.84 (with a 99.5% certainty), which means that the differences we observe in this table are not significant. We may, then, conclude that the proportion in the newspapers of Al-Jubouri precisely corresponds to the different commentaries of the newspapers of the different countries. In general articles the use of the particle *fa* almost disappears. Probably this is due to the subject dealt with. The particle *fa* probably occurs more fre-

[16] It seems to me improbable that a time span of only ten years between the Al-Jubouri corpus and the radio corpus plays a role here.

[17] Those newspapers were chosen at random, viz. the Algerian *aš-Ša'b* of 29th may 1991, The Egyptian *al-'Ahrām* of October 3rd 1995 and the Saudi *ar-Riyāḍ* of December 7th 1989.

quently in commentaries because of the style of argumentation. The question which can be raised then is whether the commentaries on the radio, which have a similar content and style of argumentation, have the same proportional use of *fa* and *wa* as the commentaries of the newspapers. An analysis of the commentaries of the control corpus gives the following picture:

Newspaper Al-Jubouri			**Commentaries radio**					
			Algeria		**Egypt**		**Saudi Arabia**	
	N	prop.	N	prop.	N	prop.	N	prop.
wa:	8452	4	32	7	2392	13	183	36
fa:	1920	1	5	1	184	1	5	1

Table 15

Application of the chi-square test on this table gives us a value of 223.53 against a table value of 12.84 (with a 99.5% certainty). This means that the differences we observe in this table are significant. From this table we deduct that the occurrence of the particle *fa* in radio commentaries is proportionally much lower than in the written commentaries. On the other hand, the particle *fa* occurs more frequently in radio commentaries than in the general news broadcasts. The difference in frequency of the particles *wa* and *fa* between the corpus newspaper articles of Al-Jubouri and our radio corpus is to be explained in the first place by the contents of the articles (commentaries versus general news).

Table 13 also shows that the nominal value of the *wa* for the radio corpus (viz. 2984; 3734; 4775) in the different countries differs, whereas the nominal value of the *fa* remains nearly equal (viz. 93; 91; 82). This means that the quantitative occurrence of the particle *fa* in relation to the total number of words (ca. 80.000) is almost equal for the different countries. A first provisional conclusion that we can draw here is that *quantitatively a regional difference can be demonstrated in the use of the particle wa.* This point too requires an explanation.

12.5. Qualitative analysis[18]

In the qualitative analysis, we look first for an explanation of the nominal difference in the use of the particle *wa* between the different

[18] We repeat here that the first three letters of the sample sentences refer to the country of origin, the following three to the type of text: 001 is a commentary, 002 a news broadcast, 003 a reportage and 004 sports news. The following numbers indicate the position of the sentence in the text.

countries. Next we will check on which domains of the syntax uniformity can be observed in the use of the particle *wa* , and on which domains there is variation. We, then, investigate whether a shift can be observed in the use of the particle *wa*, compared to the norm, such as it is described in the classical Arabic grammars. Finally we will also investigate the current use of the particle *fa*.

12.5.1. *Comparison of the use of the particle* wa *in the three countries*

A preceding observation we have to make in this respect is that, although the number of words is equal in the sample of the different countries (cf. supra 10.2.4.), this does not yield the same number of sentences (cf. supra 10.2.2. Table 1). The Algerian corpus news broadcasts contains 3025 sentences (for 80.062 words), the Egyptian, 2800 sentences (for 80242 words) and the corpus of Saudi Arabia, 2496 sentences (for 81127 words). Although the SAU corpus contains slightly more words, it contains a considerable smaller number of sentences, viz. 529 sentences (or 1/6th) less than the corpus of Algeria. This too requires an explanation. It might be due to a wrong interpretation of the transcriber, who might have interpreted the particle *wa*, in certain cases, as a conjunction between two coordinating sentences instead of interpreting it as a marker of the beginning of a sentence.[19]

In order to investigate both matters, we select a random sample from the entire corpus. Since the nominal value differs we select a sample which is directly proportional to the nominal occurrence per country. We apply the 5% rule, which means that we will investigate the use of 5% of the particles *wa* in the different corpora. This gives us the following numbers: Algeria 149 (out of 2984), Egypt 191 (out of 3834) and Saudi Arabia 238 (out of 4775). In order to compose the sample we first make a file per country, in which all the particles *wa* occur by means of the Kwic-sentence software (cf. supra 10.2.3.). Next we select a sample at random of clusters of 10 consecutive occurrences of *wa*. Further on we investigate the function of the particle *wa*. The following table offers a survey of the functions of the particle *wa* in these samples.

[19] Cf. Stetkevych: "The conjunction *wa*, which commonly introduces the classical Arabic sentence, tends to be used in modern Arabic only where actual copulative clauses exist" (Stetkevych 1970: 93-4). (cf. also supra 12.3)

Coordinating *wa*	**Algeria**		**Egypt**		**Saudi Arabia**	
	N	%	N	%	N	%
Total	**149**	100	**191**	100	**237**	100
Between sentences	31	21	34	18	32	13.5
in هاذا و	-		*(3)*		*(4)*	
Between substantives	60	40	74	39	84	35.5
Constituents	*(4)*		*(7)*		*(21)*	
Enumerations	*(3)*		*(7)*		*(10)*	
Between adjectives	8	5	10	5	12	5
Between numbers	16	11	22	11	46	20
Beginning of the sentence	32	22	46	24	60	25
Before verb	*(17)*		*(40)*		*(47)*	
Before preposition	*(14)*		*(2)*		*(9)*	
Before others	*(1)*		*(4)*		*(4)*	
Miscellany	2	1	5	3	3	1
Betw. demonstratives	*(1)*		-			
Between verbs	*(1)*		*(2)*			
wāw al-ma'īya			*(1)*			
Between adverbs			*(1)*			
ḥāl			*(1)*		*(3)*	

Table 16*

* The numbers in italics in parenthesis are a subdivision of the numbers above.

The application of the chi-square test on this table gives us a value of 12.12 against a table value of 25.19 (with a 99.5% certainty). This means that the differences which we observe in this table are not significant. This leads us to the conclusion that the *use of the particle wa as coordinating particle is largely uniform in the three countries*. However, it becomes clear from this survey that the smaller number in the SAU-corpus is not due to a wrong interpretation of the end of the sentence by the transcriber. The number of cases in which the particle *wa* holds the function of a coordinating particle between two sentences is even more restricted in Egypt than in Saudi Arabia and Algeria. The only conclusion which can be drawn with respect to the smaller number of sentences in Saudi Arabia is that those sentences are usually longer than the sentences from the other countries. The sentences in the ALG-corpus are shorter, which is due to the much more lively style (cf. infra 12.5.1.3. and 12.5.3.).

12.5.1.2. Syntactic uniformity

On the syntactic level, no variations are ascertained of the particle *wa* as coordinating element between two sentences. A limited number of sample sentences can illustrate this.

Coordination between sentences:

ALG.002.212

التقرير يتضمن فصولا متشائمة حول توسيع انشطة العصابات المتخصصة في تجارة وترويج المخدرات في العالم

← ويركّز على أنّ تلك العصابات إضافة الى كسب اموال بواسطة هذه المتاجرة اللا مشروعة تسعى إلى الاستيلاء على السلطة.

"The report contains pessimistic chapters on the expansion of the activities of the gangs specialized in trade and distribution of narcotics in the world, ***and*** *it stresses that those gangs, beside the gains by means of this illegal trade, strive to seize the power."*

EGY.002.251

فرنسا والاتحاد السوفيتي يعربان عن قلقهما إزاء التطورات الاخيرة في منطقة الشرق الاوسط

← ويحذران من اندلاع حرب جديدة بالمنطقة.

"France and the Soviet-Union express their concern about the latest developments in the Middle-East ***and*** *they warn against the outbreak of a new war in the region."*

SAU.002.607

دانت الدول التسع الاعضاء في اتحاد اروبا الغربية اليوم النظام العراقي

← وحملته السمؤولية عن بدء المعارك في الخليج العربي.

"The nine member states of the West-European Union condemned today the Iraqi regime ***and*** *held it responsible for beginning the struggles in the Arabic Gulf."*

Table 16 also reveals a striking similarity in percentage in the use of the particle *wa*. As a coordinating particle between substantives we do not obtain a significant difference in the occurrence in terms of percentage (viz. ALG 40%, EGY 39%, and SAU 35.5%). Also on a syntactic level there is little difference. The following examples from the three countries clearly show that the use of the particle *wa* as a coordinating particle between substantives is very uniform.

Coordination between substantives:

ALG.002.008

الصحافيّون

← والتقانيّون

"**Journalists and technicians**".

EGY.002.247

رسالتا بغداد

← وواشنطن.

"The (two) reports (from) **Baghdad and Washington**".

SAU.002.164

إداراتها

← وسلطاتها

"*Its* **administrations and authorities**".

We do, however, observe a difference in the occurrence of the constituents and the enumerations. The smallest number is found in Algeria. This, however, is not an indication of syntactical variation but of differences with respect to the content. As far as the constituents are concerned, often concepts are involved, such as, for instance: قطاع غزة المحتلّ ومناطق مختلفة (*The occupied Gaza strip and various areas*). Basically it is a coordination of two substantives in a construct state. The difference in the number of enumerations is also due to a cultural difference. In Saudi Arabia, and to a lesser extent in Egypt, it is customary in the case of certain events, when starting a news broadcast, to enumerate extensively all the ministers with their powers[20]. In Algeria such enumerations do not occur. Because our sample is taken at random, those enumerations are more limited than in reality. They occur, more specifically, at the beginning of news broadcasts. This is an initial explanation for the larger frequency of the particle *wa* in Egypt and Saudi Arabia. *Here, however, no syntactic variation is involved but a variation in frequency due to intrinsic factors which are culturally determined.*

[20] Below, for instance, an illustration of the enumeration of a number of personalities who attended a meeting in Saudi Arabia:

SAU0021354

عقد خادم الحرمين الشريفين الملك فهد بن عبد العزيز آل سعود ودولة رئيس وزراء إيطاليا السيد جوليو اندريوتي اجتماعًا في قصر العزيزية مساء امس وحضر الاجتماع عن الجانب السعوديّ صاحب السمو الملكيّ الامير سلطان ابن عبد العزيز النائب الثاني لرئيس مجلس الوزراء ووزير الدفاع والطيران والمفتّش العامّ ومعالي المستشار الخاصّ لخادم الحرمين الشريفين الاستاذ ابراهيم العنجري ومعالي وزير الصحّة الاستاذ فيصل الحجلان الوزير الموافق لدولة رئيس الوزراء الإيطاليّ ومعالي وزير الإعلام الاستاذ علي شاعر وسفير خادم الحرمين الشريفين في إيطاليا الاستاذ خالد ناصر التركي.

In the coordination between adjectives no syntactical variation can be registered. There is a striking similarity in the frequency in terms of percentage between the different countries, viz. 5%, which, as a matter of fact, is an indication of a high degree of uniformity. As far as content is concerned, the following examples can easily be switched between the different countries.

Coordination between adjectives:

ALG.002.738

يكون التعايش صعْبًا

← ومتوتّرًا

*"The coexistence will be **difficult and strained**."*

EGY.002.249

الإصلاح الاجتماعيّ

← والاقتصاديّ

*"The **social and economic** reform"*

SAU.002.145

على الصعيد الوطنيّ

← والإقليميّ.

*"On a **national and regional** level."*

We observe in Table 16 that many more numbers occur in the Saudi news-broadcast table. Twenty percent of the occurrences of the coordinating particle *wa* is with numbers, whereas the percentage for both Egypt and Algeria is only 11%. Although this difference is important, again not a syntactical difference is involved but a difference in content. The news broadcast in Saudi Arabia is followed by the weather forecast with the enumeration of the temperatures in the different cities of the country. In Saudi Arabia, more than in other countries, the date and the year are mentioned along with many events. *Consequently, the greater frequency of the particle wa is not due to a syntactical variation, but to factors which refer to culturally determined content.*

12.5.1.3. Syntactic variety

The occurrence of the particle *wa* in the beginning of a sentence, with respect to other coordinating functions, is almost equal for the three countries (Algeria 22%, Egypt 24% and Saudi Arabia 25%). However, there is a remarkable difference in the following word. What strikes the most is that in Algeria the particle *wa* introduces a verb in the beginning of the sentence in only 17 cases out of 32 (53%), whereas in Egypt it is 40 cases out of 46 (87%) and in Saudi Arabia 47 cases out of 60 (78%). In Algeria the particle *wa* introduces a preposition in 14 cases out of 32 (44%), whereas in Egypt only in 2 cases out of 46 (4%) and in Saudi Arabia in 9 cases out of 60 (15%).

This is a first case in which a variation can clearly be demonstrated as having more to do with word order in the sentences of the different countries than with the coordinating particle *wa*. *We can conclude that word order in the sentences which begin with the particle wa is more classical (viz. the verb first) in Egypt and Saudi Arabia than in Algeria.* This element has also been observed in the sentences which do not begin with the coordinate particle *wa*. However, a more detailed study is outside the scope of our research.

This fact is a first indication of more classical language use in Egypt and Saudi Arabia than in Algeria. Stetkevych noticed that the particle *wa* occurrs less frequently in the beginning of a sentence in Modern Arabic than in Classical Arabic. We will now investigate whether there is a significant difference in frequency between the different countries in the use of the particle *wa* at the beginning of a sentence. Thus we create, first, "a software file" to define sentences (cf. supra 10.2.2.). In the same way as we selected a sample for the particle *wa*, we will compile a representative sample of sentences on the basis of 5% with clusters of 10 sentences. We will take care that the number of sentences is directly proportional to the total number of sentences per country. The result is for Algeria 150 sentences (out of 3025), for Egypt 140 sentences (out of 2800), and for Saudi Arabia 125 sentences (out of 2496). In Table 17 there is a survey of the frequency of the number of sentences which start with and without the particle *wa*.

News broadcasts	**Algeria**		**Egypt**		**Saudi Arabia**	
	N	%	N	%	N	%
Total number of sentences	150	100	140	100	125	100
Sentences starting with *wa*	18	12	49	35	68	54
Sentences starting without *wa*	132	88	91	65	57	46

Table 17

The application of the chi-square test on this table gives a value of 56.43 against a table value of 10.60 (with a 99.5% certainty). This means that the differences which we observe in this table are significant. It is clear from this table that there is a significant difference in the use of the particle *wa* at the beginning of a sentence in the different countries. In Saudi Arabia more than half the sentences start with the particle *wa* (54%), whereas in Egypt only a minority of the sentences, only 1/3 (35%), do so. In Algeria, on the other hand, this number is even lower, viz. 12%. When we consider, with Stetkevych, the use of the particle *wa* at the beginning of a sentence as a remnant of Classical Arabic, *then we may conclude that on this point the structure of Modern Standard Arabic in news broadcasts is more classical in Saudi Arabia than those Egypt, and that Modern Standard Arabic news broadcasts in Algeria differs most significantly of the classical structure.*

12.5.2. *Shift in the use of the particle* wa *in the three countries in relation to the description in the Classical grammar*

A last element which we want to investigate is whether the higher frequency in occurrence of the particle *wa* is due to a shift in function, viz. by the fact that it has taken the place of the particle *fa* in similar functions. Since the use of the particle *fa* is reserved for those circumstances in which there is a logical or sequential order, we can only investigate this element when we have to do with a succession of events, namely the coordination between two verbs. However, in our sample this occurs only three times (cf. Table 16): once in Algeria and twice in Egypt. These are the sentences:

EGY.002.277

من اجل إعطاء العراق فرصة لكي يجمع افكاره

← ويجمع قواته.

"To give Iraq the opportunity to order its thoughts ***and*** *to combine its forces."*

ALG.002.114

الزميل علي عبود يحيّيكم

← ويقدّم لكم موجزًا لأهمّ الانباء.

"Colleague 'Alī 'Abbūd greets you ***and*** *presents a summary of the most important news."*

EGY.002.233

نحيّيكم

← ونقدّم لحضراتكم الفترة الإخبارية الثانية لهذا اليوم.

"We greet you ***and*** *present the second news broadcast of this day."*

In the first example it is clear that the act happens simultaneously. In the two other examples this is much less clear. We can raise the question whether the greeting does not always precede the presentation of the news; in my opinion, it is impossible to present the news first and to greet the listeners afterwards. Here we have clearly to do with a logical and actual succession of acts. In terms of Yaʿqūb and Al-ʿUmarī (cf. supra 12.1.1.1.) we have here a succession (or the so-called *tartīb maʿnawī*), the specific character of which is that the acts are taking place without a break. According to the grammatical norm the particle *fa* ought to be used in these cases. Of course, two examples are too little in order to be representative for the whole corpus. In order to demonstrate that the particle *wa* has indeed taken over the function of the particle *fa* in news broadcasts we will have to conduct an investigation on a wider scale.

Therefore we look for all the particles *wa* followed by a verb in the present tense by means of the KWIC-index program.[21] From a closer investigation of those sentences we can conclude the following. In the first place we notice that, when the particle *wa* is used as a conjunction between two verbs in the present tense, in most cases a normal coordination is involved where the order is not an issue (cf. supra 12.1.2.1.). In this case, often events are involved which can happen simultaneously or events of which the order is not important. We give a few examples from the three countries.

ALG.002.289

الشابّ عبد الرزاق طالب يتحدّث عن جهازه والجهود التي بذلها حتّى أصبح ذلك الجهاز حقيقةً ملموسة

← ويقول إنّ الساعة القرآنيّة كما لقبها مصنوعة من خشب الزيتون

← ويشبه شكلها شكل المسجد الأقصى بمدينة القدس الشريف

← وتعمل الكترونيًا وفقًا لحسابات ومقاييس مثبوتة.

"The young man ʿAbd al-Razzāq Ṭālib talks about his gadget and of the efforts he made to make this gadget a palpable reality ***and*** *he says that the 'Koranic watch', as he called it, is made from olive wood* ***and*** *that it resembles the form of the al-'Aqṣā mosque in the (noble) town of Jerusalem* ***and*** *that it works electronically according to fixed calculations and standards."*

In this sentence the different coordinations can easily be switched without changing the meaning of the sentence. The order is not important. It is also possible to say that: "*the watch works electronically and that it resembles in its form the al-'Aqṣā mosque in the (noble) town of Jerusalem and that it is made of the wood of the olive tree.*" The same can be observed about the following sentences:

[21] In this phase of (primary) encoding we can only ask for the verbs in the present tense. In a later phase the verbs of the past tense can also be asked for (cf. supra 10.1.).

EGY.002.129

وقد صنعت هذه العربات التي أطلق عليه اسم الثعلب في المانيا وتمّ توريدها من المصانع مباشرة الى الخليج

← وتبلغ تكلفة العربة الواحدة مليوني دولار.

*"And these cars, which were given the name 'fox' were produced in Germany **and** they were delivered directly from the factories to the Gulf **and** the cost of one car amounts to two million dollars."*

EGY.002.171

وذكرت شبكة تلفزيون CNN أنّ عددًا ليس بقليل من القوات العراقيّة في الكويت بدأ يهرب في اتّجاه السعودية

← ويقوم هؤلاء باستبدال ملابسهم العسكريّة بملابس مدنيّة حتّى يتمكّنوا من الهرب.

*"And the television station CNN reported that many (members) of the Iraqi troops began to escape out of Kuwait heading for Saudi Arabia **and** that (those) they, (literally: in order to be able to escape), substituted civilian clothing for their military clothing."*

SAU.002.879

دال: شهادة صحّيّة تثبت التطعيم ضدّ الحمّى الشوكيّة

← وتؤكّد بتلقّي الجرعة خلال مدّة لا تقلّ عن عشرة ايام ولا تزيد عن عامين.

*"D: (= fourth)· a health certificate which confirms the vaccination against fever **and** which confirms that an oral vaccination has been received in a period between not less than ten days and no longer than two years (ago)."*

SAU.002.873

ومن لم يسبق له اداء الفريضة سواء قبل قدومه للعمل بالمملكة او اثناء عمله بها

← ويرغب في اداء فريضة الحجّ فإنّ وزارة الداخلية قد وضعتْ تنظيمًا لذلك بلّغتْ به المديرية العامّة للجوازات وكافّة إداراتها في جميع المناطق ويتلخّص هذا التنظيم في الآتي.

*"For those who have not yet fulfillled their religious duties before they came to work in the kingdom or during their work (in it) **and** for those who want to fulfill their religious duty of the ḥajj, the Department of the interior has developed a special arrangement. It (the ministry) has informed the general administration for passports and all other administrations. This arrangement can be summarized as follows."*

In this last example from Saudi Arabia, the two sentences which are connected by the particle *wa* are interchangeable. It is, indeed, possible to say: *"Those who want to fulfill their religious duty of the ḥajj, and who have not fulfilled their religious duty yet either before they came to work in the kingdom or during their work there...*

The particle *wa* is also used in a connection between one event and a second one arising from it. Here we have a succession or order of events, but which flow from one to another. For instance, in the following sentences:

ALG.002.160

المخابز ومحلات بيع الخبز أغلقت ابوابها اليوم على مستوى الجزائر العاصمة
← وتبقى كذلك غدا تلبية لنداء اتّحاد التجّار والحرفيّين لولاية الجزائر.

"The bakeries and the shops which sell bread today closed their doors (on the level of) in the capital Algiers ***and*** *that will also be the case tomorrow, in compliance with a summons from the Union of merchants and professionals of the province of Algiers."*

EGY.002.101

وفي هذا الصدد أشار الدكتور عبد المجيد الى أنّ المرحلة التي تمرّ بها ازمة الخليج حاليًا تدعو للقلق خاصّة ونحن نقترب من نهاية المهلة التي أقرّها مجلس الامن للعراق بمقتضى القرار رقم ستّ مائة ثمانية وسبعين
← وتنتهي في الخامس عشر من شهر يناير الحاليّ وبالتالي يبدأ إعمال نصوص هذا القرار.

"In this respect Doctor ʿAbd al-Majīd indicated that the phase which the Gulf crisis is going through now calls for fear, especially because we are reaching the deadline which the Security Council has fixed for Iraq according to resolution NR 678 ***and*** *which ends on the fifteenth of the (current) month of January and consequently the texts of this resolution will become effective."*

EGY.002.173

وقد أصدر المجلس بيانًا عقب الاجتماع أشاد فيه بالدول الشقيقة والصديقة التي ساهمتْ
← وتساهم في عملية التحرير تنفيذًا لقرارات مجلس الامن

"After the meeting the Council published a declaration in which it praised the sister states and the friendly states which have cooperated ***and*** *still contribute to the liberation operation as implementation of the resolutions of the Security Council"*

SAU.002.372

المجالس التنفيذيّة للمؤتمر الإسلاميّ الشعبيّ تنهي جلسته الثالثة مساء اليوم
← ويعقد جلسة ختاميّة غدًا الجمعة.

"The executive councils of the Islamic people's congress end their third session this evening ***and*** *will hold their final session tomorrow, Friday."*

SAU.002.003

وسيكون قبول الطلبات اعتبارًا من السادس من الشهر القادم من شهر عشرة لعام الف واربع مائة وعشرة

← وينتهي بالثاني عشر، عشرة واربع مائة وعشرة وذلك حسب الشروط التالية.

"The acceptance of the applications will begin on the sixth of next month, on the tenth month of the year 1410 ***and*** *will end on the twelfth 1410 and this according to the following conditions."*

SAU.002.424

وقالت المصادر إنّ مسؤولين بارزين من الستّ عشرة دولة الاعضاء في الحلف اجتمعوا امس السبت

← ويجتمعون مرّة اخرى اليوم لبحث الموقف.

"The sources said that prominent officials of the sixteen member states of the alliance gathered yesterday (Saturday) ***and*** *that they will gather again today to investigate the situation."*

In all these examples we observe a certain order. For instance, the acceptance of applications can not end before it started. However, in this case there is no succession of different events, but the continuation of an event.

In many cases, however, the particle *wa* is used when a logical succession is involved. In the examples which follow, the coordinating sentences can not be switched. In the first sentence, for instance, the iron splinters can only be removed after they have penetrated the body.

ALG.002.904

الوفدان كشفا أنّ إسرائيل ستعمل او تستعمل نوعا جديدا من الرصاص المطاطيّ يحتوي على مائات المعادن والشظايا صغيرة التي تستقرّ في الجسم حالة الإصابة

← ويستحيل استئصالها لصغرها وانتشارها داخل انسجة الجسم.

"The two delegations revealed that Israel (will work or) uses a new kind of rubber bullets containing hundreds of small iron splinters which spread into the body the moment they hit (the victim) ***and*** *which cannot possibly be removed because of their small size and how they spread througout the tissues of the body."*

The same goes for the next example from Algeria.

ALG.002.698

الهجوم نفّذ تحديدا بمنطقة الرميال الواقعة على بعد حوالى سبعة وثلاثين كيلومترًا جنوب بيروت

← ويعدّ الأوّل من نوْعه منذ انتشار القوات السوريّة على الطريق الرابط بين الصيدا وبيروت عام سبعة وثمانين.

"The attack was executed (more precisely) in the region of ar-Ramyāl located approximately 37 km. south of Beirut ***and*** *this (attack) is considered to be the first of its kind since the deployment of Syrian troops on the road which connects Sidon with Beirut in 1987."*

The examination of an attack can only happen after the attack has taken place. Here too we clearly have a logical succession of events. In the following sentence as well, 'listening' is an element that can only follow the event.

ALG.002.161

نبقى مع هذه الإجراءات الاستثنائيّة ومدى تطبيقها ميدانيًا

← ونستمع الى مسؤول في احدى هذه الوحدات، وحدات الاروقة الجزائريّة ويتحدّث في الموضوع.

"We stick to these exceptional measurements and the range of the practical application of it ***and*** *we listen to an official person in one of the units of Algerian tents* ***and*** *he (as he) talks about the subject"*

The same goes for this example from Saudi Arabia. It is only possible to talk about the last part after mentioning the first part.

SAU.002.227

وقال معالي الدكتور يوم الرحمان علي شيخ أنّ هذه التمور التي امر الملك المفدّى بشرائها من المزارعين يتمّ توزيعه الجزء الأكبر منها مجانًا على من يحتاجها من المواطنين في المملكة

← ويخصّص الجزء الباقي لدعم برنامج الغذاء العالميّ التابعة للامم المتّحدة.

"And His Highness Doctor Yawm ar-Raḥmān 'Alī Šayḫ said that the major part of the dates that His Highness ordered to buy from the farmers will be distributed free among the poor citizens in the kingdom ***and*** *that the remaining part will be destined to support the world food program of the United Nations."*

However, it is not always clear whether we really have a logical succession of facts. An example from Algeria can illustrate this:

ALG.002.244

بعض المواطنين الخواصّ يتجوّلون عبر الاحياء السكنيّة للمدينة ويقومون بتوزيع مياه الشرب على المواطنين

← ويتقدّمون بالمقابل من هؤلاء نقود.

*"Some (private) citizens move around in the residential areas of the city and distribute drinking water among the citizenry (**and**) in exchange therefor they receive money from them."*

In principle the acceptance of the contribution follows the supply of an article, but this does not always have to be the case. In reality it is very well possible for a person to pay for something before he receives it. It might also be possible to say that *Some countrymen receive money in exchange for which they distribute potable water among the citizenry. In this order, however, the sentence obtains a pejorative meaning.*

Clearly, we have in the corpus many examples of sentences where the particle *wa* is used in spite of the fact that we unmistakably have to do with a succession of events.

ALG.002.208

كاتب الدولة الامريكيّ للشؤون الخارجيّة السيد جامس باكر غادر امس واشنطن باتجاه العربية السعودية التي يستقبله بها اليوم العاهل السعوديّ فهد بن عبد العزيز
← ويتباحث مع نظيره السعوديّ الامير سعود الفيصل.

*"The American Secretary of State, Mister James Baker, left Washington yesterday for Saudi Arabia where the Saudi king Fahd Ibn 'Abd al-'Azīz will greet him **and** he will conduct talks with his Saudi colleague Prince Sa'ūd al-Fayṣal."*

EGY.002.905

الرئيس حسني مبارك يستقبل غدًا الرئيس النمساويّ كورد والدهايم
← وتتركّز المباحثات حول تطوّرات ازمة الخليج والتعاون الثنائيّ بين مصر والنمسا.

*"Tomorrow President Ḥusnī Mubārak receives the Austrian President Kurt Waldheim **and** the talks will concentrate on the developments in the crisis in the Gulf and on the bilateral cooperation between Egypt and Austria."*

Of course, the talks follow the reception. The same goes for the following sentence:

ALG.002.167

السيد سيد احمد غزاليّ يسلّم بنواق شوط رسالة من الرئيس الشاذلي بن جديد الى الرئيس الموريتانيّ معاوية ولد سيد احمد الطايا
← ويشارك في اديس ابيبا في اشغال المجلس الوزاريّ لمنظّمة الوحدة الافريقيّة.

*"Mister Sayyid 'Aḥmad Ġazālī delivers in Noakchutt a letter from President aš-Šāḏlī ben Jadīd to the Mauritanian President Mu'āwīya Wuld Sayyid 'Aḥmad aṭ-Ṭāyā **and** he will (!) participate in Addis Ababa in the activities of the Council of Ministers of the Organization of African Unity."*

Also in the sentences below the succession of events is clearly noticeable.

SAU.002.153

ومن المقرّر أن يعود دوجلاس هارد الى بيروت صباح اليوم

← ويعقد مؤتمرا صحفيّا بالسفارة البريطانيّة في بيروت يتناول فيه المسائل المتعلّقة بالرهائن الغربيّين المحتجزين في لبنان.

"It has been decided that Douglas Hard will return to Beirut this morning ***and*** *that he will hold a press conference in the British embassy in Beirut in which he will deal with questions related to the western hostages who are imprisoned in Lebanon."*

EGY.002.124

وقال ديكويار للصحافيّين إنّه سيذهب للعراق

← ويقول لهم هناك إنّ العالم كلّه يريد رؤية السلام وإنّ مهمّته من اجل السلام لا يجب أن تفشل بل لا بدّ لها أن تنجح.

"And De Quellar told the journalists that he would go to Iraq ***and*** *would tell them there that the whole world wants to see peace and that his mission for peace must not fail, but on the contrary, that it must succeed."*

SAU.002.280

وأعلن كريستوف عقب اختياره أنّه سيشكّل حكومة خلال الايام القليلة القادمة

← ويقدّمها للبرلمان.

"Kristof said after his election that he would form a government within the next few days ***and*** *that he would present it to parliament."*

Here too the particle *wa* is used whereas we clearly have to do with a succession of events. In the other example it is clear that the secretary of the UN first has to go to Iraq before he can tell them something. The same goes for the next sentence: first the government has to be formed before it can be presented to parliament.

In the next sentences it becomes clear that the particle *wa* is also used in a succession of acts with a pause (the so-called *taʿqīb* cf. supra 12.1.1.1.)

EGY.002.049

نحيّيكم اخوة العروبة >>> وفي ما يلي موجز الانباء

← ويليه رسالة موسكو ثمّ حلقة في برنامج حديث الصحافة.

"We greet you, Arabic brothers, ***and*** *in what follows (is) a summary of the news* ***and*** *that will be followed by a message from Moscow and further on a sequence of the program 'discussion by the press'."*

In this example the pause between the different parts of the sentence are clearly manifested. Indeed, it is stated that the summary of the news will follow the greeting and that will be followed later on by a message from Moscow. The newsreader used the particle *ṯumma* which refers to a sequence. The same goes for the following sentence.

EGY.002.480

لحظات

← ونوافيكم بالتعليق.

"A few moments ***and*** *(then !) we will give you the commentary."*

One last sample sentence which clearly demonstrates that the particle *wa* can connect two sentences with a time span is the following:

EGY.002.073

قدّمنا لكم موجزًا لأهمّ الانباء

← وفي الثانية عشرة والنصف إن شاء الله موجزًا آخر.

"We have presented you a summary of the most important news items ***and*** *at half past twelve, God willing, another summary will follow."*

We made the same observations in the control corpus. There too the particle *wa* is used in events where it is clear that one follows another. We give one example from the sports news of the Algerian radio, and two examples from Egypt, of which one from a live (!) coverage on the Egyptian radio.

ALG.004.215

المنتخب الوطنيّ يعود غدا الى ارض الوطن

← ويستأنف يوم الثلاثاء القادم تحضيره لنهائيات كأس افريقيا:

"The national champion returns to the (territory) of the homeland tomorrow ***and*** *next Tuesday he will resume his preparations for the finals of the African Cup."*

In this case we have to do with a succession, even with a serious pause. In the next example the reporter describes the entrance of President Mubārak in parliament.

EGY.003.174

ايها الاخوة المواطنون

← وَيَدخل في هذه اللحظات السيد الرئيس محمد حسني مبارك

← ويستقبله الحاضرون في قاعة الاجتماعات الكبرى بمقرّ الحزب الوطنيّ بهذه العاصفة المدوّية من التصفيق ويقف سيادته على المنصّة

الـرئيسيّة بينما ياخذ السيد ويلي براند رئيس الحركة مكانه الى جوار السيد الرئيس

*"Dear (brothers) countrymen; (**and**) at this moment mister President Ḥusnī Mubārak enters **and** the people present greet him in the big assembly room of the headquarters of the national party with this loud storm of applause **and** His Excellency is now on the principal podium while Mr Willy Brandt, president of the movement takes his place beside the president."*

EGY.003.538

والمقاتلات تطارد منصّات الصواريخ المتحرّكة
← وَتُدمّرها.

*"The fighters chase the mobile rocket platforms **and** destroy them."*

It is logical that the fighters first have to chase the mobile rocket platforms before they can destroy them.

The preceding analysis brings us to the following conclusion. *In Modern Standard Arabic, such as it is used in radio news broadcasts, the particle wa fulfills the function of the particle fa in logical or sequential successions, more than might be expected from the Classical Arabic point of view.* This shift in function has been found in the three different countries. Consequently it seems to have become a widespread phenomenon. This phenomenon might be due to the influence of the spoken language on the written language, such as it is used on the radio. Whether the particle *wa* has completely taken over the *tartīb* and the *ta'qīb* function of the particle *fa* can be checked by examining the use of the particle *fa* in the different countries.

12.5.3. *The use of the particle* fa

In the investigation of the use of the particle *fa* the emphasis lies on the *tartīb* and *ta'qīb* function of the particle *fa*. We first give a general survey on the use of the particle *fa* in the news broadcasts.

The application of the chi-square test on this table gives us a value of 33.10 against a table value of 28.30 (with a 99.5% certainty). The difference between the $\chi 2$-value of Table 18 with the table value is big enough to be significant. In this table we observe the 'normal' use of *fa*, such as, for instance, the introduction of a sentence (cf. for example 12.1.1.4.) There are, though, also some striking elements. A first striking difference in frequency is found in the particle *fa* as introduction of the apodosis. As such it could simply mean that in Algerian news broadcasts conditional sentences occur less frequently than in other countries. It is, however, also possible that the apodosis after a conditional sentence in Algeria is less frequently introduced by the particle *fa*. This question will be investigated later on (cf. infra 13).

Function *fa* News	Algeria		Egypt		Saudi Arabia	
	N	%	N	%	N	%
Total	**93**	100	**91**	100	**82**	100
Introduction apodosis *	6	6	20	22	11*	13
Fixed form *faḥasb* **	-	-	1	1	2	2
Introductory sentence	22	24	22	24	14	17
before *qad*			*(4)*		*(6)*	
After *'amma*	10	11	18	20	18	22
After adverb. construction	31	33	13	14	12	15
Conjunction	24	26	16	18	21	26
between sentences	*(4)*		*(13)*		*(11)*	
between verbs	*(20)*		*(3)*		*(10)*	
Miscellany			1	1	4	5

Table 18

* In Saudi Arabia the protasis is introduced by a much greater variety of particles, such as *'iḏā, mahmā, man, law, 'in lā*. In the Algerian news only *'iḏā* occurs. In Egypt to a limited extent also *law* (1) and *'iḏ* (1).
** (cf. supra 12.1.1.7)

We have already pointed out that according to Beeston and Yaʿqūb (cf. supra 12.3.) the use of the particle *fa* is obligatory after the particle *'amma*. Deeper analysis of the corpus, however, shows us that the particle *fa* is not always used after *'amma*. On all the occurrences of *'amma* in the corpus both for Algeria and Saudi Arabia we found three cases in which the particle *fa* was not used after *'amma*. We give an example for each country.

ALG.002.111

← أما موقف الإدارة الامريكيّة من قضية هجرة اليهود السوفيت يَبقى متناقضاً.

"As for the attitude of the American administration, concerning the case of the emigration of the Soviet Jews, it remains contradictory ."

SAU.002.180

← اما ارتفاع المَوج من متر الى مترينَ وَدرجة حرارة المياه سبع وَعشرون درجة مئويّة.

"As far as the height of the waves is concerned, it is one up to two meters and the (degree of the) temperature of the water is 27 ° C."

We have noted that Blau (1973: 177-181 and 1981: 149) indicates that a new tendency has originated in MSA under the influence of Middle-Arabic. This tendency consists of the habit to complete the second part of adverbial constructions by means of the particle *fa*.[22] It is clear from Table 18 that the particle *fa* is abundantly used in sentences which are introduced by adverbial constructions. According to Blau, this is a distinctive characteristic of MSA compared to Classical Arabic. Our investigation of the corpus confirms this tendency. We can even observe that such constructions do occur much more frequently in Algeria (33% compared to about 15% for Egypt and Saudi Arabia). Moreover, these constructions are much more varied in Algeria than in the two other countries investigated. It would lead us too far to summarize all the possible variations such as they are used in Algeria. We limit ourselves to the observation that these constructions are, indeed, very varied, which is an indication of a much more flexible language use.

Finally the particle *fa* also has the function of a conjunction between sentences and between verbs. Especially this last point requires closer investigation since the similarity in function with the particle *wa* exists at this point. Close analysis of the corpus shows us that the particle *fa* is chiefly used between two verbs in the past tense in cases where we have an immediate succession and with a serious semantic limitation. We observe that the verbs in this construction almost always have the meaning of '*he asked him*' and '*he answered*': viz.: *sa'ala fa 'ajāba, sa'ala fa kāna radduhu, ṭalaba fa 'ajāba, ṭalaba fa jā'a, 'as'ila ṭaraḥnā fa kāna l-jawābu*.

Further on we also found one occurrence of '*he answered and said': radda fa qāla* and four occurrences of *'he met him and asked': iltaqā fa sa'ala*.

In Egypt the use of the particle *fa* as a conjunction between two verbs occurs only three times. Here too we observe a semantic limitation. Two examples are connected with the meaning *'to speak'*, viz. *'ašāra ... fa qāla (he pointed out and said)* and *radda fa qāla (he answered and said)*. In the third example we have a quotation of a speaker, i.e. the president of Egypt, where he said:

[22] Blau writes about this: "In Classical Arabic, adverbials referring to the whole sentence ("sentence adverbials"), as a rule serving a psychological subject, may stand in frontal position, connected with the rest of the sentence by *'inna, 'anna, mā* or *fa*. Yet as far as my knowlegde goes, *fa* occurs only when preceding orders. In Standard and Substandard Middle Arabic the use of such an adverbial in frontal position is continued by *fa* even before a narrative clause rather than an order. (...) This feature is one of the most outstanding traits of MSA." (Blau 1973: 177-178).

EGY.002.250

وفي يوم الغزو وبعد ساعات من وقوعه اتّصل الملك حسين وطلب الحضور الى الاسكندرية

← فرحبت بذلك.

"A few hours after the invasion, the same day, King Ḥusayn got in touch and asked (me) to be present in Alexandria ***and*** *I welcomed that."*

As far as Saudi Arabia is concerned, we have a total of 11 occurrences of the particle *fa* as a conjunction between verbs. Here too the semantic limitation is striking. In all cases the use of the particle *fa* in a succession of verbs is related to the meaning of speaking. Four occurrences concern the expression of the news reader *'aʿūdu fa 'ūjizuhā (I repeat and I summarize).* Three expressions in which the verb *taṭarraqa (go into)* stands in a relationship with another verb in the meaning of 'speaking' viz. *taṭarraqa 'ilā ... fa qāla (he went more deeply into ... and said)* and one occurrence of *taṭarraqa fa 'akkada (he went more deeply into ... and confirmed).* And finally two examples which are also related to the verb 'to speak', viz. *taḥaddaṯa fa qāla (he spoke and said)* and *istaʿraḍa l-mawqif fa qāla (he examined the situation and said).* The only remaining example is a quotation of king *Fahd* in which he says:

SAU.002.531

لقد سبق لي ان ناشدت الرئيس صدام حسين في أكثر من موقع ومناسبة بان يفي الى امر الله

← فيحقن الدماء.

"In the past I had urged President Ṣaddām Ḥusayn on more than one occasion and situation to serve the case of God ***and*** *(in that way) to avoid blood shed."*

In the last example we have to do with what Yaʿqūb and Al-ʿUmarī call a *tartīb ḏikrī* since the blood shed is an elucidation of the serving of (the case of) God. The only two examples in which the particle *fa* still fulfills this function are both found in speeches (cf. supra.). But also the previous expressions, which are all connected with the idea of speaking, according to the traditional Classical Arabic grammar fall under the *tartīb ḏikrī* (cf. supra 12.1.1.1. note 7). This way, in terms of the classical Arabic grammar, we may conclude, for the time being, that *when the particle fa in News Broadcast-MSA fulfills a similar function as the particle wa, it is replaced by the latter in the case of a tartīb maʿnawī or a ta'qīb. However, in the case of a tartīb ḏikrī the particle fa retains its function in News Broadcast-MSA.*

In order to be able to draw final conclusions we have to conduct an additional investigation. Therefore we look in the corpus for all the occurrences of the particle *wa* in collocation with the verb *qāla*. If our tentative conclusion is correct, then we should not find a verb on which the verb *qāla* gives an elucidation preceding the particle *wa* in combination with the verb *qāla*. The following table shows a survey of the occurrences of this collocation.

News broadcasts	**Algeria**		**Egypt**		**Saudi Arabia**	
wa-qāla	N	%	N	%	N	%
Total	**30**	100	**202**	100	**218**	100
introductory sentence	19	63	194	96	199	91
elucidation of verb	9	30	8	4	19	9
miscellany	2	7	-	0	-	0

Table 19

The application of the chi-square test on this table gives us a value of 53.47 compared to a table value of 14.86 (with a 99.5% certainty). This means that the differences which we observe in this table are significant. In this table we observe a very interesting element as far as the occurrence of the collocation *wa-qāla* is concerned. This occurrence seems to be very limited in Algeria, whereas it occurs both in Egypt and in Saudi Arabia with similar frequency. Moreover, what strikes one most is that the collocation *wa-qāla* chiefly occurs as an introduction to a sentence. In Algeria, however, this construction occurs much less frequently in terms of percentage. When we compare the number of sentences beginning with the collocation *wa-qāla* with the total number of sentences, we get the following distribution:

News broadcasts	**Algeria**		**Egypt**		**Saudi Arabia**	
wa-qāla	N	%	N	%	N	%
Total number of sentences	3025	100	2800	100	2496	100
sentences with *wa-qāla*	19	0.6%	194	7%	199	8%
sentences without *wa-qāla*	3006	99.4%	2606	93%	2297	92%

Table 20

The application of the chi-square test on this table gives us a value of 191.81 compared to a table value of 10.60 (with a 99.5% certainty). This means that the differences are statistically significant. Here too the difference between the three different countries in word order, or the way in which a sentence begins, is striking. Egypt and Saudi Arabia show an almost equal percentage of 'classical' structures (7 to 8%) whereas in MSA of the news broadcasts in Algeria these structures occur much less frequently (0.6 %). This confirms our previous conclusion (cf. supra 12.5.1.3) *that MSA, such as we have recorded it in our corpus of news broadcasts to a certain extent is less 'classical' in Algeria.*

In order to discuss the possible *tartīb ḏikrī* function of the particle *wa* in collocation with the verb *qāla* we recapture a subdivision of Table 19:

News broadcasts	Algeria		Egypt		Saudi Arabia	
wa-qāla	N	%	N	%	N	%
Total	**30**	100	**202**	100	**218**	100
elucidation to verb	9	30	8	4	19	9

Table 19 bis

This table clearly shows that the collocation *wa-qāla* as elucidation on a preceding verb does occur in the three countries under investigation, in spite of the fact that the nominal occurrence of this collocation is restricted. We observe that in all these cases an elucidation is involved on a verb followed by the collocation *wa-qāla*. All the preceding verbs have the meaning of speaking; note for instance, the following verbs: *'akkada (confirm), ittahama (accuse), nawwaha (praise), da'ā (call up), ṭālaba (demand), 'arraba (express), nafā (deny), ṣarraḥa (declare), 'ašāra (point at),* etc.

These data do not only clearly show that the particle *wa* has taken over the function of the particle *fa* in a *tartīb ma'nawī* and a *ta'qīb*, but also that it has taken over the function of the *tartīb ḏikrī* in the radio news broadcasts in the three different countries. The use of the particle *fa* in the *tartīb ḏikrī* function is exclusively restricted to a few fixed expressions. Indeed, in further exploring the corpus we discovered that the verbs *sa'ala* and *'awjaza* in the construction *sa'ala fa-'ajāba* (Algeria) and *'a'ūdu fa 'ūjizuhā* (Saudi Arabia) are never preceded by the particle *wa*. In other words, the use of the particle *fa* in these cases is restricted to a fixed expression. Nobody in the area investigated says *'uḥayyīkum fa-'uqaddimu* but *'uḥayyīkum wa-'uqaddimu*. The opposite is also the case, which means that the use of the particle *fa* is limited to a few expressions.

A last point which we want to investigate in this respect is whether the same tendency exists in the news commentaries. Indeed we found that the proportion of occurrences of the particles *wa* and *fa* differed in the news commentaries and the news coverages compared to the news broadcasts. We also found that this proportion closer to Al-Jubouri's newspapers commentaries (cf. supra 12.4. Table 15). Since only the Egyptian control corpus is large enough for a close investigation we limit ourselves to this particular corpus. The following table offers a survey, compared to the data of Table 18 about news commentaries from Algeria and Egypt.

Function *fa*	**Algeria/N**		**Egypt/N**		**Egypt/C**	
	N	%	N	%	N	%
Total	**93**	100	**91**	100	**184**	100
Introduction apodosis	6	6	20	22	22	12
Fixed form *faḥasb*	-	-	1	1	2	1
Introduction sentence	22	24	22	24	86	47
before *qad*			*(4)*		*(17)*	
After *'amma*	10	11	18	20	16	9
After adverb construction	31	33	13	14	48	26
Conjunction	24	26	16	18	10	5
between sentences	*(4)*		*(13)*		*(7)*	
between verbs.	*(20)*		*(3)*		*(3)*	
miscellany			1	1	-	

Table 21

Application of the chi-square test on this table gives us a value of 60.01 compared to a table value of 28.30 (with a 99.5% certainty). This means that the differences are statistically significant. This table clearly shows that in commentaries the particle *fa* is much more used to introduce a sentence than in the news broadcasts of Egypt and that it is seldom used as a conjunction between sentences and even less as a conjunction between two verbs. Since the *tartīb* function (immediate succession) and the *ta'qīb* function (succession with a pause) only occurs in a relation between two verbs , we can conclude that this function of the particle *fa* is no longer frequently used in commentaries. However, the particle *fa* does fulfill the other functions which are more closely related with the marking of styles of argumentation. The three examples of a relationship between two verbs we found in the Egyptian commentaries, all three are connected to the *tartīb ḏikrī* function. These are the sentences *nādat fa-daʿat (She called and summoned)*, *yuḥaddid fa yaqūl* (*He specifies and says*) and *yaḍaʿ fa yaqūl* (*He postulates and says*). Here too we clearly have to do with collocations which are semantically restricted to the meaning of speaking.

When searching by computer for the collocation *wa* + present tense in the control corpus we discovered that here too the particle *wa* often fulfills the function of connecting two coordinate sentences which express a concurrence in which the order of the events has no importance. But there are also a number of sentences in which the order is important and in which not the particle *fa* but the particle *wa* is used. The following examples illustrate this:

EGY.001.118

كما أتاحت الفرصة لمحدودي الدخل أن يرتفع مستواهم الاجتماعيّ
← ويلحقون ابناؤهم بمختلف مراحل التعليم.

"It also gave the opportunity to the people with a limited income to raise their social level ***and*** *to let their children participate in the different levels of education."*

EGY.001.400

والسؤال الذي يتردّد على كلّ لسان عربيّ مخلص الآن: الم يكن من الأفضل أن يعيد قادة العراق حساباتهم
← ويستجيب للنداءات المتكرّرة وَالمتعلّقة باحتواء الازمة وتنفيذ قرارات القمة العربيّة الطارئة التي عقدت بالقاهرة مؤخّرا؟

"The question, which keeps resounding on the tongue of every sincere Arab (is) now: Is it not better for the leaders of Iraq to revise their counts ***and*** *to respond to the repeated calls concerning the avoidance of a crisis and the implementation of the decisions of the extraordinary Arabic summit conference, which has been held lately in Cairo?"*

EGY.001.757

ولكنّ بعض المراقبين ياملون أن يعود = صدام حسين – الى رشده مع اقتراب الخامس عشر من يناير
← ويعلن على العالم قبوله للانسحاب.

"But some observers hope that, with the approach of January 15 Ṣaddām Ḥusayn will come to his senses again ***and*** *will announce to the world his agreement to withdraw."*

Although in the three preceding sentences we find a logical succession of facts, here too the particle *fa* has not been used. In fine, a closer investigation of the collocation *wa-qāla* in the broadcast commentaries reveals that it also occurs as an elucidation on another verb, such as, for instance, in *raḥḥaba wa-qāla* (*he welcomed and said*). Consequently, it is clear that in broadcast commentaries as well a shift in function has taken place between the particle *fa* and the particle *wa*.

12.6. Conclusion

First of all we can conclude that there is a uniformity between the three investigated countries in the use of the particles *wa* and *fa*. The regional variation which we observed in the frequency of the use of the particle *wa* is not due to a syntactical factor, but to cultural factors concerning content. We did observe a variation in syntax, but this concerned sentence word order, especially after the use of the conjunction *wa*. It would seem that in Saudi Arabia a more 'classical' style is used in the beginning of a sentence, since the majority of the sentences start with the particle *wa*.

The particle *fa* continues to fulfill its unique functions, such as its use after *'amma*. In that case the particle *fa* can sometimes be omitted but it is clearly never replaced by the particle *wa*. Moreover, our investigation confirms the tendency observed by Blau that the particle *fa* is frequently used in sentences which are introduced by an adverbial construction.

Further on our investigation clearly demonstrates that MSA, such as it is used in the news broadcasts in the media, bears specific features vis-à-vis Classical Arabic and compared to the descriptions of Modern Standard Arabic by western grammarians. The working hypothesis which we postulate, viz. that the odds are that there may be shifts in function and use in particles which have a similar function, is confirmed by this investigation. We think that we have clearly demonstrated that in the three countries investigated the particle *wa* has to a large extent taken over the function of the particle *fa* both as far as the *tartīb ma'nawī* (immediate succession), is concerned, as well as the *tartīb ḏikrī* (elucidation) and *ta'qīb* (succession with a pause). Moreover, we have demonstrated that the function of the *tartīb* and the *ta'qīb* is strictly limited to verbs of speaking.

This is not only the case in news broadcasts in general but also in the news commentaries. The ultimate question now is whether this evolution is specific to News Broadcast-MSA, or whether it can also be observed in written MSA (cf. supra 12.4.). Since Cantarino (1974) only casually mentions this function of the particle *wa* and since he only gives a few examples, we have the *impression* that the use of the particle *wa* in the literature at that moment was rather marginal. As a matter of fact, as far as we know, this function is not mentioned in any other grammar. It is not immediately clear whether in written MSA too this evolution has taken place. One single indication in that direction is to be found in a few sample sentences about the use of the particle *wa* given as an illustration by Al-Warrāqi & Ḥassanayn (1994: 13) in their recent textbook: *The Connectors in Modern Standard Arabic.* Whether this use has now become widespread can only be demonstrated by compiling a similar corpus of the written language. Only then will we know whether these functions are a specific characteristic of News Broadcast-MSA, or whether they are a general distinctive characteristic of MSA compared to Classical Arabic.

13. THE COMPLEMENTARY PARTICLES *'IḎĀ*, *'IN* AND *LAW*

The second series of complementary particles we investigate are the particles with conditional meaning, *'iḏā, 'in* and *law*. Although a lot of attention is given in traditional Arabic grammar to verb mood as a result of these particles, we will not discuss these particles in detail. Here too we will concentrate our attention on the equivalence, similarity and uniqueness of the functions of the different particles and possible shifts in their use.

13.1. THE ARABIC APPROACH

As a general classification we follow Ya'qūb's outline (1988: 78-83; 141-150 and 409-414) which is completed by Al-'Umarī's data (1993: 84-89; 167-175 and 413-418).

13.1.1. *The particle* 'iḏā

13.1.1.1. *'iḏā* with conditional meaning

The particle *'iḏā* can have a conditional as well as temporal function.[1] In that case the content of the condition refers to the future. As an example Ya'qūb quotes: إذا حضر المعلم فقفوا احتراما (*When the teacher enters, stand up out of respect.*). Further on he writes that in this case the particle *'iḏā* is often followed by a verb in the past tense with a future meaning. Only seldom is the Arabic verb found in the present tense. Al-'Umarī (1993: 84) adds that, since a particle with a conditional meaning is involved, the condition always will have to be completed by an result clause (*jawāb*) which is the case for all conditional particles. Moreover, as far as the particle *'iḏā* is concerned, Al-'Umarī argues that it is necessary that the conditional element in the sentence refer to a known case which will happen in any case. Consequently there may be no doubt about the conditions taking place. This way Al-'Umarī stresses the temporal character of the condition. Al-'Umarī quotes as an example: إذا

[1] Although Ya'qūb and Al-'Umārī use the word šarṭ (condition) they quote as examples no conditional sentences but temporal sentences.

زالت الشمس آتيك (*When the sun goes down, I will come to you*). Or, such as, for instance in the Koranic verse: 5-6: إذا قمتم الى الصلاة فاغسلوا وجوهكم (*When ye prepare for prayer, wash your faces*).

13.1.1.2. *'iḏā* referring to the future

In the second place the particle *'iḏā* can refer to the future without having a conditional meaning. Here too the verb is in the past tense, but it has a future meaning.[2] As examples Ya'qūb quotes the Koranic verses 53-1: والنجم إذا هوى (*By the star when it goes down*) and 92-1: والليل إذا يغشى (*By the Night as it conceals (the light)*.

13.1.1.3. *'iḏā* with past meaning

The temporal particle *'iḏā* can also refer to the past. Then the particle *'iḏā* holds the function of the particle *'iḏ*. As an example Ya'qūb quotes Koranic verse 62-11: وإذا رأوا تجارة او لهوا انفضوا اليها (*But when they see some bargain or some amusement, they disperse headlong to it).*).[3] In this respect Al-'Umarī refers to Koranic verse 9-92: ولا على الذين إذا ما أتوك لتحملهم قلت لا أجد ما أحملكم عليه تولوا (*Nor [is there blame] on those who came to thee to be provided with mounts, and when thou saidst "I can find no mounts for you" , they turned back).*

13.1.1.4. *'iḏā* as nominal phrase (*ism*)

Further on Ya'qūb also mentions the use of the particle *'iḏā* as a noun. In that case it is preceded by *ḥatta,* such as, for instance in Koranic verse 39-71 حتى إذا جاؤوها (*Until when they arrive there*). In this respect Al-'Umarī uses the term*'iḏā az-zā'ida* (*added 'iḏā*).

13.1.1.5. *'iḏā al-fujā'īya* (*'iḏā* of surprise)

Finally there is the *'iḏā al-fujā'īya*. This *'iḏā* differs from the previous particles because it is always followed by a noun phrase and never by a verb phrase. It also differs because the conditional particle *'iḏā* is always followed by an answer whereas this is not the case for the *'iḏā al-*

[2] Contrary to Ya'qūb, Al-'Umarī observes that in this case a future action cannot possibly be involved, but that on the contrary the action is situated in the present because of the oath.

[3] The question can be raised whether, for this reason, it would not be better to translate the verb in this Koranic verse by a past tense, viz.: *But when they saw a bargain or some amusement, they pursued it).*

fujā'īya. Moreover, the *'idā al-fujā'īya* does not refer to the future, but to the present time. According to Yaʿqūb this is an example of surprise which occurs in the present. As an example Al-ʿUmarī quotes Koranic verse 20-20: فإذا هي حية تسعى (*and behold! It was a snake, active in motion*).[4] According to both Yaʿqūb (1988: 81) and Al-ʿUmarī (1993: 86) there is no consensus among the Arab grammarians on whether *'idā al-fujā'īya* is a *ḥarf* (particle), or a *ẓarf* (adverb) or on whether it is a *ẓarf zamān* (adverb of time) or a *ẓarf makān* (adverb of place). The *'idā al-fujā'īya* can also occur in a sentence as an answer to a condition.[5] As example Yaʿqūb quotes Koranic verse 30-48: فإذا أصاب به من يشاء من عباده، إذا هم يستبشرون (*Thereof: then when He has made them reach such of His servants as He wills, behold, they do rejoice!*). Further on the *'idā al-fujā'īya* often occurs after *lammā* (*when*). Further according to Al-ʿUmarī, the *'idā al-fujā'īya* is characterized by the fact that it is always linked to the conjunction *fa*.

13.1.2. *The particle* 'in

As far as the particle *'in* is concerned, Yaʿqūb registered ten different functions with the Arab grammarians. It is important to point out here that Yaʿqūb gives an inventory of all the possible interpretations that have been given to the particle *'in*. Indeed, the use of the particle *'in* in certain Koranic verses is considered by some as *conditional* whereas other grammarians give it another function. In Yaʿqūb's work there is no systematic analysis of the particle *'in*, only an enumeration of all possible interpretations without any final judgment. Therefore we will only give a concise survey of Yaʿqūb's enumeration:

13.1.2.1. *'in aš-šarṭīya* (conditional *'in*)

This is a particle which is followed by two jussive verbs. Yaʿqūb (141) quotes a lot of Koranic verses of which we only cite Koranic verse 8-19: وإن تعودوا نعد (*If ye return, so shall We*). According to Al-ʿUmarī, however, the particle *'in* is only used when the condition is related to an uncertain event. As elucidation Al-ʿUmarī (1993: 170) writes that in the sentence *'When the sun rises'* the particle *'in* cannot be used since it is certain that the sun will rise. The conditional particle *'in* can also be fol-

[4] In this Koranic verse, given by Al-ʿUmarī as an illustration, it is rather a case of historical present.

[5] For this function Al-ʿUmari (1993: 87) provides a separate category.

lowed by the negation particle *lā* but then both are contracted to the particle *'illā* (إلا). For instance, in Koranic verse 9-40: إلا تنصروه ، فقد نصره الله (*If ye help him not ... for God did indeed help him*). It can also be followed by the particle *lam* and by the particle of negation *mā*. In that case both are contracted giving *'immā* (إمّا). For the rest Yaʿqūb pays a lot of attention to the mood of the verbs following the particle *'in*.

13.1.2.2. *'in at-tafṣīlīya aš-šarṭīya* (the separating conditional *'in*)

In English this particle has the meaning of *either*. As an example Yaʿqūb quotes the sentence: من يساعدني إن رجل وإن امرأة أساعده (*Whoever helps me, whether a man or a woman, I will help him*).

13.1.2.3 *'in al-muḫaffafa*

This *'in* has the same function as the *'inna aṯ-ṯaqīla* (*verily*). The sentence إن زيدا قائم then means: *Verily Zayd has stood up*. Yaʿqūb quotes different examples from the Koran, among which verse 86-4: إن كل نفس لما عليها حافظ (*There is no soul but has a protector over it*). In this respect Al-ʿUmarī points out that this *'in* can have the same function as *'inna (aṯ-ṯaqīla)*, but that it can also have a more soft function followed in the sentence by the particle *lam*. In order to distinguish it from the negative particle إن, it is often followed by a *lam*. Al-ʿUmarī (1993: 159) quotes different examples from the Koran of which we cite verse 39-56: وإن كنت لمن الساخرين (*And I was but among those who mocked*). In English this *'in* is mostly not translated.

13.1.2.4 The particle *'in* with the meaning of *laysa* (*not to be*)

In this function the particle *'in* only occurs in poetry.

13.1.2.5 *'in an-nāfiya* (negative *'in*)

In this function the particle *'in* is usually followed by the particle *'illā*.[6] In English this construction is mainly translated by *only*. As an example Al-ʿUmarī quotes Koranic verse 9-107: إن أردنا إلا الحسنى (*Their intention is nothing but good*) and verse 36-15: إن انتم إلا تكذبون (*Ye do nothing but lie*). When this particle is not followed by the particle *'illā* it only has a negative meaning, such as in Koranic verse 72-25: قل إن أدري أقريب ما توعدون ام يجعل له ربي أمدا (*Say: I know not whether the (punish-*

[6] According to Al-ʿUmarī (1993: 170) also by the particle *lammā*.

ment) which ye are promised is near, or whether my Lord will appoint for it a distant term).[7]

13.1.2.6 *'in az-zā'ida al-kāffa* (added negative *'in*)

This *'in* is added to the particle *mā*. However, the particle *mā* can also be concealed. Among the Koranic verses quoted by Yaʿqūb is Koranic verse 36-15, which he also quoted with the *'in an-nāfiya* (cf. supra 13.1.2.5). This clearly demonstrates that some categories overlap each other. As a matter of fact Yaʿqūb points out that not all Arab grammarians agree with this classification and he even adds that according to some the function in the previously mentioned Koranic verse is a conditional one.

13.1.2.7 *'in az-zā'ida ġayr al-kāffa* (added non-negative *'in*)

This mainly occurs in poetry and its function, according to Al-ʿUmarī, is an emphatic one.

13.1.2.8 *Other functions*

The last three categories of *'in* are, according to both Yaʿqūb and Al-ʿUmarī, interpretations by Arab grammarians of different schools of the particle *'in*. According to some it is a remnant of the particle *'imma*. It can also have the meaning of the particle *'iḏ* and according to others also of the particle *qad*. In this last case as an example Koranic verse 87-9 is quoted, viz.: فذكّر إن نفعت الذكرى (*Therefore give admonition in case the admonition profits [the hearer]*) and 2-278: اتقوا الله وذروا ما بقي من الربا إن كنتم مؤمنين (*Fear God and give up what remains of your demand for usury, if ye are indeed believers*). In our view these are both conditional in meaning.

13.1.3. The particle *law*

Here too Yaʿqūb gives a survey of all the possible classifications of the particle *law*. Although Yaʿqūb argues that there is a lack of consensus among the Arab grammarians about the classification of the particle *law* with the conditional particles, viz. the *ḥurūf aš-šarṭ*, Al-ʿUmarī (1993: 405) points out that *law* is, in all cases, a particle with a conditional function. Both authors use the same classification except for one detail.

[7] This verse is classified separately with Al-ʿUmarī.

13.1.3.1. *al-law al-imtināʿīya* (irrealis *law*)

This *law* points at the impossibility or the absence of an event because the conditional event has not been realized. As an example Yaʿqūb (1988: 409) quotes the sentence: لو زرتني أكرمتك (*If you were to visit me, I would honor you*). The underlying idea is that the first event will not occur, as a result of which the second one can impossibly be realized.[8] Further on, both Yaʿqūb and Al-ʿUmarī point at the different positive and negative combination possibilities in the apodosis and the protasis as well as the possible moods of the verbs which can follow.

13.1.3.2. *al-law aš-šarṭīya* (conditional *law*)

According to both authors, in this case a particle is involved with the meaning of *'in* which is followed by a future tense or which transforms the past tense in a future meaning. As an example Yaʿqūb refers to Koranic verse 12-17: وما انت بمؤمن لنا ولو كنا صادقين (*But thou wilt never believe us even though we tell the truth*) and Koranic verse 4-9: وليخش الذين لو تركوا من خلفهم ذرية ضعافا خافوا عليهم (*Let those have the same fear in their minds as they would have for their own, if they had left a helpless family behind*). Here too both authors allege that there is no consensus about this classification among the Arab grammarians.

13.1.3.3. *al-law al-maṣdarīya* (nominalizing *law*)

This particle replaces the particle *'an* and occurs mostly after the verb *wadda* (*to love*). This means that it holds similar functions with the particle *'an*. Yaʿqūb gives as an example Koranic verse: وَدّوا لو تُدهن فيدهنون

13.1.3.4. *law li-t-tamannī* (the *law* of wishing)

In this case the particle *law* expresses a wish such as for instance in Koranic verse 26-102: فلو أنّ لنا كرة فنكون من المؤمنين (*Now if we only had a chance of return, we shall truly be of those who believe*). In my view the particle *law* holds here a unique fiunction.

[8] Again we want to emphasize that the many examples (cf. supra 12.1.1.2.) which are quoted by Yaʿqūb and Al-ʿUmarī are not based on investigation of corpora but on the mono-introspectional method (cf. supra 7.1. note 1). Such examples are taken over by other grammarians and in that way become typical examples. Sample sentences linking a visit to be made and the possible honouring resulting from it are found not only in Yaʿqūb's and Al-ʿUmarī's books, but later on also in Fleisch (1968: 212) and Hajjar (1986: 158). Such typical sample sentences based on introspection, whether from one or several sources, soon begin to lead a life of their own; they distort the view on real current language use and lead instead to normative answers.

13.1.3.5. *law li-t-taqlīl* (the limitating *law*)

This category has been introduced by some Arab grammarians to indicate a limitation, such as, for instance, when we say: أعط المسكين ولو درهما (*Give to the poor, if only a dirham*). Ya'qūb also refers to Koranic verse 4-135: يا ايها الذين آمنوا، كونوا قوامين بالقسط شهداء لله ولو على انفسكم (*O ye who believe! Stand out firmly for justice, as witnesses to God, even as against yourselves*). In my view the particle *law* holds here too a unique function. However, the use of the particle may interfere with the particle *'in*.

From both the grammatical works we discussed above we can deduct that the complementary element of the conditional particles *'iḏā* and *'in* is to be found in the fact that,in principle, *'iḏā* has to be used when the condition is more likely than not to be realized, whereas the particle *'in,* in principle, can be used when there is some doubt about the effective realization of the condition. The other functions, such as the function of surprise of the particle *'iḏā*, are unique. On the other hand the particle *law* has, as a particle, a very specific conditional meaning: A condition which cannot possibly be realized is always involved.

13.2. The western approach

In all western approaches a distinction is made between particles which introduce possible conditional sentences, viz. *'iḏā* and *'in,* and one particle which introduces unreal conditional sentences, viz. *law*.[9] We found this fundamental distinction in all modern works on Arabic grammar. As far as the particle *law* is concerned, Cantarino points out the hypothetical character of the condition. He also observes that the particle *law* can introduce a condition which is contradictory to the facts, if the verb has a past meaning. We find the same argumentation in Kouloughli's work (1994: 289) who stresses the purely hypothetical character of the particle *law*.

In this respect Stoetzer (1991: 191) uses the term 'non-real condition'. In the description of the function of the particle *law* by Holes we find still another dimension. Besides impossibility, Holes also mentions the improbability of an event: "*law* is used to introduce conditions which are viewed as *improbable* or impossible of fulfillment" (Holes

[9] Cf. for example, Krahl (1980: 138): "Sätze, in denen die Bedingung nicht realisiert worden ist oder nicht realisiert werden kann, werden irreale Bedingungssätze genannt. (...) Im Arabischen wird der irreale Bedingungssatz durch die Konjunction لو eingeleitet."

1994: 238). It is clear from all grammatical descriptions that the particle *law* has a clearly distinguished function compared to the other conditional particles. Contrary to the particles *'iḏā* and *'in*, where the common similarity is much greater, the particle *law* holds a unique function.

In Cantarino (1974) the polysemic character of the particles *'in* and *'iḏā* is manifest. He also points out, however, that there are particles which are no longer frequently used by modern authors, such as, for example, the *'in al-muḫaffafa*. Cantarino emphasizes that the particles *'iḏā* and *'in* hold clearly distictive functions. About the particle *'iḏā* he writes: "Although إذا is used in a very broad range of meanings, it has remained primarily a temporal adverbial particle with a past meaning" (Cantarino 1974, vol. 3, 297). The possible conditional aspect of the particle *'iḏā* is heavily weakened by Cantarino. This way he completely agrees with the traditional Arabic grammar.

"The basic conditional significance of إذا normally remains so closely related to its temporal one that even in its conditional use, it generally introduces only a statement of something which is known through experience and about the eventual occurrence of which there can, therefore, be no doubt. إذا leaves uncertain the time, not the fact, of the actual event" (Cantarino 1974, vol. 3, 302). In this respect he also refers to the contrast with the function of the particle *'in* which he discusses further on in his book. In other words the particle *'iḏā* mainly has a temporal character and, according to Cantarino, there is a high certainty of the event actually taking place.

About the particle *'in* Cantarino writes: "إن, 'if,' basically states a fact or an event, the eventual occurrence of which one cannot be sure of, but which is always possible. Contrary to إذا, which presents through its conditional meaning uncertainty only about the time when the action will take place, إنْ questions whether or not the action itself as stated will occur" (Cantarino 1974, vol. 3, 312). Cantarino, further on, refers to the classical example, which according to him is often quoted to elucidate the difference between *'iḏā* and *'in* viz.: إذا مات (*when he dies*) compared to إنْ مات (*if he dies*). However, he points out that the particle *'iḏā* never can have a conditional meaning, whereas the particle *'in* never can have a temporal meaning. Cantarino also discusses the mood of the verbs which can follow both particles.

The functional distinction between the particles *'iḏā* and *'in* is confirmed by Holes (1994: 238). He quotes the same *classical* sample sentence to illustrate this distinction. However, he also observes that "in MSA *'iḏā* has to some extent encroached on the territory of CLA *'in*."

Beeston does not make this distinction between the two particles with the same emphasis. According to him, the particle *'iḏā* not only has a conditional meaning (like the particle *'in*) but also a temporal one. "The simplest of these functionals is *'in* 'if', which implies nothing more than the uncertainty of validity. *'iḏā* had originally a time significance *in addition*, 'if ever/if at any time/whenever'" (Beeston 1970: 104) (*my italics*). This contrasts sharply with the observations of Cantarino, but also with the observation of Fleisch (1968: 206) that the particle *'iḏā* essentially is a temporal one.

Krahl (1980: 437), on the other hand, observes that in modern Arabic the particle *'in* is no longer frequently used[10] Nevertheless, he too refers to the distinction which Arab grammarians make between the two particles *'iḏā* and *'in*. The first particle then ought to be translated by *when* and the second one by *if*. Monteil holds the same view when he argues that the particle *'iḏā* only expresses an eventuality and that it is translated in German (!) by *wenn*.[11] However, Krahl observes that the two particles cannot completely be distinguished from each other in meaning.[12]

13.3. Shifts in the use of the particles *'iḏā*, *'in* and *law*

The literature reveals that the particles *'iḏā* and *'in* hold new functions in Arabic which have not (yet) been described by Arab grammarians, such as Yaʿqūb and Al-ʿUmarī. Roughly we find three new shifts in use.

First of all there is the use of particles with a *conditional* meaning to introduce indirect interrogative sentences. Cantarino (1974, vol. 3, 320) observes that the particle *'in* in modern Arabic is used to introduce indirect questions. To such particles, Krahl (1980: 547) also adds the particle *'iḏā*. This tendency has already been observed by Wehr (1943: 39), who also added the particle *law*. In this respect Stetkevych (1970: 104) observes: "Considering that classical Arabic had no distinctive way of expressing an indirect question, these modern usages ought to be regarded as a formal syntactical innovation." Blau (1973: 188-189) ob-

[10] This has also been confirmed by Monteil: "*'iḏā* se substitue progressivement à *'in* et *law* et même à *hal* et *a*" (Monteil 1960: 260).

[11] "Or, *'iḏā* à toutes les époques, s'est maintenu avec un sens temporel faible, pour indiquer un éventuel: 'quand, comme, si'" (allemand *wenn*) (Monteil: 1960: 243).

[12] "Man könnte also an *wenn* als Äquivalent von إذا und an *falls* (im Sinne eines Potentialis) als Äquivalent von إنْ denken, doch tut uns der tatsächlichen Sprachgebrauch (im Deutschen wie im Arabischen) nicht den Gefallen einer reinlichen Trennung beider" (Krahl 1980: 438).

serves the same for the particles *'iḏā* and *'in*, but in a later article (1976: 161) he points out that in this meaning this construction was also extended to the combination *mā 'iḏā*.

In the second place many authors (Fleisch 1968: 215; Cantarino 1974, vol. 3, 330; Krahl 1980, vol. 2, 583; Kouloughli 1994: 294) have mentioned the possibility of forming concessive subordinate clauses with the particle *'in* preceded by the conjunction *wa*.

In the third place some authors have the impression that a shift appears in the *conditional* functions of the different particles and in their distribution. Beeston (1970: 104) but also Holes (1994: 238), for instance, observe that the particle *'iḏā* has seriously encroached into the domain of the particle *'in*. Kouloughli (1994: 289) too reaches the conclusion that the particle *'iḏā* holds more and more a conditional function and that the particle *'in* is largely ousted. "Mais dans la langue moderne, إذا originellement introducteur de circonstantielle de temps, a acquis une valeur de conditionnelle et a tendu pratiquement à évincer إنْ. (...) Quant à إنْ, il sert de plus en plus à l'expression de l'hypothèse ou de la concession." However, the textbook of Al-Warrāqi & Ḥassanayn (1994: 155) reveals the opposite. In all their examples *'in* is used in conditional sentences whereas in other cases both *'in* and *'iḏā* are used. This conveys the impression that the particle *'in* obtains a much more prominent place in conditional sentences than the particle *'iḏā*.

On the other hand there are also books, especially textbooks, where no distinction is made anymore between the two particles. In Cowan (1973: 195), for instance, no distinction is made between the particles *'iḏā* and *'in*. Stoetzer (1991: 190) does not make a fundamental distinction between the particles either. He simply observes that the particle *'in* is *more formal* than the particle *'iḏā*.

However, Holes makes some very important observations about shifts in the function of the particles *'iḏā* and *'in* in written MSA. He based himself on a small book by *an-Nafīsī* (1982, 70 pages) on the social and economic politics of the states of the cooperative body of the Gulf. According to Holes, this book reveals that the use of the particle *'in* is limited to concessive subordinate clauses. He writes: "*'in* and *'iḏā* are clearly distinguished from each other, but the distinction is connected to text function in a rhetorical sense, rather than expressive of different condition types, as it is in CLA. *'in* is found exclusively in parenthetic conditional clauses or *anti-conditional* clauses introduced by *wa 'in* 'even if'." For the rest he observes that in the great majority of conditional sentences the particle *'in* does not occur anymore, but only the particle *'iḏā*.

Before conducting a qualitative investigation, we first want to examine whether there is a significant statistical difference in the occurrence of the conditional particles: what influence does the nationality of the language user exert on the distribution of the different particles?

13.4. Quantitative analysis

In the first table we give a survey of the frequency of the different particles in the news broadcasts of the different countries. We would like to note that these numbers are totals. As these particles are polysemic, conditional functions are not always involved.

	News broadcasts					
Particles	**Algeria**		**Egypt**		**Saudi Arabia**	
	N	%	N	%	N	%
Total	**41**	100	**79**	100	**38**	100
iḏā	30	73	60	76	28	74
'in	7	17	8	10	9	24
law	4	10	11	14	1	2

Table 22

Applying the $\chi 2$-test on this table, we find that there is statistically no significant difference in the distribution of these particles in the different countries. For this table we obtained a $\chi 2$-value of 6.51 whereas the minimal $\chi 2$-table value, in this case, is 14.86. Distinguishing between the different functions of these particles, we obtain the following image:

Particles	**Algeria**		**Egypt**		**Saudi Arabia**	
	N	%	N	%	N	%
Total	**41**	100	**68**	100	**37**	100
'iḏā (total)	**30**		**60**		**28**	
(introducing question)	8		4		8	
(mā 'iḏā) (whether)	*(8)*		*(4)*		*(7)*	
(temporal)	9		11		6	
(ḥatta 'iḏā)	*(1)*		*(3)*		*(-)*	
(condition)	11		39		14	
('iḏā mā)	*(5)*		*(10)*		*(2)*	
(doubt)	2		5		0	

'in	*(total)*	**7**		**8**		**9**	
	(condition)	1		0		0	
	(parenthetic)	2		1		1	
	(introducing question)	1		0		0	
	(concessive wa-'in)	2		1		1	
	*(expression)***	0		6		8	
law		4		11		1	
	(concessive wa-law)	*(1)*		*(7)*		*(0)*	
	(condition)	*(3)*		*(4)*		*(1)*	

Table 23*

* The cursively printed numbers between brackets are a further subdivision of the above mentioned number. This means, for instance, that in Algeria *'iḏā* is used 11 times as a 'condition' of which five in the combination *'iḏā mā*.
** The expression refers to fixed uses, such as in *'in šā llāh*.

From this table it can be deducted that the particle *'in* is not often used to introduce an indirect question (only in Algeria, and limited to one occurrence). On the other hand, the customary way to introduce an indirect question is to use the collocation *mā 'iḏā*. In concessive constructions both the particle *'in* and the particle *law* are used. In the next table we only display conditional or temporal functions of the three particles. Thus we obtain the following result:

		News broadcasts					
Particles		**Algeria**		**Egypt**		**Saudi Arabia**	
		N	%	N	%	N	%
Total		**24**	100	**60**	100	**29**	100
'in		**1**		**6**		**8**	
	(condition)	1	4	0	0	0	0
	(expression)	0	0	6	10	8	28
'iḏā		**20**		**50**		**20**	
	(temporal)	9	38	11	18	6	21
	(condition)	11	46	39	65	14	48
law	*(condition)*	**3**	12	**4**	7	**1**	3

Table 24

Again, in this table we can not demonstrate a significant statistical difference in the distribution of these particles in the different countries, since we obtain a $\chi 2$-value (18.37) which is lower than the table value (21.96). Nevertheless, this table contains some interesting features. In the first place it is obvious that the particle *'in* is not used anymore with a conditional function except in fixed expressions, such as, in this case *'in šā' allāh*. Holes (1994: 241) arrives at a similar conclusion but with respect to dialectal Arabic. There too the use of the particle *'in* seems to be limited to fixed expressions. Indirectly we can observe that this expression did not occur in the Algerian news broadcasts. It might be an indication of a larger secularization of radio personnel in Algeria.[13]

The most typical particle to introduce temporal or conditional constructions seems to be the particle *'iḏā*. *These figures negate the implicit conviction of Cowan (1973: 195) and Stoetzer (1991: 189-190), but also of Al-Warrāqi and Ḥassanayn (1994: 155) that there is no fundamental distinction in the use of both particles.* They confirm the assertion of Krahl (1980: 437) that, indeed, the particle *'in* no longer occurs frequently in MSA, or at least in news broadcasts. This table clearly demonstrates that the loss of the conditional function of the particle *'in* in favour of the particle *'iḏā* is no regional phenomenon. On the contrary this phenomenon arises in those three countries which strongly differ from each other.

It seems useful to investigate whether this phenomenon is limited to news broadcasts or whether it also occurs in the reportages and the sports news. The results of this investigation are shown in the following table.

Particle Frequency		ALG/R		EGY/R		EGY/C	
		N	%	N	%	N	%
Total		**15**	100	**28**	100	**65**	100
'in	*(total)*	**7**	47	**6**	21	**15**	23
	(condition)	2		1			1
	(concessive function)	4		2			1
	(expression)	1		3		9	
	(not clear)	-		-		4	
'iḏā	*(total)*	**5**	33	**17**	61	**42**	65
	(introduction question)	-		2			1
	(mā 'iḏā) (whether)	-		*(2)*		*(1)*	
	(temporal)	2		1		20	
	(condition)	2		12		12	
	('iḏā mā)	*(2)*		*(2)*		*(2)*	
	(doubt)	1		1		5	
	('iḏā of surprise)	-		1		4	
law		**3**	20	**5**	18	**8**	12
	(concessive wa-law)	3		4		2	
	(condition)			1		6	

Table 25

[13] All broadcasts of Algeria go back to the period just before the 1991 elections, wherein radio played an important role. It is clear from different reportages that the radio journalists were no adherents of the FIS (Front Islamique du Salut).

Application of the χ2-test roughly gives no statistically significant difference in distribution between those three particles (viz. χ2-value of 5.66 against a table value of 14.86). If we only take the conditional functions of these particles we obtain the following picture:

Frequency Particles	ALG/R		EGY/R		EGY/C	
	N	%	N	%	N	%
Total	**7**	100	**18**	100	**48**	100
'in	**3**	43	**4**	22	**10**	21
(condition)	2	*(29)*	1	*(6)*	1	*(2)*
(expression)	1	*(14)*	3	*(16)*	9	*(19)*
'iḏā	**4**	57	**13**	72	**32**	67
(temporal)	2	29	1	*(6)*	20	*(42)*
(condition)	2	29	12	*(66)*	12	*(25)*
('iḏā mā)	*(2)*		*(2)*		*(2)*	
law (condition)	**0**	0	**1**	6	**6**	12

Table 26

Calculating the χ2-value of this table, we do not obtain a statistically significant difference (χ2-value of 2.86 against a table value of 14.86 with a 99.5% certainty). This means that we find exactly the same distribution of conditional particles in those three countries irrespective of the kind of text. In spite of the fact that it might be expected that in high flown speech , such as in radio commentaries, the particle *'in* might have a higher occurrence, this definitely does not seem to be the case. Also in radio commentaries and reports the particle *'in* seems to occur much less with its conditional meaning. The most frequent particle in all text types is *'iḏā*. The frequency and use of the particle *law* is much lower than the other particles. In order to investigate this phenomenon more closely a qualitative analysis is needed.

13.5. Qualitative analysis

In the qualitative analysis we will successively discuss the function of the particles mentioned such as it has been found in the corpus. First of all we will examine which functions the particle *'in* still holds.

13.5.1. *Function of the particle* 'in

When examining the corpus we notice that the particle *'in* is not only less frequently used in the positive sense in MSA of news broadcasts, but also in the negative sense *'in lā* which seems to be contracted to one particle, viz. *'illā*. Contrary to the particle of exception *'illā*, which frequently occurs in the corpus, the contraction *'in lā* does occur much less frequently. In the total corpus, main corpus and control corpus together it occurs only 8 times, more particularly in the meaning of *if not*.[14] We notice that it only occurs in this sense as the composed particle *wa-'illā* '*or else*'. In this meaning it occurs only once in the news broadcasts of Algeria and four times in Saudi Arabia. A few examples follow as an illustration:

SAU.002.149

وقال بيان أصدرته وزارة الخارجية المجريّة إنّه يجب على الحكومة الرومانيّة أن تضمن الامن الشرعيّ للمواطنين

← **والاّ** فإنّ إجراء مباحثات بين المجر ورومانيا لا معنى لها.

*"A communiqué published by the Hungarian Ministry of Foreign Affairs stated that the Romanian government must guarantee the legal safety of the fellow countrymen, and **if not**, it makes no sense to conduct negotiations between Hungary and Romania."*

SAU.002.218

وأوضح المندوب الامريكيّ توماس باكرين أنّ المجلس يطالب المبادرة العراقيّة بتصحيح فوريّ للمشكلة

← **والاّ** ستكون العواقب وخيمة.

*"The American delegate, 'Thomas Bakrin', elucidated that the (Security) Council urges the Iraqi initiative to review the problem immediately, **or else** the consequences will be disastrous."*

Also in other forms of broadcast this restriction in meaning has been observed. A last example from an Algerian report:

ALG.003.314

للتذكير فإنّ الاجتماع الاخير لمسيّري محطّات البنزين قرّر إعطاء يوم الواحد والثلاثين من الشهر الجاري كآخر اجل لحلّ مشاكلهم

← **والاّ** سيلجأون الى شنّ الإضراب.

*"We also report that in the last meeting of gasoline station managers, it was decided to set the 31st of this month as the final time limit to solve their problems, **or else** they will strike."*

[14] Because of this very restrictive meaning we did not include the occurrences of the contracted particle *wa 'illā* in previous tables.

Thus, the combination of وَ 'and' the conditional particle *'in* and the negative particle *lā* forms the fixed expression *wa-'illā* 'or else'. As mentioned above, the particle *'in* is, in its conditional function, almost exclusively used in the fixed frequent expression *'in šā' allāh*. Moreover, it also occurs in Algeria in the frequent expression *not to say:*

ALG.003.284

لعلّ اخوان المستمعين يدركون معنى هذا المثل الشعبيّ الذي سنختم به هذا التحقيق
وهو شافت حاب دبجنا فمعقول جدًّا أن نناشد المواطنين بصفة عامّة وربّات البيوت
بصفة خاصّة بضرورة ترشيد استهلاكهم$ للمياه لأنّهم على دراية تامّة بأنّ مدينتهم
تتغدّى بهذه المادّة الحيويّة بالاعتماد اساسًا على مصادر وموارد يوجد معظمها
← **إنْ** لم نقل جلّها خارج تراب ولاية وهران.

"Maybe our (brother) listeners know the meaning of this popular saying šafet ḥab dabajnā, with which we want to conclude this investigation, so it is reasonable that we advise our fellow countrymen in general and more particularly housewives on (the necessity of) proper consumption of the water. Because they are completely conscious that their city feeds on this vital resource depending mainly on sources and springs, of which the larger part ***if not*** *the greater part is situated outside the territory of Wahrān."*

Or, such as the following sports news item from Algeria:

ALG.004.418

حبيسة بوالمرك شاركت ايضا وكانت أدّت سباقا رائعا في الميل، مسافة الميل والنتيجة لم
تصلنا بعد ولكن ما هو مؤكّد أنّ هذا يكون قد حطّمت الرقم القياسيّ الجزائريّ
← **إن** لم نقل الافريقيّ في هذه المسافة.

"Ḥabīsa Boulmark participated too and ran a brilliant race for a distance of a mile, but the result has not reached us yet, but what is sure is that she will have broken the Algerian record, ***not to mention*** *the African record."*

For the rest the use of the particle *'in* is mainly restricted to concessive sentences. The use of the particle *'in* with a pure conditional function has almost completely disappeared. In the news broadcasts of Algeria, we found only one example, viz.:

ALG.002.212

وعبّرت بعدها ثماني دول عربيّة اخرى عن رفضها حضور الدورة
← **إن** تمّ عقدها بالعاصمة المصريّة.

"And after that eight other Arab countries expressed their refusal to participate in the session ***if*** *it was to be held in the Egyptian capital."*

It also occurs once in an Egyptian news commentary in a quotation from a speech by President *Mubārak*, viz.:

EGY.001.492

قال الرئيس مبارك في نداءه إنّك

← **إن** فعلت فسوف يقدّرك الشعب العربيّ والعالم كلّه.

"President Mubārak said in his appeal: ***If*** *you (Ṣaddām Ḥusayn) do so, then the whole Arab people and the whole world will hold you in esteem."*

Apart from one occurrence in a reportage, the particle *'in* does not occur with pure conditional meaning. Whether the particle *'in* in MSA has lost its importance in favor of the particle *'iḏā* can only be demonstrated from an analysis of the particle *'iḏā*.

13.5.2. *Function of the particle* 'iḏā

13.5.2.1. *'iḏā* as introduction to indirect questions

Cantarino (1974, vol. 3, 320) observed that the particle *'in* in modern Arabic may be used to introduce indirect questions. In our corpus we only found one such occurrence in an Algerian news broadcast. We also found one occurrence of the particle *'in* introducing an indirect question in a news broadcast of Saudi Arabia. For the rest it is clear from the investigation of our corpus that indirect questions are always introduced by the particle *'iḏā,* more particularly in the collocation *mā 'iḏā*. Although this construction is only mentioned by Blau (1976: 161), it is the only one which occurs in our text corpus. Moreover, the most striking feature is that this construction is used in the three countries under investigation. By way of illustration a few examples from news broadcasts:

ALG.002.113

في نفس الوقت أعلن راديو طهران أنّ الحدود بين إيران وازربيجان أغلقت وأرسلت
الى المنطقة قوات سوفيتيّة دون أن يوضّح

← **ما إذا** كان إجراء غلق الحدود اتّخذ في موسكو او طهران.

"At the same time Radio Teheran announced that the border between Iran and Azerbadjan was closed and that Soviet troops had been sent to the area without elucidating ***whether*** *the decision to close the border was taken by Moscow or Teheran."*

EGY.002.268

وردًا على سؤال حول

← **ما إذا** كان رئيس وزراء باكستان قد بلور افكارًا حول ازمة الخليج قال الدكتور عاطف صدقي إنّه يقوم بتجميع وجهات النظر ولكن ليس هناك مبادرات طرحها في هذا الشأن.

*"And in answer to the question **whether** the Pakistani prime minister already had an idea about the Gulf crisis, Doctor 'Āṭif Ṣidqī said that he was collecting points of view but that no new initiatives had been proposed in this matter."*

SAU.002.204

وقال ناراسمها راو في تصريحات للصحافيّين عقب لقائه مع الرئيس الهنديّ إنّه لم يقرّر بعد

← **ما إذا** كان سيؤدّي اليمين بمفرده او مع زملاء آخرين هذا اليوم.

*"And Narasimha Rao said in statements to journalists immediately after his meeting with the Indian president that it had not yet been decided, **whether** he will take the oath alone or with other colleagues."*

It is not only clear that a shift has taken place in the use of the appropriate particles, but also that this shift occurs in the three countries in the same direction. There is a clear tendency to introduce indirect questions by the construction *mā 'iḏā*. It is also clear that the particles *'in* and *law* lose some of their importance as far as this function is concerned (cf. supra 13.3.).

13.5.2.2. *'iḏā* as conditional particle

Investigation of the corpus clearly demonstrates that the particle *'iḏā*, indeed, has in many cases a temporal function. It is clear that conditional relations, such as they have been described by Ya'qūb and Al-'Umarī, are not always involved. We also find many connections between sentences without a real conditional relationship. For instance, the following sentences form the three countries:

ALG.002.690

ما هو الهدف من تنظيمه وماذا في جدول الاعمال خاصّة

← **إذا** علمنا أنّ هذا الملتقى يأتي بفترة قصيرة بعد زلزال التاسع والعشرين اكتوبر الماضي؟

*"What is the aim of this organization and what is the agenda, especially **when** we know that this conference is being held shortly after the earthquake of October 29th last ."*

EGY.002.101

وقال لماذا يشنّ العراق هجومًا ضدّ إسرائيل

← **إذا** كانت ليست عضوًا في التحالف الذي يواجه العراق في هذه الازمة.

"And he said, why does Iraq launch an attack against Israel ***when*** *Israel is not a member of the alliance which is confronting Iraq in this crisis?"*

SAU.002.609

وفي بيان نشر إثر اجتماع في باريس لوزراء الخارجية والدفاع أشارت الدول التسع الاعضاء في الاتّحاد الى أنّه

← **إذا** كان العراق اليوم في محنة فالمسؤولية تقع على صدام حسين الذي تجاهل كلّ دعوات السلام:

"And in a communiqué which was issued in Paris after a meeting of the ministers of Foreign Affairs and Defense of the nine member states of the Union, the ministers pointed out that ***if*** *Iraq is in a crisis today, the responsibility lies with Ṣaddām Ḥusayn who has ignored all appeals for peace."*

SAU.002.223

وأوضح شبرانجر في المؤتمر الصحفيّ الذي عقده الليلة الماضية في القاهرة أنّ المانيا لن تستجيب لمطالب إسرائيل بدفع عشرة مليارات مارك المانيّ كتعويضات لليهود خاصّة

← **إذا** كانت هذه الاموال ستخصّص لبناء مزيد من المستوطنات في الاراضي العربيّة المحتلّة.

"And Spranger elucidated at a press conference held last night in Cairo that Germany will not comply with Israel's demands to pay ten billion German Mark as compensation for the Jews, especially ***if*** *these funds will be allocated for the building of more settlements in occupied arab territories."*

On the other hand, further analysis of the corpus demonstrates that the particle *'iḏā* is also used to introduce a condition, whose occurrence is not certain. On this point the particle *'iḏā* clearly takes over the function of the particle *'in*. This shift in function is manifest in all three countries. A few examples clearly illustrate this shift.

ALG.002.207

وحول ازمة الخليج قال طارق عزيز إنّنا مستعدّون لتطبيق الجانب المتعلّق بنا من المشكلة

← **إذا** نوقشت جميع المسائل في مجلس الامن.

"And about the Gulf crisis Ṭāriq 'Azīz said: 'We are prepared to take up our side of the problem ***if*** *all questions are discussed in the Security Council'."*

Whether the condition will be fulfilled in this sentence is not at all clear. It even seems improbable given the context. Nevertheless, the particle *'iḏā* is used. Not only in Algeria but also in the other Arab countries the particle *'iḏā* introduces a condition whose realization is very incertain. For instance, in the following sentences in Egypt and Saudi Arabia:

EGY.002.216

وتضمّن التقرير ايضا أنّه

← **إذا** استمرّ هذا الاتّجاه فإنّ اربعين مليون افريقيّ سيعانون من الفقر المدقع خلال السنوات المقبلة.

*"This report also states that, **if** this tendency continues, forty million Africans will suffer from the most miserable poverty in the years to come."*

EGY.002.141

الرئيس الامريكيّ جورج بوش يصرّح بأنّ الرئيس العراقيّ صدام حسين سيرتكب خطأ فادحًا

← **إذا** رفض الانسحاب من الكويت قبل الموعد الذي حدّدته الامم المتّحدة في الخامس عشر من يناير الحاليّ.

*"The American President George Bush declared that the Iraqi President Ṣaddām Ḥusayn will commit a very serious mistake **if** he refuses to withdraw from Kuwait before the date which has been set by the Security Council on the fifteenth of this month (January)."*

SAU.002.174

وأضاف المسؤول الذي طلب عدم ذكر اسمه أنّه

← **إذا** تقرّر ذلك فسيتوجّه بيكر الى تيرانا .

*"And the person in charge, who asked that his name not be revealed, added that, **if** this is decided, Baker will head for Tirana.*

SAU.002.208

حذّر سفير الولايات المتّحدة لدى هيئة الامم المتّحدة توماس باكرين العراق من إمكانية مواجهة غضب العالم من جديد

← **إذا** استمرّ في رفض السماح بتفتيش الموادّ النوويّة التابعة له.

*"The ambassador of the United States at (the organization of) the United Nations, Thomas Bakrin, warned Iraq about the possibility of saddling itself with the anger of the world **if** it continues to refuse to have its nuclear installations inspected."*

In all these previous examples, and there are many more, it is clear that in each case a condition is involved, of which it is not 100% sure that it will be fulfilled. The observation of Cantarino (1974, vol. 3, 302) that: "The basic conditional significance of إذا normally remains so closely related to its temporal one that even in its conditional use, it generally introduces only a statement of something which is known through experience and about the eventual occurrence of which there can, therefore, be no doubt. إذا leaves uncertain the time, not the fact, of the actual event." contrasts with the data we deducted from the radio news broadcasts. Investigation of the corpus confirms the impression of Beeston (1970: 104), Holes (1994: 238) and Kouloughli (1994: 289) that the particle *'iḏā* holds more and more a conditional function, in which the particle *'in* is ousted to a large extent.[15] Moreover, with our corpus investigation we demonstrate that this shift is not a local one, but one to be found throughout the whole area dealt with.[16]

Still, there is another remarkable fact, namely that the particle *'iḏā* often occurs in collocation with the adverbial particle *mā* 'ever'. Many conditional constructions are introduced by the collocation *'iḏā mā* 'if ever'. In this case the particle *mā* should never be interpreted as a negation. When a sentence is turned into the negative after *'iḏā,* the particle *lam* is always used. For instance, in the sentence:

EGY.002.104

في تركيا بدأت اليوم حالة التعبئة لفرق الدفاع المدنيّ استعدادًا لاحتمالات نشوب الحرب في الخليج

← **إذا** لم يمتثل الرئيس العراقيّ لقرارات مجلس الامن.

"In Turkey today began the (state of) mobilization of tcivil defense teams in preparation for the possible breaking out of war in the Gulf ***if*** *the Iraqi president does not conform to the decisions of the Security Council."*

That the particle *mā* has no negative function is clear from the following two sentences. In one news broadcast the same sentence was read in the beginning and at the end of the news once with and once without the particle *mā*. The meaning of the sentence did not change.

[15] According to Fischer (1982: 47) this shift has already been observed in post-classical Arabic. However, we do not know whether it was an exceptionnal or a general phenomenon. As a matter of fact he points out that there was no uniform language use in that period.: "Seit dem 11 Jh. werden Neuerungen in Syntax und Stil allmählich zur Regel, so dass spätestens seit dieser Zeit von einer 'nachklassischen Periode' gesprochen werden kann. Sie reicht bis ins 19. Jh., stellt aber in sich keine geschlossene Einheit dar, weil die Ausdruckweise der klassisch-arabisch schreibenden Autoren während dieses langen Zeitraums sehr grosse Unterschiede aufweist" (Fischer 1982: 46).

[16] Whether this shift also occurs in contemporary Arabic literature can only be demonstrated by examining the contemporary literary language.

EGY.002.525

أعلن وزير خارجية السويد أنّ بلاده لن تتردّد في إرسال قوات الى الخليج
← **إذا** ما طلبت منها الامم المتّحدة ذلك.

EGY.002.569

أعلن اندرسون وزير خارجية السويد أنّ بلاده لن تتردّد في إرسال قوات الى الخليج
← **إذا** طلبت منها الامم المتّحدة ذلك.

"The minister of Foreign Affairs of Sweden announced that his country will not hesitate to send troops to the Gulf, ***if*** *the United Nations were to ask them to do so."*

This example shows that, with or without the addition of the particle *mā,* the particle *'iḏā* holds the same (conditional) function. According to Bravmann (1963: 368) this construction can follow verbs with or without a fixed ("phrasal") preposition. Apart from Blau (1976: 161) Cantarino (1974, vol. 3, 305-6) is the only author mentioning the construction *'iḏā mā*. According to him its use points at a general undetermined meaning, viz. *whenever*. This, however, is the classical meaning such as it has been described by Yaʿqūb (1988: 433) and which, also according to Yaʿqūb, has been used from times immemorial in this meaning in poetry. The information we found in Bravmann and Blau clearly seems to indicate that a specific conditional function is involved. We even have the impression that the use of the collocation *'iḏā mā* emphasizes the conditional function of the particle. For instance, in the sentence:

ALG.002.196

الرئيس السوفيتيّ ميخائيل جورباتشوف قال امس إنّ الاتّحاد السوفيتيّ مستعدّ لوقف كلّ التجارب النوويّة
← **إذا** ما اتّخذت الولايات المتّحدة الامريكيّة نفس القرار.

"Soviet President Michael Gorbachovsaid yesterday that the Soviet Union is prepared to stop all nuclear experiments ***if*** *the United States takes the same decision."*

ALG.002.284

وهدّد بمعاملة الرعايا الفرنسيّين نفس المعاملة التي يلاقيها الرعايا الامريكيّين
← **إذا** ما شاركت الحكومة الفرنسيّة الى جانب الولايات المتّحدة الامريكيّة في فرضها للحصار ضدّ العراق.

"He threatened to give the French citizens the same treatment as the American citizens ***if*** *the French government participates with the United States in imposing an embargo on Iraq."*

This may be an example of a shift of the particle *'iḏā* towards a composed particle *'iḏā mā*, such as has been the case for the particles *ka* towards *kamā* and *'inda* towards *'indamā*.

Finally we have to consider the question what is the specific function of the particle *law* and whether here too shifts can be observed.

13.5.3. *Function of the particle* law

Although the particle *law* does not occur frequently in the corpus, it is possible to make some interesting observations. In the first place, the use of wa 'and' plus *law* to introduce concessive sentences is widely known.

As far as the conditional function of the particle *law* is concerned we observed, in the first place, that this is the well-known function of the irrealis condition such as, for example, in the following example from the Algerian sports news:

ALG.004.250

والله ليست اسئلة ونحن في نشرة الاخبار ربّما
← **لو** كنّا في حصّة رياضيّة لطرحنا اسئلة عديدة وامامي الزميل عبد المؤمن دكار يشير لي الى الساعة على كلّ حال فيه اخبار اخرى.

*"Indeed, I don't have any more questions, at present we are in a news broadcast, **if** we **were** in a sports broadcast, we still **would** have many questions to ask, but with me is colleague 'Abd al-Mu'min Dakkār who reminds me of the time, anyhow, there still is some other news."*

In this case an unreal condition clearly is involved. The journalists are not in a sports broadcast and they lay down a condition about something which is impossible. Another example about a classical use of this particle is this sentence from an Algerian news broadcast which refers to the past

ALG.002.216

وبخصوص قمة بوش جورباتشوف المرتقبة في هيلسينكي اكتفى شيفرناتزي بالقول إنّ الرجلين سيبحثان حلا سلميًا لازمة الخليج التي
← **لو** كانت اندلعت قبل نهاية الحرب الباردة كما قال لكنّا وضعنا صواريخنا على اهبة الإطلاق وكانت حينئذ الحرب العالميّة الثالثة.

*"And more specifically about the 'Bush - Gorbachov' summit which is being held in Helsinki, Shevarnadze limited himself to saying that both men will look for a peaceful solution for the Gulf crisis, which **if** it **had** broken out before the end of the cold war, as he said, we **would** have prepared our missiles for launch and that we **would** have had a third world war."*

However, we also observe that the particle *law* is also used in possible conditions which are normally introduced by the particle *'iḏā*. For instance, in the following sentence from an Egyptian news broadcast:

EGY.002.168

أعلن مصدر رسميّ سعوديّ أنّ حاكم العراق كان يمكن أن يتفادى الحرب
← **لو** استجاب للنداءات والمبادرات التي وجّهت اليه في اللحظات الاخيرة.

"An official Saudi source announced that the Iraqi leader could avoid the war ***were*** *he to comply with the appeals and the initiatives addressed to him at the last moment."*

Similar sentences were also found in other types of broadcasts. In a way the particle *'iḏā* or *'in* might be used here. However, these particles are not used because of a specific shade of meaning. In other words, since the situation is the same, viz. the withdrawal from Iraq out of Kuwait and since this fact is not completely impossible (it is an event which still can be realized), we observe here another function of the particle *law*, viz. the indication of great doubt about the realization of a certain event.

The condition remains real, but in using the particle *law* the speaker wants to indicate that he is convinced of the improbability of the realization of this event. The fact itself is not improbable or unreal, but in using the particle *law* the speaker gives *his* impression about the improbability of the condition. It has struck us that the use of the particle *law* in this meaning occurs much more frequently in the news commentaries of Egypt. Indeed, there was a great uncertainty in Egypt about the possibility of the outbreak of a new war. The following examples can illustrate this:

EGY.001.866

وتقبّل الرجل ذلك على مضض لأنّه يدرك نبل المهمّة التي يقوم بها ويدرك الثمن الفادح الذي سوف يدفعه العراق والمنطقة
← **لو** نشبت الحرب.

"The man (the secretary general of the UN) accepted this with regret because he understands the nobility of the mission he is conducting and because he understands the heavy price that Iraq and the area ***would*** *pay if the war* ***were to*** *break out."*

والتي وصفها الرئيس مبارك بأنّها ستكون
← **لو** نشبت حربًا مدمّرة فتاكل الاخضر واليابس خاصّة وأنّ جميع المراقبين يؤكّدون أنّ الموقف خطير.

"And which President Mubārak described as — if it ***were to*** *break out — an all destructive war, especially because all the observers are convinced that the situation is dangerous."*

Consequently we record that the use of the particle *law* is not only limited to the unreal condition, but that it is also used to convey the impression that an event is improbable, even when it is real. A last example from an Algerian news broadcast can illustrate this in an even more clear way:

ALG.002.218

← **لو** قلت لكم إنّ طفلا سوفيتيًّا في السابع من عمره يزن تسعين كيلوجرام وطوله متر وثمانون سنتيمتر، هل تصدّقوني؟

"If I ***told*** *you that a Soviet child of seven years weighs ninety kilos and that he is one meter eighty tall,* ***would*** *you believe me?"*

Neither the saying by the news reader, nor the fact itself is unreal. On the contrary, both elements are real. Indeed, the news reader continues by saying, 'and yet it is the truth', and then recounts the story of the boy. In this case too it is not the impossibility of the occurrence which is involved but the improbability of a real event is emphasized. These observations confirm the comment by Holes that the particle *law* not only points at the impossibility but also can point at the improbability of an event (Holes 1994: 238).

In the corpus the expression *if the necessity demands it,* occurs quite frequently. In all cases in such expressions the particle *'iḏā* is used such as, for instance, in *'iḏā iqtaḍathā ḍ-ḍarūra* or *'iḏā lazima l-'amr*. Only in one case in a reportage in Egypt did the journalist use the particle *law*. In this case too I hold the view that the particle *law* performs a separate function and that the meaning of the sentence with *law* differs from the meaning of the sentence with *'iḏā. law lazima l-'amr* expresses a much greater uncertainty than the expression *'iḏā lazima l-'amr*. In my view this construction, introduced by the particle *law,* ought to be translated as *if the necessity* ***were to*** *demand so.*

13.6. Conclusion

Regional variation of Modern Standard Arabic of the news broadcasts in the use of the conditional particles has not been observed. It is clear, however, that the use of these particles in MSA strongly deviates from the norm such as it is prescribed by contemporary Arab grammarians. We ascertain an important shift in function of the particles concerned compared to 'classical Arabic' such as it is described in these grammars.

Our previous investigation demonstrates, in the first place, that a far-reaching standardization has taken place in favor of the collocation *mā 'iḏā*, as far as the introduction of indirect questions is concerned in MSA such as we observed it in the news broadcasts on the radio. Except for one case this collocation was used in all indirect questions.

In the second place we can conclude that the particle *'iḏā* in News Broadcast-MSA has taken almost completely over the conditional function of the particle *'in*,6 whereas the particle *law* retains its specific function. However, besides the well known function of introducing an unreal condition, this particle also holds a new function, viz. to convey the impression of the speaker about the improbability of an event. It is remarkable that the particle *law* maintains its function whereas the other particles are subject to a striking shift in function. This confirms our hypothesis that the internal language evolution chiefly takes place where elements operate which hold a similar function.

14. THE COMPLEMENTARY PARTICLES OF NEGATION *MĀ* AND *LAM*

The word *mā* is polysemic. It can as well be a pronoun as a particle. In this investigation we limit ourselves to *mā* as a particle of negation. It is not very clear whether the particles of negation *mā* and *lam* have equivalent or similar functions, whether they are mutually interchangeable without producing a shift in meaning of the sentence. Views on that matter differ. On any event, the Arabic approach by Al-ʿUmarī and Yaʿqūb seems to consider them as being equivalent.

14.1. The Arabic approach

The information on these particles found in both Yaʿqūb (1988: 427-433 and 401-403) and Al-ʿUmarī (1993: 398-399 and 478-479) is very limited. As for the negative aspect, no distinction is made between both particles; only the mood of the following verbs differs. We will briefly discuss the particles in turn.

14.1.1. *The particle* mā

As far as the particle of negation *mā* is concerned, Yaʿqūb distinguishes between the *mā al-ḥijāzīya* (the *Ḥijāzī mā*) (which precedes a nominal phrase) and the *mā an-nāfiya ad-dāḫila ʿalā jumla fiʿlīya* (the *mā* of negation which precedes a verbal clause). As an example Yaʿqūb quotes the sentence: ما الكسول ناجحا (*The idler is not successful*). In this form and meaning the particle *mā* has the negation function of the verb *laysa* (*not to be*). When the particle *mā* is used to introduce a verbal clause, the negation particle *mā* can be followed by a verb in the present tense or a verb in the past tense. Yaʿqūb quotes Koranic verse 7-72 as an example: وما كانوا مؤمنين (*And did not believe*) and Koranic verse 74-31: وما يعلم جنود ربّك إلا هو (*And none can know the forces of thy Lord, except He*). Al-ʿUmarī (1993: 478) lumps both functions of the particle *mā* together, viz. the negation function of the particle *mā*. According to both authors the negation function of the particle *mā* was called the *Ḥijāzī mā* because it was used in this manner by the inhabitants of the Ḥijāz. In this function it is always placed before a nominal phrase.

14.1.2. *The particle* lam

The particle *lam* negates the verb. It converts the present meaning of a verb into a past meaning by putting the verb in the jussive[1] such as, for instance, in Koranic verse 112-3: لم يلد ولم يولد *(He begetteth not, nor is He begotten)*.[2] Further Yaʿqūb points out that the verb after the particle *lam* can not be omitted except under certain circumstances in poetry. In poetry too the particle *lam* can be separated from the verb by another word.

14.2. The western approach

Most western authors likewise hold the view that the two particles are equivalent. Kouloughli (1988: 56-60) gives a long list of authors who either don't pay attention to the problem, or don't see a difference in meaning[3], or hold the view that there is only a difference in style. However Kouloughli observes that classical grammarians, among others Ibn Yaʿīš, clearly distinguish the meaning of the particles. This distinction in meaning by Ibn Yaʿīš is described by Kouloughli as follows: "Si on demandait: 'quel besoin a-t-on de *lam* pour la négation et pourquoi ne se contente-t-on pas du *mā* de *mā qāma zaydun* (Zayd ne s'est pas levé)?', il faudrait répondre: '*lam* à une valeur supplémentaire qui n'est pas dans *mā* à savoir que *mā* lorsqu'elle nie le passé porte sur ce qui a été rapproché du présent mais ne nie pas le passé de façon absolue" (Kouloughli 1988: 54). On this basis Kouloughli concludes that in Classical Arabic only those events which are characterized by a link to the present can be made negative by the particle *mā*. No Arabic author, according to Kouloughli, has clearly explained what this link exactly consists of. Moreover in the Koran certain verses which contain the particle *mā* do refer to a past discrete from the present.

The question whether both particles are really mutually interchangeable was asked by Hans Wehr long before Kouloughli: "Bereits dem Anfänger im Arabischen fällt es auf, dass er scheinbar die Wahl hat, im

[1] Although, according to Al-ʿUmarī (1993: 397) some hold the view that the verb can be put in the subjunctive.
[2] Al-ʿUmarī (1993: 397) quotes the same Koranic verse as an example.
[3] Cf. Stoetzer (1991: 153)

präteritalen Sinn *lam 'aktub* und *mā katabtu* zu gebrauchen (...) Aber sind die genannten Paare wirklich vertauschbar? Wir dürfen a priori voraussetzen, dass dies kaum denkbar ist" (Wehr 1953: 27). When conducting a closer investigation of smaller classical corpora, also statistically, Wehr comes to the conclusion that the particle *mā* is chiefly used in direct speech. Moreover, he observes: "Ferner fällt es auf, dass in *mā* Sätzen in durchschnittlich der Hälfte oder mehr aller überhaupt vorkommenden Fälle die 1. und 2. Person subjekt ist. Es handelt sich also um lebhafte Rede und Gegenrede" (Wehr 1953: 30).[4]

Wehr concludes that it is much more appropriate to use the particle *mā* when the negation is subjective and the content of the negation is heavily emotional. In those cases the use of the particle *lam*, according to Wehr, is much less appropriate.[5] In other words, the affective emotional emphasis of the negation is much stronger in the particle *mā* than in the particle *lam*. In the latter case we rather have *objective* negations which also occur in direct speech, but even more in tales.

According to Wehr, this does not exclude the link of the particle *mā* with the present. As an example he takes the verb *qatala*. Preceded by the particle *lam (yaqtul)* it ought to be translated by: *he killed*, whereas preceded by *mā (qatala)* it ought to be translated by *he has killed*, which in particular emphasizes the result of the act.[6] The most important distinction between the two particles , however, lies in the emotional tension. "Der primäre Unterschied zwischen *lam yaktub* und *mā kataba* ist nicht im Tempus, sondern in der personlichen Anteilnahme des Sprechers an der Aussage, also im Affektgrad zu sehen" (Wehr 1953: 31). Whether this still plays a role in Modern Standard Arabic is not quite clear. We do find, however, some indications in Cantarino's work.

14.3. Evolution in the use of the particles of negation *mā* and *lam*

Cantarino (1974 vol. 1, 108 et seq.) observes that the particle *mā* is only rarely used to make a noun phrase negative. As for the use of this

[4] Cf. also Holes (1994: 262)

[5] As another example of emotionally heavily loaded expressions Wehr refers to the incantations, in which, according to his investigation, the particle *mā* is exclusively used. Even the expression *lā budda* (*no doubt*), according to Wehr (1953: 32-34), is converted to *mā budda*after an incantation.

[6] This principle has been confirmed by Kouloughli (1988: 60): "On ne peut donc que souscrire, au moins au niveau du principe général, à la règle de traduction de *mā fa'ala* par un parfait (en français ce sera un 'passé composé') et non par un prétérit (en français un 'passé simple')".

particle in modern literary works, Cantarino shares Wehr's view. The particle *mā* is preferably used in direct speech and consequently with a verb following in the first or the second person. More often than not the particle is placed at the head of the sentence immediately before the verb. It is also used before a present tense as a negation of the present. Moreover, it often occurs as the first part of the compound of exception *mā ... 'illā* and as the first part of the compound *mā ... ḥattā*.

As a matter of fact, Cantarino (1974 vol. 1: 127 et seq.) observes that the negative particle *mā* is much less frequently used than was the case in former days. Even if it does occur in a certain kind of prose, there too it ought to be considered as an archaism.[7] The same view is held by Krahl (1980 vol. 1: 136): "Statt ما + Perfektform wird in der Schriftsprache fast ausschliesslich لم + Apokopat gebraucht." However, further on he remarks, as does Kouloughli (1988: 49), that it is still often used in fixed expressions: "Es gibt aber mit ما eine ganze Reihe lexikalisierter Ausdrücke sowohl verbaler als auch nominaler Konstruktion, wie z.B. ما زال يشرب (*Er hat nicht aufgehört zu trinken*)."[8]

The reason why the particle *mā* does not occur so frequently any more in MSA is, according to Cantarino, a stylistic one. The negative particle *mā* is indeed very often used in colloquial language, and writers want to avoid forms and constructions from the colloquial language. Kouloughli (1988: 69) does not agree with this view when he writes: "Une telle 'explication' est, pour le moins, arbitraire: pourquoi l'aversion supposée des auteurs pour ce qui fait dialectal se serait-elle particulièrement portée sur ce schéma d'énoncé plutôt que sur des dizaines d'autres que l'arabe écrit partage de bon gré avec l'arabe parlé?. En outre, peut-on sérieusement supposer que nos auteurs ignoraient que cette construction est très largement employée dans le Koran considéré comme le modèle inimitable de la perfection littéraire?".

At first one might agree with Kouloughli. Indeed, our investigation too demonstrates that the use of the particle *'iḏā* (which is also prevalent in the dialects) is increasing in comparison with the more 'classical' particle *'in*. The same goes for the particle *wa* which is used much more

[7] See, for instance, Holes (1990: 71 et seq.) and Palva (1969: 37). This, however, completely contradicts the allegations of Cowan who writes (1973: 56 and 87) that for the negation of the past tense, the particle *mā* is put before a past tense and that the negation of an imperfect is performed by putting the prefix *lā* or *mā* before a present tense!

[8] Fischer (1982, I: 325) agrees with this view but observes too that "مَا wird gelegentlich im Verbalsatz gebraucht als nachdrückliche Negation im Sinne von 'überhaupt nicht'."

frequently than the particle *fa*.[9] If Cantarino's reasoning holds water, one might wonder why we do not observe the same conduct of avoidance vis-à-vis the other particles. On the other hand, it is generally known that such an approach in language use does exist. Why the use of one particle is avoided whereas the use of another is not may be due to the fact that this approach is not based on *objective* criteria, but on *subjective* impressions, viz. Arabs' perception of MSA. The speaker, often erroneously, fears that a certain construction is dialectal, which is why he will try to avoid its use in the standard language.

As a matter of fact, the image and the impression of the contradiction of *mā* as a dialectal particle compared to *lam* as an MSA particle is widespread. Even if we observe in the work of both Al-ʿUmarī and Yaʿqūb that the negative particle *mā* is definitely acceptable as a norm because of its use in the dialects, the impression still remains widespread that *mā* is a typical dialectal particle. Holes, for instance, describes the particle *lam* as a 'saliently MSA negative' (1994: 303). Elsewhere he writes: 'The use of the *mā* construction has come to be associated either with a consciously 'literary' style, or with dialectal usage; on both accounts it is avoided in non-literary MSA writing (Holes 1994: 263)."

This proposition clearly demonstrates that the negative particle *m* not be used as a parameter for *dialectal language use*, since it occurs in the contemporary normative grammars by Al-ʿUmarī and Yaʿqūb who clearly argue that it is a possible, negative form in Classical Arabic. Consequently, the use of the negative particle *mā* alone is not a sufficient indication of whether an author is influenced by classical Arabic or dialectal Arabic.[10]

According to Wehr, the cause of the less frequent occurrence of the particle *mā* in MSA lies elsewhere. According to him the particle *mā* is much less frequently used in prose precisely because more and more it

[9] This proposition clearly goes against Holes' observation that 'written Arabic' is moving away from the dialectal Arabic: "These developments (the decline in use of the particle *mā* in the written language) are another example (...) of the conscious distancing of written Arabic from anything which smacks of dialect" (Holes 1994: 263).

[10] Except, for instance, for the discontinuous ngative morpheme *mā - š* 'not', such as, for instance, in the expression *mā fī-š* 'there is not' (cf. also infra 14.4.). The same goes for the conjunction *wa*: it is not because the conjunction *wa* occurs much more frequently in the dialects that the increase in use which we have observed in MSA of the particle *wa* compared to the particle *fa* can be interpreted as an influence of dialectal Arabic on MSA. The use of the particle *wa* in the dialects is already an influence of MSA on the dialects (cf. Palva 1969). In Moroccan Arabic the most used form of the conjunction was *u* (cf. Van Mol 1981: 11), but under influence of the standard language the conjunction *wa* penetrated more and more in Moroccan Arabic.

has become a written language, a 'Papiersprache', in which the emotional stresses play a much less important role. Further on he remarks: "Heute muss man in einer Zeitung sehr lange suchen, bis man einmal auf einen durch *mā* verneinten Satz stöszt" (Wehr 1953: 38). We can only add in this respect that the rare occurrence of the particle *mā* can also be due to the type of text in which Wehr was looking for it, viz. newspaper language in which direct speech occurs much less frequently.

About the less frequent occurrence of the particle *mā* in MSA, Kouloughli postulates another not uninteresting hypothesis. In the pair *mā* - *lam*, Kouloughli presents the particle *lam* as the *unmarked* form because, according to him, a negative with *lam* is possible in all contexts, whereas this is not the case for the particle *mā*. He argues: "Il paraît raisonable de faire l'hypothèse que, si une opposition tend à disparaître d'un système, c'est toujours, quand il existe, au profit du terme non marqué" (Kouloughli 1988: 69). Due to the lack of *specialization* the unmarked form can adopt the functions of a marked term much more easily.

In the first place we have to admit that the term *marking* is not very univocal. Lyons (1984: 305-311), for instance, points out that the term *marking* can easily lead to confusion. He distinguishes between a) the original meaning of the term, viz. the *formal marking*, in which a word is marked by a suffix (for instance, *friendly* as an unmarked term and *unfriendly* as a marked term), b) a *distributional marking*, in which the most frequent word is the unmarked form, whereas the least frequent word is the marked one (for instance, *lion* as unmarked form compared to *lioness* as marked form) and c) a *semantic marking* (for instance, the word *dog* as semantic unmarked form compared to the word *bitch* as semantic marked form).[11]

We have the impression that marking as presented by Kouloughli does not fit in the classification by Lyons. Kouloughli discusses a new kind of marking which we might call a *functional marking*. The particle *lam* could then be the *functional* unmarked form contrary to *mā*. Whether Kouloughli's hypothesis can be an explanation for the less frequent occurrence of the particle *mā* in MSA is not quite sure.

Indeed, Kouloughli himself elsewhere in his article refers to Middle Arabic where the use of the particle *lam* had completely disappeared in the current language use of those days. Moreover, when it did occurr it was seen as a kind of hypercorrection. These data suggest that the particle *mā*, in spite of the fact that it was the *functional* marked form, did

[11] For this terminology also see Leech (1976: 17-20).

not gain the upper hand over the particle *lam*, since, according to Blau, in Middle Arabic (cited in Kouloughli p. 67): "*lam* avait, semble t-il, disparu de l'usage vivant."

However, we can argue that the particle *mā*, purely on the basis of its frequency, was *distributionally* the unmarked term. In this sense, the hypothesis such as it has been formulated by Kouloughli is not a very conclusive one. As a matter of fact Kouloughli (p. 71) himself admits that the real reason has not yet been found, nor will it unless we gather corpora of different periods in history. We will start with an investigation in our corpus of contemporary media language into the distribution of the negative particles in the three countries under investigation.

14.4. Quantitative analysis

First we investigate the distribution of the negative particles *mā* and *lam* with the following results:

	News broadcasts					
negative particles	**Algeria**		**Egypt**		**Saudi Arabia**	
N		%	N	%	N	%
Total	**120**	100	**111**	100	**86**	100
lam	101	84	83	75	65	76
mā	19	16	28	25	21	24

Table 26

Starting from the zero hypothesis and assuming that there is no regional difference in distribution of the two particles for the different countries, we can check this by applying the $\chi 2$-test. This test yields for this table a value of 3.64, whereas the table-value with a certainty of 99.5% is 10.60. This means that we can not determine a statistically significant difference in the distribution of the two particles in the different countries. Conducting the same investigation on the control corpus we obtain the following results:

	ALG/R		**ALG/S**		**EGY/R**		**EGY/C**	
	N	%	N	%	N	%	N	%
Tot	**38**	100	**25**	100	**41**	100	**52**	100
lam	29	76	23	92	35	85	44	85
mā	9	24	2	8	6	15	8	15

Table 27

Here too the application of the $\chi 2$-test shows that there is no significant difference in the distribution of the two particles in the different types of broadcast. Indeed we obtain a $\chi 2$-value of 2.92, whereas the table value is 12.84. This means that in Modern Standard Arabic, such as it is used in different Arabic countries in the radio news broadcasts, no statistically significant difference can be determined in the distribution of the negative particles *mā* and *lam*. In the qualitative analysis we will investigate the circumstances under which the particles are used.

14.5. Qualitative analysis

A rough investigation of the use of the particle *mā* in news broadcasts confirms what other scholars already assumed or demonstrated with regard to Arabic literature. The use of the negative particle *mā* is very limited. Moreover, what strikes one most is Krahl's observation (cf. supra 14.3.) that the negative particle *mā* exclusively occurs in a large series of *lexikalisierter Ausdrücke* is indeed correct. Krahl, however, creates the impression that a large variety of expressions is involved. Our investigation reveals that the *collocations* with the negative particle *mā* are very limited. Prior to studying the collocations in detail we present the exceptional sentences in which the particle *mā* was used to make a verb negative. Beside the fixed expressions, the particle *mā* occurred only twice in an Egyptian news broadcast and once in a Saudi Arabia commentary. These are the sentences:

EGY.002.255

وأنّ العراق إذا كان قد تعرّض لغزو اجنبيّ او عربيّ

← **ما** كان لنا نفس الموقف.

"And that we would ***not*** *have the same attitude, if Iraq had already been exposed to a foreign or Arabic attack."*

We note here that the negation of the verb *kāna* by means of the particle *lam* occurred seventeen times in the whole corpus. We can consider the negation of the verb *kāna* by means of the negation particle *mā* as an exception. Further it occurs only once in the whole corpus followed by an imperfect, in the following sentence:

EGY.002.025

اكّد الامين العامّ لمنظّمة المؤتمر الإسلاميّ السيد حامد الغابط أنّ تدفّق المهاجرين اليهود السوفيت الى فلسطين المحتلّة يحمل مخاطر

← **ما** تقلّ عن مخاطر الهجرة التي ادّت الى اغتصاب فلسطين وإنشاء الكيان الصهيوني".

"The secretary general of the Islamic congress organization, mister Ḥāmid al-Ġābiṭ, confirmed that the flow of Jewish immigrants from the USSR to occupied Palestine carries dangers which are ***not*** *less than the dangers of the emigration which led to the occupation of Palestine and the creation of the Zionist state."*

This is the only case in the corpus in which the negation particle *mā* is used before a verb in the present tense. This might be a rare case of dialectal interference. We could only identify the particle *mā* as a dialectal interference elsewhere twice because it was followed by the complementary element *š*.

ALG.002.250

يبدو أنّنا على اتّصال مباشر،

← **ما** في ش# اتّصال يقول خير الدين رجيمي".

"It seems that we are in direct contact?!... "There is no contact", says Ḫayr ad-Dīn Rajīmī."

ALG.002.250

← **ما** في ش#.

"There is none."

As a negative of nominal phrases, the particle *mā* does not occur at all in the corpus except in the fixed expression *mā ... 'illā* which in general we can translate by *it is nothing but only.*[12]:

ALG.002.328

وأضاف قائلا إنّ نبيه برّي أغرم على قبول هذا الاتّفاق خوفًا من توسّع سيطرة حزب الله وإنّ قبوله هذا

← **ما** هو إلاّ تمثيليّة لوقف المعارك.

"And he added (saying) that Nabīh Berrī felt compelled to accept this agreement for fear of the expansion of the dominion of the Ḥizb Allāh and that his acceptance of it ***is nothing but*** *a masquerade to stop the struggle."*

[12] One may wonder whether there is a negative particle in this sentence. Besides, Wehr (1953) observes that the negative particle *mā* is an evolution out of the interrogative *mā*.

ALG.002.974

فالكلّ يجمع على أنّ ما روّجته وسائل الإعلام

← **ما** هي إلاّ ادعاءات مؤسفة لا اساس لها.

*"All agree that what the media diffuse **is nothing but** painful baseless accusations."*

SAU.002.923

وقال

← **وما** هذه الجائزة إلاّ احدى المشاريع السعوديّة العربيّة الإسلاميّة العالميّة التي تحظى باهتمام ورعاية ملكنا المفدّى رعاه الله.

*"And he said: This prize **is only** one of the Saudi Arabian Islamic world projects which have the attention and the protection of our beloved king, May God protect him'."*

Another fixed expression in which the negative particle *mā* occurs is the expression *mā ʿadā*. According to Stetkevych (1970: 99) this construction is new in MSA and is probably introduced by way of translations from French. *Ne plus* was then translated by *mā ʿadā*. Stetkevych adds that *ʿadā* occurs in the Koran and in the traditions but never in a negative construction. In our text corpus *mā ʿadā* has the meaning *with the exception of*. In the whole corpus this expression occurs only three times, viz. in the following sentences:

EGY.002.162

وقد شهدت هذه الساعات الاخيرة قبل انتهاء المهلة التي حدّدها مجلس الامن لانسحاب العراق من الكويت نداءات عديدة لإقناعه بتنفيذ النداءات الدوليّة وكان لهذه النداءات صدى كبير في ارجاء العالم كلّه

← **ما عدا** العراق الذي لم تجد هذه النداءات لديه اذنا صاغية.

*"These last moments before the end of the deadline which had been set by the Security Council for Iraq's withdrawal from Kuwait, have witnessed many appeals aiming at convincing him to carry out the international appeals, which have resounded loudly in all regions of the world, **with the exception** of Iraq, which remains deaf."*

SAU.002.165

طقس صحو على كافّة مناطق المملكة

← **ما عدا** المرتفعات الجنوبيّة الغربيّة حيث تتشكّل عليها سحب منخفضة خاصّة في فترة بعد الظهر.

*"Clear weather in all the regions of the kingdom **with the exception** of the south-western heights where especially in the afternoon low clouds will be formed."*

ALG.003.228

← **ما عدا** اختلافات في بعض المسائل، الوزراء أقرّوا حسب مصدر مطلّع جملة من التوصيات والاقتراحات كانت أعدّتها لجنة المتابعة المشكّلة من الخبراء وكتّاب الدولة للشؤون المغاربيّة.

*"**With the exception of** disagreements about some questions, the ministers have approved, according to a reliable source, a whole list of recommendations and proposals which the follow-up commission composed of experts and secretaries of state for Maghrebi affairs had prepared."*

Only once (in a sports broadcast from Algeria) does the negative particle *mā* occur in collocation with the verb *kāda* (*to be on the point of*). In the remaining cases, the majority, the negative particle *mā* is used before the verb *zāla* (*cease to be*). The verb *zāla* shows great variation both as regards the negative particle which can precede the verb *zāla* and its. In the following table a survey is given of all the possibilities.

	News broadcasts					
verb *zāla*	Algeria		Egypt		Saudi Arabia	
	N	%	N	%	N	%
Total *zāla*	**24**	100	**44**	100	**33**	100
mā + present zāla	8	33	3	7	2	6
mā + past zāla	7	29	23	52	13	39
lā + present zāla	5	21	18	41	15	46
lā +past zāla	4	17	0*	0	3	9

Table 28

* However this collocation does occur twice in Egyptian radio reportages.

Application of the χ2-test on this table gives us a χ2-value of 21.32 with a 99.5% certainty, whereas the χ2-table value is 21.96. In other words we did not find a statistically significant difference between the different countries in the different possibilities of negation for the verb *zāla*. Given the great range of possibilities, this is remarkable. Indeed, we have the *impression* that in the whole corpus not one verb in the past tense follows the particle *lā*. This seems to occur only with the verb *zāla*. It clearly is only an impression, since we do not have the possibility yet of exploring the grammatical categories and verb tenses in the corpus due to its rudimentary encoding. This small example, however, shows the importance of corpus linguistics and of techniques to explore corpora, because it is the only possible means of providing decisive answers about certain grammatical questions.

A second important fact is that in the corpus the verb *zāla* is never preceded by the negative particle *lam*. Whether this is always the case in MSA can only be demonstrated if we compile a comparably encoded corpus of the written language. The data we found suffice to reformulate certain rules and aspects about the verb *zāla,* such as we have described it in our textbook *Handboek Modern Arabisch* (Van Mol 1984: 307). We stated there that the verb *zāla* is seldom used in the jussive. Moreover, we argued that the verb *zāla* is seldom used in the present tense.

The above table demonstrates that these data are not completely correct. In Algeria the verb *zāla* in 54% of the cases is in the present tense; in Egypt, in 48% of the cases and in Saudi Arabia, in 54% of the cases. It is even possible to state that in a light majority of the cases the verb *zāla* is clearly used with the present tense.[13] We also proposed in the textbook *Handboek Modern Arabisch* (Van Mol 1984: 307) *lā* as only possibility for the negation of the verb *zāla* in the present tense, whereas *mā* is also common. It is possible that we have consciously not presented this form in the handbook for fear of introducing a dialectal form as Modern Standard Arabic (cf. supra).[14]

Whether differences in tense and negative particle correspond to differences in meaning is to be examined by comparing a few sentences which are roughly similar in meaning:

ALG.002.119

الوضع في المعسكر الشرقيّ يبقى في واجهة الاحداث الدوليّة وفي مقدّمته الاوضاع
في جنوب شرقيّ يوغسلافيا حيث التوتّر
← **ما يزال** قائمًا، والتفاصيل مع صليحة بحري.

"The situation in the Eastern camp remains on the front page of international events, with the situation in South-East Yugoslavia in the forefront, where tension ***still*** *exists; further details by Ṣalīḥa Baḥrī."*

13 In Stoetzer's grammar (1991: 178) it is stated that the verb *zāla* occurs in the form *mā zāla* and *lā yazālu.* The other two possibilities, viz. *lā zāla* and *mā yazālu* are not mentioned. Besides, in his sample sentences Stoetzer only uses the form *mā zāla,* which conveys the impression that this is the most commonly used form.

14 Neither does Krahl mention the possible negation of the verb *zāla* in the present tense by the particle *mā*. He (1980: vol. 2, 358-362) gives four possibilities, including the jussive *lam yazal*. In his sample sentences this form does not occur at all. We also found the negation with the jussive in Fischer's textbook (1982, vol 1, 234). He does not mention, however, the occurrence of the negative particle *lā* followed by the verb *zāla* in the past tense. Cantarino (1974: vol. 1, 83; vol. 3, 259) gives the three familiar possibilities, viz. *lā zāla, lā yazālu* and *mā zāla*. He adds that the negation *lā* + *zāla* is indicative of emphasis. We did find, however, in another chapter about word order one sample sentence with the form *mā yazālu* which is not discussed elsewhere (Cantarino 1974: vol. 2, 521).

EGY.001.104

وهو الامر الذي رفضته المجموعة الاوربيّة بدورها معرّبةً عن اسفها للرفض العراقيّ السابق ومؤكّدةً في الوقت نفسه أنّ اقتراحها

← **لا يزال** قائما.

*"And this is the case which in turn has been rejected by the European community, expressing its regret about the former Iraqi refusal, but confirming at the same time that its proposition is **still** valid."*

ALG.002.288

وبشأن الاوضاع الامنيّة بالمنطقة، التعزيزات العسكريّة لا زالت تصل الى الخليج في وقت يعلن فيه وزير الدفاع الإماراتيّ أنّ فرص نجاح الجهود العربيّة والدوليّة

← **لا زالت** قائمة.

*"And about the security situation in the territory: at the moment that the minister of defense of the Emirates announces that the chances of success for the international and Arab efforts **still** exist, military reinforcements are still arriving in the Gulf."*

Although in the preceding samples three different negative forms are used, viz. *mā yazālu, lā yazālu* and *lā zālat*, it is not possible to determine any difference in meaning. The same is clear in the following sentences:

ALG.002.541

على إثر صدور البيان الإعلاميّ المشترك من جانب نقابة عمال قطاع التربية ووزارة التربية صدر بيان ثاني# من توقيع لجنة المتابعة عن النقابة الوطنيّة للتعليم الاساسيّ يقول إنّ لجنة المتابعة برئاسة امين عامّ النقابة الوطنيّة للتعليم الاساسيّ تعلم جميع عمال القطاع أنّ الحوار **لا**

← **يزال** متواصلا ولا نتيجة لحدّ الساعة نظرًا لتصلّب موقف الوزارة الوصيّة.

*"Immediately after the publication of the joint press communiqué by the union of the workers of the educational sector and the ministry of education, a second communiqué was published, signed by the (?) commission of the national union of primary education, which says that the (?) commission, under the presidency of the secretary general of the national union for primary education, informs all workers in the sector that the talks are **still continuing** but that there is no result yet because of the tough attitude of the mandatory ministry."*

ALG.002.193

انباء موسكو أفادت أنّ المعارك **ما**

← **تزال** متواصلة بين الازربيجانيّين والارمن خاصّة في مقاطعة ناجورني كرباخ.

*"Messages from Moscow inform that the struggle between the inhabitants of Azerbaijan and the Armenians, especially in the province of Nagorni Karabach, **still continues**."*

ALG.002.183

وكالة تاس أعلنت اليوم أنّ عملية تطبيع الوضع في ازربيجان **ما**
← **زالت** متواصلةً باعتقالات جديدة وتبادل للرهائن.

"The press agency 'Tass' announced today that the operation to normalize the situation in Azerbaijan ***still continues*** *with new arrests and the exchange of hostages."*

ALG.002.100

← **ما يزال** التحقيق في قضية اقتحام مركز الشرطة، الدائرة الثامنة يوم الثلاثاء الماضي متواصلا بمحكمة الجزائر حيث تمّ إيداع ستّة اشخاص الحبس بامر من قاضي التحقيق بالمحكمة من بين سبعة اشخاص الذين أحيلوا على النيابة بتهمة تعدّ على رجال الامن اثناء ممارسة مهامهم وإهانة الهيئة العموميّة والعصيان والإخلال بالنظام العامّ في حين أفرج مؤقّتًا عن واحد منهم.

"The judicial inquiry in the case of the attack on the police station (eighth district) last Tuesday ***still continues*** *in the court of Algiers where by an order of the examining magistrate, six of the seven persons who were handed over to the prosecutor on a charge of aggression against security officers in the execution of their function, insult of the public body, insubordination and disturbance of the public order, were arrested, and that one of them has been freed temporarily."*

Here too, in spite of the fact that different possibilities of negation are used, no difference in meaning can be demonstrated. We finally quote three sentences with an identical collocation, but with different negation forms.

EGY.001.827

جيمس بيكر وزير الخارجية الامريكيّ يؤكّد عقب لقائه بالرئيس مبارك أنّ الباب
← **لا يزال** مفتوحًا للحلّ السلميّ لازمة الخليج والامر متروك للعراق إذا أراد السلام وانسحب من الكويت.

"James Baker, The American Foreign Secretary, confirms after his meeting with President Mubārak that ***the door is still open*** *for a peaceful solution to the Gulf crisis and that the case is left now to Iraq whether they want peace and withdrawal from Kuwait or not."*

EGY.001.103

على أيّة حال فإنّ الباب كما اكّد بوش في مؤتمره الصحفيّ
← **ما يزال** مفتوحًا امام أيّة مبادرات عربيّة او دوليّة.

"In any case, ***the door****, as Bush confirmed at his press conference,* ***is still open*** *to any Arab or international initiative."*

EGY.003.685

وتسارع على الفور الى التسليم بالإرادة الدوليّة والانسحاب الفوريّ من الكويت خاصّة بعدما أعلنت واشنطن أنّ باب التراجع

← **لا زال** مفتوحًا امام الرئيس العراقيّ إن أراد أن يجنّب شعبه وبلده بقية فصول الكارثة.

*"That they (Iraq) immediately hasten to subject themselves to the international will and withdraw from Kuwait, especially after the announcement by Washington that **the door** of withdrawal **is still open** for the Iraqi president, if he wants to avoid further disasters for his people and his country."*

In this expression in particular it is clear that there is no distinction in meaning in the use of the different forms. It is also clear that these forms are mutually interchangeable.

14.6. Conclusion

We can not find regional variation in the use of the negative particles *mā* and *lam*. What strikes one most, however, is that its use in the three countries contrasts in the same way with 'classical Arabic grammar'. The particle *mā* certainly keeps its specific function of referring to the present, but this function seems to be almost exclusively limited to the collocation with the verb *zāla*. The particle *lam* has become generally common for the negation of the past tense. We also found no indications of whether the particle *mā* is still used in direct speech as an emotional emphasis, but this may be due to the type of text investigated in which direct speech does not frequently occur. Contrary to what was generally accepted, the negation of the verb *zāla* by the particle *lam* does not occur and the negation of the verb *zāla* in the present tense by *mā* does indeed occur. The choice of the different particles of negation or of verb tense is of no influence on its meaning. No regional variation has been found in its use.

15. OTHER COMPLEMENTARY PARTICLES

Of the other particles, viz. *sawfa* and *sa*, *'a* and *hal* and *'aw* and *'am* the description found in literature is much more limited. We discuss these three pairs together in this last chapter, starting from the information to be found with the contemporary Arab grammarians Ya'qūb and Al-'Umarī.

15.1. THE COMPLEMENTARY PARTICLES *SAWFA* AND *SA*

15.1.1. *The Arabic approach*

The particle *sa* refers to the future. It is also called the particle of expansion (*ḥarf tawsī'*) because it transforms a verb from a limited time (*zamān ḍayyiq;* in this case a present tense) to a wider time (*zaman wāsi'*; in this case the future tense). As an illustration Ya'qūb (1988: 269) quotes Koranic verse 26: 227: وسيعلم الذين ظلموا أي منقلب ينقلبون (*And soon will the unjust assailants know what vicissitudes their affairs will take*). Moreover, it is also called *ḥarf istiqbāl*, viz. particle of the future. According to the Kufa grammarians, the particle *sa* was a derivation from the particle *sawfa*. On the other hand, according to the grammarians of Baṣra it is an original particle because it has a very specific meaning. In their view the particle *sawfa* indicates a lassitude (*tarāḥin*) in the future. In other words it refers to an event in the later future. Both Ya'qūb and Al-'Umarī observe that the opinions on the difference in meaning of both particles are divided. Indeed, *sa* and *sawfa,* are similar in meaning if not completely equivalent.

Al-'Umarī adds that the particle *sa* preceding a verb with high emotional value also indicates the complete certainty and the inevitable character of an event in the future.[1] As an example he quotes Koranic verse 2-137: فسيكفيكهم الله (*but God will suffice thee as against them*). In this meaning the particle *sa* refers to an inevitable event in the future. This is not without importance because, as we will see later, we can have different shades of meaning when we translate the particle *sa* into English.

[1] Al-'Umarī (1993: 263) uses the term *fi'l maḥbūb 'aw makrūh*.

Finally Al-ʿUmarī observes that the particle *sa* can also refer to a duration (*istimrār*) in the future.

15.1.2. *The western approach*

In contemporary western grammatical works, there is hardly any differentiation in the meaning between both particles. Blohm & Reuschel (1981: 462) do not even mention a difference in meaning between them. The same goes for Cowan (1973: 88) and Stoetzer (1991: 182). In Cantarino's work nothing is said about a difference in meaning between both particles. He confines himself to the argument that the particle *sa* is only used in positive statements, whereas the particle *sawfa* is also used by 'some authors' in negative statements, with the negative particle *lā*.

Blau (1973: 207) recognizes that such a construction occurs in MSA, but he argues that this is contrary to the grammatical rules of 'Classical Arabic'. Moreover, Blau also observes that the combination *lā sa* and even *sawfa lan* occur in MSA! Contrary to 'Classical Arabic', the particle *sa* in MSA is often used in questions and concessive sentences. Finally Blau remarks that the particle *sa* plus indicative following the verb *kāna* (*to be*) refers to an event in the past which could not be realized, such as, for instance, in the sentence: من يدري ماذا كان سيقول (*Who knows what he would have said*). Before focusing on the syntax and the meaning of the particles *sa* and *sawfa,* we check whether in the MSA radio broadcasts there is a difference in distribution or function of the two particles.

15.1.3. *Quantitative analysis*

In the quantitative investigation we will also include the future negative particle *lan*. The distribution of the particles *sa*, *sawfa* and the future negative *lan* in the different countries is as follows:

	News broadcasts					
future particles	**Algeria**		**Egypt**		**Saudi Arabia**	
	N	%	N	%	N	%
Total	**254**	100	**263**	100	**270**	100
sa	218	86	212	81	220	82
sawfa	4	2	25	9	26	10
lan	32	12	26	10	24	8

Table 29

Starting from the zero hypothesis that there is no regional difference in the distribution of the particles mentioned above for the different countries, we can check this by applying the χ^2-test. This gives us for this table a value of 18.05 whereas the table value is 14.86 with a certainty of 99.5%. This means that we were able to determine a statistically significant difference in the distribution of the particles of the future throughout the different countries. By examining the different cell-values of the χ^2 we can determine which elements determine this significant difference. A survey of the χ^2-values per cell follows in the next table:

	News broadcasts					
future particles	**Algeria**		**Egypt**		**Saudi Arabia**	
	N	χ^2	N	χ^2	N	χ^2
Total	**254**		**263**		**270**	
sa	218	0.32	212	0.12	220	0.04
sawfa	4	10.65	25	2.38	26	2.69
lan	32	1.15	26	0.07	24	0.60

Table 30

This survey clearly shows that the high χ^2-value is caused by the χ^2-cell-value which is formed by the Algeria column and the future particle *sawfa* where the χ^2-value is 10.65.[2] The percentages from Table 29 also clearly show that the particle *sawfa* occurs much less frequently in the Algerian news broadcasts than in the other two countries. We have also demonstrated with the χ^2-test that the difference is significant. Since we use a certainty degree of 99.5% for the χ^2-test, we have a chance of 1 to 200 that the difference is caused by the random sample. For this reason it is interesting to compare this fact with the results we found in the control corpus. A survey of the occurrence of the particles of the future is given in the following table:

	ALG/R		**ALG/S**		**EGY/R**		**EGY/C**	
	N	%	N	%	N	%	N	%
Tot	**53**	100	**71**	100	**74**	100	**109**	100
sa	45	85	66	93	57	77	60	55
sawfa	1	2	1	1	9	12	33	30
lan	7	13	4	6	8	11	16	15

Table 31

[2] According to Prof. Billiet of the centre for statistics (Leuven) the cell values are only relevant when the χ^2-value is higher than 2.5.

The χ^2-value of this table is 46.49 compared to a table value of 18.55 with a certainty of 99.5%. The χ^2-cell-values are as follows:

	ALG/R		**ALG/S**		**EGY/R**		**EGY/C**	
	N	χ^2	N	χ^2	N	χ^2	N	χ^2
Tot	**53**		**71**		**74**		**109**	
sa	45	0.80	66	3.33	57	0.07	60	5.42
sawfa	1	5.72	1	8.27	9	0.24	33	19.33
lan	7	0.15	4	2.07	8	0.02	16	1.02

Table 32

The tables above show that there is no variation in the distribution of the particle *lan* in the different countries. The most ample variation occurs with the particle *sawfa*. The table confirms what has already been demonstrated for the news broadcasts, viz. that the particle *sawfa* occurs significantly much less frequently in Algeria than in the other two countries under investigation. Moreover, it is remarkable that in the two cases in which the particle *sawfa* occurs, viz. in an Algerian report and in an Algerian sports broadcast, the collocation *sawfa lan* is involved! This might be a slip of the tongue (cf. supra 9.2.2.). Conversely a counter-indication is Blau's finding (cf. supra 15.1.2.) that the collocation *sawfa lan* also occurs in literature. However, we do not know at all how many times Blau has recorded this collocation in literature. There too its occurrence can be exceptional. Another remarkable fact is that the collocation *sawfa lā* does not occur in the corpus at all. Except for the two exceptional occurrences of *sawfa lan,* the negation of the future happens always by means of the particle *lan* alone.

Furthermore we observe that there is a significantly higher frequency in the use of the particle *sawfa* in commentaries on the Egyptian radio. In these broadcasts this goes together with a significantly (!) lower occurrence of the particle *sa*. In all countries and in all types of broadcasts the particle *sa* has a minimal share of 77%. In most cases the share is higher than 80%. In the broadcast commentaries the share decreases to 55% in favor of a wider use of the particle *sawfa*. This might be due to the fact that the use of the particle *sawfa* lends a text a more elevated, even more serious style. We can only give a decisive answer about this topic if we can demonstrate that both particles have no difference in meaning, because otherwise the difference in frequency might be determined by the meaning. This we will investigate in the qualitative analysis.

15.1.4. *Qualitative analysis*

As far as the news broadcasts of Algeria are concerned, three of the four occurrences of *sawfa* involve a later future and one of four, the near future, expressed by the word *lāḥiqan* (*subsequently*). Given the limited number of occurrences it is very difficult to make a comparison for Algeria. As far as Egypt is concerned, we could not find a difference in time span between the particles *sa* and *sawfa*. Both particles occur with precisely the same time indications. In what follows we will give a few examples.

EGY.002.104

كما أعلنت وكالة الانباء التركيّة الرسميّة أنّ مجلس الامن القوميّ
← **سوف** يعقد جلسة طارئة في وقت لاحق مساء اليوم برئاسة الرئيس التركيّ تورجوت اوزال.

"The official Turkish press agency also announced that the National Security Council will ***later on this evening*** *hold an extra ordinary session under the chairmanship of the Turkish President Turgut Özal."*

EGY.002.567

وقد أقلّت المجموعة قافلة مكوّنة من احدى عشرة سيارة
← وستغادر تركيا في وقت لاحق اليوم.

"The group transports a caravan composed of eleven cars, and it will leave Turkey ***later on today****."*

Furthermore we also found the particles *sawfa* and *sa* in collocation with the word *today* (اليوم).

EGY.002.745

صرّح خفير بيريز ديكوييار السكرتير العامّ للامم المتّحدة بأنّ وزيري خارجية إيران والعراق
← **سوف** يعقدان اجتماعًا مباشرًا اليوم في مقرّ الامم المتّحدة في جنيف.

"Javier Perez De Cuellar, the secretary-general of the United Nations, declared that the ministers of Foreign Affairs of Iraq and Iran will ***today*** *hold a meeting at the UN headquarters in Geneva."*

EGY.002.156

وقال متحدّث باسم الرئاسة في باريس إنّ ميتاران
← سيلتقي مع اعضاء مجلس الوزراء قبل اجتماع البرلمان اليوم.

"A spokesman for the president in Paris said that Mitterrand will meet with the members of the cabinet before the meeting of the parliament ***today****."*

Both particles also occur with the word *tomorrow* (غدا), as well as with temporal clauses which indicate a more remote future such as, for instance *the following months*.

EGY.002.782

← **وسوف** تبدأ اعمال التصدير خلال الشهرين القادمين.

*"The export activities will start during the **next two months**."*

EGY.002.157

وذكر راديو مونتي كارلو أنّ هذه الموادّ من طبّيّة وغيرها

← ستساعد على استقبال ما بين ثلاثين واربعين الف لاجئ خلال الاشهر

الثلاثة المقبلة في حالة اندلاع الحرب.

*"Radio Monte Carlo announced that, in case war breaks out, this medical and other materiel will help to receive about thirty to forty thousand refugees during the **next three coming months**."*

Finally both particles are also used to indicate indefinite future.

EGY.002.155

الذي اكّد فيه أنّ مصر

← **سوف** تتحمّل نفقات عودة المصريّين وتسيير عملية انتقالهم.

*"In which he confirmed that Egypt **will** bear the costs of the return of and the organization of the operation of transporting the Egyptians."*

EGY.002.054

فقالت صحيفة الخليج الصادرة في دولة الإمارات إنّ المنظور الاقتصاديّ لزيارة الرئيس

مبارك لموسكو يشكّل جانبًا متميّزًا

← ستنعكس نتائجه على مسار العلاقة بين البلدين.

*"The newspaper 'the Gulf', which is published in (the state of) the Emirates, said that the economic aspect of President Mubārak's visit to Moscow has a distinctive dimension whose results **will** have repercussions on the relations between the two countries."*

The same variation in the aspect of time for both particles can be found in the news broadcasts of Saudi Arabia. We limit ourselves to two striking examples showing a larger span of time.

SAU.002.154

وأضاف المتحدّث أنّ الرئيس بوش أبلغ جورباتشوف بقرار القروض التي

← ستمنح لموسكو على ثلاثة مراحل خلال الاشهر التسعة القادمة.

*"The spokesman added that President Bush announced to Gorbachov the decision concerning the loans which will be given in three phases to Moscow during the **next nine months**."*

SAU.002.296

العاهل المغربيّ يعلن أنّ قضية الصحراء

← **سوف** تحلّ خلال الاشهر الستّة القادمة.

"The Moroccan monarch announced that the problem of the Sahara will be solved during the ***coming six months****."*

All these illustrative sentences and many others lead us to conclude, indeed, that in MSA such as it is used in present-day Arabic news broadcasts there is no difference anymore in meaning concerning time. The more frequent occurrence of the particle *sawfa* at the expense of the particle *sa* in the Egyptian radio commentaries is in our view due to a difference in style.

In 15.1.1. we have argued that, according to Al-ʿUmarī the particle *sa* points at the complete security and the inevitable character of an event in the future, if it precedes a verb with strong emotional value. Furthermore we have mentioned Blau's observation (cf. supra 15.1.2.) that the particle *sa* (preceded by the verb *kāna*) refers to an event in the past which could not be realized. In the first case we have to translate the particle *sa* and the verb in English by a simple future and in the second case by a conditional perfect.

Further analysis of the corpus reveals in the first place that the particle *sa* after the verb *kāna* does not have to refer exclusively to an event in the past which which could not be realized. In this construction it can also refer to an event in the future which may or may not be realized such as, for instance, in the following sentences:

SAU.002.293

بريطانيا تعلن أنّها لن تشارك في اجتماع لوكسمبورج غدًا إذا كان هذا الاجتماع

← سيؤدّي الى خرق الإجماع الدوليّ ضدّ العراق.

"Great Britain announced that it would not participate in the Luxembourg meeting if this meeting ***were to*** *lead to the breach of the international consensus against Iraq."*

SAU.002.223

وأوضح شبرانجر في المؤتمر الصحفيّ الذي عقده الليلة الماضية في القاهرة أنّ المانيا لن تستجيب لمطالب إسرائيل بدفع عشرة مليارات مارك المانيّ كتعويضات لليهود خاصّة إذا كانت هذه الاموال

← ستخصّص لبناء مزيد من المستوطنات في الاراضي العربيّة المحتلّة.

"And Spranger elucidated in a press conference he held last night in Cairo that Germany will not comply with the demands of Israel to pay ten billion

German Marks as compensation for the Jews, especially if these funds ***were to*** *be used for the building of more settlements in the occupied Arab territories."*

Analysis of the corpus clearly shows that the particle *sawfa* never follows the verb *kāna*. This means that it is never used with regard to an uncertain event in the future which might be translated in English by a future perfect. In other words, all sample sentences show that, irrespective of the following verb, the particle *sawfa* is always used for an event in the future of which there is no doubt about the certainty of its taking place. This may be illustrated in the following sentences:

EGY.002.195

وقال الرئيس بوش إنّ القوات الامريكيّة

← **سوف** تنسحب من منطقة الخليج فور إنهاء الانسحاب العراقيّ من الكويت.

"And President Bush said that the American armed forces ***would*** *be withdrawn from the Gulf region immediately after the Iraqi withdrawal from Kuwait."*

SAU.002.457

أعلن مسؤولون حكوميّون في طوكيو اليوم أنّ اليابان

← **سوف** تجلي آخر دبلوماسيّيها الستّة من سفارتها في بغداد يوم غد الثلاثاء.

"Government officials in Tokyo announced today that Japan ***will*** *evacuate its six last diplomats from its embassy in Baghad tomorrow (Tuesday) ."*

However, next to the indication of a certainty about an event in the future, the particle *sa* can also indicate an uncertainty with respect to an event in the future. And not necessarily after the verb *kāna* (*to be*).[3] For instance, in the following sentence:

EGY.002.200

ولكنّه قال إنّ الحديث عن الانسحاب قبل بدء المفاوضات

← سيكون امر غير مفيد وغير مبدع.

"But he said that the discussion about the withdrawal before the beginning of the talks ***would*** *be a useless and unproductive matter."*

[3] It is clear also from other corpus material from the radio (Van Mol 1991) that the particle *sa* in such cases does not necessarily have to be preceded by the verb *kāna*. The context alone suffices sometimes to indicate that an event did not happen, such as, for example, in this sentence from a news broadcast of Kuwait: ووقع الانفجار قبل وقت قصير من اجتماع ستعقده لجنة التنسيق. *'The explosion took place shortly before a meeting which the coordination council* ***would*** *hold.'* (Van Mol 1991: 63). Or, for instance, this sentence in a documentary from Kuwait: ظل يحلمون بانّ الجاسوس الفرنسي سينهار قبيل إعدامه *'They continued dreaming that the French spy* ***would*** *collapse before his execution'*. (Van Mol 1991: 21), where the end of the story tells that he did not collapse.

15.1.5. *Conclusion*

The difference in time between the particles of the future, such as it has been presented by Ya'qūb and Al-ʿUmarī, plays no role anymore in MSA. Contemporary grammarians, such as Blohm & Reuschel, Cowan, Stoetzer and Cantarino, rightly do not distinguish between those two anymore. Furthermore the collocation *sawfa lā* does not occur in the broadcast corpus. For the negation of the future, the particle *lan* is used in all countries. It is possible that in contemporary written modern Arabic, the collocation *sawfa lā* is disappearing completely. Investigation of a comparable corpus of written modern Arabic might demonstrate this or the opposite. The occurrence of the collocation *sawfa lan* in Algeria is to be considered an exception.

Since there is no difference in time span we may assume that the frequent use of the particle *sawfa* at the expense of the particle *sa* in the radio commentaries on the Egyptian radio is rather linked to a difference in style. It occurs much less on the Algerian radio possibly for this reason. In order to establish this for a 100% certainty additional investigation is necessary. This might be done by examining other genres of literature or by interrogating informants about their impressions on both particles. By applying other methods of investigation (cf. supra 7) interesting additional data might be gathered.

Finally we observe that, in spite of the fact that Al-ʿUmarī gives the particle *sa* in certain circumstances the meaning of a certain event in the future, we demonstrated that the opposite with the particle *sa* is also the case. The particle *sa* is polysemic. It can indicate a certain event in the future, but in certain contexts it can also indicate a future event of which the occurrence is not certain. We demonstrated that this is not only the case when the particle *sa* follows the verb *kāna* in the perfect tense. On the contrary, the particle *sawfa* never occurs in a construction which ought to be translated in English by a conditional perfect. In this way we may state that both particles are not completely equivalent.

15.2. The complementary particles *'aw* and *'am*

15.2.1. *The Arabic approach*

According to Ya'qūb the particle *'am* is a conjunction (*ḥarf 'aṭf*) which can be placed after the *hamza of nivellation* (*hamzat at-taswiya*), such as, for instance in Koranic verse 63-6: سواء عليهم أستغفرت لهم أم لم

تستغفر لهم لن يغفر الله لهم (*It is equal to them whether thou pray for their forgiveness or not, God will not forgive them*). It can also be in collocation with the interrogative particle *'a* (*hamzat al-istifhām*), such as, for instance, in the sentence: أزيد نجح أم عمرو (*Did Zayd succeed or 'Amr?*). According to Ya'qūb the particle *'aw* can also be introduced by the interrogative *'a*. On the contrary, according to Al-'Umarī (1993: 123) the particle *'aw* can only be introduced by the particle *hal*, whereas the particle *'am* can only be introduced by the particle *'a*. This is contradictory to the allegation of Ya'qūb that, according to some Arab grammarians, the particle *'am* can be preceded by *hal* (Ya'qūb 1988: 125). As a matter of fact, further in his work Ya'qūb quotes a Koranic verse (13-16)[4] in which the collocation *hal - 'am* occurs. Furthermore Ya'qūb points out that not all grammarians agree that after the noun *sawā'* the particle *'am* is obligatory. According to some, the use of the particle *'aw* is also possible there. On this point Ya'qūb (126) does not agree.

The particle *'aw* is a conjunction (*ḥarf 'aṭf*) which connects single words with each other or with phrases. According to Ya'qūb this particle has the following meanings:

a) *doubt* (*šakk*) such as, for instance, in Koranic verse 23-113: قالوا لبثنا يوما او بعض يوم (*They will say: "We stayed a day or a part of a day*).[5]

b) *ambiguity* (*'ibhām*) such as, in Koranic verse 34-24: وإنا وإياكم لعلى هدى او في ضلال مبين (*And certain it is that either we or ye are on right guidance or in manifest error*).

c) *option-* (*'ibāḥa*) such as, for instance, in the sentence: تعلم الفقه او النحو (*Study law or grammar*).[6] In this respect Al-'Umarī also quotes Koranic verse 76-24: ولا تطع منهم آثما او كفورا (*and hearken not to the sinner or the ingrate among them*).

d) a *division* (*taqsīm*, also called *tafṣīl* by Al-'Umarī) such as, for instance, in the sentence: الكلمة اسم او فعل او حرف (*The word is either a noun, or a verb or a particle).*

e) a *particle of* (*'iḍrāb*) in the meaning of *bal* (*rather*) such as, for instance in Koranic verse 37-147: وارسلناه الى مائة الف او يزيدون (*And We sent him to a hundred thousand or more*). Next to this Koranic verse Al-'Umarī adds the following example: ضربت زيدا او عمرا (*I hit Zayd, I rather mean 'Amr*). He assumes in this case that the particle *'aw* in this sentence has the same meaning as the particle *bal* viz. *rather*.

[4] This verse runs as follows: قل هل يستوى الأعمى والبصير ام هل تستوى الظلمات والنور (*Say: Are the blind equal with those who see? Or the depths of darkness equal with light?*).

[5] Almost everywhere Al-'Umarī quotes the same Koranic verses.

[6] Al-'Umarī quotes the same sample sentence.

Furthermore it can have the meaning of the conjunction *wa* (*and*)[7], or of the particle of exception *'illā* such as, for instance, in the sentence: يموت العطشان او يشرب الماء (*The thirsty person dies, unless he drinks water*), of the particles *'ilā* (*to*), the conditional *'in*, and the particle *ḥattā* (*in order that*). For the last function Ya'qūb gives as an example the sentence: ادرس او تنجح (*study in order to succeed*). The question is whether the particle *'aw* nowadays still has these meanings in MSA.

Except for the above-mentioned divisions Al-'Umarī also mentions the use of the particle *'aw* as a choice (*taḫyīr*) such as, for instance, in Koranic verse 5-89 فكفارته إطعام عشرة مساكين من اوسط ما تطعمون اهليكم او كسوتهم او تحرير رقبة (*For expiation feed ten indigent persons, on a scale of the average for the food of your families; or clothe them, or give a slave his freedom*).[8]

In an interrogative sentence the difference between the particle *'am* and the particle *'aw* lies, according to Ya'qūb, in the fact that in the first case, as an answer, one of both choices is expected, whereas in the other case only a *yes* or a *no* is expected. He writes: When somebody asks you: *'a Zayd 'indak 'aw 'Amr* (*Is Zayd or 'Amr with you?*) then the meaning of this question is: 'Is one of them with you or not?' The answer in that case ought to be: *yes* or *no*. However, when somebody asks you: *'a Zayd 'indak 'am 'Amr* (*Is Zayd or 'Amr with you?*), then you have to specify who was with you. In that case it is impossible to answer with *yes* or *no*.

This proposition is elucidated by Al-'Umarī (1993: 122) with another example. He argues that the question: *'a Zayd qāma 'am 'Amr? (Did Zayd get up or did 'Amr?*), has to be answered by specifying which of the two stood up. When in such a case the particle *'aw* is used, then the question is not directed to the persons but to the verb, viz. the question of whether either one of them stood up. The answer to this sentence is *yes* or *no*. We would like to observe here that the same shade of meaning exists in English by changing the word order in the sentence. In English too the answer differs depending on whether the question is put as *'Is Zayd or 'Amr with you?'* or *'Is Zayd with you or 'Amr?'*. In English, the intonation of the question can also be meaningful. Al-'Umarī's reasoning, however, becomes more complicated when he argues that this is also the case for the question: *'a taqūm 'aw taq'ud* (*Will you stand up or*

[7] However, further on in his book Ya'qūb (p. 177) argues that not all grammarians agree about this.

[8] In the translation of Yusuf Ali (1975: 270) the number of this verse is 92. However, in the *al mu'jam al-mufahras* by *al-Bāqī* this verse is numbered 59.

sit down?). According to him, here too the question ought to be answered by *yes* or *no.*

The foregoing makes clear that the complementarity of the two particles lies in a subtle shade of meaning between them, which manifests itself mainly in the expected answer to the question. Furthermore we notice the contradiction between Al-ʿUmarī who argues that the particle *'aw* can only be introduced by the interrogative *hal,* whereas the particle *'am* can only be introduced by the interrogative *'a*, and Yaʿqūb who argues that the interrogative *'a* can be used for both. According to Yaʿqūb, the use of the particle *'am* after the word *sawā'* is obligatory.

15.2.2. *The western approach*

According to Cantarino (1974 vol. 3, 49) the particle *'aw* is the most frequently occurring *separating conjunction.* He claims the particle *'aw* can only be used in affirmative interrogative sentences. Furthermore Cantarino (1974 vol. 2, 500) argues that the particle *'am* is often used in MSA as an equivalent of the particle *'aw* and that usually it implies a dilemma, that is, a choice between two options. It seems that the particle *'aw* on the other hand indicates a simple disjunction. The particle *'am* is also used in indirect questions.

As far as the use of the particles *'am* and *'aw* after *sawā'* is concerned, we notice in Cantarino's work that the particle *'am* is used in five out of six sample sentences which he quotes (vol. 3, 104) and, *'aw* only once. In Al-Warrāqi & Ḥassanayn's textbook (1994: 175) both possibilities are referred to in the theoretical part of their work, albeit the particle *'aw* is mentioned only between brackets. In the sample sentences the particle *'aw* is sometimes mentioned between brackets following the particle *'am.* All this indicates that there clearly seems to be a kind of preference for the particle *'am* in collocation with *sawā'*.

Furthermore Al-Warrāqi & Ḥassanayn (1994: 13) point out that the particle *'am* is mainly used in interrogative sentences. On the other hand, Tapiéro observes a shift in use of both particles in MSA compared to their use in Classical Arabic. According to Tapiéro, the particle *'aw* was reserved in classical Arabic for an affirmative or negative statement, whereas the particle *'am* was only used in an interrogative sentence.[9] Furthermore he writes: "En arabe moderne cette spécificité semble ne

[9] This is contrary to Al-ʿUmarī and Yaʿqūb's allegation that both the particle *'am* and the particle *'aw* are used in interrogative sentences (cf. supra).

plus se maintenir d'une manière aussi stricte et *'am* et *'aw* sont employés indifféremment quelle que soit la nature de la première proposition" (Tapiéro: 1976: 95) . Moreover, he adds that in case of hypothetical alternatives a 'faux interrogatif' is placed at the head of the sentence and that in MSA, the particle *'am* is prefered above the particle *'aw*.

We will first examine the distribution of the two particles in the corpus of radio broadcasts.

15.2.3. *Quantitative analysis*

Table 33 offers a survey of the distribution of the particles *'aw* and *'am*:

	News broadcasts					
particles *'aw* and *'am*	**Algeria**		**Egypt**		**Saudi Arabia**	
	N	%	N	%	N	%
Total	**82**	100	**74**	100	**62**	100
'aw	76	93	74	100	59	95
'am	6	7	0	0	3	5

Table 33

Application of the χ^2-test gives an χ^2-value of 5.37 compared to a table value of 10.60 with a 99.5% certainty. In other words, statistically there is no significant difference between the different countries. Never theless we notice that the particle *'am* is completely absent from the news broadcasts in Egypt. A closer investigation into the control corpus yields the following distribution:

	ALG/R		**ALG/S**		**EGY/R**		**EGY/C**	
	N	%	N	%	N	%	N	%
Tot	**29**	100	**13**	100	**25**	100	**71**	100
'aw	28	97	12	92	25	100	70	99
'am	1	3	1	8	0	0	1	1

Table 34

Application of the χ^2-test on this table gives an χ^2-value of 2.83 against a table value of 12.84 with a 99.5% certainty. Here too we do not obtain a statistically significant difference. We notice that the particle *'am* is seldom used in either table. In the Egyptian reports it does not occur at all and in the Egyptian commentaries extremely rarely, viz.

compared to *'aw* only 1%. On the other hand, in the countries where it is used more frequently, the proportion is an average of 6%. When investigating the functions of both particles we can check whether in Egypt the particle *'aw* has adopted certain functions of the particle *'am*.

15.2.4. *Qualitative analysis*

For the qualitative analysis we base ourselves on the information about both particles as it is known from literature. We have already stated that Yaʿqūb holds the view that the use of the particle *'am* after the word *sawā'* (*equal*) is obligatory and that its use corroborates with the findings of Cantarino. Analysis of the corpus reveals that, in these cases, the particle *'am* only occurs in Saudi Arabia and even then relatively seldom. A survey of the use of the particle *'am* and *'aw* after the word *sawā'* follows in Table 35.

	News broadcasts					
particles after *sawā'*	**Algeria**		**Egypt**		**Saudi Arabia**	
	N	%	N	%	N	%
Total	**4**	100	**9**	100	**15**	100
'aw	4	100	9	100	13	87
'am	0	0	0	0	2	13

Table 35

Only in the Saudi Arabia corpus does the particle *'am* occur (only two times) after the word *sawā'*. In the other countries the particle *'aw* is used exclusively, contrary to the norm proposed by Yaʿqūb. The same results occur in the control corpus. There too the particle *'aw* is used exclusively after the word *sawā'*, viz. ten times in Egyptian broadcast commentaries, twice in Algerian and three times in Egyptian reports.

Apart from its rare use after the word *sawā'*, the particle *'am* still occurs, albeit in a more limited scope in the following two cases,[10] (a) after the interrogative *hal*. A purely positive question introduced by the particle *'a* occurs in the broadcast corpus only after the word *sawā'* and followed by the verb *kāna*. Otherwise positive questions are exclusively introduced by the particle *hal*. The only occurrence of the particle *'am* in an Algerian reportage and the only occurrence in an Algerian sports item are to be found after the interrogative *hal*. In the Algerian news broad-

[10] We are leaving a third case out of consideration, viz. the unique occurrence of the particle *'am* in an Egyptian news commentary in the dichotomic construction حرب ام سلام (*war or peace*).

casts both particles *'am* and *'aw* occur three times in positive questions. The examples below reveal that in such a case, both particles have the same function.[11]

ALG.002.145

هل أنّ الازمة سببها اشتراك السيد عجريد في حصّة امس

← **ام** أنّ الازمة لها خلفيات اخرى.

*"Is the cause of the crisis Mr 'Ajrīd's participation in a broadcast **or** does the crisis have other backgrounds?"*

ALG.002.463

وهل سيكون الموحّد الكبير لكلّ اتّجاهات المعارضة الافريقيّة

← **او** سيجد نفسه مغمورًا باحداث بلد لم يعشها منذ أكثر من ربع قرن.

*"Will he be the big unifier of all the trends of the African opposition **or** will he find himself submerged under the events of a country in which he has not lived for half a century?"*

The allegation by Al-ʿUmarī (cf. supra 15.2.1.) that the particle *'am* can only be introduced by the interrogative particle *'a* is contradicted by the facts. The findings from the corpus correspond to the rules such as they are described by Yaʿqūb.

The particle *'am* also occurs in the fixed expression *'am lā* (*or not, whether or not*). This fixed expression occurs both in Algeria and in Saudi Arabia. Two illustrative sentences follow:

ALG.002.648

لكن شيفرناتزا لم يقل ما إذا كان عرض

← **ام** لا على جيمس بيكر المخطّط المذكور.

*"But Shevardnadze did not say **whether or not** he had presented the mentioned plan to James Baker."*

SAU.002.665

وقالت مصادر مطّلعة في بغداد إنّ المسؤول الكرديّ اقترح على صدام حسين أنّه في حالة رفض ذلك المطلب فإنّه لا بدّ من إجراء إحصاء في هذه المناطق باتّفاق الفريقين لتحديد ما إذا كان يجب أن تنضمّ الى منطقة الحكم الذاتيّ

← **ام** لا.

*"Well-informed sources in Baghdad said that the Kurdish person in charge had suggested to Ṣaddām Ḥusayn that if the demand were refused, it would be inevitable, with the agreement of both parties, to conduct a count in those territories to define **whether** they must join the self-rule zone or **not**."*

[11] These data contrast with the observation by Fischer (1982 vol. 1, 327): "Bei Alternativfragen wird 'oder' nicht durch أَوْ, sondern durch أَمْ /'am/ ausgedrückt."

In all other cases the particle *'aw* is used. In most cases a simple choice is involved, such as, for instance:

ALG.002.519

على الصعيد الوطنيّ

← **او المحلّيّ**

*"On a national or l**ocal level.**"*

EGY.002.377

في نيو يورك

← **او** جنيف.

*"In New York **or** Geneva."*

SAU.002.155

عدّة ايام

← **او** شهرًا.

*"A number of days **or** a month."*

In this meaning it also often occurs in all countries in the fixed expression: دون قيد او شرط (*with no condition or restriction*). This choice can also be used between constituents.

ALG.002.145

لكن يبدو أنّ هناك بعض الصعوبات التقانيّة التي تحول دون هذا الاتّصال ولكن رجائي فقط سي عبد الرحمن أن تبقى في اتّصال معنا

← او سنتّصل معك في حتّى نهاية هذه الجريدة رجائي أن تبقى إذن معنا او أن تتّصل بنا في رقم ستّين تسعين واحد وعشرين.

*"But there seem to be some technical difficulties which interfere with this contact, but I only hope, Mr 'Abd ar-Raḥmān, that you keep in touch with us **or** that we shall contact you before the end of this broadcast, so I hope that you stay with us or that you contact us on the number sixty, ninety, twenty one."*

It can also be used to express a choice, for instance:

SAU.002.203

ولم يؤكّد احدهما

← **او** ينفي.

*"None of them affirmed **or** denied."*

EGY.002.131

في الرياض حثّ خادم الحرمين الشريفين الملك فهد بن عبد العزيز عاهل السعودية الرئيس العراقيّ صدام حسين على الانسحاب من الكويت

← **او** تحمّل مسؤولية الكارثة التي ستحلّ بالعراق.

"In Riyāḍ the 'Servant of the two Holy Places', King Fahd Ibn 'Abd al-'Azīz, the sovereign of Saudi Arabia, urged the Iraqi President Ṣaddām Ḥusayn to withdraw from Kuwait ***or*** *to bear the responsibility for the catastrophe which will fall on Iraq."*

Finally the particle *'aw* is, mainly in Algeria, also used to correct slips of the tongue or to adapt the choice of words (cf. supra 15.2.1. the use of the particle in the meaning of *bal*). This meaning occurs, with the exception of one occurrence in Saudi Arabia, exclusively and quite frequently in Algeria. This has also to do with the other, more spontaneous style of presentation in Algeria. The only example from Saudi Arabia is the following sentence:

SAU.002.587

ونقلت الإذاعة عن مصادر وصفتها بأنّها عليمة أنّ الإجراءات التي ستتّخذها تلك الحكومة

← **او** اللجنة هي ما يلي.

"And the radio learned from sources, described as well informed, that the measures which this government will take ***or rather*** *which this council will take, are the following:"*

ALG.002.179

كانت هذه سيداتي وسادتي آراء واصداء الشارع، شارع العاصمة هذا الصباح بعد أن تفضّلت التلفزة الموقّرة بتقديم برنامج قيل عنه الكثير

← **او** حصّة وقيل بأنّها ستدفع الكثير ممن اشتركوا في الهوائيات المقعّرة الى متابعة برامج التليفزيون الجزائريّ.

"These, ladies and gentlemen, were the views and echoes from the street, the street of the capital this morning after the respectable television was so kind as to present a program ***or rather*** *an episode on which a lot has been said, and it is said that it will urge many who participated in these obscure antics to further watch the programs of the Algerian television."*

In Algeria this particle is also often used to correct faults. For instance, the correction of the finite form of the verb in the next sentence:

ALG.002.036

الحصار العسكريّ الذي يخضع له

← **او** تخضع له العاصمة باكو

"The military blocade to which the capital Bakou is subjected..."

Or, for instance, the correction of a passive verb form to an active verb form, such as, in the following sentence:

ALG.002.299

المجلس الوطنيّ الفلسطينيّ لن يُعقد

← او لن يَعقد اجتماعًا له في الايام المقبلة.

"The National Palestinian Council will not hold a meeting the next coming days."

In Algeria the particle *'aw* occurs nineteen times in this corrective function.

15.2.5. *Conclusion*

If the norm, indeed, is postulated that, following the word *sawā'*, the use of the particle *'am* is obligatory, then we record that in language usage on the radio there seems to be a shift towards the particle *'aw*. It is clear that the use of the particle *'am* in relation to the particle *'aw* has become marginal. As far as questions are concerned, we observed that after the particle *hal* both particles *'aw* and *'am* are used.

15.3. THE COMPLEMENTARY PARTICLES *'A* AND *HAL*

15.3.1. *The Arabic approach*

According to Yaʿqūb the interrogative particle *'a* is used in questions inquiring after an idea (*taṣawwur*) and in questions which can possibly be followed by a *confirmation* (*taṣdīq*). The first are of the type أزيد نجح أو عمرو (*Did Zayd or ʿAmr succeed?*). The second are of the type أنجح زيد (*Did Zayd succeed?*). If the latter is preceded by the particle *hal* instead of *'a*, then we have, according to Yaʿqūb, to do with an obligating confirmation (*taṣdīq mawjib*), viz. a question to which the answer *yes* is obligatory.[12]

According to Yaʿqūb and Al-ʿUmarī the particle *'a* has different functions. First of all it is used as a *hamza of nivellation* (*hamzat at-taswiya*), viz. after the word *sawā'* (cf. supra 15.2.1.). In the second place it refers

[12] Furthermore Yaʿqūb points out that unlike the interrogative *'a*, the particle *hal* can not follow the particle *'am* such as, for instance, in the sentence *'a-qāma Zayd 'am 'a-qaʿada* (*Did Zayd sit down or did he stand up*?). In the beginning of a sentence the interrogative particle *'a*, unlike the particle *hal*, can also be placed before the particle *wa*, the particle *fa* or the particle *ṯumma*.

to a *complete negation* (*'inkār 'ibṭālī*). In this case the fact is emphasized that the sentence which follows is untrue and that the person who claims such a thing is a liar. As an example Yaʿqūb refers to Koranic verse 17-40: أفأصفاكم ربكم بالبنين واتخذ من الملائكة إناثا إنكم لتقولون قولا عظيما (*Has then your Lord, preferred for you Sons, and taken for Himself daughters among the angels? Truly ye utter a most dreadful saying!*). Also according to Yaʿqūb the particle *'a*, as such, bears in itself a negation. When it is followed by another negation, then the sentence is made positive. According to Yaʿqūb the meaning of the sentence *'a lam našraḥ* (*Didn't we explain*) is positive because the real meaning of this sentence is that we have, indeed, explained it.

In the third place, the particle *'a* has the meaning of a *reproaching negation* (*'inkār tawbīḫī*). The sentence which follows the particle is true, but the fact itself is reproachable such as, for instance, in Koranic verse 37-95: أتعبدون ما تنحتون؟ (*Worship ye that which ye have carved?*).[13]

In the fourth place it has the function of obtaining a decision (*taqrīr*) from the listener by a simple question such as, for instance in: أكافأت زيدا؟ (*Did you reward Zayd?*). Finally in an interrogative sense the particle can also have the connotation of scorn (*tahakkum*), amazement (*taʿajjub*), patience (*istibṭā'*), threat (*tahdīd*) and warning (*tanbīh*).

As far as the particle *hal* is concerned, Yaʿqūb (1988: 493) argues that it is an interrogative particle (*ḥarf istifhām*) which can be placed before nouns or verbs. Unlike the particle *'a*, *hal* can not be placed before a conditional particle. Both Yaʿqūb and Al-ʿUmarī allege that the particle *hal* asks a question for a *positive confirmation* (*taṣdīq 'īǧābī*). It is not possible to answer such question with *no* or with a concrete idea (*taṣawwur*). The distinction between the particle *hal* and *'a* (*hamzat al-istifhām*) lies, according to Yaʿqūb (1988: 495-496), in the next ten points:

(1) The interrogative particle *hal* is very specifically used for a confirmation whereas the particle *'a* can also be used in order to obtain a concrete answer.[14] (2) Unlike the particle *'a*, the particle *hal* can not be followed by a negative particle. (3) The particle *hal* is used for the present or future tense, whereas the particle *'a* can also ask questions in the past, such as, for instance, in the sentence: أتظنه ناجحا (*Do you think he succeeded?*). (4) The particle *hal* cannot be placed before a conditional particle nor (5) before the particle *'inna*. However, it can have the meaning of the particle *'inna* (Al-ʿUmarī 1993: 507). (6) Contrary to the particle

[13] We found identical examples in Al-ʿUmarī (1993: 75)

[14] This is also asserted by Al-ʿUmarī (1993: 71)

'a, after *hal* a verb can not follow a noun. The verb has to precede the noun.[15] (7) The particle *hal* follows the conjunctions *wa* and *fa* and can not precede these, contrary to the particle *'a*. (8) It also can not be placed before the particle *'am* but has to follow it. (9) If the question has to be made negative it is followed by the particle *'illā* such as, for instance, in Koranic verse 55-60: هل جزاء الإحسان إلا الإحسان؟ (*Is there any Reward for Good - other than Good?*). In such a question the use of the particle *'a* is not permitted.[16] (10) Finally, contrary to the particle *'a*, the particle *hal* can, according to Al-ʿUmarī and Yaʿqūb, have the meaning of *qad* such as, for instance, in Koranic verse 76-1: هل أتى على الإنسان حين من الدهر؟ (*Has there not been over Man a long period of Time, when he was nothing - mentioned?*).[17]

According to Al-ʿUmarī the particle *hal,* contrary to the interrogative particle *'a,* can not be used together with the particle *'am,* but it can be used with the particle *'aw* (cf supra 15.2.1). Finally, according to Al-ʿUmarī the particle *hal* can also contain the meaning of a wish such as, for instance, in Koranic verse 7-53: فهل لنا من شفعاء فيشفعوا لنا (*Have we no intercessors now to intercede on our behalf?*). According to Al-ʿUmarī the interrogative particle *'a* is the most original of all the interrogative particles.

15.3.2. *The western approach*

Cantarino (1974 vol. 2, 139), Cowan (1973: 11) and Beeston (1970: 102) hold the view that there is no fundamental difference between the particles *'a* and *hal*. The same goes for Abu-Absi (1990: 38) who characterizes both particles as "the two question markers *'a*- and *hal*, both of which are used for *yes-no* questions in MSA." Furthermore, Cantarino, like Yaʿqūb and Al-ʿUmarī, points out that the particle *hal* follows conjunctions such as *fa* and *wa,* whereas the interrogative particle *'a* precedes them. The particle *hal* resembles the particle *'a* to a great extent , but it emphasizes the declaration on which the question is asked.

[15] This contrary to Al-ʿUmarī (1993: 506) who gives both possibilities, viz. *hal qāma Zayd* or *hal Zayd qāma* (*Did Zayd got up?*). Al-ʿUmarī specifies that the noun cannot precede the verb, if it is a direct object, such as, for instance, in the sentence: * *hal Zaydan ḍarabta?* (*Did you hit Zayd?*).

[16] Cf. also Al-ʿUmarī who, moreover, refers to Koranic verse 46-35: فهل يهلك إلا القوم الفاسقون (*But shall any be destroyed except those who transgress?*).

[17] Al-ʿUmarī endorses the viewpoint of Yaʿqūb that the particle *hal* can have the meaning of *qad*, but he also points out that a number of Arab grammarians do not agree on this point. (AlʿUmarī 1993: 507-508)

Stoetzer does not observe any difference in the function of both particles, but he does observe that "the word *'a* is mainly used before the words لا *lā*, لم *lam* and the forms of ليس *laysa*" (Stoetzer 1991: 149). Both according to Cantarino (vol. 2, 141) and Stoetzer (1991: 149) the particle *hal* can be followed by a negation, in the contracted form *hallā* هلا, which is in contrast with the allegation of Yaʿqūb that no negation particle can follow the particle *hal* (cf. supra 15.3.1.). Fischer (1982, vol. 1, 67) agrees with Yaʿqūb: "In negativen Sätzen wird jedoch nur die Partikel أ verwendet".[18]

15.3.3. *Quantitative analysis*

In the first place we have to observe that interrogative particles do not occur very frequently in the broadcast corpus because of the type of texts, viz. news broadcasts and reports. Those do occur, of course, much more frequently in, for instance, stage plays, which contain a lot of dialogues. Nevertheless, we found some interesting data about the distribution of the particles *hal* and *'a* in the radio corpus. The following table gives a survey of the news broadcasts:

	News broadcasts					
particles *hal* and *'a*	**Algeria**		**Egypt**		**Saudi Arabia**	
	N	%	N	%	N	%
Total	**14**	100	**3**	100	**2**	100
hal	14	100	2	67	0	0
'a	0	0	1	33	2	100

Table 36

A survey of the control corpus offers the following image:

	ALG/R		**ALG/S**		**EGY/R**		**EGY/C**	
	N	%	N	%	N	%	N	%
Tot	**1**	100	**2**	100	**8**	100	**17**	100
hal	1	100	1	50	8	100	13	76
'a	0	0	1	50	0	0	4	24

Table 37

[18] Fischer (1982, vol 2, 188) points out that in case of هَلَّا another meaning is involved, viz. 'why not'.

Given the limited number of occurrences the application of a χ^2-test is not meaningful, also because the expected values are too low (cf. Moore 1993: 515). Nevertheless, it is possible to make a few, albeit limited, observations which we discuss in the next paragraph.

15.3.4. *Qualitative analysis*

Analysis of the KWIC sentence indexes reveals that the particle *hal* is used in all countries and in all text types exclusively in positive questions, whereas the particle *'a* only occurs in negative questions.[19] Stoetzer's observation (cf. supra.), that the particle *'a* is *chiefly* used before the words لا *lā*, لم *lam* and the forms of ليس *laysa*", is certainly not contradicted by our investigation. For instance, these two questions from Egyptian radio commentaries:

EGY.001.401

← ألم يكن من الأفضل أن تحلّ جميع المشاكل العربيّة تحت مظلّة عربيّة دون تدخّلات اجنبيّة؟

"Would it not be better that all Arab problems are solved within an Arab context (literally: under an Arab umbrella) without foreign interference?"

EGY.001.551

← فهل هذا ممكن؟

"And is this possible ?"

Also when occuring in indirect questions the particle *hal* is kept for positive questions and the particle *'a,* for negative questions.

EGY.002.260

وتساءل الرئيس

← أليست الكويت بلدًا إسلاميًا مثل إيران.

"And the president wondered ***whether*** *Kuwait is not an Islamic country, like Iran."*

EGY.002.257

وتساءل الرئيس:

← هل سيتصوّر احد أنّ مصر تعرف عن التحرّكات على الحدود السعوديّة أكثر ممّا تعرفه السعودية.

"And the president wondered ***whether*** *somebody can imagine that Egypt knows more about the movements on the Saudi border than Saudi Arabia."*

[19] With the exception of the two occurrences of the particle *'a* after the noun *sawā'* (cf supra. 12.2.4.)

On the other hand the question can be raised whether the above-mentioned cases really are examples of indirect questions, since those questions can also be put in a direct way.

15.3.5. *Conclusion*

The use of the interrogative particle *'a* in the broadcast corpus is mainly limited to negative questions, whereas the interrogative particle *hal* is used for positive questions.

16. GENERAL CONCLUSION

In this study we have tried to conduct an empirical investigation into variation in Modern Standard Arabic in news broadcasts on the radio. In the first chapter we have discussed the specific characteristics of modern standard languages.

Next we have made an analysis of the Arabic language situation and the place of MSA in the Arabic language spectrum on the basis of existing scientific knowledge. This analysis revealed that there are many contradictory views on different points as far as the Arabic language situation is concerned. In the first place we discovered that there is a "great" distinction between Classical Arabic and Modern Standard Arabic. According to some authors there is no fundamental difference between them, but according to others differences do exist (cf. supra 2.3.3.). As a matter of fact, however, the differences between the two variants are discussed only in very vague terms.

Moreover, we have shown the confusion both in the Arab world and among western investigators about the use of the terminology to design different Arabic variants. In the Arab world, in most cases, *fuṣḥā* is seen as an indivisible whole which comprises both the language of the Middle Ages and Modern Standard Arabic. On the other hand we have observed that many western scholars still write about MSA in terms of Classical Arabic.

We have found similar contradictions in the description of 'Arabic' in the continuum going from *pure* dialectal Arabic to the modern standard language. Besides the initial dichotomy, better known under the name diglossia, there are also divisions into several language levels. Some scholars make a subdivision into three levels, others into four or five levels. However, those scholars are not always able to define the precise characteristics of these different language levels. In this respect we have pursued the contradictory views of the investigators of the 'Leeds corpus' in the definition of what they understand by Educated Spoken Arabic.

We have observed that the difficulty of a precise description of different language varieties is linked to the fact that those language varieties are no isolated systems, but that they influence each other and that they are, on the contrary, subdivisions of the greater whole, which is called

'Arabic'. That doesn't alter the fact that under certain influences, among others political measures, a standard variant can be purified more and more. By means of statistical data we also demonstrated that MSA is propagated more and more in the Arab world through education and the media, and that it probably is gaining ground.

When we want to investigate the standard language we have to solve a few methodological problems. One of these is the way of investigation. We have pointed out that there are many investigations, mainly with regard to the spoken language, in which the conclusions are based on impressions rather than on actual facts. We started from the assumption that we need a *written* corpus of standard language read aloud in order to obtain valuable results. When conducting an investigation into the 'spoken language' we have to make use of both recordings and the whole transcription. This way other researchers may be able to verify certain elements of the investigation. In chapter seven we have discussed and assessed the different possible methods of investigation. The corpus linguistic approach seemed to us the most interesting in order to investigate variation within a standard language. It is, however, very important in this method to structure the corpus extremely well both internally and externally.

For the compilation of the corpus we have chosen three countries with a maximum in variation on background, viz. Algeria, Egypt and Saudi Arabia. In order to make the comparison between the three countries as accurate as possible, we have limited the investigation to radio news broadcasts. Those were subdivided into two large parts viz.: the *main corpus* of approximately 240,000 words (80,000 per country), which contains exclusively *'pure'* news broadcasts, and a *control corpus* of approximately 80.000 words, which contains reports, commentaries and sports news. For well-considered reasons (9.2.1.) we opted for an *orthographic* transcription. We have also paid attention to the specific problems which are related to the transcription of a corpus of the 'spoken' language. Those are the problems of slips of the tongue and also the problem of the unintelligibility of words, a problem that until now has never been given attention in the scientific literature.

The whole corpus has been encoded primarily to make it ready to be explored by special computer programs (cf. supra 10.2.). This encoding has been performed both on a morphological and syntactical basis. This way we could strongly reduce the well-known problem of ambiguity. The encoding we have designed not only makes it possible to identify every word and its affixes and to tag them but also to count words automatically. As far as the attribution of grammatical categories is concerned, we have demonstrated that the traditional mixed grammar is an adequate instrument for analyzing corpora.

For the investigation of syntactical variation between the different countries we wanted to limit ourselves to the use of the particles. In this investigation we also paid attention to the relation between the function of certain particles such as they have been used in Classical Arabic and the internal language evolution. We assumed that in every language there is *institutional* variation. We can make a distinction between grammatical elements and constructions which are *equal* and grammatical elements and constructions which are *similar*. With similar constructions or grammatical elements we mean *constructions or elements which have a comparable but not identical function*. We assumed that precisely because of the similarity, the chance might be the highest that shifts in function can occur with those elements.

The following particles have been identified as complementary: (1) the particles *wa* and *fa*, *(2) 'iḏā, 'in* and *law*, (3) the negative particles *mā* and *lam*, (4) the particles *sa* and *sawfa*, *(5) 'aw* and *'am* and finally (6) the interrogative particles *hal* and *'a*. For the analysis of the data we always worked according to the following strategy. First we checked how contemporary Arab grammarians depict the functions of these complementary particles in order to define precisely which functions of these particles are equal, which are similar and which are unique. It is clear that those Arab grammarians assume that the Arabic language is an *indivisible fuṣḥā*. In order to describe this *fuṣḥā* they base themselves on the Koran and some typical sample sentences. Those works are strictly normative. Next we have investigated how western grammarians, or Arab grammarians in the West, describe the functions of these particles. Meanwhile we also investigated whether there were demonstrable data indicating an evolution in the use of the particles. We found that the findings of a number of western scholars often corroborate those normative Arabic grammars.

Next we tested those data against a quantitative and qualitative analysis of the corpus. For the determination of possible statistical differences in the use of the particles in the different countries we made use of the chi-square test. Both the quantitative and qualitative analysis leads us to the following conclusions.

In the first place, we observe that regional differences in the standard language are mainly limited to differences in style. We have indicated the word order in Algeria differs strongly from the word order in Egypt and Saudi Arabia. This mainly has to do with the much more lively style which is used in Algeria. This style manifests itself not only in the structure of the sentence, but also in the structure of the program and in the much more lively way of presenting the programs. In general we can state that, as far as the standard language is concerned, such as it is used in radio news broadcasts, there is no reason to believe that in the Arabic language territory different standards are evolving. On the syntactical level we were not able to demonstrate regional variation for any particle. On many points the analogy in the use of the particles is even striking. In this respect we refer in particular to the different possibilities of negation of the verb *zāla*.

We would like to emphasize that we have chosen those elements of the grammar, where we expected to find the greatest variation. But even when these results are negative, this does not mean that there is no regional variation in other domains. This does not rule out the possibility that on other points of syntax or on a phonological, lexical and even morphological level variation occurs. Through corpus investigation those elements can be examined in future.

On the other hand, we have found important differences between the use of these particles in News Broadcast-MSA, and the grammatical rules about their use such as they have been discussed in different contemporary Arabic grammars and many modern western grammars which often adopt the classical rules on different points. We have demonstrated empirically that one of each pair of complementary particles loses its importance in frequency in favor of the other element of the pair in each of the three countries under investigation. Consequently it seems to be a widespread phenomenon. The particles *fa*, *'in, mā, sawfa* and *'am* occur much less frequently than their respective complementary counterparts *wa, 'iḏā, lam, sa* and *'aw*. Because of the limited number of occurrences of the interrogative particles *hal* and *'a* we do not want to include these in this conclusion.

Qualitative analysis has revealed that the low frequency of certain particles is due to the fact that their function has been adopted by the other complementary particle. The thesis which we have postulated, viz. that particles holding similar functions can evolve more easily in function because the shade of meaning is very small, has been confirmed by this investigation. We have clearly demonstrated that the particle *wa* has taken over the function of the particle *fa* in case of a logical or sequential succession of events. The same goes for the conditional function which has been completely taken over by the particle *'iḏā,* which originally had only a temporal function. We have also demonstrated that the particle *'aw* has taken over certain functions which have been reserved by the Arab grammarians for the particle *'am*.

Furthermore it seems that the function of the complementary particle which loses importance is often reduced to fixed expressions or semantic relations. The use of the particle *fa*, for instance, seems to be limited to expressions which are semantically limited to speech. The use of the particle *'in* is also limited to fixed expressions. The same goes for the negative particle *mā,* which is almost completely limited to collocation with the verb *zāla*. As far as the particle of the future *sawfa* is concerned we notice that it is only rarely used in Algeria. It does occur significantly more frequently in Egyptian radio commentaries, which might mean that the particle *sawfa* has another more elevated style contents than the particle *sa*. Other additional multi-introspectionel analyses are required, however, to confirm this observation.

Why one particle is limited in use and the other one takes over certain functions is not immediately clear. Different hypotheses might be formulated about this topic. We have demonstrated that the thesis which classifies the particles as marked and unmarked categories is difficult to maintain. We have also pointed out that some researchers have presented the thesis of the avoidance conduct more specifically about the negative particles. This means that the particle *lam* is used much more frequently than the particle *mā,* because the latter is often seen as dialectical. Even when this is not the case objectively, we can understand that Arabs have the impression *subjectively* that the particle *mā* has a rather dialectal character. Our other results of investigation, however, demonstrate that this thesis can hardly be maintained. The particles *fa* and *'in*, and to a lesser extent *'am,* which are unmistakably characterized as *fuṣḥā*, lose their importance under the influence of particles, such as, *wa, 'iḏā* and *'aw,* which are frequently used in certain dialects, unless we assume that those particles are *subjectively* less seen as dialectical. In order to demonstrate this, other methods of investigation are required based on interviews of native speakers.

Anyhow, we have clearly demonstrated that MSA such as it is used in different countries in the radio news broadcasts occasionally follows new patterns which we do not find in the descriptions of contemporary Arab grammarians. We also notice that those new patterns do not correspond with the descriptions made by western grammarians on the written language. This is partly due to the fact that a number of grammars are not based on empirical investigations, but simply take over the patterns described in other grammars.

The question arises now whether the evolution which we have demonstrated also occurs in written MSA. There are some indications that this is, indeed, the case. The indications which we have found in the literature, however, are not based on a systematic and thorough analysis of empirical material. In order to be certain about this, a comparative investigation of a corpus of written standard language is necessary. This means that this investigation has not yet come to an end. We have investigated *only* one element out of a gigantic number of grammatical elements which can be investigated. Moreover, we have worked with a language sample which is, even if it is representative of the language of radio news broadcasts, still relatively small compared to the whole universe of words and sentences which are produced every day in the whole Arab world.

The next step in the further investigation will have to concentrate on the secondary encoding of the corpus. This is a task for corpus linguistics. Furthermore, many software porgrams can be improved. On the basis of the existing material a program can be developed which for the greater part might encode new written corpora automatically. However, we always have to keep in mind that the encoding of a written corpus of MSA is no sinecure. Moreover, it would also seem interesting to encode classical corpora. Only then will we be able to obtain more and new insights in the structure of the classical language and its evolution based on empirical data.

17. BIBLIOGRAPHY

Aarts, Jan, & Oostdijk, Nelleke (1988). "Corpus-Related Research at Nijmegen University". Proc. of Eighth International Conf. on English Language Research on Computerized Corpora. In Merja Kyto, Ossi Ihalainen, & Matti Rissanen (Eds.), *Corpus Linguistics, Hard and Soft*, Amsterdam, pp. 1-14.

Abboud, Peter F. (1970). "Spoken Arabic". In Thomas A. Sebeok (Eds.), *Current Trends in Linguistics VI: Linguistics in So. West Asia and No. Africa*, Den Haag, pp. 439-466.

Abboud, Peter F., & McCarus, Ernest N. (1983). *Elementary Modern Standard Arabic, parts 1 & 2*, Cambridge.

Abboud, Peter F. (1986). "The *Ḥāl* Construction and the Main Verb in the Sentence". In Joshua A. Fishman, Andree Tabouret-Keller, Michael Clyne, Bh. Krishnamurti & Mohamed Abdulaziz (Eds.), *The Fergusonian Impact: In Honor of Charles A. Ferguson on the Occasion of His 65th Birthday*, I: From Phonology to Society; II: Sociolinguistics and the Sociology of Language, Berlin, pp. 191-196.

ʿAbd al-Ḥalīm & Al-Fiqī (1988). *al-ʿArabīya fī l-'iʿlām, al-'uṣūl wa-l-qawāʿid wa-l-'aḫṭā' aš-šā'iʿa*, Kairo, 206 p.

ʿAbd al-Munʿam, Sayyid ʿAbd al-ʿĀl (1968). *Lahjat šamāl al-maġrib, Tiṭwān wa-mā ḥawlahā*, Kairo, 432 p.

ʿAbd al-Munʿam, Sayyid ʿAbd al-ʿĀl (1968). *Muʿjam šamāl al-maġrib, Tiṭwān wa-mā ḥawlahā*, Kairo, 255 p.

Abdelfattah, Nabil, M. S. (1996). "Reflections on the Sociolinguistic Force of Journalism in the Process of Language Development in Egypt". In Elgibali, A.,*Understanding Arabic, Essays in Contemporary Arabic Linguistics in Honor of El-Said Badawi*, Kairo, pp. 129-136.

Abdel-Jawad, Hassan Rashid, & Abu-Salim, Issam (1987). "Slips of the tongue in Arabic and their theoretical implications". *Language Sciences*, 9, pp. 145-171.

Abdel-Karim, Abdin (1990). "From a free Arabic text to its word frequency table: the search for the solution". In Pierre A. MacKay (Eds.), *Computers and the Arabic Language*, New York, pp. 218-221.

Abdel-Massih, Ernest T. (1975). *An introduction to Egyptian-Arabic*, Center for Near Eastern and North African Studies, University of Michigan, Ann Arbor, 358 p.

Abdel-Nour, Jabbour (1983). *Dictionnaire Arabe-Français*, Beiroet, 1126 p.

Abdulaziz, Mohamed H. (1986). "Factors in the development of modern Arabic usage". *International Journal of the Sociology of Language*, 62, pp. 11-24.

Abi Farah, Anis (1986). "La reconnaissance automatique de l'auteur inconnu d'un texte arabe". In *Méthodes quantitatives et informatiques dans l'étude des textes*, Genève-Paris, 2 dln., pp. 15-18.

Abu-Absi, Samir (1986). "The modernization of Arabic: problems and prospects".

Anthropological Linguistics, 28(3), pp. 337-348.

Abu-Absi, Samir (1990). "A Characterization of the Language of Iftaḥ yā Simsim: Sociolinguistic and Educational Implications for Arabic". *Language Problems and Language Planning*, 14(1), pp. 33-46.

Abu-Haidar, Farida (1992). "Shifting Boundaries: The effect of MSA on dialect convergence in Baghdad". In E. Broselow, Mushira Eid, & John McCarthy (Eds.), *Perspectives on Arabic Linguistics IV*, Amsterdam & Philadelphia, pp. 91-106.

Abuhamdia, Zakaria A. (1988). "The Arabic Language regions". In Ulrich Ammon, Norbert Dittmar, & Klaus J. Mattheier (Eds.), *Sociolinguistics: an international handbook of the science of language and society*, Berlin, pp. 1238 -1244.

Abu-Melhim, Abdel-Rahman (1991). "Code-Switching and Linguistic Accommodation in Arabic". Papers from 3rd Annual Symposium on Arabic Linguistics. In Bernard Comrie & Mushira Eid (Eds.), *Perspectives on Arabic Linguistics* III, Amsterdam, pp. 231-250.

Ad-Daḥdāḥ, 'Anṭwān (1990). *Mu'jam qawā'id al-'arabīya al-'ālamīya*, Beiroet, 249 p. (toegevoegde titel: A dictionary of Universal Arabic Grammar).

Al, B.P.F. (1987). "Franse taalnormen". In Rooij, J. de, *Variatie en Norm in de Standaardtaal*, Amsterdam, pp. 35-41.

Al-'Adnānī, Muḥammad (1989). *Mu'jam al-'aġlāṭ al-luġawīya al-mu'āṣira*, Beiroet, 870 p. (toegevoegde titel: A Dictionary of Common Mistakes in Modern Written Arabic).

Al-Akhdar, Boujemaa (1990). "De l'ordre des mots en arabe". In Pleines, Jochen, *La linguistique au Maghreb*, Rabat, pp. 37-45.

Al-'Antāki, Moḥammad (s.d.). *al-Manhaj fī l-qawā'id wa-l-'i'rāb*, Beiroet, 352 p.

Al-Ġalāyīnī, Muṣṭafā (1995). *Jāmi' ad-durūs al-'arabīya*, Beiroet, (1ste uitgave 1912).

Al-Ḥusrī, S. (1957). *Fī l-luġa wa-l-'ādāb*, Beiroet

Al-Jubouri, Adnan J. R. & Knowles, Frank E. (1988). "A Computer-Assisted Study of Cohesion Based on English and Arabic Corpora: An Interim Report". Proceedings of Thirteenth International Conference, University. of E. Anglia (Norwich), 1-4 Apr. 1986. In John P. G. Roper (Eds.), *Computers in Literary and Linguistic Research*, Paris, Geneva, pp. 59-77.

Allard, Michel (1970). "Note sur l'informatique au service de la langue arabe", *Actes du Vme congres international d'arabisants et d'islamisants à Bruxelles*, pp. 31-33.

Al-Munjid al-Faransī - al-'Arabī (1972). Beiroet

Al-Munjid fī l-luġa wa-l-'i'lām (1986). Beiroet

Al-Shabbab, Omar & Swales, John (1986). "Rhetorical features of Arab and British news broadcasts". *Anthropological Linguistics*, 28(1), pp. 31-42.

Al-'Umarī (1993). *Maṣābīḥ al-ma'ānī fī ḥurūf al-ma'ānī*, Kairo, 701 p.

Alverny, D. A. (1959). *Cours de langue Arabe*, Beirut, 462 p.

Al-Warrāqī, Nārīmān Nā'ilī & Ḥassanayn, 'Aḥmad Ṭāhir (1994). *'Adawāt ar-rabṭ fī l-'arabīya al-mu'āṣira*, (bijgevoegde titel: The Connectors in Modern Standard Arabic), Kairo, 209 p.

Altoma, Salih J. (1980). "Toward unified linguistics terminology". *Al-'Arabiyya*, 13(1-2), pp. 51-64.

Amaireh, Khalil (1981). "Various Elements Ascertaining Meaning in Arabic Grammar". *Journal of Semitic Studies*, 26 (Spring), pp. 31-45.

Amaireh, Khalil (1982). "The affective meaning of some exclamatory styles in Arabic grammar". *Al-'Arabiyya*, 15(1-2), pp. 66-81.

Anghelescu, Nadia (1970). "Observations sur les démonstratifs pronominaux dans l'arabe moderne", *Revue Roumaine de Linguistique*, 15, 377-83.

Anwar, Mohamed Sami (1989). "Computer-Based Lexicography: How much Grammar can be Included?" In *Proceedings of the 1st Seminar on Bilingual Computing in Arabic and English*, 6-7 Sept. 1989, Cambridge University, UK., pp. 1-9.

Appel, René, Hubers, Gerard & Meijer, Guus (1979). *Sociolinguïstiek*, Antwerpen, 247 p.

Ashtiany, Julia (1993). *Media Arabic*, Edinburgh.

Aṣ-Ṣayyād, Muḥammad Maḥmūd (s.d.). *'Aṭlas jumhūrīyat Miṣr al-'arabīya wa-l-'ālam*, Beiroet, 100 p.

Atoui, H. (1979). *l'Arabe langue vivante*, 3 Vol., Edicef, Parijs.

Auwera, J. van der & W. Vandeweghe (red.). (1984). *Studies over Nederlandse partikels*, Antwerpen, U.I.A., 15 p.

Ayalon, Ami (1987). *Language and Change in the Arab Middle East. The evolution of Modern Arabic Political Discourse*, Oxford, 196 p.

Ayoub, Georgine, & Bohas, Georges (1981). "Les grammairiens Arabes, la phrase nominale et le bon sens". *Historiographia Linguistica*, 8(2-3), pp. 267-284.

Baalbaki, Ramzi (1990). "'I'rāb and Binā' from Linguistic Reality to Grammatical Theory". Proceedings. of 2nd Symposium on History of Arabic Grammar, Nijmegen, 27 Apr.-1 May 1987. In Kees Versteegh & Michael G. Carter (Eds.), *Studies in the History of Arabic Grammar*, Amsterdam, pp. 17-33.

Baccouche, Belkacem & Sanaa, Azmi (s.d.). *Conversations in Modern Standard Arabic*, New Haven & London, 400 p.

Badawī, As-Sa'īd Muḥammad (1973). *Mustawayāt al-'arabīya al-mu'āṣira fī Miṣr. Baḥṯ fī 'alāqat al-luġa bi-l-ḥaḍāra*, Kairo, 212 p.

Badawī, As-Sa'īd Muḥammad (1985). "Educated Spoken Arabic: A problem in teaching Arabic as a foreign language" In Jankowsky, Kurt. R., *Scientific and humanistic dimensions of language*, Festschrift for Robert Lado, John Benjamins, pp. 15-22.

Bahloul, Maher (1993). "The Copula in Modern Standard Arabic". In Mushira Eid & Clive Holes (Eds.), *Perspectives on Arabic Linguistics V*, Amsterdam & Philadelphia, pp. 209-230.

Bakalla, M.H. (1983). *Arabic Linguistics*: An Introduction and Bibliography, London, 740 p.

Bakir, Murtadha (1986). "Sex differences in the approximation to standard Arabic: a case study". *Anthropological Linguistics*, 28(1), pp. 3-9.

Barber, David (1988).; "Automatic Analysis and Tagging of Arabic Words". In Shivtiel, A., (Ed.): *Proceedings of the 2nd Leeds Symposium*, pp. 30-35.

Barbot, Michel (1981). *Evolution de l'arabe contemporain*, I: Bibliographie d'arabe moderne et du Levant; Introduction au parler de Damas; II: Les Sons du parler de Damas. Paris.

Barbot, Michel (1983). "Réflexions sur les réformes modernes de l'arabe littéral". In Istvan Fodor & Claude Hagege (Eds.), *Language Reform: History and Future*, Hamburg, pp. 127-154.

Barnouw, Victor (1973). *Culture and Personality*, Illinois, 511 p.

Al-Batal, Mahmoud (1990). "Connectives as Cohesive Elements in a Modern Expository Arabic Text". Papers from Second Annual Symposium on Arabic Linguistics. In Mushira Eid & John McCarthy (Eds.), *Perspectives on Arabic Linguistics II* , Amsterdam, pp. 234-268.

Bateson, M.C., (1967). *Arabic Language Handbook*, Language Handbook Series, Washington, DC, Center for Applied Linguistics, XV, 125 pp.

Bathurst, R.D (1971). "Automatic alphabetization of Arabic words; a problem of graphic morphology and combinatorial logic". In Wisbey, R.A. (Ed.) *The computer in literary and linguistic research*, Papers from a Cambridge symposium, Cambrigde, pp. 185-190.

Bausch, Karl-Heinz (1979). "Intuition und Datenerhebung in der Linguistik". In Bergenholtz, Henning, *Empirische Textwissenschaft, Aufbau und Auswertung von Text-Corpora*, Frankfurt, pp. 71-87.

Baybars, 'Aḥmad Samīr (1990). *al-Wāqi' al-luġawī wa-l-huwīya al-'arabīya,* Kairo, 199 p.

Beersmans, F. (1987). "Variatie en norm in het Duitse taalgebied". In Rooij, J. de, *Variatie en Norm in de Standaardtaal*, Amsterdam, pp. 43-55.

Beesley, Kenneth R., T. Buckwalter and S. Newton (1989). "Two-Level Finite State Analysis of Arabic Morphology". In *Proceedings of the 1st Seminar on Bilingual Computing in Arabic and English,* 6-7 Sept. 1989, Cambridge University, UK., pp. 1-10.

Beesley, Kenneth R. (1991). "Computer Analysis of Arabic Morphology: A Two-Level Approach with Detours". Papers from 3rd Annual Symposium on Arabic Linguistics. In Bernard Comrie & Mushira Eid (Eds.), *Perspectives on Arabic Linguistics III* , Amsterdam, pp. 155-172.

Beeston, Alfred Felix Landon (1968). *Written Arabic: An Approach to the Basic Structures,* London, xii, 118 p.

Beeston, Alfred Felix Landon (1970). *The Arabic language today*, London, 125 p.

Beeston, Alfred Felix Landon (1975). "Some features of Modern Standard Arabic". *Journal of Semitic Studies.*, 20 pp. 62-68.

Beeston, Alfred Felix Landon. (1981). "Some Notes on Classical Arabic Syntax". *Journal of Semitic Studies*, 26 (1981 Spring), pp. 21-30.

Behnstedt, Peter & Woidich, Manfred (1985). *Die Ägyptisch-arabischen Dialekte,* Wiesbaden.

Behnstedt, Peter & Woidich, M. (1988). *Die Ägyptisch-arabischen Dialekte*: Band 3, Texte: II. Niltaldialekte, III. Oasendialekte, Wiesbaden.

Belemans, R. (red.) & van de Wijngaard, H.H.A. (1995). *Het Dialektenboek 3. Dialekt in beweging,* Stichting Nederlandse Dialekten, Goesbeek.

Belmore, Nancy (1988). "The use of tagged corpora in defining informationaly relevant word classes". Proc. of Eighth International Conf. on English Lang. Research on Computerized Corpora. In Merja Kyto, Ossi Ihalainen, & Matti Rissanen (Eds.), *Corpus Linguistics, Hard and Soft*, Amsterdam, pp. 71-82.

Belnap, R. Kirk & Shabaneh, Osama (1992). "Variable Agreement with Non-human Controllers in Classical and Modern Standard Arabic". In Ellen Broselow, Mushira Eid, & John McCarthy (Eds.), *Perspectives on Arabic Linguistics IV*, Amsterdam & Philadelphia, pp. 245-262.

Benabdi, Linda C. (1986). "Lexical expansion in the Maghrib: the functional linguistic corpus". *International Journal of the Sociology of Language*, 61, pp. 65-78.

Benjelloun, Said (1990). "L'arabe: de la langue maternelle à la langue de l'enseignement". In Pleines, Jochen, *La linguistique au Maghreb*, Rabat, pp. 353-361.

Benmamoun, E. (1991). "Negation and Verb Movement". In *Proceedings of NELS 21*, GLSA, University of Massachusetts at Amherst, pp. 17-31.

Bentahila, Abdelali & Davies, Eirlys E. (1991). "Standards for Arabic: One, Two or Many?" *Indian Journal of Applied Linguistics*, 17(1), pp. 69-88.

Berens, Franz Joseph. (1979). "Das Freiburger Korpus gesprochener deutscher Standardsprache: Möglichkeiten seiner Auswertung am Beispiel der Untersuchung der Lexeme Freude und freuen und ihrer Ableitungen". In Bergenholtz, Henning, *Empirische Textwissenschaft, Aufbau und Auswertung von Text-Corpora*, Frankfurt, pp. 268-281.

Berns, J.B. (1992). *Variatie in de Nederlandse standaardtaal*, Amsterdam, 65 p.

Berque, J. (1974). *Langages arabes du présent*, Paris, 400 p.

Bihnām, Faḍīl ʿAfāṣ (1984). *Tārīḫ aṭ-ṭibāʿāt wa-l-maṭbūʿāt al-ʿirāqīya*, Bagdad, 379 p.

Billiet, Jaak B. (1995). *Methoden van Sociaal-Wetenschappelijk Onderzoek*, Leuven, 320 p.

Bishai, Wilson B. (1966). "Modern Inter-Arabic". *Journal of the Oriental Society*, 82, pp. 41-63.

Blachère, R. & Gaudefroy-Demombynes, M. (1952). *Grammaire de l'arabe classique*, Paris, Maissonneuve, 508 p.

Blake, N.F. (1988). *Traditional English Grammar and beyond*, London, 155 p.

Blanc, Haim (1960). "Style variations in spoken Arabic, A sample of interdialectal educated conversation". In Ferguson, Ch.A. et al., *Contributions to Arabic linguistics*, Cambridge, 1960, pp. 81-161.

Blanc, Haim (1971). "Arabic". In Thomas A. Sebeok & others (Eds.), *Current Trends in Linguistics VII: Linguistics in Sub-Saharan Africa,* Den Haag, pp. 501-509.

Blau, Joshua (1969). "L'apparition du type linguistique néo-arabe", *Revue des Etudes Islamiques*, 37, pp. 191-201.

Blau, Joshua (1973). "Remarks on some syntactic trends in Modern Standard Arabic", *Israel Oriental Studies*, pp. 172-231.

Blau, Joshua (1976). "Some additional observations on syntactic trends in Modern Standard Arabic", *Israel Oriental Studies*, pp. 159-190.

Blau, Joshua (1981). *The Renaissance of Modern Hebrew and Modern Standard Arabic, Parallels and Differences in the Revival of Two Semitic Languages*, University of California Press, Berkeley, 200 p.

Bloch, Ariel A. (1986). *Studies in Arabic Syntax and Semantics*, Wiesbaden, 140 p.

Blohm, Dieter, Reuschel, Wolfgang & Samarraie, Abed (1981). *Lehrbuch des Modernen Arabisch,* Leipzig: Verlag Enzyklopädie, Vol. 2, 1112 p.

Blohm, Dieter (1991). "Some Remarks on Writing a Grammar of Modern Standard Arabic". *Folia Orientalia*, 28, pp. 89-98.

Bobzin, Hartmut (1980). "Zur Häufigkeit von Verben im Neuhocharabischen". *Zeitschrift für Arabische Linguistik*, 5, pp. 35-69.

Bohas, Georges (1993). *Développements récents en linguistique arabe et sémitique*, Institut Français de Damas, Damascus.

Bohas, Georges (1998). "Des faits, des grammairiens et des linguistes". *Arabica: Revue d'Etudes Arabes*, 45, pp. 297-319.

Borrmans, M. & Müller, A. (1977). *Arabe littéraire Moderne*, Institut Pontifical d'Etudes Arabes, Rome.

Boucherit, Aziza (1987). "Discours alternatif arabe-francais à Alger". *La Linguistique*, 23(2), pp. 117-129.

Branca, Paolo (1986). "La lemmatisation de l'arabe". In *Méthodes quantitatives et informatiques dans l'étude des textes*, Genève-Paris, 2 dln., pp. 119-123.

Bravmann (1963). "Review of the dictionary of Hans Wehr". *Journal of the American Oriental Society*, 23, p. 368.

Brill, Moshe, & al. (1940). *The Basic Word List of the Arabic Daily Newspaper*, Jerusalem, 180 p.

Briscoe, Ted (1994). "Prospects for practical parsing of unrestricted text: Robust statistical parsing techniques". In Oostdijk, Nelleke & de Haan, Pieter (Eds.), *Corpus-based research into language, in honour of Jan Aarts*, Amsterdam, pp. 97-119

Brockelmann, C. (1992, 24ste uitgave). *Arabische Grammatik, Paradigmen*, 16, Leipzig

Brunot, Louis (1931). *Textes arabes de Rabat*, Vol. 1. Textes, transcription et traduction annotée, Paris, 207 p.

Buckwalter, Timothy A. (1994). "Computer-generated Concordances in Arabic Lexicography", MESA Conference '94, 7 p.

Bungarten, Theo (1979). "Das Korpus als empirische Grundlage in der Linguistik und Literaturwissenschaft". In Bergenholtz, Henning, *Empirische Textwissenschaft, Aufbau und Auswertung von Text-Corpora*, Frankfurt, pp. 29-51.

Cachia, P.J.E. (1967). "The use of the colloquial in modern Arabic literature". *Journal of the American Oriental Society*, 82, pp. 12-22.

Cachia, P.J.E. (1973). *The Monitor, a Dictionary of Arabic Grammatical Terms*, Beiroet, 88 p. en 110 p.

Cadora, Frederick J. (1966). "The Concept of Compatibility in the Study of Language Varieties". *Word*, 22 (1, 2, & 3), pp. 310-317.

Cantarino, Vicente (1974-75). *Syntax of modern Arabic prose*, 3 Vol, Bloomington, London.

Cohen, David (1970). *Etudes de Linguistique Sémitique et Arabe*, Janua Linguarum, Series Practica, 81, Den Haag, 178 p.

Colin, Georges (1951). *Chrestomathie Marocaine*, Paris, 248 p.

Comrie, Bernard (1991). "On the Importance of Arabic for General Linguistic Theory". Papers from 3rd Annual Symposium on Arabic Linguistics. In Bernard Comrie & Mushira Eid (Eds.), *Perspectives on Arabic Linguistics III*, Amsterdam, pp. 3-30.

Comrie, Bernard & Eid, Mushira (Ed.) (1991). *Perspectives on Arabic Linguistics III*, Amsterdam & Philadelphia.

Corduck, Edward Scott Mc. (1993). *Grammatical information in ESL Dictionaries*, Tübingen

Cowan, D. (1970). *An Introduction to Modern Literary Arabic*, London, xi, 205 p.

Cowan, William (1968). "Notes toward a definition of modern standard Arabic". *Language Learning*, 18, Ann Arbor, pp. 29-34.

Dahl, Osten & Talmoudi, Fathi (1979). "Qad and Laqad: Tense/Aspect and Pragmatics in Arabic". In *Fifth Scandinavian Conference of Linguistics.*, Frostavallen: Almqvist and Wiksell, pp. 51-68.

Darke, Diana (1985). "Arabic: unifying factor of the Islamic world". *Language Monthly*, 25, 16-17.

Ḍayf, Šawqī (1990). *Tajdīd an-naḥw*, Kairo, 284 p.

Debili, Fathi & Souissi, Emna (1998). "Traitement automatique de l'arabe voyellé ou non" In *Workshop on Computational Approaches to Semitic Languages, COLING-ACL98*, University of Montreal, http://www.irmcmaghreb.org/corres/textes/debili. htm

de Jong, E.D. (1977). *Spreektaal. Woordfrequenties in gesproken Nederlands*, Utrecht.

DeMiller, A.L. (1988). "Syntax and semantics of the Form II Modern Standard Arabic verb". *Al-'Arabiyya*, 21(1-2), pp. 19-50.

de Moor, Ed. (1984). *Arabisch voor beginners*, Muiderberg, 208 p.

Denz, Adolf (1982). "Die Struktur des Klassischen Arabisch". In Fischer, Wolfdietrich, *Grundriss der arabischen Philologie, I: Sprachwissenschaft*, Wiesbaden, pp. 58-82.

Deprez, K. (1986). "De aard van het Nederlands in Vlaanderen". In Gillaerts, Paul, *Verscheidenheid in eenheid, een bloemlezing taalpolitieke artikelen over normering en standaardisering van het Nederlands*, Leuven, pp. 205-229.

Deville, G. en Fekhar, M. (1984). *Ecouter et comprendre les informations en Arabe Moderne*, Paris, 183 p.

de Vries, J.W. (1987). "De standaardtaal in Nederland". In Rooij, J. de, *Variatie en Norm in de Standaardtaal*, Amsterdam, pp. 127-141.

Dichy, Joseph (1990). "Grammatologie de l'arabe, I: Les Sens du mot ḥarf ou le labyrinthe d'une évidence". Proc. of 2nd Symposium on History of Arabic Grammar, Nijmegen, 27 Apr.-1 May 1987. In Kees Versteegh & Michael G. Carter (Eds.), *Studies in the History of Arabic Grammar*, Amsterdam, pp. 111-128.

Dichy, Joseph (1994). "La Pluriglossie de l'Arabe". In Pierre Larcher (ed.), 19-32 *Langue et littérature arabes. Bulletin d'Études Orientales* 46.

Dichy, Joseph (2001). "On Lemmatization in Arabic, A formal definition of the Arabic entries of multilingual Lexical databases, In *ACL/EACL 2001 Workshop, Arabic Language Processing: Status and Prospects*, Toulouse

Diem, Werner (1971). "Über eine Einführung in die Europäische Sprachwissenschaft auf Arabisch". *Die Welt des Islams*, 13, pp. 11-19.

Diem, Werner (1974). *Hochsprache und Dialekt im Arabischen*, Untersuchungen zur heutigen arabischen Zweisprachigkeit, Wiesbaden, 183 p.

Ditters, Everhard (1986). "An Extended Affix Grammar for the Noun Phrase in Modern Standard Arabic". In Jan Aarts & Willem Meijs (Eds.), *Corpus Linguistics II: New Studies in the Analysis and Exploration of Computer Corpora*, Amsterdam, pp. 47-78.

Ditters, Everhard (1987). "Progress-report ASCAMSA". *Processing Arabic*, Report 2, pp. 40-51.

Ditters, Everhard (1988a). "CAI and Related Research". In *Processing Arabic*, Report 3, pp. 1-9.

Ditters, Everhard (1988b). "Report on activities concerning the Computer and Arabic at Nijmegen University, Holland". In Shivtiel, A. (Ed.), *Proceedings of the 2nd Leeds Symposium*, pp. 32-40.

Ditters, Everhard (1989a). "Arabisch in Bits en Bytes". In Aarts, P. (Ed.): *Midden-Oosten en Islam Publicaties*, No. 14, Nijmegen, 28-60.

Ditters, Everhard (1989b). "Arabic in Bits, Bytes and Words". *Processing Arabic*, Report 4, pp. 29-65.

Ditters, Everhard (1990a). "Arabic Corpus Linguistics in Past and Present". Proc. of 2nd Symposium on Hist. of Arabic Grammar. In Kees Versteegh & Michael Carter (Eds.), *Studies in the History of Arabic Grammar II*, Amsterdam, pp. 129-141.

Ditters, Everhard (1990b). "Current bibliography on computer applications and Arabic". *Processing Arabic*, Report 5, pp. 1-109.

Ditters, Everhard (1991a). "Arabic". In Lancashire I (Eds.), *Humanities Computing Yearbook* 1989-90, Oxford, pp. 285-291.

Ditters, Everhard (1991b). "A modern standard Arabic sentence grammar". *Bulletin d'Études Orientales*, Damas: IFEAD, pp. 197-236.

Ditters, Everhard (1992). *A Formal Approach to Arabic Syntax: the Noun Phrase and the Verb Phrase*, Amsterdam, 475 p.

Dobrisan, Nicolae (1985). "Tendencies in the Verbal System of Contemporary Standard Arabic". *Revue Roumaine de Linguistique*, 30(3), pp. 281-291.

Doniach, N. S. (1985). *The Concise Oxford English-Arabic Dictionary of Current Usage*, New York.

Douglas, Allen & Malti-Douglas, Fedwa (1994). *Arab Comic Strips*, Bloomington & Indianapolis, 263 p.

Eid, Mushira (1982). "The non-randomness of diglossic variation in Arabic". *Glossa: An International Journal of Linguistics*, 16, pp. 54-84.

Eid, Mushira (1988). "Principles for Code-Switching between Standard and Egyptian Arabic". *Al-'Arabiyya*, 21, pp. 51-80.

Eid, Mushira (1990a). "Arabic Linguistics: The Current Scene". Papers from the First Annual Symposium on Arabic Linguistics. In Mushira Eid (Ed.), *Perspectives on Arabic Linguistics I* , Amsterdam, pp. 3-37.

Eid, Mushira (Ed.) (1990b). *Perspectives on Arabic Linguistics I*, Amsterdam & Philadelphia.

Eid, Mushira & McCarthy, John (Eds.) (1990c). *Perspectives on Arabic Linguistics II*, Papers from Second Annual Symposium on Arabic Linguistics (series no: 72 ed.), Amsterdam.

El-Ayoubi, H. (1973). *Untersuchungen zur Wortstellung in der heutigen arabischen Sprache*, Nürnberg

El-Dash, Linda & Tucker, Richard (1975). "Subjective Reactions to various speech styles in Egypt". *Linguistics*, 166, pp. 33-54.

El-Ezabi, Yehia A. (1967). "The Sectors of Written Arabic". In Edward L. Jr. Blansitt (Ed.), *Report of the Eighteenth Annual Round Table Meeting on Linguistics and Language Studies* , Washington DC, pp. 175-180.

Elgibali, Alaa (Ed.) (1996). *Understanding Arabic, Essays in Contemporary Arabic Linguistics in Honor of El-Said Badawi*, Kairo, 274 p.

El-Hassan, Shahir A. (1977). "Educated spoken Arabic in Egypt and the Levant: a critical review of diglossia and related concepts". *Archivum Linguisticum*, 8, pp. 112-132.

El-Hassan, Shahir A. (1978). "Variation in the demonstrative system in Educated Spoken Arabic". *Archivum Linguisticum*, 9, pp. 32-57.

El-Sayed, Dawood H. (1984). "Notes on the Arabization of the terminology of modern linguistics". *LEXeter* '83, Exeter, pp. 333-338.

Ezzat, A. (1974). *Intelligibility among Arabic Dialects*, Beirut Arab University

Farhat, Mohamad (1989). "Issues in the Development of a Comprehensive Arabic Lexical Database". In *Proceedings of the 1st Seminar on Bilingual Computing in Arabic and English,* 6-7 Sept. 1989, Cambridge University, UK., session 1.3, pp. 1-14.

Fehri, Abdelkader Fassi (1981). "Théorie lexicale-fonctionelle, controle et accord en arabe moderne". *Arabica: Revue d'Etudes Arabes*, 28 (1981 June-Sept.), pp. 299-332.

Feitsma, A. (1987). "Geschiedenis en karakter van de Friese norm". In Rooij, J. de,*Variatie en Norm in de Standaardtaal*, Amsterdam, pp. 57-69.

Ferguson, Charles (1959a). "Diglossia". *Word* ,15, pp. 325-340.

Ferguson, Charles (1959b). "The Arabic koine". *Language* , 35, pp. 616-630

Ferguson, Charles (1959c). "Myths about Arabic". In *Monograph Series on Language and Languages*, Georgetown University, 12, pp. 75-82.

Ferguson, Charles (1960). *Contributions to Arabic linguistics*, Cambridge, Mass., 161 p.

Ferguson, Charles (1989). "Grammatical agreement in Classical Arabic and the modern dialects: a response to Versteegh's pidginization hypothesis". *Al-'Arabiyya*, 22 (1-2), pp. 5-18.

Ferguson, Charles (1990). "'Come Forth with a Surah Like It': Arabic as a Measure of Arab Society". In Mushira Eid (Eds.), *Perspectives on Arabic Linguistics I*, Amsterdam, pp. 39-51.

Ferguson, Charles (1996). "Epilogue: Diglossia Revisited". In Elgibali, A., *Understanding Arabic, Essays in Contemporary Arabic Linguistics in Honor of El-Said Badawi,* Kairo, pp. 49-67.

Fischer, Wolfdietrich (1959). *Die Demonstrativen Bildungen der Neuarabischen Dialekte.* Ein Beitrag zur Historischen Grammatik des Arabischen, Den Haag, viii, 221 p.

Fischer, Wolfdietrich (1972). *Grammatik des Klassischen Arabisch.* Porta Linguarum Orientalum, N.S. XI, Wiesbaden, xvi, 262 p.

Fischer, Wolfdietrich & Jastrow, Otto (1980). *Handbuch der Arabischen Dialekte*, Wiesbaden

Fischer, Wolfdietrich & Jastrow, Otto (1982a). *Lehrgang für die Arabische Schriftsprache der Gegenwart*, Wiesbaden, 400 p.

Fischer, Wolfdietrich (1982b). *Grundriss der arabischen Philologie, I: Sprachwissenschaft.* Wiesbaden.

Fischer, Wolfdietrich (1986). *Lehrgang für die Arabische Schriftsprache der Gegenwart, Band II* , Wiesbaden, 404 p.

Fischer, Wolfdietrich (1989). "Zur Herkunft des grammatischen Terminus *ḥarf*". *Jerusalem Studies in Arabic and Islam,* 12, pp. 135-145.

Fleisch, Henri (1968). *l'Arabe classique, esquisse d'une structure linguistique*, Beiroet, 271 p.

Forkel, Fritz (1980). *Die sprachliche Situation im heutigen Marokko*: eine soziolinguistische Untersuchung, Hamburg.

Forkel, Fritz (1987). "Die Entwicklung einer Modernen Hocharabischen Aussprachenorm im Mashriq und im Maghreb", *Der Islam*, 64, pp. 289-291.

Francis, W. Nelson (1979). "Problems of Assembling and Computerizing Large Corpora". In Bergenholtz, Henning, *Empirische Textwissenschaft, Aufbau und Auswertung von Text-Corpora*, Frankfurt, pp. 111-123.

Frazier, W. (1976). *A demonstration of a computer technique for investigating Arabic morphology*, Ann Arbor, Michigan.

Gai, Amikam (1981). "Two Points of Arabic Grammar". *Arabica: Revue d'Etudes Arabes*, 28, pp. 293-298.

Galinski, J. (1989). "The human reading process in Arabic: toward an experimental investigation". *Processing Arabic*, Report 4, pp. 13-21.

Geeraerts, Dirk (1989). *Wat er in een woord zit*, Leuven, 268 p.

Geerts, Guido (1987). "Variatie en norm in de standaarduitspraak". In Rooij, J. de, *Variatie en Norm in de Standaardtaal*, Amsterdam, pp. 165-173.

Goossens, J. (1986). "Taal". In Gillaerts, Paul, *Verscheidenheid in eenheid, een bloemlezing taalpolitieke artikelen over normering en standaardisering van het Nederlands*, Leuven, pp. 9-14.

Gran, L. & Taylor, C. (1990). *Aspects of Applied and Experimental research on Conference interpretation*, Trieste, 253 p.

Greenbaum, Sidney & Ni, Yibin (1994). "Tagging the British ICE Corpus: English word classes". In Oostdijk, Nelleke & de Haan, Pieter (Eds.), *Corpus-based research into language, in honour of Jan Aarts*, Amsterdam, pp. 34-45.

Guillaume, Jean-Patrick (1988). "'Le Discours tout entier est nom, verbe et particule': Elaboration et constitution de la theorie des parties du discours dans la tradition grammaticale arabe". *Languages*, 92 (Dec 1988), pp. 25-36.

Gully, Adrian John (1993). "The Changing Face of Modern Arabic". *Al-'Arabiyya*, 26, pp. 19-59.

Gussenhoven, C.H.M. (1987). "Norm en variatie in het Standaard Engels". In Rooij, J. de, *Variatie en Norm in de Standaardtaal*, Amsterdam, pp. 13-33.

Guthrie, Louise, Joe Guthrie & Jim Cowie (1994). "Resolving lexical ambiguity". In Oostdijk, Nelleke & de Haan, Pieter (Eds.), *Corpus-based research into language, in honour of Jan Aarts*, Amsterdam, pp. 79-93.

Haas, W. (Ed.) (1982a). *Standard Languages: Spoken and Written*, Manchester.

Haas, W. (1982b). "On the normative character of language". In Haas, W. (Ed.), *Standard Languages: Spoken and Written*, Manchester.

Haeseryn, W. (1986). "De Algemene Nederlandse Spraakkunst en Normativiteit". In Gillaerts, Paul, *Verscheidenheid in eenheid, een bloemlezing taalpolitieke artikelen over normering en standaardisering van het Nederlands*, Leuven, 1986, pp. 175-182.

Haeseryn, W. (1987). *Normen en taal*, Groningen, 25 p.

Hajjar, Joseph N. (1986). *Traité de Traduction*, Beiroet, 428 p.

Hamzaoui, R. (1965). *l'Académie arabe de Damas et le problème de la modernisation de la langue arabe*, Leiden, 84 p.

Hamzaoui, R. (1975). *l'Académie de langue arabe du Caire, histoire et œuvre*, Tunis, 661 p.

Harrell, Richard Slade (1960). "A linguistic analysis of Egyptian Radio Arabic". in Ferguson, Ch.A. et al., *Contributions to Arabic linguistics*, Cambridge, Mass., pp. 81-161.

Harvey, David (1979). *Spoken Arabic*, London.

Hary, Benjamin (1989). "Middle Arabic, proposels for New Terminology". *Al-'Arabiyya*, 22, pp. 19-36.

Hary, Benjamin (1996). "The Importance of the Language Continuum in Arabic Multiglossia". In Elgibali, A., *Understanding Arabic, Essays in Contemporary Arabic Linguistics in Honor of El-Said Badawi*, Kairo, pp. 69-90.

Haugen, Einar (1977). "Some Issues in Sociolinguistics". In Uribe-Villegas, Oscar (Ed.), *Issues in Sociolinguistics*, Den Haag, pp. 113-143.

Haywood, J.A. & Nahmad, H.M. (1962). *A new Arabic Grammar of the Written Language*, London.

Heidbuchel, H. & Luyten, G.J. (1985). *Hoe zeg en schrijf ik het?*, Antwerpen, 125 p.

Heliel, Mohamed H. (1987). "Definitions of Linguistic Terms in an English-Arabic Dictionary". *Journal of the Dictionary Society of North America*, 9, pp. 133-148.

Hlal, Yahya (1988). "Morpho-syntactic analysis and generation". *Processing Arabic*, Report 3, Nijmegen, pp. 45-50.

Hlal, Yahya (1990). "Morphology and Syntax of the Arabic Language". In Pierre A. MacKay (Ed.), *Computers and the Arabic Language*, New York, pp. 201-207.

Holes, Clive, & Ingham, Bruce (1987). *Language Variation and Change in a Modernising Arab State: The Case of Bahrain*, London.

Holes, Clive & M. Baker (1988). "The Use of a Computerised Text Concordancer in Arabic Language Teaching and Translating", in Shivtiel, A. (ed), *Proceedings of the 2nd Leeds Symposium*, pp. 5-29.

Holes, Clive (1990). *Gulf Arabic*, Routledge, London & New York, 302 p.

Holes, Clive (1993). "The Uses of Variation: A Study of the Political Speeches of Gamal Abdal al-Nasir". In Mushira Eid & Clive Holes (Eds.), *Perspectives on Arabic Linguistics V*, Amsterdam & Philadelphia, pp. 13-46.

Holes, Clive (1995). *Modern Arabic, Structures, Functions and Varieties*, Longman Linguistics Library, London & New York, 343 p.

Holt, Mike (1994). "Algeria: language, nation and state". In Suleiman, Yasir, *Arabic Sociolinguistics, Issues & Perspectives*, London, pp. 25-41.

Huber, Onno (1988). "Representatie van tekstcorpora in de computer". In van Reenen-Stein K.H. en Dees A. (Eds.), *Corpusgebaseerde woordanalyse*, Vrije Universiteit Amsterdam, pp. 61-65.

Hug, Marc (1986). "Le role des données quantitatives dans l'étude syntaxique d'une langue". In *Méthodes quantitatives et informatiques dans l'étude des textes*, Genève-Paris, 2 dln., pp. 483-493.

Hussein, Riyad F. & El-Ali, Nasser (1989). "Subjective Reactions of Rural University Students toward Different Varieties of Arabic". *Al-'Arabiyya*, 22 (1-2), pp. 37-54.

Ibrahim, Amr Helmy (1991). "Arabes et argots sont-ils compatibles?" *Bulletin d'Études Orientales XLIII*, Damas: IFEAD, pp. 33-45.

Ibrahim, Muhammad H. (1983). "Linguistic distance and literacy in Arabic". *Journal of Pragmatics*, 7(5), pp. 507-515.

Ibrahim, Muhammad H. (1986). "Standard and prestige language: a problem in Arabic sociolinguistics". *Anthropological linguistics*, 28(1), pp. 115-26.

Isesco (1989). *al-Muʿjam al-ʿarabī al-'asāsī*, Parijs.

Jabal, Moḥammad Ḥasan Ḥasan (1987). *Ḫaṣā'iṣ al-luġa al-ʿarabīya, tafṣīl wa-taḥqīq*, Kairo, 156 p.

Janssen, Sylvia (1990). "Automatic Sense Disambiguation with LDOCE: Enriching Syntactically Analysed Corpora with semantic Data". In Aarts, Jan & Meijs, Willem (Eds.), *Theory and Practice in Corpus Linguistics*, Amsterdam, pp. 105-131.

Jārī, Ḥamza e.a. (1992). *al-Qirā'a*, al-Maʿhad at-tarbawī al-waṭanī, Algiers.

Jelinek, Eloise (1981). "Person-subject marking in AUX in Egyptian Arabic". In R. Heny & B. Richards (Eds.), *Linguistic Categories*, University of Arizona, pp. 21-46.

Jernudd, Björn H. (1986). "Language Mentions in Jordanian Newspapers (The English-Language Press)". In Joshua A. Fishman, Andree Tabouret-Keller, Michael Clyne, Bh. Krishnamurti, & Mohamed Abdulaziz (Eds.), *The Fergusonian Impact: In Honor of Charles A. Ferguson on the Occasion of His 65th Birthday*, I: From Phonology to Society; II: Sociolinguistics and the Sociology of Language, Berlin, pp. 253-269.

Johansson, Stig (1987). "The tagged Lob corpus: Description and analyses". In Meijs, Willem, *Corpus linguistics and beyond*, Proceedings of the 7th International Conference on English language research on Computerized Corpora, Amsterdam, pp. 1-20.

Johansson, Stig (1994). "Continuity and change in the encoding of computer corpora". In Oostdijk, Nelleke & de Haan, Pieter (Eds.), *Corpus-based research into language, in honour of Jan Aarts*, Amsterdam, pp. 13-31.

Johnstone, Barbara (1990). "'Orality' and Discourse Structure in Modern Standard Arabic". Papers from the First Annual Symposium on Arabic Linguistics. In Mushira Eid (Eds.), *Perspectives on Arabic Linguistics I*, Amsterdam, pp. 215-233.

Jolivet, Rémi (1986). "Aspect statistique de la structure linguistique". In *Méthodes quantitatives et informatiques dans l'étude des textes*, Genève-Paris, 2 dln., pp. 509-517.

Jomier, J. en Khouzam, J. (1977). *Manuel d'Arabe Egyptien*, Paris.

Joseph, John Earl (1987). *Eloquence and Power, The Rise of Language Standards and Standard Languages*, Frances Pinter, Open Linguistics Series, London, 177 p.

Jundī, 'Aḥmad ʿAlam ad-Dīn (1981). *Fī qawāʿid al-ʿArabīya*, Kairo, 582 p.

Justice, David (1987). *The semantics of Form in Arabic*, Amsterdam, 434 p.

Kampffmeyer, G. (1909). "Texte aus Fes. Mit einem Text aus Tanger". *Mitteilungen des Seminars für Orientalische Sprachen*, 12 (2), pp. 51-98.

Karlsson, Fred (1994). "Robust Parsing of unconstrained text". In Oostdijk, Nelleke & de Haan, Pieter (Eds.), *Corpus-based research into language, in honour of Jan Aarts*, Amsterdam, pp. 121-141.

Kästner, Hartmut (1981). *Phonetik und Phonologie des modernen Hocharabisch*, Leipzig.

Kästner, Hartmut (1987). "Die gepressten Konsonanten des Hocharabischen und ihre phonologische Interpretation". *Zeitschrift für Phonetik, Sprachwissenschaft und Kommunikationsforschung*, 40(6), pp. 814-817.

Kaye, Alan S. (1969-70). "Modern Standard Arabic and the colloquials", *Lingua*, 24, pp. 374-391.

Kaye, Alan S. (1972). "Arabic /*jīm*/: A synchronic and diachronic study". *Linguistics*, 79, pp. 31-72.

Kaye, Alan S. (1987). "Arabic". In Bernard Comrie (Eds.), *The World's Major Languages*, Oxford, London, pp. 664-685.

Kaye, Alan S. (1991). "The hamzat al-waṣl in contemporary Modern Standard Arabic". *Journal of the American Oriental Society*, 111(3), pp. 572-573.

Kaye, Alan S. (1992). "Orthographic Variation in Arabic Loan Words". *English Today: The International Review of the English Language*, 8(2), pp. 32-41.

Kechaou, Salah (1982). "Adjectifs et formes apparentées". *IBLA, Revue de l'Institut des Belles Lettres Arabes a Tunis*, 45 (1), (149), pp. 149-157.

Kechaou, Salah (1984). "Frontières entre noms et verbes". *IBLA, Revue de l'Institut des Belles Lettres Arabes a Tunis, 47* (1), (153), pp. 125-37.

Kelly, Peter (1991). "Lexical Ignorance: The main obstacle to listening comprehension with advanced foreign language learners". *International Review of Applied Linguistics in Language Teaching*, XXIX/2, pp. 135-149.

Kempeneers, P. (1979). *Elementaire begrippen uit de Nederlandse Taalkunde.*

Khalafallah, Ahmad Muhammad (1971). "The role and future of Classical Arabic in the life and thought of the modern Arab people". *Proceedings of the 27th Congress of Orientalists*, Michigan, August 13-19 1967, Wiesbaden, pp. 197-199.

Khalil, Esam N. (1985). "News discourse: a strategy of recasting". *Journal of Pragmatics*, 9(5), pp. 621-643.

Khan, Geoffrey (1988). *Studies in Semitic Syntax*, London Oriental Series, Vol. 38, 252 p.

Killean, Carolyn G. (1970). "Classical Arabic". In Thomas A. Sebeok (Ed.), *Current Trends in Linguistics VI: Linguistics in So. West Asia and No. Africa*, Den Haag, pp. 413-424.

Killean, Carolyn G. (1980). "Demonstrative variation in oral media Arabic in Egypt". *Studies in the Linguistic Sciences*, 10(2), pp. 165-178.

Killean, Carolyn G. (1984). "The Development of Western Grammars in Arabic". *Journal of Near Eastern Studies*, 43(3), pp. 223-230.

Kjellmer, Göran (1990). "Patterns of Collocability". In Aarts, Jan & Meijs, Willem (Eds.), *Theory and Practice in Corpus Linguistics*, Amsterdam, pp. 163-178.

Klooster, W.G. (1971). *Inleiding tot de syntaxis*, Keulen, 152 p.

Klopfer, H. (1970). *Modernes Arabisch*. Eine Einführung ins heutige Zeitungsschriftarabisch, Heidelberg, 2nd revised edn, 136 p.

Koefoed, G.A.T. (1987). "Verzorgd Nederlands, Verzorgd Surinaams-Nederlands of zorgvuldige taal?" In Rooij, J. de, *Variatie en Norm in de Standaardtaal*, Amsterdam, pp. 115-125.

Kouloughli, Djamel-Eddine (1980). "Grammaire de transfert dans le domaine arabe. Perspectives et problèmes". *l'Arabisant*, pp. 57-66.

Kouloughli, Djamel-Eddine (1987). "Les particules ont-elles un sens? Autour d'une controverse dans la tradition grammaticale arabe". *Bulletin de linguistique appliquée et générale*, 13, pp. 215-237.

Kouloughli, Djamel-Eddine (1988a). "Renouvellement énonciatif et valeur aoristique: à propos de l'opposition mā/lam en arabe". *Langues Orientales Anciennes, Philologie et Linguistique*, 1, pp. 49-72.

Kouloughli, Djamel-Eddine & J. Feat (1988b). "The Dynamic Binding Approach to Automatic Text Understanding". *Processing Arabic*, Report 3, pp. 13-44.

Kouloughli, Djamel-Eddine (1991). *Lexique fondamental de l'arabe standard moderne/Basic lexicon of modern standard arabic*, Paris, 287 p.

Kouloughli, Djamel-Eddine (1994). *Grammaire de l'arabe d'aujourd'hui*, Langues pour tous, Paris, 350 p.

Krahl, Günther & Reuschel, Wolfgang (1974). *Lehrbuch des modernen Arabisch*, Leipzig, Vol 1, 620 p.

Kropfitsch, Lorenz (1980). "Semantische Tendenzen im Neuhocharabischen". *Zeitschrift für Arabische Linguistik*, 5, pp. 118-136.

Lagarde, J.P. (1988). "Les parties du discours dans la linguistique moderne et contemporaine". *Languages*, 92 (Dec 1988), pp. 93-108.

Lagarde, M. (1981). *La radio Arabe* 1980-1981, Pontificio Instituto di Studi Arabi, Rome, 123 p.

Landau, Jacob M. (1959). *A Word Count of Modern Arabic Prose*, New York

Larcher, Pierre & Girod, Alain (1990). "Passif grammatical, passif periphrastique et categorie d'auxiliaire en arabe classique moderne". *Arabica: Revue d'Etudes Arabes*, 37(2), pp. 137-150.

Larcher, Pierre (1994). "Mā fa'ala vs lam yaf'al: Une hypothèse pragmatique". *Arabica: Revue d'Etudes Arabes*, 41, pp. 388-415.

Larcher, Pierre (2001). "Moyen arabe et arabe moyen". *Arabica: Revue d'Etudes Arabes*, 48, pp. 578-609.

Lecerf, J. (1933). "L'arabe contemporain comme langage de civilisation". *Revue Africaine*, 74, pp. 269-96.

Lecomte, Gérard (1968). *Grammaire de l'Arabe*, Paris P.U.F. (Que Sais-Je?), 128 p.

Lecomte, Gérard & Ghedira, A. (1970). *Méthode d'Arabe littéral*, Paris, 2 delen, 240 p. en 179 p.

Lecomte, Gérard (1978). *Elements d'arabe de presse et de radio*, Paris, 1978, 99 p.

Leech, Geoffrey & Fligelstone, Steven (1992). "Computers and Corpus Analysis". In Butler, Christopher S. (Ed.), *Computers and Written Texts*, Oxford, pp. 115-140.

Leech, Geoffrey, Roger Garside & Michael Bryant (1994). "The large-scale grammatical tagging of text: Experience with the British National Corpus". In Oostdijk, Nelleke & de Haan, Pieter (Eds.), *Corpus-based research into language, in honour of Jan Aarts*, Amsterdam, pp. 47-63.

Leemhuis, Fred (1992). *De Koran*, Houten, 436 p.

Le Gassick, Trevor, J. (1979). *Major Themes in Modern Arabic Thought: An Anthology*, Ann Arbor, 71 p. en 152 p.

Lenoble, Michel (1986). "Statistique lexicale et critique littéraire; le marriage impossible". In *Méthodes quantitatives et informatiques dans l'étude des textes*, Genève-Paris, 2 dln., pp. 567-573.

Lévy-Provençal, E. (1922). *Textes arabes de l'Ouargha, dialecte des Jbala*, Paris.

Lory, P. (1988). "Quelques remarques sur l'expression du temps, de l'espace et du corps humain en arabe littéral". *Revue de Phonétique Appliquée*, 87-89, pp. 173-176.

Lyne, A.A. (1986). "In praise of Juilland's 'D'; a contribution to the empirical evaluation of various measures of dispersion applied to word frequencies". In *Méthodes quantitatives et informatiques dans l'étude des textes*, Genève-Paris, 2 dln., pp. 589-597.

Lyons, John (1984). *Semantics,* Vol 1., Cambridge.

Lyons, M.C. (1962). *An elementary Classical Arabic Reader*, Cambridge, 237 p.

Mahmoud, N.C. (1985). "Landmarks in Arabic". *Verbatim*, 12(2), p. 2.

Mahmoud, Youssef (1982). "Towards a functional Arabic". *Al-'Arabiyya*, 15(1-2), pp. 82-89.

Mahmoud, Youssef (1986). "Arabic after Diglossia". In Joshua A. Fishman, Andree Tabouret-Keller, Michael Clyne, Bh. Krishnamurti & Mohamed Abdulaziz (Eds.), *The Fergusonian Impact: In Honor of Charles A. Ferguson on the Occasion of His 65th Birthday*, I: From Phonology to Society; II: Sociolinguistics and the Sociology of Language, Berlin, pp. 239-251.

Marçais, Philippe (1977). *Esquisse grammaticale de l'arabe maghrébin*, Paris, Librairie d'Amérique et d'Orient, 284 p.

Marçais, William (1911). *Textes arabes de Tanger*, Paris, Bibliothèque de l'Ecole des langues Orientales vivantes, 8, 213 p.

Marçais, William (1930a). "La diglossie arabe". *l'Enseignement Public*, XCVII, pp. 401-409.

Marçais, William (1930b). "La langue arabe dans l'Afrique du Nord". *l'Enseignement Public*, XCVII, pp. 20-39.

Marçais, William (1930c). "l'Arabe écrit et l'arabe parlé dans l'enseignement secondaire". *l'Enseignement Public*, XCVII, pp. 121-133.

Martin, Willy (1989). "Corpora voor Woordenboeken". In Dees, T., *Corpusgebaseerde Woordanalyse*, Amsterdam, pp. 91-99.

Martinet (1955). *Économie des changements phonétiques*, Berne-Francke.

Mattar, Antoine C. (1986). "Disparité linguistique arabe et communication de masse", *Cahiers de l'Orient*, 3, pp. 249-280.

McLoughlin, L.J. (1972). "Towards a definition of Modern Standard Arabic". *Archivum Linguisticum*, New Series 3, Menston, Yorkshire, pp. 57-73.

Meiseles, Gustav (1975). *Oral Literary Arabic, Its main features in Speech and Reading,* Hebrew University.

Meiseles, Gustav (1977). "Restitution of 'word-endings' in Modern Literary Arabic", *Israel Oriental Studies*, pp. 173-195.

Meiseles, Gustav (1979). "Informal Written Arabic, a preliminary evaluation of data", *Israel Oriental Studies*, pp. 273-313.

Meiseles, Gustav (1980a). "Educated spoken Arabic and the Arabic language continuum". *Archivum Linguisticum*, New Series 11(2), Menston, Yorkshire, pp. 118-48.

Meiseles, Gustav (1980b). "Ḥawla al-waḍʿ al-luġawī fī l-ʿālam al-ʿarabī l-muʿāṣir". In Somekh, Sasson (Ed.), *'Abḥāṯ fī l-luġa wa-l-'uslūb*, Tell Aviv, pp. 75-94.
Meiseles, Gustav (1981). "Hybrid versus symbiotic constructions: a case study of contemporary Arabic". *Linguistics*, 19, pp. 1077-1093.
Mitchell, Terry F. (1978). "Educated spoken Arabic in Egypt and the Levant, with special reference to participle and tense". *Journal of Linguistics*, 14, pp. 227-258.
Mitchell, Terry F. (1980). "Dimensions of style in a grammar of educated spoken Arabic". *Archivum Linguisticum*, New Series 11(2), Menston, Yorkshire, pp. 89-106.
Mitchell, Terry F. (1982). "More than a matter of 'writing with the learned, pronouncing with the vulgar' some preliminary observations on the Arabic Koine". In Haas, W. (Ed.). *Standard Languages: Spoken and Written*. Manchester, pp. 123-155.
Mitchell, Terry F. (1986). "What is educated spoken Arabic?" *International Journal of the Sociology of Language*, 61, pp. 7-32.
Mitchell, Terry F. & El-Hassan, Shahir (1994). *Modality, Mood and Aspect in Spoken Arabic: With Special Reference to Egypt and the Levant*, New York, 129 p.
Monteil, Vincent (1960). *L'arabe moderne*, Paris, 386 p.
Moore, David S. & McCabe, George P. (1993). *Statistiek in de Praktijk*, Schoonhoven, 681 p.
Morsly, Dalila (1986). "Multilingualism in Algeria". In Joshua A. Fishman, Andree Tabouret-Keller, Michael Clyne, Bh. Krishnamurti & Mohamed Abdulaziz (Eds.), *The Fergusonian Impact: In Honor of Charles A. Ferguson on the Occasion of His 65th Birthday*, I: From Phonology to Society; II: Sociolinguistics and the Sociology of Language, Berlin, pp. 253-263.
Morsly, Dalila (1990). "En arabe classique le journal télévisé?" In Pleines, Jochen, *La linguistique au Maghreb*, Rabat, pp. 163-174.
Moser, C.A. & Kalton G. (1971). *Survey Methods in Social Investigation*, London, 549 p.
Mrayati, Mohamed (1990). "Statistical Studies in Arabic Linguistics". In Pierre A. MacKay (Ed.), *Computers and the Arabic Language*, New York, pp. 190-200.
Naḥlaḥ, Maḥmūd 'Aḥmad (1987). *'Uṣūl an-naḥw al-ʿarabī*, Beiroet, 160 p.
Najock, Dietmar (1986). "Bootstrap Experiments for the Evaluation of Expected Values and Variances of Vocabulary Sizes". In *Méthodes quantitatives et informatiques dans l'étude des textes*, Genève-Paris, 2 dln. pp. 659-667.
Neter, J., Wasserman, W. & Whitmore, G.A. (1988). *Applied Statistics*, Boston.
Niʿma, Fu'ād (1973). *Qawāʿid al-luġa al-ʿarabīya*, Kairo, 2 delen, 142 p. en 164 p.
Nofal, Loutfy M. (1980). *Language Function Analysis in Modern Standard Arabic*. With Pedagogical Implications for the Teaching of Arabic as a Foreign Language, Erlangen-Nürnberg.
Oostdijk, Nelleke (1984). "An Extended Affix Grammar for the English Noun Phrase". In Aarts, Jan & Meijs, Willem (Eds.), *Corpus Linguistics*, Amsterdam, 1984, pp. 95-122.

Oostdijk, Nelleke & de Haan, Pieter (1994). *Corpus-based research into language, in honour of Jan Aarts*, Amsterdam, 279 p.

Otten, R. (1983). *Basiswoordenboek van het Marokkaans Arabisch. Marokkaans/Nederlands, Nederlands /Marokkaans*, Muiderberg.

Ouersighni, Riadh (2001). "A major offshoot of the DIINAR-MBC project, a morpho-syntactic analyzer for unvoiwelled Arabic texts, In *ACL/EACL 2001 Workshop, Arabic Language Processing: Status and Prospects*, Toulouse

Owens, Jonathan (1984). "Structure, Class and Dependency: Modern Linguistic Theory and the Arabic Grammatical Tradition". *Lingua: International Review of General Linguistics*, 64(1), pp. 25-62.

Owens, Jonathan (1989). "The Syntactic Basis of Arabic Word Classificaiton". *Arabica: Revue d'Etudes Arabes*, 36 (2), pp. 211-234.

Owens, Jonathan & Bani-Yasin, Raslan (1991). "Spoken Arabic and language mixture". *Bulletin d'Études Orientales, XLIII*, Damas: IFEAD, pp. 17-31.

Owens, Jonathan (2001). "Arabic sociolinguistics". *Arabica: Revue d'Études Arabes*, 48, pp. 419-469.

Palva, H. (1969). *Notes on classicization in modern colloquial Arabic*, Helsinki, 41 p.

Parkinson, Dilworth B. (1975)." The agreement of baʿḍ and kull in Modern Literary Arabic". *Nashra,* 8, (1/2), pp. 52-68.

Parkinson, Dilworth B. (1990). "Orthographic variation in Modern Standard Arabic: The case of the hamza". In Mushira Eid & John McCarthy (Eds.), *Perspectives on Arabic Linguistics*, Amsterdam, pp. 269-295.

Parkinson, Dilworth B. (1991). "Searching for Modern Fuṣḥā: Real Life Formal Arabic". *Al-'Arabiyya*, 24, pp. 31-64.

Parkinson, Dilworth B. (1993). "Knowing Standard Arabic: Testing Egyptians' MSA Abilities". In Mushira Eid & Clive Holes (Eds.), *Perspectives on Arabic Linguistics V*, Philadelphia/Amsterdam, pp. 47-74.

Parkinson, Dilworth B. (1994). "Speaking fuṣḥā in Cairo: The role of the ending vowels". In Suleiman, Yasir, *Arabic Sociolinguistics, Issues & Perspectives*, London, pp. 179-211.

Parkinson, Dilworth B. (1996). "Variability In Standard Arabic Grammar Skills". In Elgibali, A., *Understanding Arabic, Essays in Contemporary Arabic Linguistics in Honor of El-Said Badawi,* Kairo, pp. 91-101.

Paulussen, Hans (1992). *Automatic Grammatical Tagging: Description, comparison and proposal for augmentation*, Universitaire Instelling Antwerpen, Wilrijk, 83 p. + 32 p.

Pauwels, J.L. (1986). "Dialecten en algemeen Nederlands". In Gillaerts, Paul, *Verscheidenheid in eenheid, een bloemlezing taalpolitieke artikelen over normering en standaardisering van het Nederlands*, Leuven, 1986, pp. 77-81.

Pellat, Charles (1970a). *Introduction à l'Arabe Moderne*, Paris; 248 p.

Pellat, Charles (1970b). *Langue et littérature arabes*, Paris, 240 p.

Pellat, Charles (1971). *L'Arabe Vivant. Mots Arabes Groupés d'après le Sens et Vocabulaire Fondamental de l'Arabe Moderne,* Paris, 338, 77 pp.

Penninckx, Willy & Buyse, Paul (1988). *Vertaalgids*, 194 p.

Penninckx, Willy & Buyse, Paul (1991). *Correct Taalgebruik*, 259 p.

Pensart, L. en Van der Sande, L. (1991). *Grammaticaal & Taalkundig Lexicon, op basis van de Algemene Nederlandse Spraakkunst*, Antwerpen, 71 p.

Plunkett, Bernadette (1993). "The Position of Subjects in Modern Standard Arabic". In Mushira Eid & Clive Holes (Eds.), *Perspectives on Arabic Linguistics V*, Amsterdam & Philadelphia, pp. 231-260.

Quirk, Randolph (1979). "A Corpus of Modern English". In Bergenholtz, Henning, *Empirische Textwissenschaft, Aufbau und Auswertung von Text-Corpora*, Frankfurt, pp. 205-218.

Quirk, Randolph (1985). *A comprehensive grammar of the English Language*, London.

Rebhan, Helga (1986). *Geschichte und Funktion einiger politischer Termini im Arabischen des 19. Jahrhunderts* (1789-1882), Wiesbaden, 205 p.

Reckendorf, H. (1921). *Arabische Syntax*, Heidelberg, 567 p.

Reig, Daniel (1983). *Dictionnaire Arabe-Français*, As-Sabil, Paris.

Renouf, Antoinette (1988). "Coding metalanguage: issues raised in the creation and processing of specialised corpora". Proceedings of Eighth International Conference on English Lang. Research on Computerized Corpora. In Merja Kyto, Ossi Ihalainen, & Matti Rissanen (Eds.), *Corpus Linguistics, Hard and Soft*, Amsterdam, pp. 197-206.

Rieger, Burghard (1979). "Repräsentativität: von der Unangemessenheit eines Begriffs zur Kennzeichnung eines Problems linguistischer Korpusbildung". In Bergenholtz, Henning, *Empirische Textwissenschaft, Aufbau und Auswertung von Text-Corpora*, Frankfurt, pp. 53-69.

Rooij, J. de (1987). *Variatie en Norm in de Standaardtaal*, P.J. Meertens-Instituut voor Dialectologie, Volkskunde en Naamkunde, Amsterdam, 174 p.

Roman, Andre (1987). "Des causes de l'évolution des langues; l'exemple de l'évolution de la langue arabe". *Arabica: Revue d'Etudes Arabes*, 34, pp. 129-146.

Safi-Stagni, Sabah (1990). "Slips of the Tongue in Arabic". Papers from the First Annual Symposium on Arabic Linguistics. In Mushira Eid (Ed.), *Perspectives on Arabic Linguistics* I, Amsterdam, pp. 271-290.

Safi-Stagni, Sabah (1994). "Arabic Segmental Errors and Segmental Phonology". In Mushira Eid, Vincente Cantarino & Keith Walters (Eds.), *Perspectives on Arabic Linguistics VI: Papers from the sixth symposium on Arabic Linguistics*, Amsterdam & Philadelphia, pp. 169-184.

Sami, Waheed (1996). "Computer Word Frequency counting in Arabic". In Elgibali, A.,*Understanding Arabic, Essays in Contemporary Arabic Linguistics in Honor of El-Said Badawi*, Kairo, pp. 259-271.

Sampson, Geoffrey (1994). "Susanne: A Demesday Book of English grammar". In Oostdijk, Nelleke & de Haan Pieter (Eds.), *Corpus-based research into language, in honour of Jan Aarts*, Amsterdam, pp. 169-187.

Sapir, Eduard (1921). *Language*

Schall, Anton (1982). "Geschichte des Arabischen Wortschatzes, Lehn- und Fremdwörter im Klassischen Arabisch". In Fischer, Wolfdietrich, *Grundriss der arabischen Philologie, I: Sprachwissenschaft,* Wiesbaden, pp. 142-153.

Schippers, Arie en Versteegh, Kees (1987). *Het Arabisch, Norm en realiteit*, Muiderberg, 206 p.

Schmidt, Richard Wilbur (1974). *Sociostylistic Variation in spoken Egyptian Arabic: A Re-examination of the Concept of Diglossia*, PH.D., Brown University, 311 p.

Schulz, David E. (1981). *Diglossia and variation in Formal Spoken Arabic in Egypt*, Ann Arbor, Michigan, 294 p.

Serruys, W. (1897). *L'arabe moderne étudié dans les journaux et les pièces officiëles*, Beirut, 143 p.

Sethom, Hafedh & Bachrouch, T. (1989). "A propos du Dictionnaire de géographie (franco-arabe)". *IBLA: Revue de l'Institut des Belles Lettres Arabes*, 52 (2), pp. 327-332.

Šarīf, Muḥammad 'Abū al-Futūḥ (1984). *an-Naḥw al-jāmi'ī,* Kairo, 309 p.

Shalaby, Ahmad (1985). *Qawā'id al-luġa al-'arabīya wa-t-taṭbīq 'alayhā*, Kairo, 288 p.

Shorrab, Ghazi (1984). "Garvin's Standardization Model and Arabic: A Case in Language Planning". *Journal of College of Arts, King Saud University*, 11(2), pp. 211-223.

Siemund, Rainer (2002). "OrienTel - Arabic speech resources for the IT market". In Choukri, Khaled (ed.), *Arabic Language Resources and Evaluation - Status and Prospects*, A Post Workshop of LREC 2002, Las Palmas

Somekh, Sasson (1993). "Colloqialized *Fuṣḥā* in Modern Arabic Prose Fiction". *Jerusalem Studies in Arabic and Islam* , 16, pp. 176-194.

Souter, Clive & Atwell, Eric (1994). "Using parsed corpora: A review of current practice". In Oostdijk, Nelleke & de Haan, Pieter (Eds.), *Corpus-based research into language, in honour of Jan Aarts*, Amsterdam, pp. 143-157.

Stetkevych, Jaroslav (1970). *The modern Arabic literary language, lexical and stylistic developments*, Chicago-London, UCP, 135 p.

Stoetzer, Willem (1991). *Arabische Grammatica in schema's en regels*, Muiderberg, 337 p.

Suleiman, Saleh M. (1989). "On the Pragmatics of Subject Preposing in Standard Arabic". *Language Sciences*, 11(2), pp. 215-235.

Suleiman, Yasir (1994). "Nationalism and the arabic language: an historical overview". In Suleiman, Yasir, *Arabic Sociolinguistics, Issues & Perspectives.*, London, pp. 3-23.

Suleiman, Yasir (1994). *Arabic Sociolinguistics, Issues & Perspectives*, London, 273 p.

Suleiman, Yasir (1996). "The simplification of Arabic Grammar and the problematic nature of the sources". *Journal of Semitic Studies, XLI*, pp. 99-119.

Talmoudi, Fathi (1984). *The Diglossic Situation in North Africa:* A Study of Classical Arabic/Dialectal Arabic Diglossia with Sample Text in 'Mixed Arabic', Acta Univ. Gothoburgensis, Gothenburg.

Tapiéro, Norbert (1971). *Manuel d'Arabe Algérien Moderne*. Études Arabes et Islamiques, Série A, Manuels, Vol. 5. Paris, 3rd edn., 176 p.

Tapiéro, Norbert (1976). *Pour une didactique de l'arabe moderne, langue de communication, problématique et solutions*, Paris , 2 Vol.

Tapiéro, Norbert (1984). "Methode d'analyse semiologique du discours arabe moderne". *Arabica: Revue d'Etudes Arabes*, 31(3), pp. 239-273.

Tarrier, Jean-Michel (1991). "A propos de sociolinguistique de l'arabe, présentation de quelques difficultés". *Bulletin d'Études Orientales, XLIII*, Damas: IFEAD, pp. 1-15.

Tarrier, Jean-Michel (1993). "Contribution à l'étude de l'arabe parlé formel. Un essai méthodologique pour une analyse variationniste". In Bohas, Georges (Ed.), *Développements récents en linguistique arabe et sémitique*, Institut Français de Damas, Damascus. pp. 93-120.

Taylor, Lita & Knowles Gerry (1988). "Progress report on the spoken English corpus". Proceedings of Eighth International Conference on English Language Research on Computerized Corpora. In Merja Kyto, Ossi Ihalainen, & Matti Rissanen (Eds.), *Corpus Linguistics, Hard and Soft*, Amsterdam, pp. 237-244.

Thalji, Abdel-Majid Ibrahim (1986a). "Marked vs. unmarked structures in modern written Arabic (Part I)". *Al-'Arabiyya*, 19(1-2), pp. 106-26.

Thalji, Abdel-Majid Ibrahim (1986b). "The absence of VP in Arabic basic unmarked order (part II)". *Al-'Arabiyya*, 19(1-2), pp. 127-136.

Thalouth, Boutros & Al-Dannan Abdullah (1990). "A Comprehensive Arabic Morphological Analyser Generator". In Pierre A. MacKay (Ed.), *Computers and the Arabic Language*, New York, pp. 208-217.

Theissen, S., Gehlen, L. & Vromans, J. (1995). *Woordenboek voor Correct Taalgebruik*, Leuven, 375 p.

Thiry, Jacques (1985). *Arabe Moderne, Arabe classique*. Rapport d'Activités de l'Institut de Phonétique, 20, Université Libre de Bruxelles, pp. 95-126.

Thompson-Panos, Karyn & Thomas-Ruzic, Maria (1983). "The Least You Should Know about Arabic: Implications for the ESL Writing Instructor". *TESOL Quarterly*, 17(4), pp. 609-623.

Tomiche, Nada (1964). *Le parler arabe du Caire*, Maison des sciences de l'homme, Recherches méditterranéennes, Textes et études linguistiques, 3, Den Haag, 1964, 236 p.

Tomiche, Nada (1969). "Sur la langue de la presse du Caire, Le style nouveau d'une culture vivante". *Annales islamologiques*, 8, pp. 183-188.

Touratier, Christian (1989). "Structure de la phrase simple en arabe". *Bulletin de la Société de Linguistique de Paris*, 84(1), pp. 345-359.

Uit den Boogaart, P.C. (red.) (1975). *Woordfrequenties in geschreven en gesproken Nederlands*, Utrecht.

Troupeau, Gerard (1976). *Lexique-Index du kitāb de Sībawayhi*, Etudes Arabes et Islamiques, Paris, 266 p.

Ulvestad, Bjarne (1979). "Corpus vs. Intuition in Syntactical Research". In Bergenholtz, Henning, *Empirische Textwissenschaft, Aufbau und Auswertung von Text-Corpora*, Frankfurt, pp. 89-108.

UNESCO (1992). *Statistisch Jaarboek*, Parijs

Vaane, Eveline (1982). "Subjective Estimation of Speech Rate". *Phonetica*, 39(2-3), pp. 136-149.

Van de Poel, Kristien (1992). "Nederlands en Frans in Vlaanderen". In Berns, J.B., *Variatie in de Nederlandse standaardtaal*, Amsterdam, pp. 49-57.

Van der Voort van der Kleij, J., Raaijmakers e.a. (1994). "Een automatisch geanalyseerd corpus hedendaags Nederlands in een flexibel retrievalsysteem. In: Noordman, L.G.M. & Vroomen, W.A.M. de (red.), *Informatiewetenschap 1994. Wetenschappelijke bijdragen aan de derde STINFON-conferentie*, Tilburg, pp. 181-194.

van de Velde, R.G. (1979). "Probleme der linguistischen Theoriebildung einer empirischen Textwissenschaft". In Bergenholtz Henning, *Empirische Textwissenschaft, Aufbau und Auswertung von Text-Corpora*, Frankfurt, pp. 10-27.

Van Marle, J. (1992). "Iets over het werk van Jaap de Rooij". In Berns, J.B., *Variatie in de Nederlandse standaardtaal*, Amsterdam, pp. 3-21.

Van Mol, Mark (1976). *De participerende Observatie als methodiek van onderzoek*, Leuven, 44 p.

Van Mol, Mark (1979). "Cultuur, gedragsverandering en de migrant". *Streven*, nov 1979, pp. 152-165.

Van Mol, Mark (1980a). "Een poging tot classificatie van ziekte bij Marokkaanse gastarbeiders". *Nederlands Tijdschrift voor Geneeskunde*, 124, (28), pp. 1162-1165.

Van Mol, Mark (1980b). *Le verbe dans les parlers arabes de Rabat et du Caire, Etude comparative*, Bruxelles, ULB, 109 p.

Van Mol, Mark (1981). *Marokkaans voor Nederlandstaligen, al-Lahja l-maġribīya*, Antwerpen-Deventer, 360 p.

Van Mol, Mark (1983). *Marokkaans voor Nederlandstaligen, Qāmūs maġrabī*, Woordenboek en Oplossingenboek, Antwerpen-Deventer, 570 p.

Van Mol, Mark (1984). *Handboek Modern Arabisch*, Leuven, 422 p.

Van Mol, Mark (1986). "Oorzaken van klachten en uitingsmogelijkheden bij Marokkanen". In *Migranten en Geestelijke Gezondheidszorg*, Nationale Vereniging voor Geestelijke Gezondheidszorg, pp. 37-64.

Van Mol, Mark (1990a). *Kennisniveau van het Arabisch in het Secundair Onderwijs*, Verslag van een onderzoek bij Marokkaanse kinderen, EG-experiment, Talen en culturen in het secundair onderwijs, Antwerpen, april 1990, 24 p.

Van Mol, Mark (1990b). *Tussentijdse evaluatie Lessenpakket Arabisch*, EG-experiment, Talen en culturen in het secundair onderwijs, Antwerpen; oktober 1990, 13 p.

Van Mol, Mark (1991a). *Eindevaluatie EG-experiment, Arabisch in het secundair Onderwijs*, EG-experiment, Talen en culturen in het secundair onderwijs, Antwerpen, augustus 1991

Van Mol, Mark (1991b). *Modern gesproken Standaard Arabisch op de radio, al-luġa al-'arabīya l-mu'āṣira fī l-'iḏā'a*, deel 1, formeel taalgebruik, nieuwsuitzendingen, documentaires, reportages, toespraken, Instituut voor Levende Talen, KU Leuven, teksten 91 p., woordenlijst, 57 p.

Van Mol, Mark (1992). *Modern gesproken Standaard Arabisch op de radio, al-luġa al-'arabīya l-mu'āṣira fī l-'iḏā'a*, deel 2, informeel taalgebruik, interviews en perconferenties, Instituut voor Levende Talen, KU Leuven, 101 p.

Van Mol, Mark (2000a) *Arabic language and vocabulary acquisition*, In MIDEO, 24, 2000, pp. 434-440

Van Mol, Mark (2000b) Exploring annotated Arabic corpora, preliminary results, In *Corpora and Natural Language Processing, proceedings of the International Conference on Artificial and Computational Intelligence for Decision, Control and Automation in Engineering and Industrial Applications*, Monastir, pp. 94-98

Van Mol, Mark (2000c) The development of a new learner's dictionary for Modern Standard Arabic, the corpus linguistic approach, *In Proceedings of the Ninth EURALEX international Congress*, Stuttgart, 8-12 august 2000, pp. 831-836

Van Mol, Mark & Bergman, Koen (2001a) *Leerwoordenboek Modern Arabisch-Nederlands*, De Nederlandse Taalunie, Bulaaq, 520 p.

Van Mol, Mark & Bergman, Koen (2001b) *Leerwoordenboek Nederlands-Modern Arabisch*, De Nederlandse Taalunie, Bulaaq, 530 p.

Van Mol, Mark & Paulussen, Hans (2001c) AraLat: a relational database for the development of bilingual Arabic dictionaries, In Asialex 2001 proceedings, Asian Bilingualism and the Dictionary, Seoel 8-10 augustus 2001, pp. 206-211.

Van Mol, Mark (2002). "The Semi-automatic Tagging of Arabic Corpora". In Choukri, Khaled (ed.), *Arabic Language Resources and Evaluation - Status and Prospects*, A Post Workshop of LREC 2002, Las Palmas

Verrept, S. (1986). "De derde fase in de ontwikkeling naar een algemene taal?" In Gillaerts, Paul, *Verscheidenheid in eenheid, een bloemlezing taalpolitieke artikelen over normering en standaardisering van het Nederlands*, Leuven, 1986, pp. 83-91.

Versteegh, Kees & Carter, Michael (Eds.) (1990). *Studies in the History of Arabic Grammar II*, Amsterdam.

Versteegh, Kees (1997). *The Arabic Language*, Edinburgh University Press.

Versteegh, Kees (2001). "Linguistic contacts between Arabic and other languages" *Arabica: Revue d'Etudes Arabes*, 48, pp. 470-508.

Voortman, Berber (1992). "Regionale variatie in de taal van de elite: een onderzoek naar de aanwezigheid van dialectismen". In Berns, J.B., *Variatie in de Nederlandse standaardtaal*, Amsterdam, pp. 23-47.

Vooys, de C.G.N. (1986). "Het gezag van een 'algemeen beschaafd'". In Gillaerts, Paul, *Verscheidenheid in eenheid, een bloemlezing taalpolitieke artikelen over normering en standaardisering van het Nederlands*, Leuven, 1986, pp. 15-41.

Vreese, de W. (1986). "Algemeen beschaafde omgangstaal in Zuid-Nederland". In Gillaerts, Paul, *Verscheidenheid in eenheid, een bloemlezing taalpolitieke artikelen over normering en standaardisering van het Nederlands*, Leuven, 1986, pp. 45-53.

Wehr, Hans (1943). "Entwicklung und traditionelle Pflege der arabischen Schriftsprache in der Gegenwart". *Zeitschrift der Deutschen Morgenländischen Gesellschaft*, 97, Wiesbaden, pp. 16-46.

Wehr, Hans (1953). "Zur Funktion arabischer Negationen", *Zeitschrift der Deutschen Morgenländischen Gesellschaft*, 103, Wiesbaden, pp. 27-39.

Wehr, Hans (1979). *A Dictionary of Modern Written Arabic*, Ed. J. Milton Cowan, Wiesbaden, xvii, 1301 pp.

Weijnen, A.A. (1974). *Het Algemeen Beschaafd Nederlands historisch beschouwd*, Assen, 35 p.

Whitson, Valerie (1972). "The Correlation of Auditory Comprehension with General Language Proficiency". *Audio-Visual Language Journal*, 10/2, pp. 89-91.

Wickens, G.M. (1980). *Arabic Grammar: A First Workbook*, New York, Cambridge.

Wild, Stefan (1982). "Arabische Lexikographie". In Fischer, Wolfdietrich, *Grundriss der arabischen Philologie, I: Sprachwissenschaft*, Wiesbaden, pp. 136-176.

Willemyns, R. (1987). "Norm en variatie in Vlaanderen". In Rooij, J. de, *Variatie en Norm in de Standaardtaal*, Amsterdam, pp. 143-163.

Wilmsen, David William (1995). *The word play's the Thing: Educated Spoken Arabic in a Theatrical Community*, University of Michigan, 297 p.

Witteboon, S. (1972). "De radionieuwsdienst en de Nederlandse Taal". In Geerts, G., *Taal of taaltje, een bloemlezing taalpolitieke beschouwingen over het Nederlands*, pp. 237-250.

Wittig, Sabine (1991). "Fa- als Indikator arabischer Kausalsatze". *Zeitschrift für Phonetik, Sprachwissenschaft und Kommunikationsforschung*, 44(2), pp. 180-189.

Woidich, Manfred & Heinen-Nasr, Rabha (1996). *kullu tamām, Inleiding tot de Egyptische omgangstaal*, Amsterdam, 313 p.

Wood, Richard E. (1979). "Language Choice in Transnational Radio Broadcasting". *Journal of Communication*, 29 (2), pp. 112-123.

Wright, W. (1971). *A Grammar of the Arabic Language*. Translated from the German of Caspari and edited with numerous additions and corrections. 3rd edn. revised by W.R. Smith and M.J. de Goeje, London, 2 vols., I: xviii, 317pp.; II: xx, 450 pp.

Yaʿqūb, 'Imīl Badīʿ (1986). *Mawsū'at an-naḥw wa-ṣ-ṣarf wa-l-'iʿrāb*, Beiroet, 584 p.

Yaʿqūb, 'Imīl Badīʿ (1988). *Mawsū'at al-ḥurūf*, Beiroet, 662 p.

Ziadeh, F.J. (1955). *An Introduction to Modern Arabic*, Princeton, x, 331 pp.

ORIENTALIA LOVANIENSIA ANALECTA

1. E. Lipiński, Studies in Aramaic Inscriptions and Onomastics I.
2. J. Quaegebeur, Le dieu égyptien Shaï dans la religion et l'onomastique.
3. P.H.L. Eggermont, Alexander's Campaigns in Sind and Baluchistan and the Siege of the Brahmin Town of Harmatelia.
4. W.M. Callewaert, The Sarvāṅgī of the Dādūpanthī Rajab.
5. E. Lipiński (ed.), State and Temple Economy in the Ancient Near East I.
6. E. Lipiński (ed.), State and Temple Economy in the Ancient Near East II.
7. M.-C. De Graeve, The Ships of the Ancient Near East (c. 2000-500 B.C.).
8. W.M. Callewaert (ed.), Early Hindī Devotional Literature in Current Research.
9. F.L. Damen, Crisis and Religious Renewal in the Brahmo Samaj Movement (1860-1884).
10. R.Y. Ebied - A. Van Roey - L.R. Wickham, Peter of Callinicum, Anti-Tritheist Dossier.
11. A. Rammant-Peeters, Les pyramidions égyptiens du Nouvel Empire.
12. S. Scheers (ed.), Studia Paulo Naster Oblata I. Numismatica Antiqua.
13. J. Quaegebeur (ed.), Studia Paulo Naster Oblata II. Orientalia Antiqua.
14. E. Platti, Yaḥyā ibn ʿAdī, théologien chrétien et philosophe arabe.
15. E. Gubel - E. Lipiński - B. Servais-Soyez (eds.), Studia Phoenicia I-II.
16. W. Skalmowski - A. Van Tongerloo (ed.), Middle Iranian Studies.
17. M. van Mol, Handboek Modern Arabisch.
18. C. Laga - J.A. Munitiz - L. Van Rompay (eds.), After Chalcedon. Studies in Theology and Church History.
19. E. Lipiński (ed.), The Land of Israel: Cross-Roads of Civilizations.
20. S. Wachsmann, Aegeans in the Theban Tombs.
21. K. Van Lerberghe, Old Babylonian Legal and Administrative Texts from Philadelphia.
22. E. Lipiński (ed.), Phoenicia and the East Mediterranean in the First Millennium B.C.
23. M. Heltzer - E. Lipiński (eds.), Society and Economy in the Eastern Mediterranean (1500-1000 B.C.).
24. M. Van de Mieroop, Crafts in the Early Isin Period.
25. G. Pollet (ed.), India and the Ancient World.
26. E. Lipiński (ed.), Carthago.
27. E. Verreet, Modi Ugaritici.
28. R. Zadok, The Pre-Hellenistic Israelite Anthroponomy and Prosopography.
29. W. Callewaert - M. Lath, The Hindī Songs of Nāmdev.
30. A. Shisha-Halevy, Coptic Grammatical Chrestomathy.
31. N. Baum, Arbres et arbustes de l'Égypte ancienne.
32. J.-M. Kruchten, Les Annales des prêtres de Karnak.
33. H. Devijver - E. Lipiński (eds.), Punic Wars.
34. E. Vassilika, Ptolemaic Philae.
35. A. Ghaith, La Pensée Religieuse chez Ǧubrân Ḫalil Ǧubrân et Miḫâ'îl Nuʿayma.
36. N. Beaux, Le Cabinet de curiosités de Thoutmosis III.
37. G. Pollet - P. Eggermont - G. Van Damme, Archaeological Sites of Ancient India.
38. S.-A. Naguib, Le Clergé féminin d'Amon thébain à la 21e dynastie.
39. U. Verhoeven - E. Graefe (eds.), Religion und Philosophie im Alten Ägypten.
40. A.R. George, Babylonian Topographical Texts.
41. A. Schoors, The Preacher Sought to Find Pleasing Words.
42. G. Reinink - H.E.J. Van Stiphout (eds.), Dispute Poems and Dialogues in the Ancient and Mediaeval Near East.

43. C. TRAUNECKER, Coptos. Hommes et dieux sur le parvis de Geb.
44. E. LIPIŃSKI (ed.), Phoenicia and the Bible.
45. L. ISEBAERT (ed.), Studia Etymologica Indoeuropaea Memoriae A.J. Van Windekens dicata.
46. F. BRIQUEL-CHATONNET, Les relations entre les cités de la côte phénicienne et les royaumes d'Israël et de Juda.
47. W.J. VAN BEKKUM, A Hebrew Alexander Romance according to MS London, Jews' College no. 145.
48. W. SKALMOWSKI - A. VAN TONGERLOO (eds.), Medioiranica.
49. L. LAUWERS, Igor'-Severjanin, His Life and Work — The Formal Aspects of His Poetry.
50. R.L. VOS, The Apis Embalming Ritual. P. Vindob. 3873.
51. Fr. LABRIQUE, Stylistique et Théologie à Edfou. Le rituel de l'offrande de la campagne: étude de la composition.
52. F. DE JONG (ed.), Miscellanea Arabica et Islamica.
53. G. BREYER, Etruskisches Sprachgut im Lateinischen unter Ausschluß des spezifisch onomastischen Bereiches.
54. P.H.L. EGGERMONT, Alexander's Campaign in Southern Punjab.
55. J. QUAEGEBEUR (ed.), Ritual and Sacrifice in the Ancient Near East.
56. A. VAN ROEY - P. ALLEN, Monophysite Texts of the Sixth Century.
57. E. LIPIŃSKI, Studies in Aramaic Inscriptions and Onomastics II.
58. F.R. HERBIN, Le livre de parcourir l'éternité.
59. K. GEUS, Prosopographie der literarisch bezeugten Karthager.
60. A. SCHOORS - P. VAN DEUN (eds.), Philohistor. Miscellanea in honorem Caroli Laga septuagenarii.
61. M. KRAUSE - S. GIVERSEN - P. NAGEL (eds.), Coptology. Past, Present and Future. Studies in Honour of R. Kasser.
62. C. LEITZ, Altägyptische Sternuhren.
63. J.J. CLÈRE, Les Chauves d'Hathor.
64. E. LIPIŃSKI, Dieux et déesses de l'univers phénicien et punique.
65. K. VAN LERBERGHE - A. SCHOORS (eds.), Immigration and Emigration within the Ancient Near East. Festschrift E. Lipiński.
66. G. POLLET (ed.), Indian Epic Values. *Rāmāyaṇa* and its impact.
67. D. DE SMET, La quiétude de l'Intellect. Néoplatonisme et gnose ismaélienne dans l'œuvre de Ḥamîd ad-Dîn al-Kirmânî (X^e^-XIe s.).
68. M.L. FOLMER, The Aramaic Language in the Achaemenid Period. A Study in Linguistic Variation.
69. S. IKRAM, Choice Cuts: Meat Production in Ancient Egypt.
70. H. WILLEMS, The Coffin of Heqata (Cairo JdE 36418). A Case Study of Egyptian Funerary Culture of the Early Middle Kingdom.
71. C. EDER, Die Ägyptischen Motive in der Glyptik des Östlichen Mittelmeerraumes zu Anfang des 2. Jts. v. Chr.
72. J. THIRY, Le Sahara libyen dans l'Afrique du Nord médiévale.
73. U. VERMEULEN - D. DE SMET (eds.), Egypt and Syria in the Fatimid, Ayyubid and Mamluk Eras. Proceedings of the 1st, 2nd and 3rd International Colloquium organized at the Katholieke Universiteit Leuven in May 1992, 1993 and 1994.
74. P. ARÈNES, La déesse Sgrol-Ma (Tara). Recherches sur la nature et le statut d'une divinité du bouddhisme tibétain.
75. K. CIGGAAR - A. DAVIDS - H. TEULE (eds.), East and West in the Crusader States. Context - Contacts - Confrontations. Acta of the Congress Held at Hernen Castle in May 1993.
76. M. BROZE, Mythe et Roman en Egypte ancienne. Les Aventures d'Horus et Seth dans le papyrus Chester Beatty I.
77. L. DEPUYDT, Civil Calendar and Lunar Calendar in Ancient Egypt.
78. P. WILSON, A Ptolemaic Lexikon. A Lexicographical Study of the Texts in the Temple of Edfu.
79. A. HASNAWI - A. ELAMRANI - M. JAMAL - M. AOUAD (eds.), Perspectives arabes et médiévales sur le tradition scientifique et philosophique grecque.

80. E. LIPIŃSKI, Semitic Languages: Outline of a Comparative Grammar.
81. S. CAUVILLE, Dendara I. Traduction.
82. C. EYRE (ed.), Proceedings of the Seventh International Congress of Egyptologists.
83. U. VERMEULEN - D. DE SMET (eds.), Egypt and Syria in the Fatimid, Ayyubid and Mamluk Eras II.
84-85. W. CLARYSSE - A. SCHOORS - H. WILLEMS (eds.), Egyptian Religion. The Last Thousand Years.
86. U. VERMEULEN - J.M. VAN REETH (eds.), Law, Christianity and Modernism in Islamic Society.
87. D. DE SMET - U. VERMEULEN (eds.), Philosophy and Acts in the Islamic World Proceedings of the Eighteenth Congress of the Union européenne des Arabisants et Islamisants held at the Katholieke Universiteit Leuven.
88. S. CAUVILLE, Dendara II. Traduction.
89. G.J. REININK - A.C. KLUGKIST (eds.), After Bardaisan. Studies on Continuity and Change in Syriac Christianity in Honour of Professor Han J.W. Drijvers.
90. C.R. KRAHMALKOV, Phoenician-Punic Dictionary.
91. M. TAHTAH, Entre pragmatisme, réformisme et modernisme. Le rôle politico-religieux des Khattabi dans le Rif (Maroc) jusqu'à 1926.
92. K. CIGGAAR - H. TEULE (eds.), East and West in the Crusader States. Context — Contact — Confrontations II. Acta of the Congress held at Hernen Castle, the Netherlands, in May 1997.
93. A.C.J. VERHEIJ, Bits, Bytes, and Binyanim. A Quantitative Study of Verbal Lexeme Formations in the Hebrew Bible.
94. W.M. CALLEWAERT - D. TAILLIEU - F. LALEMAN, A Descriptive Bibliography of Allama Muhammad Iqbal (1877-1938).
95. S. CAUVILLE, Dendara III. Traduction.
96. K. VAN LERBERGHE - G. VOET (eds.), Languages and Cultures in Contact: At the Crossroads of Civilizations in the Syro-Mesopotamian Realm.
97. A. CABROL, Les voies processionnelles de Thèbes.
98. J. PATRICH, The Sabaite Heritage in the Orthodox Church from the Fifth Century to the Present. Monastic Life, Liturgy, Theology, Literature, Art, Archaeology.
99. U. VERHOEVEN, Untersuchungen zur Späthieratischen Buchschrift.
100. E. LIPIŃSKI, The Aramaeans: Their Ancient History, Culture, Religion.
101. S. CAUVILLE, Dendara IV. Traduction.
102. U. VERMEULEN - J. VAN STEENBERGEN (eds.), Egypt and Syria in the Fatimid, Ayyubid and Mamluk Eras.
103. H. WILLEMS (ed.), Social Aspects of Funerary Culture in the Egyptian Old and Middle Kingdoms.
104. K. GEUS - K. ZIMMERMANN (eds.), Punica — Libyca — Ptolemaica. Festschrift für Werner Huß, zum 65. Geburtstag dargebracht von Schülern, Freunden und Kollegen.
105. S. CAUVILLE, Dendara. Les fêtes d'Hathor.
106. R. PREYS, Les complexes de la demeure du sistre et du trône de Rê. Théologie et décoration dans le temple d'Hathor à Dendera.
107. A. BLASIUS - B.U. SCHIPPER (eds.), Apokalyptik und Ägypten. Eine kritische Analyse der relevanten Texte aus dem griechisch-römischen Ägypten.
108. S. LEDER (ed.), Studies in Arabic and Islam.

PRINTED ON PERMANENT PAPER • IMPRIME SUR PAPIER PERMANENT • GEDRUKT OP DUURZAAM PAPIER - ISO 9706

N.V. PEETERS S.A., WAROTSTRAAT 50, B-3020 HERENT